ROUTLEDGE LIBRARY EDITIONS:
ANCIENT PHILOSOPHY

Volume 1

LUDWIG EDELSTEIN: SELECTED PHILOSOPHICAL PAPERS BY LUDWIG EDELSTEIN

LUDWIG EDELSTEIN: SELECTED PHILOSOPHICAL PAPERS BY LUDWIG EDELSTEIN

EDITED WITH AN INTRODUCTION BY
LEONARDO TARÁN

Routledge
Taylor & Francis Group
LONDON AND NEW YORK

First published in 1987 by Garland Publishing, Inc.

This edition first published in 2017
by Routledge
2 Park Square, Milton Park, Abingdon, Oxon OX14 4RN

and by Routledge
711 Third Avenue, New York, NY 10017

Routledge is an imprint of the Taylor & Francis Group, an informa business

British Library Cataloguing in Publication Data
A catalogue record for this book is available from the British Library

ISBN: 978-1-138-20063-0 (Set)
ISBN: 978-1-315-47325-3 (Set) (ebk)
ISBN: 978-1-138-69727-0 (Volume 1) (hbk)
ISBN: 978-1-138-69731-7 (Volume 1) (pbk)
ISBN: 978-1-315-52221-0 (Volume 1) (ebk)

Publisher's Note
The publisher has gone to great lengths to ensure the quality of this reprint but points out that some imperfections in the original copies may be apparent.

Disclaimer
The publisher has made every effort to trace copyright holders and would welcome correspondence from those they have been unable to trace.

LUDWIG EDELSTEIN

SELECTED PHILOSOPHICAL PAPERS BY LUDWIG EDELSTEIN

Edited with an Introduction by
Leonardo Tarán

GARLAND PUBLISHING, INC.
NEW YORK & LONDON 1987

For a complete list of Garland's
publications in this series,
please see the final pages of this volume.

Library of Congress Cataloging-in-Publication Data

Edelstein, Ludwig, 1902-1965.
Selected philosophical papers.

(Greek and Roman philosophy ; 15)
1. Philosophy, Ancient. I. Tarán, Leonardo.
II. Title. III. Series.
B335.E342 1987 180 86-29542
ISBN 0-8240-6914-5

The volumes in this series are printed on
acid-free, 250-year-life paper.

Printed in the United States of America

INTRODUCTION

Like many German scholars of his generation who were of Jewish ancestry, Ludwig Edelstein's life and academic career received a most severe and prolonged blow with the Nazis' accession to power in 1933. He eventually moved to the United States where he became a professor and a well known, highly esteemed scholar.

Edelstein was born in Berlin on April 23, 1902, the son of an affluent Jewish businessman. He attended the Joachim Friederich Gymnasium in Berlin and after graduation entered the University of Berlin in 1921. He remained there until 1924, studying Greek and Latin mainly with Werner Jaeger and Philosophy and Sociology with Edward Spranger. He then went to the University of Heidelberg, where in 1929 he received a doctorate in Greek, Latin, and Philosophy with a doctoral dissertation on the Hippocratic treatise *Peri Aeron,* written under the sponsorship of Otto Regenbogen. This work, revised and enlarged, was published two years later with the title *Peri Aeron und die Sammlung der hippokratischen Schriften* (Berlin, 1931. *Problemata* Heft 4). From 1930 to 1932 Edelstein was an assistant at the Institute of the History of Medicine in Berlin. In 1932 he became a lecturer in the History of the Exact Sciences in Classical Antiquity at the University of Berlin, but lost the job the following year when Hitler came to power. After spending several months in Italy doing research in the history of Greek medicine and in ancient philosophy, he came to the United States in 1934, having accepted a position as Associate in the Institute of the History of Medicine at Johns Hopkins University. In 1939 he became Associate Professor of the History of Medicine, and remained at the Institute until 1947, when he accepted an offer from the University of Washington in Seattle to become Associate Professor of Classical Languages and Literature. But he remained there one year only, for in 1948 he moved to the University of California at Berkeley where he became a Professor of Greek. But Edelstein's tenure at Berkeley was also brief: when he had been in his new position for a little more than a year, he became involved in the fight against the Regents of the University of California over the "loyalty oath." He was one of a small group of faculty members who finally won the case when the Supreme Court of California decided that the Regents had acted unconstitutionally in requiring the oath and in denying reappointment to the faculty for failure to take it. By that time, however, Edelstein had accepted an appointment as Visiting Professor of Philosophy at the Johns Hopkins University (1951-52) and in the following year he became Professor of Humanistic Studies there. In 1960 he accepted a position as Professor of Classical Philosophy and as Lecturer in the History of Medicine at the Rockefeller Institute (later Rockefeller University). He died in New York City on August 16, 1965.

In 1953 he was Fullbright Lecturer at Oxford, where he delivered a series of lectures on the history of ancient science. In 1956 he delivered the Martin Classical Lectures at Oberlin on the subject of Stoicism. In 1954 he was made a member of the American Philosophical Society and in 1959-60 he was a member of the Institute for Advanced Study (Princeton, N.J.).

Edelstein had two different though, especially in his own view, related fields of research: the history of ancient medicine and of ancient philosophy, and to both he made contributions of primary importance. During his lifetime he published three books: his doctoral dissertation already referred to; *The Hippocratic Oath: Text, Translation, and Interpretation* (Baltimore: Johns Hopkins Press, 1943. *Supplements to the Bulletin of the History of Medicine,* No. 1); and with his wife Emma J. Edelstein, *Asclepius: A Collection and Interpretation of the Testimonies,* 2 vols. (Baltimore: Johns Hopkins Press, 1945). A fourth book, which he had finished and sent to his publisher but of which he did not correct proof, appeared after his death: *Plato's Seventh Letter* (Leiden: E.J. Brill, 1966. *Philosophia Antiqua.* Vol. XIV). Death also prevented him from finishing three additional monographs on which he had been working for many years. Parts of two of them have been published: *The Meaning of Stoicism* (Cambridge, Mass., 1966. Martin Classical Lectures. Vol. XXI) and *The Idea of Progress in Classical Antiquity* (Baltimore: The Johns Hopkins Press, 1967). The materials for the third, a collection of the fragments of Posidonius with commentary, have been utilized in *Posidonius.* I. *The Fragments,* edited by L. Edelstein and I.G. Kidd (Cambridge: Cambridge University Press, 1972). (The volume containing the commentary is now in the press.)

In addition a collection of his papers on the history of medicine has been published: *Ancient Medicine. Selected Papers of Ludwig Edelstein,* edited by Owsei Temkin and C. Lilian Temkin (Baltimore: The Johns Hopkins Press, 1967). One may therefore say that with the publication of the present volume containing his main papers on ancient philosophy most of Edelstein's *Opuscula* are now more easily available to scholars and students. (I understand that the Johns Hopkins Press plans soon to re-issue in paperback *Ancient Medicine.*) Of the twenty-three papers published here, four (Nos. 5, 6, 9, and 12) have also been included in *Ancient Medicine.* The reason for reprinting them here is to make the present volume as complete and self-contained as possible. I have placed at the beginning three papers of a more general nature. Thereafter they are arranged in chronological order of subjects; also in each case the more general papers have been placed first.

It is to be hoped that one or another of Edelstein's students will one day give a picture of him as a teacher. But his books and papers reveal clearly, I believe, a man for whom humanistic research and the study of classical antiquity were integrated into his own life and thought and were not only of antiquarian interest. I heard him lecture twice: once at the Institute for Advanced Study on the idea of progress in antiquity and later at Johns Hopkins, where I attended the first meeting of his Plotinus seminar. The latter occasion especially left on me an indelible impression of an assessment of Plotinus as a philosopher who is alive and important for us today.[1]

Leonardo Tarán
Department of Classics
Columbia University

1. On Edelstein's life cf. Harold Cherniss, "Ludwig Edelstein," *Year Book of the American Philosophical Society* (1965), pp. 130-137 and Owsei Temkin, "In Memory of Ludwig Edelstein," *Bulletin of the History of Medicine* 40 (1966), pp. 1-13. The latter contains a complete bibliography up to 1966, which I have supplemented here with Edelstein's posthumous publications.

Contents

Introduction

1. "Philosophy—The Pilot of Life." (Phi Beta Kappa Address at Columbia University).
   Teachers College Record 65 (1964).
2. "The Greco-Roman Concept of Scientific Progress."
   ITHACA, Actes du Xeme Congrès International d'Histoire des Sciences 26 VIII–2 IX 1962. (Paris: Hermann, 1965).
3. "Motives and Incentives for Science in Antiquity."
   A. C. Crombie (editor), *Scientific Change.* Historical studies in the intellectual, social and technical conditions for scientific discovery and technical invention, from antiquity to the present. (New York: Basic Books, 1963).
4. "The Golden Chain of Homer."
   Studies in Intellectual History (Baltimore: The Johns Hopkins Press, 1953).
5. "The Relation of Ancient Philosophy to Medicine."
   Bulletin of the History of Medicine 26 (1952).
6. Review of M. Pohlenz, *Hippokrates und die Begründung der wissenschaftlichen Medizin.*
   American Journal of Philosophy 61 (1940).
7. "The Function of the Myth in Plato's Philosophy."
   Journal of the History of Ideas 10 (1949).
8. "Platonic Anonymity."
   American Journal of Philology 83 (1962).

9. "The Role of Eryximachus in Plato's *Symposium.*" *Transactions of the American Philological Association* 76 (1945).
10. "Randall on Aristotle, a Review." *Journal of Philosophy* 59 (1962).
11. "Aristotle and the Concept of Evolution." *Classical Weekly* (now *Classical World*) 37 (1944).
12. Review of W. Jaeger, *Diokles von Karystos. Die griechische Medizin und die Schule des Aristoteles.* *American Journal of Philology* 61 (1940).
13. Review of F. Wehrli, *Die Schule des Aristoteles, Texte und Kommentar.* Heft IV: *Demetrios von Phaleron.* Heft V: *Straton von Lampsakos.* Heft VI: *Lykon und Ariston von Keos.* Heft VII: *Herakleides Pontikos.* *American Journal of Philology* 76 (1955).
14. Review of K. Deichgräber, *Die griechische Empirikerschule.* *Deutsche Literaturzeitung* 24 (1931).
15. Review of M. Pohlenz, *Die Stoa.* *American Journal of Philology* 72 (1951).
16. Review of M. van Straaten, *Panétius, sa vie, ses écrits et sa doctrine avec une édition des fragments.* *American Journal of Philology* 71 (1950).
17. Review of L. Labowsky, *Die Ethik des Panaitios.* *American Journal of Philology* 59 (1938).
18. "The Philosophical System of Posidonius." *American Journal of Philology* 57 (1936).
19. "Primum Graius Homo (Lucretius 1. 66)." *Transactions of the American Philological Association* 71 (1940).
20. Review of P. Boyancé, *Études sur le Songe de Scipion.* *American Journal of Philology* 59 (1938).
21. "Cicero: De Natura Deorum, II." *Studi Italiani di Filologia Classica* n. s. 11 (1934).
22. Review of R. Walzer, *Galen on Medical Experience.* *The Philosophical Review* 56 (1947).
23. Review of E. O. Wallace, *The Notes on Philosophy in the Commentary of Servius on the Eclogues, the Georgics, and the Aeneid of Vergil.* *American Journal of Philology* 65 (1944).

Teachers College
RECORD

VOLUME 65 NO. 4 JANUARY 1964

LUDWIG EDELSTEIN
The Rockefeller Institute
New York City

Philosophy—the pilot of life

IN THE BEGINNING, the ideal of Phi Beta Kappa was shrouded in becoming secrecy. The minutes of the first meeting of the Founding Fathers give only the initials of the motto adopted as the name of their society (*21*, p. 1). Now, the words to be spelled out are well known. *Philosophia biou kybernetes*, philosophy, the pilot of life: This has, from the very first, been the proud contention, the message of Phi Beta Kappa. The handshake, the brotherly love that one member owes the other, the friendly communion designed "as a recreation to the philosophic mind, satiate with investigating the various springs of human nature and human actions" (*21*, p. 9; cf. *14*)—such an outward sign, such a bond of attachment, and such a community of thought and discussion are but the manifestations of the lofty creed which inspired the founders of the Society, of their conviction that philosophy must be and is, in fact, the true and only steersman of life.

Yet, if we are honest, can we deny that their belief is not ours? To be sure, we still compare human life with traveling on the high seas, but the voyage in our opinion, is guided by altogether different forces. The windows of our

Are we captains of our own destiny or pawns of circumstance? How we answer largely decides the stance we take toward education. In this adaptation of a Phi Beta Kappa address at Columbia University, Dr. Edelstein, a philosopher-in-residence among the scientists of the Rockefeller Institute, makes a moving case for self-determination, proving that rationalism still speaks for as well as to us.

bookstores are replete with copies of novels called *The Ship of Fools* or *The Black Ship to Hell.* Our historians and sociologists and statesmen, and even most of our philosophers, are no more sanguine than are our novelists. "We sail a boundless and bottomless sea," they are fond of saying, "where there is neither starting point nor appointed destination, and where our sole aim can be to keep afloat on an even keel" (*16*, p. 22). Our ship has no pilot. And were we to complain, like Odysseus, that we are being sent on a long and dangerous voyage without a steersman "to guide us on our way," the only consolation we would receive (or would accept) is the one given to Odysseus by Circe, the sorceress: "The winds will carry you" (*Odyssey* X, 501 ff.)—that is, in our language, I suppose, external circumstances and powers other than our own.

The ideal of 1775, engraved on Phi Beta Kappa keys, is, then, no longer engraved on our hearts. We disregard it, we even slight it. Are we right in doing so? This, it seems to me, is a question no one can avoid asking in the present situation as in all times, for it touches upon the fundamental problems of human existence. To give an answer is difficult and hazardous. I venture to prepare the ground for finding it by recalling what has been said and can be said in favor of the message of the motto. Undoubtedly, the ideals which we reject deserve that much attention. Otherwise, their rejection is in danger of becoming dogmatic and unreasoned.

Philosophy as Reason

Let me begin by tracing the source from which the words *philosophia biou kybernetes* were taken, clarifying the teaching they embody and our quarrel with it. Certainly, the saying was not an invention *ex nihilo*. As has long been recognized, it is probably the Gre adaptation of a phrase of Cicero's, its taken from a Greek author: *O vitae ph losophia dux* (*Tusc. Disp.* V, 2, 5), " philosophy, you leader of life" (6 Speaking of philosophy as "the leade of life, Cicero thinks of it as the for that civilized men, founded their citi created their laws, and secured their e istence. In short, he thinks of philosoph as the instigator of practical and theore ical life; he defines the task of philosoph in its broadest sense. The Greek rende ing that makes of philosophy "the pilo of life shifts the emphasis not insigni cantly and stresses the role that philo ophy plays in an *individual's* life. As o pilot, philosophy gives direction to o voyage; it tells us where we ought go. It brings us to the port of destinatio or, if this proves impossible, it at lea tells us what is the right course a makes us follow it. "Let us steer our ow ship," says Seneca, "and not allow (ou side) powers to sweep us from th course. He is a sorry steersman who le the waves tear the helm from his hand who has left the sails to the mercy the winds and abandoned the ship to th storm; but he deserves praise, even am shipwreck, whom the sea overwhelm still gripping the rudder and unyielding (*Cons. ad Marc.* VI).

As regards the word "philosophy neither Cicero nor he who translat him into Greek does, I believe, use it its formal sense.[1] Both think of philos phy as the representative of reason, th reason which is able to discern the trut He for whom philosophy is the pil steers his ship by the light of those sta which shine in the world of true know ledge, "visible only to the mind, the pil of the soul," as Plato has it (*Phaedr* 247 C). On the square medal of Phi Be Kappa, devised "for the better establish

[1] The contrary is maintained by Ducasse (5

ment and sanctitude of our unanimity," there is, in addition to the Greek letters, "an index imparting a philosophical design, extended to the three stars, a part of the planetary orbit" (*21*, p. 1). These stars are, I take it, the Sun, the Moon, and Venus, the triad distinguished as the most brilliant of the planets, the great rulers of the zodiac (*4*, p. 47; cf. pp. 79, 22). They symbolize the regular and undeviating course of the heavenly signs in which the eternity of truth becomes manifest to our bodily eye, and which, as the *Timeaeus* (90 B ff.) puts it, our souls are destined to imitate as far as possible—the eternal truth of the heavenly abode from which the soul has come into the world here below (41 D ff.).

I hasten to add that the young men who adopted the motto, though young, can hardly have been naïve in their endorsement of reason, in their belief in its power as a pilot. Almost half a century before, a very different view of reason had been expressed, one still widely acclaimed at the end of the eighteenth century, and one of which they cannot have been ignorant. As Pope says in his *Essay on Man* (II, 107 f.),

> On life's vast ocean diversely we sail,
> Reason's the card, but Passion is the gale.

Here reason and insight have no power. "The card, the compass, neither propels the ship nor determines the direction in which it is to sail." It merely enables the mariner to know in which direction he is moving. It is the passions that provide "the sole dynamic factor in human behavior." And these passions are not only diverse, they are antagonistic to one another. "Every individual's will is dominated by some obsessing 'Master Passion,' which is the 'mind's disease':

> Reason itself but gives it edge and pow'r,
> As Heaven's blest beam turns vinegar
> more sour" (13, p. 43).

How modern is the theory, even though the conclusion is not! For this chaos of individual passions in the end becomes a cosmos of harmonious living; the selfishness of the one individual is counteracted by the selfishness of the others; taken together, they mysteriously create an "according music," "the joy, the peace, the glory of mankind." For God has so ordained things; his invisible hand has arranged them in such a way that private vices become public virtues.

Vision of Greatness

This was perhaps the basic belief also of the fathers of the American Constitution (*13*, pp. 46 ff.). It was *not* the belief that brought the founders of Phi Beta Kappa together to discuss the problems they were interested in, "remembering that everything transacted is transacted *sub rosa* and detested is he that discloses it" (*21*, p. 10). Their questions were youthful questions—whether duelling is to be abolished, whether it is advantageous to a scholar to be in love—as well as questions, if not of greater depth, at least of more general concern—for instance, whether public education is preferable to private education, whether stealing in extreme want is morally permissible, whether there is anything more dangerous to civil liberty than a standing army in peace time, whether Brutus was justified in killing Caesar, whether all affections and principles are not in some measure deducible from self-love (*21*, pp. 13 f.; 58). In asking such questions, they sought for the true, the right, the better, for what the individual ought to do; and they hoped to ascertain it through reason, through continuous and reasonable argumentation. For they believed in what has been called the Heavenly City of the eighteenth-century philosophers (*1*). To them, man, guided by the light of reason, seemed capable of finding out what is the good life and thus of achieving it. Certainly, he can fail in his efforts if the circumstances are against him. Even then, however, he has the consolation of knowing that he is doing the right thing, persevering in it so that his cause may have another day—here or there. Those who founded Phi Beta Kappa subscribed to Seneca's verdict that "no fortune can shut off the wise man, the reasonable man from action . . . he is ready for either outcome: If it brings goods, he controls them; if evils, he conquers them . . . neither poverty, nor pain, nor anything else that deflects the inexperienced and drives them headlong restrains him from his course" (*Ep.* 85, 38 f.).

I need not say that such an attitude is the very antithesis of the attitude which, in our time, tends more and more to be endorsed in matters of private and public concern. As individuals, we hardly trust in life until we can control it. Our mood is not to judge situations but to work them out by giving particular answers to particular problems. Sorrow and mental anguish, we have learned, need not be conquered by the mind; they can be removed from the domain of the mind once it is tranquillized by drugs. Even at the death of those whom we love, we shrink from dying a little ourselves, from withdrawing from the world of the living. This at least is the wisdom we are disposed to cherish. It is the wisdom of adjustment. We live in the moment and for it. Reality, as we call it, takes precedence over principle.

And concerning affairs of the common weal, we are wont to say that the less man clogs the free play of his mind with political doctrine and dogma, the better for his thinking. Some, to be sure, still complain of a "tired lull" and the absence at present of argument on general politics and are disturbed by the fact that programs and ideals are forgotten by all parties. Many more, I a afraid, will agree that it is a token greater national maturity to be und turbed by the workings of political p losophy, hoping that we will long co tinue to be undisturbed by them (*15*, p 5-7). We are empiricists; we are prac cal, and we take pride in both. We a determined by events, not by intellectu movements. Our criterion is success o if you prefer, "what works best." Pre nant failures, not unknown in histor which turn out to have made vital co tributions to the achievement of tomo row, go without acclaim (*2*, p. 171).

Man and Nature

In short, neither in private nor public life do we trust in the pilot of th ship who says, to quote Plato's famo parable (*Republic*, VI), that he mu give his attention not only to the sh and its present condition, but also to th time of the year, the seasons, the sk the winds, the stars, and all that pertai to his art, if he is to be a true ruler of ship (489 D-E). Such a pilot, to us, "in very deed . . . a star-gazer, an id babbler, a useless fellow" (E). For the *is* no art or science of life or politi that prescribes "the right course." It not that we argue that a ship "navigate in the happy-go-lucky manner coul ever arrive into port" (*3*, ch. 1). W question whether there is a port int which we are destined to arrive, an whether, if there were one, we coul discover it.

The Platonic parable, the plea that th ship be steered by a "true ruler" (497 D) announced a new enterprise, a new ad venture in human history. Throug Greek philosophy, man, for the firs time, saw and experienced himself a entirely different from nature; for th first time, he understood that he had possession peculiarly his own, reason or spirit or however you wish to translate the Greek term *logos* (*18*, pp. 66, 71). Thus philosophers, as the Greeks would say, invented, or as we would put it, proposed the interpretation of man as a rational being. Their belief in his rationality was to constitute the common ground of the metaphysical systems that reigned through the ages up to the eighteenth century, while the counterargument of the materialists and biologists remained a weak undercurrent (*19*, p. 63). The nineteenth century became doubtful of the Greek venture. We are convinced—and it is not a matter of mere whim—that it has failed. For the proud claim of the past, we hold, has been shown, by stubborn and irrefutable facts of nature and history, to be an illusion. This is our mature judgment, in which, despite a feeling of superiority, there is perhaps, as so often in the judgment of the aged and the more mature, an overtone of regret, of sadness that the dreams of youth should have proved to be dreams.

Are we right in our contention? I would surely go beyond all bounds of propriety, and far beyond the limits of my knowledge, were I now to indulge in a metaphysical discourse on idealism and naturalism. But there are certain experiences that have given rise to the concept of the *homo sapiens*, the rational being, just as others have given rise to other interpretations of human nature, such as the concept of the *homo faber*, man the maker, the empirical, positivistic, pragmatic being, and to many more which the philosophical anthropologist, the student of man's self-interpretations, is fond of distinguishing. And I stay within my province, I think, in raising the question of whether the data which the concept of man as a rational being summarizes are not still data to which no other concept of his self-interpretation does equal justice.

No—in Rational Thunder

To start with, I shall quote two texts that describe what in the parlance of modern philosophy is called the human situation. I have selected them not from poetry or novels, for the poets and the novelists, though to be sure the Muses have given to them to tell the truth, are not infrequently also tellers of lies, as the old proverb has it. Nor do my examples come from philosophical textbooks, which one may suspect of bias. They are taken from the book of reality. They are simple records of what happens, not, to be sure, in times of prosperity, not in happy times when men usually recoil from facing the ultimate questions, but in situations where they act under the duress of conflict, of that life-and-death struggle which, since the First World War, has been faced almost daily in some parts of the world by people put in prisons, in concentration camps. In short, my examples are taken from accounts of members of the German and French Resistance.

The last words of one of the leaders in the German opposition to Hitler, who committed suicide, were these:

> Everybody will now turn upon us and cover us with abuse. But my conviction remains unshaken: We have done the right thing. Hitler is not only the arch enemy of Germany; he is the archenemy of the world. In a few hours I shall stand before God answering for my actions and my omissions. I think I shall be able to uphold with a clear conscience all that I have done in the fight against Hitler. . . . Whosoever joined the Resistance movement put on the shirt of Nessus. The worth of a man is certain only if he is prepared to sacrifice his life for his convictions (*20*, p. 1395).

Sartre, simply reporting on what everyone in the Resistance experienced, speaks no differently:

> Exile, captivity, and especially death . . . became for us the habitual objects of our concern. We learned that they were neither inevitable accidents, nor even constant and exterior dangers, but that they must be considered as our lot itself, our destiny, the profound source of our reality as men. At every instant we lived up to the full sense of this commonplace little phrase: Man is mortal. And the choice that each of us made of his life and of his being was an authentic choice because it was made face to face with death, because it could always have been expressed in these terms: "Rather death than. . . ." And here I am not speaking of the élite among us who were real Resistants, but of all Frenchmen who, at every hour of the night and day throughout four years, answered No (*17*, pp. 498-500).

The power to say "No" in a given situation, the experience described in these two documents, is, I believe, the starting point for the interpretation of man as a rational being. For although this power does not always appear with the dramatic emphasis which it has at crucial points of life, it pervades our whole existence. The ability to say *no* to the moment constitutes our humanity, and for the rationalist, it is the gift of reason. For reason is not only capable of formulating principles of insight or of action; it is first of all a liberating force, the power to negate.

To Conceive a World

One aspect of this reason which restrains us like a golden cord is set forth by Plato with great precision. Our appetites, he says in the *Republic*, our drives—thirst, for instance—is just thirst, "neither of much nor little nor good nor bad, nor in a word of any kind" (439 A). The thirsty man, in so far as he thirsts, wishes nothing else than to drink, and his impulse is toward this. But something "draws him back" (B). There is not only that which "bids" him to drink but also that which "forbids" him to drink (C). And while the one "draws and drags," the other calculates and reckons (D). While thirst "drives man like a beast" (439 B), reason, instead of "bidding," forbids; it says, "Thou must not" (440 B), and asks us to choose. But it is not only with regard to drives and passions that reason makes us abandon unconscious responses. Living within the domain of concrete reality, we are subject to the everchanging sense perceptions which impinge upon us. Reason opposes to these fleeting impressions of the Here and Now an emphatic No, building out of the momentary and the passing a world of permanence—of concepts, of essences. All understanding is bought at the price of denying the truth of the moment. By negating the world of perceptions, we conceive another world through reason (*19*, p. 52).

In this sense, man, compared with the animal that always says *yes* to drives and perceptions, even when it avoids them or flees from them—man, the animal endowed with reason, the being who can and does say *no*, is "the ascetic of life," "the protestant par excellence" against sensual reality (*19*, pp. 54 f.). And it was through the use of his reason that he conquered himself and the world. The passage in Cicero from which Phi Beta Kappa's motto is derived means just this. Whatever the role played by need, as the ancients say, by the instinct of self-preservation, by the necessities of survival, at the very beginnings of human history, it was under the leadership of reason that cities were founded, that laws were formulated and governments instituted, that science arose, an objective analysis of phenomena replacing the fancies of mythology. Thus civilization was created; and with it arose the concept of humanity, of the unity of mankind, as well as the belief in continuous progress which leads man from a stage of savage and barbaric existence, where he is no more than another animal, to ever higher states of life.

This ancient philosophy of culture was obscured in the Middle Ages. The pilot of the boat was supplanted by Fortune—sometimes glad, sometimes sad—and her wheel on which men climb and fall. The lesson was that we should turn from earthly things to the contemplation of the eternal. The Renaissance spoke of Fortune as the goddess with the sail; but while she is directing the boat, man sits at the oar and rows. Resignation had given place to new trust in human strength. Soon, reason as the pilot was rediscovered. In the eighteenth century, belief in it became a commonplace. Dare to use your reason (*sapere aude*), urges Kant in the little essay in which he explains the meaning of "Enlightenment." Through daring to use reason, man leaves behind the state of non-age, grows to maturity, goes farther and farther.

The Questions

But has reason such power? Can one assume with the rationalists of the old school that there are in man two forces entirely different in origin? Can one, in the old-fashioned way, distinguish between body and soul and maintain that reason controls impulses? Is it not in reality led by them? Does reason not evolve out of life? One cannot fail to ask these questions. In answering them, I shall again not rely on metaphysical deductions, but point to the situations and to the reflections upon them that underlie the metaphor of the ship and the pilot and the self-interpretation of man as a rational being.

"It cannot be," Plato asserts in the *Republic*, "that the same thing with the same part of itself at the same time acts in opposite ways about the same thing . . . (For) I fancy it is not well said of the archer that his hands at the same time thrust away the bow and draw it nigh, but we should rather say that there is one hand that puts it away and another that draws it to" (439 B). And the one hand we call irrational, the other, rational. We are forbidden to proceed otherwise by the law of contradiction Or, to translate Plato's words into categories more fitting to the modern mode of thinking, the principle that transcends what we call life in the most general sense cannot be merely an element of life which belongs to the psychic and vital functions and capacities and thus falls into the provinces of psychology and biology. As a principle opposed to life, even to life in man, it is outside the realm of evolution, "and if reducible to anything, leads back to the ultimate ground of Being of which life itself is a particular manifestation." It is therefore that *logos*, reason or spirit, cannot be thought of as "an episodic fact of earthly life"; it is, as it were, of the fabric of the whole that comprises us and everything which exists (*19*, p. 36).[2]

This dualism does not, of course, gainsay the fact that these antagonistic principles are not mutually exclusive. Some rationalists, it is true, have assumed that man must make a choice between life and reason, that reason by itself is creative even of action. This, I think, was not the conviction of Plato, or of any of the great ancient rationalists, or of those who later followed their lead Rather, they assigned each force its own and indispensable role. The impulse to act comes from life. But it is mere response to what happens. By saying *no* to

[2]This essay is perhaps the most searching analysis of the symbol of the *homo sapiens*.

the moment, to the immediate and blind reaction, reason opens the possibility of proceeding in another way and, in addition, kindles a light through which reaction becomes action. Having liberated or released man from his servitude to the data of experience, having repressed his momentary wishes and instinctual drives, it proposes to the impulse to act, which it cannot itself create, other images that provide guidance. Becoming "the pilot of the boat," reason brings about the realization of the ideas and values of which it is the source (*18*, p. 2).

Of course, the voice of reason which says "you ought not" or "you ought rather" does not necessarily provide an altogether unfailing sense of direction. No age would have claimed this. The insight into the relativity of rational thought or into the historicity of human knowledge has merely been formulated more clearly in the nineteenth and twentieth centuries; it was not foreign to the ancient rationalists or to those of the eighteenth century. Herodotus expatiated on the variety of the interpretations of the lawful which is to be found among the nations of the globe. Plato and Kant emphasized the dialectical nature of reason. But for the rationalist, neither the dialectic of reason nor its involvement in the historical process proves its impotence. The good, the true, the beautiful, the planets to which the index on the Phi Beta Kappa plaque points, run their immutable and eternal course, though when we look at them from our station here on earth, they seem to have irregular motions. Likewise, the fact that mountains appear to take on different shapes from different angles of vision does not argue that there are no mountains or that they have no shape at all or any shape imaginable. The relativity and historicity of so many values must not deceive us into believing that no standards are generally accepted.[8] The light of truth, broken as it is into the spectrum of individual existence, still is the reflection of the light of a truth absolute, not relative, everlasting and not waning. Through discussion, through argument, through ever renewed consideration of problems, we do find the better in the course of time—as much of the truth as mortal eyes are able to discover. That is why the unexamined life is not worth living, why the rational man indulges in matters of speculation and never desists from argumentation.

Pain of Prometheus

Not only is the voyage undertaken with a fallible sense of direction; not only do new vistas come into sight where the old landscape appears in a changed form; it is also a voyage that may be stormy, that may even end in shipwreck. Suffering is an ineradicable part of life. There are victories and defeats in the history of individuals as well as of societies. And especially in the story of the spirit of liberty, the protagonist is often cast in the role of Prometheus, "defying the Powers of this world," powers that "are ruthless, competent, and strong, and among the properties in the play there are real lightning and a real eagle" (*9*, p. 154). Yet whether we think of man as an individual or as a member of the community, it is just in the inevitable vicissitudes of life that the force of reason shows itself most strongly. The rationalist, suffering pain, asks not only "What caused it?" or "How can it be removed?" This is a matter of practical intelligence, and the answer lies with such sciences as physiology, psychology, or medicine. He asks also, "What is pain itself?" and

[8]This is beginning to be admitted also by anthropologists and sociologists; see Merlan (*14*, p. 49). I have borrowed the metaphor of the mountain from Carr (*2*, p. 30).

"What must be the nature of things that such a phenomenon as pain is possible?" If encountering a poor man or seeing a man dying, he asks, "What is poverty or death?" and "What is a world in which such things happen?" Thus distinguishing essence from existence, he reaches out into another realm. He becomes conscious of the fact that he is at home not only here, but also there—that he has a dual citizenship, as it were. The suspension of the momentary impressions, the entering into "those regions where the pure forms dwell," makes him superior to "the anguish of earthly existence" as well as to the fear and anxiety of the existentialist, unable to "realize the general, the universal," as Kierkegaard said of himself (*8*, p. 39).

It is not that suffering ceases, that through understanding the hardship of life is annihilated. The pilot, say the ancients, "is harmed by any circumstance which does not permit him to make port, frustrates all his efforts, and either carries him out to sea, or holds the ship in irons, or strips her masts"; but he is harmed "not as a pilot, but only as a voyager" (Seneca, *Ep.* 85, 34). The two are, so to say, two different persons, two different roles, and he must not mistake one for the other. Although as a passenger, as a voyager, the pilot can be harmed and his concerns be thwarted; although in playing this role and in suffering even the destruction of his individuality, he is forlorn and forsaken, he is not alone in his role of pilot. His art brings him into communication with all who have reason. For reason, by its very nature, is universal, and he who clings to it is united with all who share in reason, even with those before or after him.

This, at least in broad outlines, is an account of the situations, of the reflections upon them, which gave rise to the metaphor of the pilot and the boat. But as I have indicated before, though we may find ourselves in the same situations, we understand them quite differently. We cannot persuade ourselves that reason teaches the truth, that to some degree it makes us masters of our fate. And it sounds paradoxical to us when we are told that "there are times when a man ought to be more afraid of living than of dying" (*10*, p. 13). To us, experience, the observation of "facts," rather than reason, is the great teacher. Moreover, whatever our verdict on events in our own life or in the world at large, there is, it seems, nothing we can do about them. Things happen to us; history is made without us. Last though not least, whether men be driven by desires or guided by reason, they seek the realization of their wishes and hopes; fulfillment in this life is the goal, and failure to reach it is the refutation of our aspirations. With such convictions in our hearts and minds, how can there still be belief in reason as the pilot?

What Knowing Is

Yet it is well to remember, first of all, that it is not self-evident that knowledge is the knowledge of facts. Epistemological analysis inevitably leads to the result that all statements of fact involve interpretation—that is, an act of mind. Experience is made up of both the given and our thought about it. Facts ar data of experience are arrived at through conclusions (*12*, pp. 169 ff.). This is most obvious in the very sciences in which we trust most. For it is (or ought to be) a truism that they do *not* study facts in the commonly acknowledged sense of the word. The phenomena the natural sciences scrutinize, the world they analyze, is a world of constructs. Knowledge and its objects, as applied to nature, are one and the same. The study of atoms, electrons, and all the other natural constituents presupposes, as perhaps its most important piece of apparatus, not merely the inquiring mind, but the scientific mind as it has been shaped by the entire history of the human race, particularly by the history of western civilization. Each stage of theoretical knowledge and practical skill is dependent on the one previously reached, on the progress made in the past, just as it prepares for the progress to be made in the future. Once the general hypothesis was made that the world could be understood by reason, nature became, in principle, understandable. Through more specific hypotheses, constantly reformulated, understanding has increased and will increase. Thus, it makes good sense to say that nature, as that which is known or knowable, exists independently of our knowledge merely as a "potential reality" that is actualized in the process of understanding itself (7, pp. 396 f.; also pp. 390 f.).

As for the problem of actions, individually performed or taken by the body politic, wherever one stands with regard to the issue of freedom and determinism, of whether men or impersonal forces are more decisive for the course of events, he will admit that not everything is possible in human affairs. We cannot discount the objective forces which we encounter and which not infrequently subdue even the greatest and strongest. Yet we are not on that account at the mercy of circumstances. Rather, we all, whatever our place, have an ineluctable share in the things to come.

For when we are on the point of making a decision but not yet committed to one, we must choose among alternatives. No matter what our convictions, we cannot take refuge behind the dogma that events are inevitable. And while all options are still open, the future does not as yet exist as an object, as it were, at which we may look; it is still in th making. Deliberating on the possibilitie before us, we are not least influenced b what we want, by our aims and concern These, as much as the forces existin outside, become themselves factors de termining the future which we ma theoretically hold to be decided; the become a criterion of choice. Therefor the most stubborn fact about a give situation is the way we look at it. Ou understanding of ourselves is part of ou destiny. This is true of the individu with regard to his own life, as well a of the statesman with regard to the pub lic good. It is not a sign of maturity, bu rather of self-deception, to ignore poli ical ideals or ambitions and hopes. Fo we cannot escape our responsibility fo the events that take place. To some ex tent, we bring them about, as the mome of decision attests (7, pp. 400 f.).

Finally, there is no denying that bot idealists and materialists desire to g what they want, that they wish for th fulfillment of their intentions, that the crave the possession of the objects f which they strive. Yet, strange as th phenomenon may be from the point view of the naturalist, and unique as is in the animal kingdom, man, in add tion, *judges* himself and his actions. Bei a self-conscious animal, he is "both act and spectator, both performer and co mentator on or critic of the perform ance." And while as actor and perform he seeks his own satisfaction, as spectat and commentator, he has a desire f distinction, for superiority, an emulativ ness which is independent of what ha pens to him; he has an eagerness f self-esteem and the esteem of others, approbativeness, that is founded not what he accomplishes, but on what endeavors to achieve (*13*, especially p 82; 92; 100; 106; 112). These gifts fr us from considering as values merely th acquisition and possession of the things we desire to attain; they allow us to appreciate the significance of the aims envisaged. Strength is given to the principle, "Do unto others as ye would that they should do unto you." The phrase, "I ought to do this," in contradistinction to the phrase, "I desire to do this," becomes meaningful (*13*, pp. 104 f.).

Pilot, Not Voyager

At this point we begin to think of ourselves as moral agents, as men who choose values, and to want others to think of us as moral agents; we draw the balance of our life and take account not of particular acts alone, but of the sum total of our existence; in short, we do not think of ourselves as voyagers, but assess our merit as pilots of the boat. The issue is not one of whether we have gotten into port, but whether we have chosen the right route and steered the right course. For this is what makes the good pilot; even shipwreck, if it is caused by uncontrollable circumstances rather than lack of skill and insight, does not lower our esteem for the pilot. The requirements of his art are fulfilled when he can say, as did the Rhodian of old, "Neptune, you shall never sink this ship except on her course" (Seneca, *Ep.* 85, 33).

The art of life, the reasonable steering of existence, makes no greater demand upon us. We pray and hope, as we must, that we will be fortunate in carrying out our decisions. But we learn and have to learn that even when we are defeated, our aims and ideals are not yet refuted. To be worthy of the esteem of oneself and of others whom one respects, then, counts as much as success or failure. And we realize that the satisfaction of our desires dies with the moment that brings it, whereas the judgment on ourselves stays with us throughout our lives. In the shipwreck of today, we look to the future, when others may be luckier in the struggle whose outlines in the past we barely discern and whose final outcome we cannot predict.

If we view our earthly voyage in this light, if we want to do what is right, if we want to be able to approve of ourselves and to have the approval of others for the right reason, in order that the divine gift does not lead to our debasement, reason alone, philosophy, can show us which course to follow. The Ship of Fools may arrive in port, but not even all of its passengers truly desire to go where it anchors. The Black Ship to Hell surely reaches its destination, but those who land in Orcus have been turned into shadows. The ship of the skeptic, said Kant after he had completed the work in which he attempted to vindicate reason against skepticism and dogmatism, runs ashore for safety's sake, remains lying there, and rots. Reason is the only pilot who "may steer the ship safely whither he listeth" (*11*, Introduction, p. 10). Philosophy, the pilot of life—it is still a message which we neglect at the peril of life itself.

REFERENCES

1. Becker, C. L. *The heavenly city of the eighteenth-century philosophers.* New Haven: Yale Univer. Press, 1932.
2. Carr, E. H. *What is history?* New York: Knopf, 1962.
3. Conrad, J. *Chance.* Garden City, N. Y.: Doubleday, 1921.
4. Cumont, F. *Astrology and religion among the Greeks and Romans.* New York: Putnam, 1912.
5. Ducasse, C. J. The guide of life. *The Key Reporter*, 1958, *2*, 2-6.
6. Fitch, E. Phi Beta Kappa. *The Classical Weekly*, 1909, *2*, 143.
7. Frank, E. "Nature and history" and "Time and eternity." In Edelstein, L. (Ed.), *Knowledge, will, and belief.* Zürich and Stuttgart: Artemis-Verlag, 1955.
8. Grene, Marjorie. *Dreadful freedom.* Univer. Chicago Press, 1948.
9. Hand, L. *The spirit of liberty.* New York: Knopf, 1960.

10. Hook, S. Pragmatism and the tragic sense of life. *Proceedings and Addresses of the American Philosophical Association*, 1959, 23, 5-26.
11. Kant, I. *Prolegomena to any future metaphysics*. New York: Liberal Arts Press, 1950 (1783).
12. Loewenberg, J. The futile flight from interpretation. *University of California Publications in Philosophy*, 1950, 25, 169-352.
13. Lovejoy, A. O. *Reflections on human nature*. Baltimore: The Johns Hopkins Press, 1961.
14. Merlan, P. Existentialism—a third way. *Proceedings and Addresses of the American Philosophical Association*, 1960, 33, 43-68.
15. Namier, L. *Personalities and powers*. London: Hamish Hamilton, 1955.
16. Oakeshott, M. *Political education*. New York: Cambridge Univer. Press, 1951.
17. Sartre, J.-P. *The republic of silence*. New York: Harcourt Brace, 1947.
18. Scheler, M. Man and history. In *Philosophical perspectives*. Boston: Beacon Press, 1958.
19. Scheler. *Man's place in nature*. Boston: Beacon Press, 1961.
20. Shirer, W. L. *The rise and fall of the Third Reich*. New York: Crest Books, 1962.
21. Voorhees, O. M. *The history of Phi Beta Kappa*. New York: Crown, 1945.

The Greco-Roman Concept of Scientific Progress

LUDWIG EDELSTEIN
Rockefeller Institute, New York, U.S.A.

In modern parlance, the word progress in its widest sense denotes, to quote Professor Lovejoy, "a tendency inherent in nature or in man to pass through a regular sequence of stages of development in the past, present and future, the later stages being—with perhaps occasional retardations or minor retrogressions—superior to the earlier" [1]. Such a concept, it has become commonplace to assert, was unknown to the ancients. More often than not, it is even said that the Greeks and Romans were unfamiliar with the idea of scientific progress; the belief that science is produced by the cooperation of succeeding generations, that it is an enterprise which leads further and further, is held instead to be a discovery of the Renaissance.

To this common view, I venture to oppose another thesis. The concept of scientific progress was, I suggest, first formulated in antiquity. Moreover, it played a pivotal rôle in shaping a general theory of progress not very different from the modern one. And the resulting philosophy of history was a strong competitor of the other ancient philosophies of history, such as the belief in a Golden Age of the past or the theory of a continuous decay of the human race.

Any discussion of the subject is beset by the difficulty that the evidence is scattered and disparate. No treatise survives in which the topic under investigation is dealt with on principle. In order to gain an understanding of the movement of progressivism one must integrate into a composite picture occasional remarks in tragedies, comedies, lyric poetry, philosophical, historical and scientific works, the only sources of information still available. Here, I cannot, of course, go through the process of reconstruction itself, or argue details; I must on the whole speak dogmatically. And I must restrict myself to raising three of the many questions involved, those which are perhaps of the greatest general interest. When was the concept of scientific progress formulated in all its aspects and how did it come to be formulated? What influence did it have on historical and philosophical thought? Finally, what was the relation of progressivism to the other philosophies of history, including that of the early Christians who still lived

*. The lecture given at the meeting is printed in the extended version written for the discussant. It is based on a book on the same topic which I hope will go to print next year and which should treat the problem in all its ramifications and more adequately than can be done even in the longer paper now published. J.T.C.

under the sway of ancient civilization, and whose view of history is more and more considered the origin of all progressive thought?

To begin with, it might be best to quote some testimony which puts it beyond any doubt, I think, that the concept of scientific progress is an ancient one. "The time will come," Seneca says [2], "when mental acumen and prolonged study will bring to light what now lies hidden... the time will come when our successors will wonder how we could have been ignorant of things so obvious." And he continues," many things unknown to us will be understood by men of future centuries, many are reserved for ages yet to come, when our memories will have perished. It is a petty world in which there would be no questions worth asking for every generation" [3]. Progress, then, will go on forever; it requires "long succeeding ages to unfold all" [4]. Knowledge is not a matter to be gained by one man, it is too great an undertaking "for a single lifetime"; it needs the cooperation of past and future generations [5]. Surely these assertions contain all the essential implications of what has been meant by continuous scientific progress even in modern centuries.

But Seneca, of course, was not expressing a thought peculiarly his own. In his time, belief in scientific progress was widespread. "Let no one lose hope that the ages will always progress in knowledge," exclaims Pliny [6]. "Use is always finding the seeds of new things in the old," contends Manilius [7]. Nor is the progressivism of the first century a novelty. Behind these substantially identical statements of the writers quoted, one can still descry their common source, the philosophy of the Middle Stoa, which is reflected in the writings of Cicero, especially in the second book of his *De natura deorum*. Whether the particular author whom he follows be Panaetius or Posidonius, it is certain that among philosophers at the end of the second century or the beginning of the first century BC the idea of scientific progress was taken for granted.

It was no less familiar to scientists of the 2nd century BC. Hipparchus, refusing to draw a new map of the earth though the old one seemed to him antiquated, asked for a combined research project by means of which the data would gradually be accumulated [8]. He prepared a list of the fixed stars observed in his own time for future astronomers, for the future solution of problems [9]. Polybius, proud of how much had been accomplished, especially in his own time [10], nevertheless realized how much was still unknown and would remain unknown until someone in years to come started upon further investigations [11].

Clearly, however, Hipparchus and Polybius, speaking as they did, echoed a sentiment that had been characteristic of Hellenistic science from its beginning. Both in philosophy and science, I think, an awareness of progress past, present and future can be found still much earlier, in fact, since the 5th century, and to an increasing degree. Yet, in all the passages that one might adduce from medical writings, historical works, essays on economics, the dialogues of Plato or the Aristotelian treatises, what definitively constitutes the concept of scientific progress and is so obvious in the Hellenistic evidence I have quoted, is missing, or at most, indistinctly expressed—I mean the full consciousness that the individual is but a link in the chain of generations. However, it is clearly formulated in the memorable words of Archimedes, written a hundred years before Hipparchus and Polybius:myself in the position of having "I am first made the discovery of the theorem now to be published, and I deem it necessary to expound the method, partly because I have already spoken of it and I do not want to have been thought to have uttered vain words, but equally because I am persuaded that it will be of no little service to mathematics; for I apprehend that some, either of my contemporaries or of my successors, will, by means of the method when once established, be able to discover other theorems in addition, which have not yet occurred to me " [12].

That it was the Hellenistic age which overcame completely the illusion of finality, so natural to men even when they talk about progress in the future, that it was Hellenistic scholars who not only foresaw further advances, but worked with a view toward them, realizing that they were but preparing the ground for the results to come, is confirmed even by the terminology they use in talking about progress. The 5th and 4th centuries had spoken of "growth" or "increase" *(epidosis)* in knowledge. And what Aristotle said seemed to express the general opinion: "The first start is the main thing, as the saying goes"; afterwards, it is easier to make additions, to attain considerable knowledge or skill [13]. The 3rd century replaced the term "growth" by another one, using the equivalent to the Latin word from which the modern "progress" is derived. It spoke of *prokope*, of cutting a new road that leads further. Here, the stress was no longer on adding something to the findings of old, on filling in gaps, on the continuity with the past; the emphasis was on what was being done at the moment. Man leaves behind him that point on the road at which he finds himself; he marches on. He faces forward, not backward; his concern is with what lies ahead, rather than with the distance already covered.

Why should it have been the early Hellenistic period that fully realized and expressed the meaning of scientific progress? That knowledge progresses, that man does not find everything to be known at one stroke, is an idea that was first formulated in the famous lines of Xenophanes. "The gods have not revealed to men all things from the beginning. Rather are men, through their own search, finding in the course of time that which is better" (Fr. 18). The 7th and 6th centuries BC had been a period of great advance in all departments of knowledge and in all technical skills. The political and economic situation had undergone decisive changes. Moral values were being re-examined, new standards sought and defended. Xenophanes was but reading the signs of his time when he objected to the philosophy of the Homeric epic which had made men the pupils of the gods in all they knew and did, the recipients of an insight and a skill that were unchangeable because they are god-given. But when Xenophanes pondered on the fact that the generations to follow would achieve even more than had so far been achieved—and he must have speculated about this; the Greeks were eager to penetrate the future—his forecast no doubt amounted to no more than a prediction in general terms. It is hard to succeed in realizing as a fact that things ahead will be as different from the present as the present is from the past; or even more so. Discoveries for him were still "inventions" *(heuremata)*. Once made, they are taken over, they may be improved, but neither their number nor the possibilities of varying them will have seemed to him inexhaustible.

The view which Xenophanes had put into words found almost general acceptance among the intellectuals of the 5th century, at least as far as the past and present of mankind was concerned. For most of the Presocratics and the Sophists, it was a foregone conclusion that man had gradually risen from primitive conditions to the level of civilized existence; animal-like at the very beginning, life had gradually become human. The present, too, continued to progress. But the thinkers of that period were fatalistic believers in the factual; they emphasized the limitations set to man. He has initiative, he can do much; but he cannot go beyond a certain point. In the 5th century, which witnessed not only an amazing expansion of knowledge all over Greece, as Aristotle testifies, but also a rapid advance in knowledge, the expectations for the future can hardly have been too great.

The 4th century was no less successful in extending the frontiers of science. It added many more discoveries and foresaw others. But though there was much talk about future progress, Plato's was the only voice heard in advocacy of a progress without end [14]. In general, what counted most with the intelligent observer of events was that which had been accomplished. This was especially true of Aristotle and his school in which scientific research was furthered most. Small wonder! For, as Bacon was to point out: "When a man looks at the variety and the beauty of the provisions brought together... he will certainly be more inclined to admire the wealth of man than to feel his wants" [15], and the thought that nothing or nothing much can be done naturally presents itself "to men grave and of great judgement" [16]. One began to understand the organic development of knowledge which the 5th century had failed to see. No longer was the history of civilization explained by a diffusion theory. The torch of knowledge is handed down, from one generation to the other as in a relay race [17]. Yet, for the Aristotelians, at any rate, an end was in sight.

Their expectations were not fulfilled. If progress had been great in the 4th century, it was greater still in the 3rd. The revolutionary advances in mathematics and geography, in anatomy and physiology, ushered in a new phase in the development of science. How could Hellenistic scientists, aware of the claims made by their predecessors, have the courage to believe that they were near the goal? Should not succeeding generations repeat their experience, outdoing vaunted predecessors, as they themselves had done? It was, I suggest, three hundred years of almost uninterrupted progress in science that finally gave rise to the belief—for it is a belief, rational to be sure, as it derives from certain experiences, but not a demonstrable truth—that the voyage of discovery is unending, that whenever man seems to come to the edge of the horizon, the horizon recedes anew.

As will be clear from what I have said, I take it that the concept of progress is derived from a comparison of past and present which allows a forecast of the future. To put it differently, it implies historical consciousness, an awareness of the relativity of particular situations, an appreciation of what is antiquated and what is modern. All these categories, recent interpreters are wont to deny to the ancients. They have no historical consciousness, one says. Instead, their historical analysis is concerned with eternal laws of human life, with typical, ever-recurrent factors. I shall not argue that this is too limited a view even of ancient political history. It certainly is an untenable view as regards ancient history of civilization or cultural history. Greeks and Romans wrote the history of the human race, as distinct from the history of cities or states, in terms of development and progress. Time and place determine the possibilities of man. In antiquity, too, there is a *Querelle des anciens et des modernes*. Documents from the 5th century BC, to the 2nd century AD attest to its violence and significance. And consciously taking the point of view of the moderns, the cultural historian treats the history of civilization as the gradual rise, the step-by-step development, of the arts and sciences, very much in the manner in which this history was still written in the 18th century, for instance by Hume.

One is, therefore, not astonished to find that the concept of progress comes to constitute a political ideal. Roman writers of the 1st century BC, as they preserved the most explicit definition of scientific progress, also stated most clearly its political implications. Man, being a citizen of the world in addition to being a citizen of his state or empire, has the obligation to work for the progress of the human race. Nor is the state exempt from the claims that scientific progress makes on human life. It has a cultural mission. Mastery over the sea is not given to men merely for the sake of bringing back products that increase luxury, but, above all, in order to spread to the furthest corners of the world knowledge and insight [18]. Pacification of the world is to be sought not merely for the sake of the security of the empire, but, above all, as a guarantee of cultural activities [19]. In short, there grows out of the reflection on progress a view of the state again almost identical with the view held by the great thinkers and historians of the 18th century, Shaftesbury, Voltaire, Hume and Robertson.

But long before the progressivist movement had led to the formulation of such a political ideal, the fact of scientific progress and of progress in general had become a problem for political philosophy, and more particularly, the philosophies of Plato and Aristotle. Both take it for granted that man's life is not static, but changing, and feel constrained to submit this datum of experience to critical analysis. As Plato put it, there is a double progressive development of a civilization in virtue and vice [20], a development which, in his opinion, is related to the growth of the arts and sciences. It is the task of the statesman to prevent any changes that may lead to moral corruption, and to insure moral improvement. In order to achieve this aim, progress must be supervised. One cannot leave to chance or the arbitrariness of an individual what should be done. A specially selected body of experienced persons must make the decision [21]. Aristotle on the other hand, tried to distinguish between progress in the arts and sciences and progress in political affairs. Discussing the law proposed by Hippodamus that all those who discover something of advantage to the state should receive honour [22], he drew a sharp distinction between changes in the constitution and changes in the arts and sciences. They are more dangerous in the former than in the latter. It would take me too far away from my subject were I to enter into a discussion of the details of Platonic and Aristotelian political theory. The point I wish to make is simply that in the 4th century BC the idea of progress was so well established that it could not be discarded by political theory.

A more decisive and more positive influence of the progressive movement can, I think, be detected in Greek philosophy of the second half of the Hellenistic period, in Scepticism, Epicureanism and Stoicism alike. To speak of the Sceptic school first, it had for centuries maintained that in view of the dissension among philosophers, nothing was left except to suspend judgement on all questions. Truth is beyond the reach of man. In this sense, Scepticism was the antithesis of progressivism. But Antiochus thought it unlikely that nothing should have been discovered since the first thinkers made an attempt to find a solution to the riddle of the world, that men of great genius, engaged in most earnest investigations, should in the course of so many centuries have got nowhere [23]. He therefore accepted Zeno's theory of cognition, which he considered superior to those of Plato and Aristotle. The individual, he held, must supplement the mere beginnings implanted in his own nature by searching further, just as in man written large, that is, in humanity, nature developed gradually with the assistance of the arts [24]. Thus, at least for a moment, Scepticism, the eternal shadow of dogmatism, disappeared before the light cast upon human nature by progress.

Far-reaching, if not revolutionary, changes were wrought in Stoicism as well as in Epicureanism. As for the latter, the founder of the school had been unconcerned with a life of learning. He asked his pupils to free themselves from the prison of the liberal arts and political life [25]. The wisdom and insight he taught were to be unalterable. Yet the Epicureans around Philodemus began to look with favour on mathematical investigations, as well as on historical studies. They worked out the principles guiding empirical research. In Lucretius' grandiose representation of the development of mankind this greater regard for the realities of life, even for politics, comes to the fore. The outlines of the story are not new. Instead, under the cloak of Epicurus' doctrine it gives the traditional picture that had been elaborated ever since the days of the Presocratics. The poet is not a blind admirer of progress either. He does not, I think, believe in an infinite advance of mankind. Nevertheless, it remains true that Epicureanism had changed in the atmosphere of a world for which the idea of progress was a commonplace.

The Stoa, even in its beginning, had not been as antagonistic to the arts and sciences as was Epicureanism. But even to Zeno, the arts and sciences, the means by which man had progressed, were useless after the task had been accomplished. The wise man is concerned with moral conduct. Moral improvement, progress of the individual on the road to virtue, is the true goal. With Panaetius and Posidonius, as I have already indicated, the matter stands differently. Man now finds his fulfilment in the cultivation of all his gifts, practical and theoretical. His *imperium in imperio* is the realm of civilization which he builds through his own efforts. The reformed Stoicism includes the detailed treatment of nature and history which had been absent from the teaching of the Old Stoa [26]. And moral perfectionism is transformed into a perfectionism pertaining to all products of the human mind and human hand. The task of man, the "caretaker of the earth," beautifying the land and preventing it from becoming a desert, adorning it with houses and cities [27], will continue as long as the world itself may last.

The influence exercized by the progressivist movement starting at the end of the 6th century on historical and philosophical thought in the classical and Hellenistic periods clearly indicated its rising significance. From the 2nd century AD, the importance of progressivism diminished and gradually became extinct. But the historian of the concept of progress cannot rest satisfied with such a general characterization of the rôle played by the idea of progress within ancient intellectual history. He will want a more definite estimate of the acceptance of progressivism, and especially of its strength relative to competing philosophies of history.

To attempt such an estimate is most difficult. For surely it will not do to argue, as one usually does, about *the* Greek or Roman attitude in such matters. It is not likely that within the thousand years of ancient history people always felt the same about the meaning of history. Granted that the national character shapes the peoples' judgement of what happens in this world, it is not an invariable constant, and different situations, brought about by changing events, call forth different responses. One must, then, try to proceed historically, that is, to evaluate the situation as it existed in the various phases of the history of antiquity.

The different intellectual trends competing with progressivism differ in time, too. Their evaluation, as far as it has been undertaken at all, is all too often vitiated by the same fault I have noted with regard to the evaluation of progressivism : they are taken as unchanging, as invariables. In every respect, then, the enterprise I propose, necessary as it is, is hazardous. Nor is it always certain which are the antagonistic forces to be dealt with. I shall leave out of consideration two concepts which are usually considered most inimical to progressive thought : the concept of eternal recurrence, and that of the final destruction of the world. In my opinion, they have no bearing on the problem at hand.

For even if it were true that belief in the cyclical return of things was as widespread as is commonly assumed, this belief is neutral as regards theories of development. Philosophers who speak of a repetition in number, to use the technical term, need not, and usually do not, deny development within each cycle. And though being repeated it loses the quality of uniqueness in the strict sense, it is still development. Where recurrence is but recurrence in kind, development can even have distinguishing features. On the other hand, the prophecy of a dissolution of the world impaired the progressivist creed in antiquity as little as it has in modern times. The proverbial running down of the clock of the universe was no hindrance to 19th century optimism and has little bearing in the 20th century on philosophies of history. It is surely not an intrinsic quality of the concept of progress that infinity must mean absolute infinity rather than infinite extension during the span of time in which the universe exists. Not infrequently, the progressivist will glory in the work to be done just because the visible cosmos will one day be shattered. Seneca's is a good example of this attitude [28].

To take up my topic proper, progressivism arose in opposition to the Homeric view of the world as static. The latter was still the predominant view of the 6th century. If men in the prosperous cities of Ionia, where Greek rationalism originated, took cognizance of Hesiod's song of the five ages, they will hardly have mistaken his tale for a philosophy of culture, as one did so often later on. The mysticism of the Orphics, the other-worldliness of Pythagoras may have had a strong appeal; the glorification of distant countries, of a happy past of yore was not absent; and pessimism about the fortunes of man abounded. But the main obstacle to the acceptance of Xenophanes' vision was, I think, the fact that though the achievements of the arts and crafts and of the beginning sciences were gladly enjoyed, those who practiced them were not appreciated. That man is the maker of all things in this world, and that it is characteristic of him to create a civilization, was a thesis that can have carried weight only with a very few. The city, business and the athletic *agon* were higher ideals of life.

The 5th century took learning and knowledge more seriously. Intellectual values began to find a place, even though they were still subordinate to the values of political existence. The concern with cultural history is evidenced by Thucydides' *Archaeology* and by the fact that, as Hippias says, his audiences were eager to listen to his story about the beginnings of culture. [29] Moreover, politics itself was imbued with progressivism;

the 5th century was the century of political Utopianism. And Thucydides attests that ever new changes were taken for granted also by people of sober judgment : "In politics, as in the arts, the new must always prevail over the old". [30] In such a climate the progressivist philosophy should have been given a sympathetic hearing.

Among the educated of the 4th century, progressivism of some form or other was undoubtedly a common belief. Plato, Aristotle, Xenophon, Isocrates, to mention only some of those whom one could quote, reckoned with the idea of progress as a self-evident constituent of philosophical analysis. The beginning rationalization of life, the increasing specialization in the social apparatus, as well as in economic matters, is itself an indication of the progressivist temper. Insight and skill were now appreciated more and more for the fruits they bore. The serious threat to progressivism lay not in dreams about the past, though they were dreamt, not in pessimistic complaints of the decay of the present and a greater decay to come, though they were not foreign to observers of the political scene; the true danger arose from a trenchant criticism of the value of civilization as such. Cynic philosophy was the first revolution of the civilized against civilization, one has rightly remarked, a civilization that had become burdensome and seemed to destroy man's moral character, or what the Cynics were fond of calling "natural life."This revolution left a mark on the whole subsequent development. Its influence on early Stoicism and Epicureanism, I have noted before.

The Hellenistic age, the modern age of antiquity, was modern also in its endorsement of progress. But while scientists and philosophers and even the general public with whose enlightenment scientific and philosophical writers were equally concerned, revelled in progress, a new sentimentalism is found in poetry, and poets became dreamers praising a past that was irrevocably lost. When Protagoras spoke about those who cherish the life of the noble savage, he had added bitingly that were they to live among the primitives, they would sorrowfully long to revisit "the rascality of this part of the world." For compared with the savage, the most unjust of the here and now would seem to be "a just man and a master of justice" [31]. The poet Aratus, putting into verse the astronomical teaching of Eudoxus, inserted into his account the story of the Golden Age [32]. From then on this story was a stock in trade of escapism, an escapism equally promoted by dissatisfaction with a highly organized and technicalized society and, I think, by political events, the final loss of Greek independence.

Perhaps progressivism would have come to an end with the close of the Hellenistic age, had not the Romans of that time shown a native affinity to it. "Our republic," the older Cato, the most Roman of all Romans, used to assert, "was not created by the genius of any individual, nor in the lifetime of one man, but through countless centuries and generations." And he observed that "there never was a being so perspicacious that nothing could escape him, nor have the combined talents of any single age been such that it could look forward and anticipate all probabilities without the lessons of time and experience" [33]. The creation of Roman law is but the most impressive testimony to the Romans' pragmatic progressivism. Cicero, in his forensic and political speeches, talks of progress as orators and lawyers of the later 19th century or the beginning of the 20th used to talk of Darwinism. One must not be misled by the crisis poetry of Horace and Vergil, so often quoted as evidence for ancient primitivism, the glorification of the past. When the civil wars were over, even these poets wrote in a different mood.

The early empire had an optimistic outlook. The scientific and philosophical works took progress for granted; nor were the historians oblivious of it [34]. Even the early Greek archaism, the theory of imitation, advocated a selection of the best of the past, a selection which allowed one to be original. And the Emperor Claudius could say in a debate in the Senate : "All things which are now considered old, once were new... what we are doing will become old too, and what today we try to aver with reference to examples, will itself one day be among the examples" [35].

It was also in the first century AD, however, that romantic longing for the past was voiced more earnestly perhaps than ever before. New cultural theories that are basically hostile to progressive thought made their appearance. I am thinking of the place assigned to the genius in the formation of the arts and sciences, of the so-called law of reaction governing the extension of knowledge, and of the concept of renaissance.

In its beginnings and for a long time afterwards the history of civilization had made no distinction between practical skills, sciences, and the fine arts and literature. All of them were subject to progress because they were estimated in categories of greater or lesser mastery over the material or of technical problems solved. A new aesthetics, from the 3rd century BC, had tended to separate the *belles lettres* and the arts of painting and sculpture from merely technical skills and the sciences. One began to understand the incomparable greatness of the genius, who seems independent of historical time and space. If the progressivist found fault with Homer and considered it natural that he should be deficient in many things because he lived in a rude, nay, a barbaric age, the believer in the genius of the poet thought him perfect and declared that to the great the truth is accessible whenever and wherever they are born. Allied with the latter conviction was the acceptance of certain centuries as classical. Observing that for unaccountable reasons the arts flourish at a certain period to such an extent that the poets then living seem to exhaust all possibilities of the genre they cultivate, one came to recognize standard works that could at most be reproduced. This habit was to be transferred to other fields, oratory for instance; it soon infected more and more areas of human activities. As the law of reaction has it, the late-born who wants to do something novel, must select a subject not worked on before. Often, it seems, no other choice was regarded as open except the compilation and integration of the results that had been reached earlier. Thus the possibilities of progress began to be severly circumscribed, the chance of extending knowledge began to be narrowed down. The theory of renaissance had an effect not too dissimilar. There is an acme of the development; once it is reached, decay is inevitable. To be sure, return to what was, is possible; there can even be additions and improvements. But it is a cyclic movement that dominates; the belief in going forward step by step is abandoned.

Although these philosophies of history, or even those which I mentioned earlier, did not gain supremacy or put an end to progressivism. from the 3rd century AD, progressive thought was certainly on the retreat, and by the 6th century it had almost completely vanished. The very few who still spoke of advance were called revolutionary and chided [36]. And though the concept of progress was not altogether forgotten— "human nature in the course of time always is prone to produce new ideas about things, "said Procopius [37]—although advances were still made in science and especially in techniques, not least in military matters, it is clear that the prevailing spirit of the last centuries was that of traditionalism rather than of progressivism.

Many factors, political and intellectual, combined to bring about this change of temper. For the historian of scientific progress it is important to note that science itself, which once had so greatly contributed to the rise of the progressive attitude, in late antiquity favoured the traditionalist movement. The great masters of science in the 2nd century AD, Galen and Ptolemy, had tried to put an end to the dissension that previously had rent ancient science for many centuries. Down to their time the presuppositions and methods of science had been optional and sectarian, as it were; rival systems of science had existed side by side, in geography, history, medicine, even in mathematics. Both Galen and Ptolemy aimed at establishing a sect above all sects, a *scientia aeterna* equally shared by everybody. Their achievement was the final contribution the ancients made to the creation of science, as important as any of the other contributions, for it constituted science in its formal sense, as a system about the foundation of which, despite temporary conflicts, there must be, and is, agreement of all concerned. Doing what they did, neither Galen nor Ptolemy excluded the possibility of all further progress; they themselves added considerably to the knowledge they took over from others. Yet the effect of the systematization of science which they accomplished was to establish traditionalism in science. One began to search for an insight eternally true and everlasting, as Rome and the Roman empire were expected to last forever. Justinian's code was the final and most exemplary instance of this petrification in all departments of knowledge which went together with the traditionalism taking hold of all provinces of human existence.

The victory of the new view of history was the more complete because the latter corresponded also to the metaphysics that reigned supreme among the pagans and had many followers among the Christians. Here too, science, once the instigator of a progressive philosophy, had its share in the building of a quite different teaching. For it can be shown that Plotinus' re-interpretation of Plato owes its systematic character to a large extent to Galen's theory of science. At any rate, Plotinian philosophizing did justify men in looking back rather than forward. He considered himself the heir of a long tradition; he believed that venerable philosophers of old had discovered the truth [38]; it had only to be re-interpreted and to be understood in its entirety, as an organic unity which allowed one to deduce from one detail the rest by force of sequence [39]. On the other hand, such an approach to the problems of a philosophy intended to be scientific reflects the metaphysical truth that what comes first in the process of emanation, the oldest, is by its very nature the best, because perfection there finds its fullest expression; that the divine in the course of its descent into reality loses in power; that what is later and more distant from the original source is weaker and, so to say, at a disadvantage.

There was in these last centuries only one short-lived revival of progressivism. I am thinking of the belief in progress so noticeable in the early Christian writers. Whether or not such progressivism is reconcilable with the Christian doctrine as set forth in the New Testament, it is a fact that the Apologists of the 2nd century AD, and not a few of the Church Fathers of the 3rd and 4th centuries emphasized the progressive moment in history. Indeed, modern interpreters are inclined to maintain that this belief in progress was their discovery, that every progressivist understanding of history depends on the Christian experience of time, on its appreciation of the unique importance of the historical moment, as it was first revealed to men through the life and death of Christ. I have no desire to deny that the specifically modern concept of progress is determined by a rationalization of the Christian experience and derives from it many of its important and distinctive characteristics. But that the Greeks and Romans were familiar not only with "cycles of time," but with "the sound doctrine of a rectilinear course" of time, which Augustine seems to deny to them [40], that they were progressivists in their own way, it has been the burden of my whole argument to show.

It also seems clear to me that when the early Christians talked about progress in history they were merely "despoiling the Egyptians," to use the famous phrase, and turning the tables on their adversaries. This is most obvious in the writings of the Apologists. Faced with the objection that, were Christianity the truth, it would have become known to men long ago, they said as did the pagans themselves, that truth is the daughter of time; reason in its entirety has come to the fore gradually [41]. Also, the Montanist theory of a continuous inspiration even after the time of Christ was merely the Christian formulation of the conviction that knowledge is arrived at "step by step." In the works of the Greek Church Fathers the idea of progress is deeply interwoven with the other concepts they took over from Greek philosophy. Eusebius' conviction [42] that under the Roman empire men had progressed more than ever since the birth of Christ, that the Christian empire would increase in the future, presents the history of civilization from the point of view of the faithful in categories that remind one of Seneca and Pliny [43].

It is true, then, that while paganism in its old age began to plead for the authority of the old, most memorably in the fight about the worship of Victoria in the Roman Senate, the new creed had taken over that philosophy which paganism itself inaugurated in its youth. But Christian progressivism was not to last. Augustine's *City of God* recalled the Church to the other-worldly message of its doctrine and soon put an end to speculations on past, present, and future here.

Having spoken of the origin of the idea of scientific progress, of its influence on history and philosophy, of its relative importance within the ancient world, it remains to add at least a few words on some general questions that have always been asked in connection with progressivism. What is the betterment of life, the betterment that progress brings about? How far does it extend? Do disadvantages go with advantages? Opinions on these matters differed in antiquity as they do today. Progress was hymned and execrated, as the word in our times is a blessed or a cursed word. But some generalizations can, I think, be attempted.

To the believers in progressivism, progress naturally was a good thing. When told about resulting dangers or damages, they would first of all point out that any harm that might conceivably arise from the new was due to the misuse of it; and misuse of a good is not an argument against the good. Such a mode of reasoning carried the more conviction since in antiquity the force that prompted men to change conditions, to search further, was without exception held to reside in man and not in nature. It was regarded as a human faculty, not as a biological fact or as part of a necessary evolution. It is true, at the very beginning of the history of mankind, certain inventions and improvements were indispensable to the preservation of human life. After a short period, what is added is an *embarras de richesse*. It is due to the free creativity of the human spirit. The ancients, therefore, were always conscious of the possibility that progress might cease at any moment. They would have agreed with Bossuet's verdict that the possibilities of the human spirit are inexhaustible, though laziness may well set them limits [44]. They therefore did not feel at the mercy of progress as an extraneous force; it seemed reasonable to them that man can control a work of his own creation.

Moreover, the expectations that the ancients had with regard to progress were in some ways greater and in some ways humbler than those of the moderns. Being by no means adverse to a progress that can be measured in statistics of export and import, in an increase in good living in peace-time, and better defensive weapons in war-time, they never dissociated progress from the spread of culture. The process of civilization to them meant, above all, that the individual, as well as society at large, becomes humanized. Last but not least, as regards knowledge and its extension, they never forgot that understanding is a value in itself and is its own reward.

On the other hand, asked whether through progress man becomes happier or morally better, the ancients, I think, would have answered almost unanimously that progress has little bearing on these issues. Greater wealth, improved conditions, more facilities and knowledge may help to produce better men. True moral progress of the community or the individual will come only if there is in addition greater wisdom, a clearer perception of man's duties and obligations, in other words, moral and metaphysical insight. Progress itself is no philosophy. As for a happiness consisting in the absence of pain, in freedom from misfortune and suffering—if it can be had at all—this was held to be accessible only to him who had learned to master life such as it is, under the guidance of reason.

In fine, one may say perhaps that in the judgment of the ancients, man through working for the progress of civilization acquires dignity and worth. It is, therefore, his obligation to further progress. As regards the balance of the good and bad in the course of doing one's duty, they were resigned to the truth, elevating and humbling at the same time, which summarizes much of what I have been trying to express in my discussion : "Mankind always progresses; man always remains the same."

References

[1] Lovejoy. *Introduction to Primitivism and Related Ideas in Antiquity.*
[2] Seneca. *Naturales Quaestiones*, VII, 25, 4.
[3] *Ibid.*, VII, 30, 5; cf. VI, 5, 3.
[4] *Ibid.*, VII, 25, 4.
[5] *Ibid.*, VI, 5, 3.
[6] Pliny. II, 15, 62.
[7] Manilius. *Astronomicon*, I, v. 90.
[8] Strabo, p. 69.
[9] Pliny. II, 26, 95; cf. Ptolemy. *Almagest*, IX, 2.
[10] Polybius, X, 47, 12.
[11] *Ibid.*, III, 38, 2-3.
[12] Archimedes. *Method*, Introduction p. 69 (Heiberg).
[13] *Soph. Ref.* 34, 183 b 17 ff.
[14] Plato. *Politicus*, 299.
[15] Bacon. *Novum Organum*, 1, 85.

[16] *Ibid.*, 92.
[17] 183 b 29-31.
[18] Seneca. *Naturales Quaestiones*, V, 18, 14.
[19] Pliny. II, 45, 117, cf. XIV, *Praefatio*; Seneca. *De providentia*, 4, 14.
[20] Plato. *Laws*, III, 676 A.
[21] *Ibid.*, XII, 951 B ff.
[22] *Politics*, II, 8, 1268 a 6-8; b 22 ff.
[23] Cicero. *Academica*, II, 6, 16 ff.
[24] Cicero. *De finibus*, IV, 7,16.
[25] *Gnomologicum Vaticanum* 58.
[26] Cicero. *De finibus*, IV, 5, 12.
[27] *De natura deorum*, II, 39, 99.
[28] Seneca. *Naturales Quaestiones*, III, 30, 1 ff.; 27, 1 ff.
[29] Plato. *Hippias Major*, 285 D-E.
[30] I, 71, 2.
[31] Plato. *Protagoras* 327 C-D.
[32] *Phaenomena*, vv. 100 ff.
[33] Cicero. *De republica*, II, 1, 2.
[34] Livy. IV, 4, 4.
[35] Tacitus, *Annales*. XI, 24.
[36] Iamblichus. *De mysteriis*, VII, 5; cf. III, 26.
[37] *Bellum Gothicum*, IV, 11, 28.
[38] III, 7, 1.
[39] IV, 9, 5.
[40] *De civitate dei*, XII, 13.
[41] Justinus. II, 8; 10; 13.
[42] *Praep*. I, 4, 6 ff.
[43] *Praise of Constantine*, 16, 8; cf. Meleto *apud* Eusebius, *Eccles. Hist.*, IV, 26, 7-8.
[44] *Traité de la Connaissance de Dieu et de soi-même*, 5, 28.

Comments on Edelstein's paper by J. T. Clark.

Under the provocative title of "The Graeco-Roman Concept of Scientific Progress" a vintage scholar of internationally established reputation, exceptionally equipped with the multiple philological resources requisite for the volunteer task, has here explored with enviable expertness and enthusiastic empathy a vast and incredibly wide spatial and temporal expanse of ancient literature. What impressed me most on first reading the advance copy of the manuscript was the awesomely colossal and truly stupendous scope of the author's enterprise.

But despite all the merits of the essay's profound scolarship and warmly humanistic interpretation of the manifold texts, both explicitly cited and allusively mentioned, at the close I was vaguely uneasy but definitely unhappy.

A first diagnosis of my psychotic malaise was to the effect that if the paper was so truly and admirable broad in scope, then this reader must presently be too narrow-minded to appreciate its superb excellence.

2

Motives and Incentives for Science in Antiquity

LUDWIG EDELSTEIN

The knowledge of the arts and crafts (the *technai*), derived from experience and employed for practical purposes, in the opinion of the ancients was coeval with man. Scientific knowledge (the knowledge of the *mathemata* or *epistemai*, or *scientiae* in the strict sense of the word) to them was a discovery of a relatively late period of history, the seventh and sixth centuries B.C. Then for the first time, they agreed, an attempt was made to give a consistently rational picture of nature, to classify phenomena systematically and to explain them, to establish a limited number of principles and to deduce their consequences. But the implications of this new enterprise were understood differently at different times during the thousand years or so that ancient science lasted. And as the meaning of science itself changed, motives and incentives for it changed too. It is therefore impossible to proceed as if there were one answer to the question at issue. One can but try to discuss the various positions that were taken and to indicate their relative importance within the development of ancient science.[1]

I

The science arising in the pre-Socratic age undoubtedly aimed at understanding, at contemplation of the truth, of the essence of things. This vaunted theoretical attitude is glorified in Democritus's saying that it is greater gain to find an ætiology than to become King of Persia[2]; it is caricatured in the Socrates of the Aristophanic *Clouds* who is made to pose the question, "How many times the length of its legs does a flea jump?"

[1] Little work seems to have been done on the topic here under investigation. Those studies I have found most helpful will be referred to in the course of my discussion. In the main my material is drawn from a history of ancient science which I am preparing, and from a book, *The Idea of Progress in Antiquity*, scheduled to appear shortly.

[2] 68B 118, *Die Fragmente der Vorsokratiker*, ed. H. Diels and W. Kranz (5th ed., Berlin, 1934–5).

(v. 145.) The investigations of problems which to the comic poet seemed useless and meaningless were to the adherents of science worth everything. They wished to know what it is all about, if I may use this expression. To be born seemed to them preferable to not being born, "for the sake of viewing the heavens and the whole order of the universe".[1]

Such an attitude of course includes traits noticeable even in earlier periods. To give a picture of the world 'as it is', to describe it 'objectively', without the intrusion of the observer as it were, is characteristic already of the Homeric epic. With his panoramic ability, the poet, clinging closely to reality, encompasses in his work great things and small. The Greek artist was the first to try to represent a body as it appears in nature, showing it not from the front or the side but plastically. Again, explanation, classification and systematization are not foreign to Homeric or Hesiodic mythology. The epic knows well that what is truly seducing in the song of the Sirens is "their professions of knowledge".[2]

But although the wish to see things as they are, to explain, to systematize, to find out, has its share also in the ideal of theoretical knowledge, there is in the latter from the beginning something other and new. A life devoted to science is considered a life of happiness. "Blessed is he", says Euripides, "who has taken knowledge of science . . . contemplating the ageless order of deathless Nature — how it came to be formed, its manner, its way."[3] And such 'beatitudes' recur again and again in later literature. They attest the belief that scientific inquiry is one form of the human quest for *eudæmonia*. The pleasure sought by all men, yet found by most in the enjoyment of the senses or in the winning of glory, is found by the man of science in knowledge itself.[4]

[1] Anaxagoras, 59A 30, Diels-Kranz. See in general F. Boll, "Vita Contemplativa", *Sitzungsberichte d. Heidelberger Akademie d. Wissenschaften*, Philol. Hist. Klasse, VIII (1920).

[2] Odyssey, XII, v. 189; cf. Cicero, *De finibus*, V, 18, 49. Concerning the Cicero passage see below p. 19, n. 1. The 'theoretical' character of the Homeric epic has been noted, e.g. by S. H. Butcher, "The Greek love of knowledge", in *Harvard Lectures on Greek Subjects* (London and New York, 1904) 82 ff., 86 ff.

[3] A. Nauck, *Tragicorum Græcorum Fragmenta* (2nd ed., Leipzig, 1889) Fr. 910.

[4] For these 'beatitudes' cf. G. L. Dirichlet ("De veterum macarismis", *Religionsgeschichtliche Versuche und Vorarbeiten* XIV, 4, Giessen, 1914, p. 66), who, however, in my opinion does not discriminate sharply enough between testimonies concerned with science and those concerned with philosophy.

Such an emotion must not be confounded with that which still today a scientist may experience in his work. He feels pleasure when he solves a particular problem with which he has wrestled for a long time, and things at last fall into place; he enjoys playing the game of science successfully. Such a feeling has subjective grounds. The pleasure which the ancient scientist experienced, as the beatitudes indicate, is objectively determined. It is derived from "contemplating the ageless order of deathless Nature".

What is here at stake can be elucidated I think by a famous statement of Kant. The discovery of order in nature, he says,

> is the business of the understanding, which is designedly borne toward a necessary purpose, viz. the bringing of unity of principles into nature, which purpose then the judgment must ascribe to nature, because the understanding cannot here prescribe any law to it. The attainment of that design is bound up with the feeling of pleasure. . . . We no longer find, it is true, any marked pleasure in the comprehensibility of nature and in the unity of its divisions into genera and species, by which all empirical concepts are possible, through which we cognize it according to its particular laws. But this pleasure has certainly been present at one time, and it is only because the commonest experience would be impossible without it that it is gradually confounded with mere cognition and no longer arrests particular attention.[1]

To put it differently, science whose aim it is to understand nature must start from the presupposition that nature can be understood by reason. When this hypothesis for the first time proved to be correct, when scientists as it were by "a lucky chance" favouring their design met under empirical laws with such a systematic unity as they had assumed to exist, they were "rejoiced".[2] Disorder became rational order; chaos, cosmos. Definitions, classifications, general rules of coming-to-be and passing-away, could be devised and could be shown to exist in nature. For those to whom the fact of science is self-evident,

[1] I. Kant, *Critique of Judgment*, trans. J. H. Bernard (The Hafner Library of Classics, New York, 1951) Introduction, VI, pp. 23 f. What Kant says here about the original scientific experience in terms of critical idealism, Darwin, the reflective empirical scientist, expresses in his observation that the relation of species to one another "is a truly wonderful fact, the wonder of which we are apt to overlook from familiarity" (*The Origin of Species*, London, 1859, Ch. 4, pp. 128 f.). On the identity of the point of view in the two statements see B. Bauch, *Immanuel Kant* (2nd ed., Berlin and Leipzig, 1921) 418 ff.

[2] Kant, op. cit. Introduction, V, p. 20.

a commonplace of their life, this is a truism evoking pleasure at most for the flash of a moment. For the ancients who started the scientific enterprise, it was a wonder to which they had not yet become accustomed.[1]

Moroever it would seem that the scientific analysis of data was thought to provide a short cut to insight and, even if no practical results followed from it, was considered the basis of superior knowledge. Theætetus, distinguishing rational and irrational numbers and setting forth their characteristics, emphasizes that he is thereby freed from the necessity of dealing empirically with each succeeding number.[2] With the magic wand of definition the infinity of instances is made finite, as it were. On the other hand, when the scientific physician, instead of judging that a certain remedy benefited Callias and similarly Socrates, comes to judge "that it benefits all persons of a certain type, considered as a class, who suffer from this or that disease", he may not be able to treat better, but he knows more.[3] When everything is understood as made up of elements changing from one form into another, the manifoldness of all appearances is reduced to unity and uniformity and thus becomes manageable by the intellect. "Learning increaseth wisdom."[4]

Finally, although truth is independent of the human mind and is not made by men, theoretical cognition is not passive. Contemplation is an "activity" of the mind, Aristotle says.[5] It is a "theoretical virtue", the highest virtue of man. Such a definition is to be found in all philosophical systems to which ancient scientists owed allegiance.[6] As Cicero puts it following Antiochus,

> it is therefore at all events manifest that we are designed by nature for activity. Activities vary in kind, so much so that the more important actually eclipse the less, but the most important are, first, . . . the contemplation and the study of the heavenly bodies

[1] In Greek philosophy one may for instance note a sentiment similar to that expressed by Kant and Darwin in Plato's theory of the κοινόν of the ideas, which is also concerned with the fact that if no identities could be found, if reality consisted of incomparable units, knowledge would be impossible (cf. Bauch, op. cit. p. 419).

[2] Plato, *Theaetetus*, 147C ff.

[3] Aristotle, *Metaphysics*, I, 981a 7 ff.

[4] Empedocles, 31B 17, l. 14, Diels-Kranz. This sense of power over nature through mere cognition is, I suggest, part of the original scientific experience of which Kant and Darwin speak.

[5] *Nicomachean Ethics*, X, 7, 1177a 20.

[6] For the relation between philosophy and science cf. below p. 29 and p. 25, n. 1.

and of those secrets and mysteries of nature which reason has the capacity to penetrate; secondly, the practice and the theory of politics; thirdly, the principles of Prudence, Temperance, Courage and Justice, with the remaining virtues.[1]

Three factors then seem to constitute the ancient ideal of theoretical knowledge: objective pleasure; a sense of bringing to a sudden halt the rush of experience together with a sense of heightened insight; an experience of active accomplishment. This was the original ideal with which Greek science started and of which it never completely lost sight, although its various aspects had probably greater or lesser significance depending on the individual and also on the age in which he lived. While the activeness of reason appears to have been felt throughout Antiquity, joy in the order of the world and wisdom in its ways certainly meant something other to a scientist who sided with Plotinus than to a follower of Aristotle.[2] Moreover, the theoretical ideal and its motivating force soon merged with another ideal destined to become no less important for scientific research.

II

At the very beginning of Greek science, the individual scientist works in almost complete isolation and on his own. There is as yet no scientific dialogue. Other workers in the field are mentioned at most in order to reject summarily their point of view. The opening words of the oldest historical treatise — "Hecatæus of Miletus speaks thus: I put down things as they seem to me to be true: for the accounts given by the Greeks are manifold and ridiculous, as it appears to me"[3] — are symbolic of the early attitude of 'going it alone'.[4]

But by the time of Plato and Aristotle, an entirely different concept of research had taken shape. Xenophanes's theory of progress[5] is now more generally accepted and has changed the

[1] *De finibus*, V, 21, 58. The Ciceronian analysis of the theoretical ideal (V, 18, 48–21, 60), from which I have quoted, is perhaps the most explicit and most comprehensive which is preserved from Antiquity.

[2] Cf. below p. 21, n. 5.

[3] 1 F 1, *Die Fragmente der Griechischen Historiker*, ed. F. Jacoby (Berlin, 1923) I.

[4] The isolation of the early scientist has been stressed by W. A. Heidel, *The Heroic Age of Science* (Baltimore, 1933) 73. See also below p. 27.

[5] 21B 18, Diels-Kranz.

scientist's relation to his predecessors, his contemporaries, and his successors. The search for truth, he realizes, is a co-operative undertaking. Every step forward on the road to the solution of a problem presupposes those previously taken and prepares those to be taken in the future. At the height of the Hellenistic era the belief begins to spread that such progress must of necessity be infinite. The individual is no more than a link in the chain of generations working together for a common purpose. How much or how little insight he possesses depends also on the point of time at which he stands in the gradually unfolding process of discovery.[1]

This expectation of progress does not carry with it the conclusion that since later generations will know so much more, the present generation knows too little to lay hold on anything that could properly be called knowledge. Such a sceptical resignation, if I am not mistaken, was not to prevail before the nineteenth century.[2] Enjoyment of what has been accomplished is quite possible, for what will be known better in the future is essentially the same truth. And through the progressivist creed the personal motive for gaining insight is associated with another and ulterior motive: that of making a contribution to the life of others, of helping to build up an edifice that will outlast him and grow beyond what he himself is privileged to see and to enjoy.

As Seneca puts it, summarizing the development of thought down to his own time, science is an inheritance, a patrimony left to us by earlier generations. We administer it and should leave it enriched to those who come after us. As we are grateful to our predecessors for what they have done for us and this is their reward, so the gratitude of our successors for what we have done for them is our reward. It motivates our endeavour as much as does our wish to understand. At the same time science, growing out of the efforts of the past, added to by those now alive and to be increased further in the future, is no longer the property of an individual, but of all men, of mankind. Thus the scientist becomes a citizen of two cities, the one on

[1] That, contrary to the current view, the idea of scientific progress is not modern but ancient, I have pointed out in "Recent trends in the interpretations of ancient science", *Journal of the History of Ideas*, XIII (1952) 575 f. This article will be quoted in the following as "Ancient science".

[2] Cf. M. Weber, "Wissenschaft als Beruf", *Gesammelte Aufsätze zur Wissenschaftslehre* (Tübingen, 1922) 536 f., who illustrates his thesis by Tolstoy's analysis of modern life.

earth in which he happens to be born and which is perishable, the other imperishable and voluntarily chosen. As a member of that eternal community comprising men of all ages, he works not for the tasks of the day, for mundane affairs, but for the enlightenment of the world — for the growth of civilization, to put it in modern teminology.[1]

Through civilization, the Stoics asserted, man erects over nature a second nature as it were, an *altera natura.*[2] In the same way, one may say that the history of the sciences is an *altera historia* over political history. While the latter is filled with wars, with fights for power, with destruction, this second history, unstained by blood and human passions, is devoted to the realization of man's intellectual gifts. Science and its discoveries, together with poetry and the fine arts, are the subjects of this truly humane story in which man transcends himself, or as the ancients would say, becomes most like the divine.[3]

Also in another respect, however, does ancient science touch upon the divine — the divine not in man, but in nature itself. Whenever the Greek or Roman confronts phenomena that reflect eternal laws, he hears in the eternal the voice of the divine; "eternal" and "divine" are interchangeable expressions. In later stages of science the divine becomes its concern in a still more specific sense. Teleological thought leads everywhere to the discovery of the working of God. Aristotle, having treated of "things divine" — that is, astronomy — turns to biology and shows his students that in this field too the divine is not missing, though to be sure it is present only to a lesser degree: "Come in; don't be afraid; there are gods even here."[4] In the second century A.D. Galen the anatomist writes:

> This [book on the Use of Parts] is a sacred book which I composed as a true hymn of the god who has created us, in the belief that I am truly pious not if I sacrifice many hecatombs of oxen to him and burn thousands of talents of cassia, but if I first recognize myself and then explain also to the others the wisdom of God, his power, his excellence. (III, 10)[5]

[1] For Seneca see *Naturales quaestiones*, Praefatio and e.g. VI, 5, 3; VII, 25, 4 f.; 30, 5. His views reflect theories of the Middle Stoa, which is itself indebted to earlier doctrines.

[2] Cicero, *De natura deorum*, II, 60, 152.

[3] Cf. below p. 37.

[4] *De partibus animalium*, I, 5, 645a 22.

[5] Cf. L. Edelstein, "Greek medicine in its relation to religion and magic", *Bulletin of the Institute of the History of Medicine*, V (1937) 215 f. and also 229. The neo-Platonists too find God in nature. Their explanation may seem

It is sometimes claimed that it was seventeenth-century science which, imbued with the spirit of Protestantism and Puritanism, for the first time promised to lead men to God. But when Swammerdam proposed to show divine providence at work in the anatomy of the flea — an animal as insignificant as that for whose study Aristophanes had ridiculed Socrates — he was not doing anything new.[1] Long before, pagan science was a way to God and taught men to read the book of the world as a book written by a divine author and thus to understand its meaning rightly. This one must remember in order to grasp the full significance of the words in which Ptolemy sets forth the dignity and value of astronomy: "I know that I am mortal, a creature of a day; but when I search into the multitudinous revolving spirals of the stars, my feet no longer rest on the earth, but, standing by Zeus himself, I take my fill of ambrosia, the food of the Gods." The scientist of late centuries, just as he was a servant of mankind, was a servant and worshipper of the deity. Ancient science was not mere knowledge nor was it mere technique; it preserved an awareness of the meaning of the universe and retained a place for values within the world of facts.[2]

III

So far I have considered science merely as theoretical understanding and have left out of consideration its usefulness for practical ends. Of the applicability of their findings the scientists were of course quite conscious, as the testimony shows. Archytas's studies in the theory of mechanics led him to construct instruments and machines, and even a rattle, "a good inven-

unscientific to the modern interpreter even in comparison with Aristotle's physics and biology, but it was of course meant to be scientific and was considered so by those who accepted it; see below p. 38. About the early "science of the cosmos" and "Greek monotheism" see W. Dilthey, "Einleitung in die Geisteswissenschaften", *Gesammelte Schriften* I (Leipzig and Berlin, 1922) 165 ff.

[1] That Swammerdam's statement is at least indirectly influenced by Christian ideas current in his time has been suggested by Weber, op. cit. p. 539.

[2] For modern science and the concept of meaning cf. e.g. Weber, op. cit. pp. 539 ff. He identifies all Greek science with knowledge through concepts and thus knowledge of eternal truth, which is sought for the purpose of right political action. This to me seems a much too narrow definition of the Greek concept of science. For Ptolemy's epigram see *Anthologia Palatina*, IX, 577.

tion", Aristotle says, "which people give to children in order that while occupied with this they may not break any furniture, for young things cannot keep still."[1] Archimedes, the "geometrical Briareus" as the Roman aggressors called him, invented weapons for the defence of his native city. Astronomers and geographers applied their knowledge to drawing maps that could be used by sailors and travellers. It is true, scientists did not undertake their research with practical purposes in mind; they did not feel that their labours were more valuable or justifiable on account of the practical fruits they bore. The latter rather were by-products, so to say. Yet science did not shy away from technology, as is often assumed.[2]

On the other hand, one cannot deny that applied science, as all ancient technology, did not advance as far as it could conceivably have done. During the thousand years of scientific studies in which the intellect on its "flight through the universe" revolutionized man's understanding of nature and achieved ever greater triumphs, the forms of daily existence changed relatively little, less perhaps than during the later Middle Ages, surely much less than in some of the decades since the middle of the nineteenth century. That the usefulness of science in Graeco-Roman times was comparatively unexploited, that it was, strictly speaking, no motive for developing scientific knowledge, is due I think mainly to three factors.[3]

First, the 'empirical' scientists, who considered speculation and theory of less importance, if of importance at all, and who on account of their prevalent concern with reality might have

[1] *Politics*, 1340b 28.

[2] For the place of technology in antiquity cf. A. Rehm, "Zur Rolle der Technik in der griechisch-römischen Antike", *Archiv f. Kulturgeschichte*, XXVIII (1938) 135 ff. (on Archimedes and the various traditions on his work, p. 145, n. 27); see also "Ancient science", pp. 579 f. (The brief outline of the development of ancient science given in this article is taken as the starting point for my discussion of the topics dealt with in this and in the following section.) The modern attitude, so different from that of the ancients, is I think best illustrated by Pasteur's saying: "To him who devotes his life to science, nothing can give more happiness than increasing the number of discoveries, but his cup of joy is full when the results of his studies immediately find practical application" (René J. Dubos, *Louis Pasteur*, Boston, 1950, p. 85).

[3] That the technological shortcomings of ancient civilization were not the consequences of economic conditions, of the existence of slavery, I have tried to show: "Ancient science", pp. 580 ff. Here I am concerned mainly with those factors inherent in the nature of ancient science itself that appear to have limited the interest in applied science.

taken a special interest in applying their knowledge, were the ones to curtail research and thereby to curtail also the chances of mastering the phenomena. For in the Hellenistic theory of empiricism, the possibility of comprehending nature is severely narrowed down. Everything inaccessible to the senses is regarded as hidden from exploration and thus closed to scientific study. It was the empirical physician who denied that anatomy and physiology could become sciences and rendered useful for medical treatment. Also, reading of books — the treasured-up experience of the past — for him took precedence over making new experiments and accumulating more data. Extension of knowledge, the opening-up of new opportunities for applied science, was therefore left almost exclusively to the 'theoretical' scientists — the "dogmatists" as they were derisively called by their opponents, and yet in fact the only ones to venture beyond the already known. But with them, of course, knowledge for the sake of knowledge was the prime motive and the prime concern.[1]

Second, one must not forget that ancient sciences have by their very nature so to say a slant towards the theoretical rather than the practical. Some, physics and psychology for instance, were really 'philosophical' sciences. For they remained in the domain of the philosopher and were studied by him as part of his analysis of the physical world and of human nature. When the original unity of philosophy and all the sciences, obtaining in the pre-Socratic period, dissolved, and independent, particular sciences were established — sciences pursued by specialists — they still kept in close touch with philosophy. Their first principles, their methodology rested on philosophical grounds. The issue between mechanism and teleology, the controversy about the respective values of empirical observation and theoretical reasoning were fought not with scientific but with philosophical arguments, and these discussions occupied

[1] Medicine by chance of tradition best represents the type of ancient empirical science, and F. M. Cornford (*Principium Sapientiae*, Cambridge, 1952, pp. 31 ff.) ascribes to the very first physicians an empirical theory of knowledge (p. 42), an interrogation of Nature "prepared to accept the answers she gives" (p. 38), a theoretical science based on particular observations (p. 8). This I think could be asserted not even of Hellenistic medicine (see "Ancient science", pp. 576 f. and p. 596, n. 59). In the light of modern historical hindsight empiricism may seem to be the most promising method. In Antiquity paradoxically enough it proved no more fruitful than the seemingly sound atomic theory of Democritus and Epicurus (cf. Dilthey, op. cit. pp. 169 ff., and "Ancient science", pp. 594 ff.).

a much larger part of scientific writing than they would in later science. Not that the scientist slavishly followed the dictates of a philosophic law-giver. Rather he took an active interest in philosophy, he became himself a philosopher. The title of Galen's essay "That the best physician is also a philosopher" epitomizes the prevailing attitude.[1] On the other hand, there was a feeling that men of experience, as Aristotle[2] says, are better in practical matters, better equipped to handle particulars, than is the scientist who knows the universals. Thus the improvement of the technical apparatus remained largely in the hands of artisans and craftsmen, who changed things slowly and cautiously in their traditional conservative manner.[3]

[1] Modern interpreters assume the existence of independent sciences at least from Hellenistic times (e.g. W. Jaeger, *Aristoteles*, Berlin, 1923, pp. 431 f.; L. Robin, *La Pensée grecque et les origines de l'ésprit scientifique*, Paris 1923, p. 433). But the original connexion between philosophical and scientific thought continues not only in medicine (as Robin would admit, p. 434), but for instance also in astronomy. According to the Stoa, the school most influential on scientific research, the mathematician calculates the movements of the stars and so forth, but in questions of aetiology or hypotheses to be made he must cooperate with the "physicist", the philosopher (e.g. Diogenes Laertius, VII, 132–133). No outstanding ancient scientist took an attitude similar to that of the modern positivist, for whom the description of the phenomenal world in concepts and the proof of the validity of law and order through experiment are the whole content of science (W. Dilthey, "Das Wesen der Philosophie", *Gesammelte Schriften*, V, Leipzig and Berlin, 1924, pp. 358 f.), and who believes in a fundamental conflict between metaphysics and science. On the relation between philosophy and science see also "Ancient science", pp. 578 f.

[2] *Metaphysics*, I, 4, 981a 13 ff.

[3] It is as difficult to draw the demarcation line between science and the arts and crafts as between science and philosophy. The arts and crafts were so to say the laboratory of the scientist. The study of medical theories and the deductions drawn from them had to be checked by medical practice; one cannot write about warfare, Polybius says, without military experience (XII, 25g, cf. 25d). According to Hiero the science of mechanics has, as well as a theoretical part, a practical part, consisting of the study of "metal-working, architecture, carpentry, painting, and the manual activities connected with these arts". Skill in such arts makes "the ablest inventor" (Pappus, *Mathematical Collection*, VIII, 1 ff.). Clearly, then, the Aristotelian passage to which I have referred expresses the more general feeling that practical invention properly speaking comes from an experience outside science. But behind such an attitude, as Aristotle implies, there is also the recognition of a philosophical problem which throughout the development of Greek philosophy and science presented great difficulty, namely, how any law can do justice to the particularity, the ineffability of individual phenomena. The answer always seems to be that the handling of reality requires a certain 'tact'. In addition, it may be true that ancient scientific

Last though not least, the relative neglect of the practical must I think be viewed against the background of the ancients' general attitude towards life, of which it seems characteristic that they acknowledged and respected boundaries set to their actions. They would, to be sure, aim at perfection in rational insight and in right conduct; they would fashion their cities or states in accordance with political ideals; they would above all civilize human existence so that it became truly human. They did not feel that it was their business to take the world over altogether. Men no more claimed than did their gods to be creators out of nothing, to act with a free will that imposes its law on things that have no nature of their own. Rather did they feel called upon to shape matter that was given and, here below at any rate, refractory to reason. The gods but mould, or to use a Platonic phrase, persuade the physical universe to accommodate itself to their wishes as far as possible. It does not stand otherwise with that universe which men build. Having accomplished what appeared possible and essential, the pagans were satisfied to use knowledge mostly for taking care of their daily wants which were modest, for defending their country when there was need, for adorning temple services and festivals, for increasing pleasure through play and amusement.[1]

laws in general, no less than Aristotle's laws of motion, lacked the abstraction from actual conditions characteristic of modern scientific laws, and therefore were less serviceable for the mastery of phenomena. This whole issue, like the relation between philosophy and science, still needs further elaboration.

[1] "In themselves inventions are passive"; a force is needed "to set them working" (Brooks Adams, *The Law of Civilization and Decay*, New York, 1955, p. 256). If in the modern age inventions are promoted primarily by capitalistic interests, the situation was quite different in Antiquity. Although the capitalistic spirit was not absent altogether, the "element of play" was far stronger. Even definitions of mechanics always include references to the art of contriving "marvellous devices" (Pappus, loc. cit., and Geminus apud Proclus, *In Euclid.*, ed. Friedlein, p. 41, 8). On the other hand, it would seem to be true that the increase in practical inventions noticeable since the Renaissance is in part due to the fact that man wished to participate "in the creative passion" of his God (cf. A. O. Lovejoy, *The Great Chain of Being*, 3rd ed., Cambridge, Mass., 1948, p. 84, and in general on this and the previous topic "Ancient science", pp. 583–5). To the ancients, confronted with the teaching of Moses, its strangest aspect was that according to him God was a creator *ex nihilo*, in contrast to their gods; such a concept seemed irrational to them and irreconcilable with their philosophy (Galen, *De usu partium*, XI, 14). And this fundamental difference between pagan and Christian thought did not, in my opinion, remain without influence on the later attitude towards reality. The ancients' zest

It is mainly for such reasons, I think, that ancient science remained relatively useless, that changes which in principle were within reach were actually not made. But to a certain extent the ineffectiveness of science in altering conditions depended also on social factors, as should become clear from the discussion of the incentives for science, to which I shall now turn.

IV

The new venture of science which started in the pre-Socratic centuries was a venture undertaken by individuals; it lacked the support of society. In the opinion of the citizens of the Greek communities, the scientist's "activity" was "idleness" — indeed withdrawal from the realities of life. They neither cared to be like him nor had they any use for him. Why then should they have given support to science? Far from supporting it, they did not even pay homage to it, as they did honour and reward poets or athletes. One who wished to engage in scientific studies had to be a man of independent means, free to indulge his fancies. At most he might maintain himself by teaching converts to the new cause. He certainly had no other hope of making a living. There were no schools with which one could be associated, no careers that one could follow as a scientist. The few who favoured the scientific movement advocated redress of the situation, for they were well aware of the fact that what society does not pay for or prize does not flourish.[1] No one listened to their remonstrances. Throughout the classical age science remained beyond the pale of society.

Matters changed in the Hellenistic world only to a certain extent. For on the whole the cost for his own maintenance, for travelling and books[2] and all the paraphernalia of scholarship

for reshaping themselves rather than the world is well expressed by Socrates's saying that in human matters one argues in order to produce corresponding action, but no one would argue about winds, rains and seasons in the hope of "producing" winds and rains and seasons (Xenophon, *Memorabilia*, I, 1, 15). Empedocles's dream of achieving the latter feats (31 B 111, Diels-Kranz) is to my knowledge quite exceptional (contrary to what Heidel, *Heroic Age of Science*, p. 58, appears to think).

[1] E.g. Plato, *Republic*, VII, 528 C. Cf. in general "Ancient science", pp. 597 ff. For the *ἀργία* of the philosopher see e.g. Aristophanes, *Frogs*, v. 1498, and Boll, "Vita contemplativa", p. 30. That in the early centuries of science one cannot speak of schools but only of personal associations has been pointed out by Heidel, op. cit. pp. 73 f.

[2] Polybius, XII, 27–8.

had still to be paid for by the individual. It was but in a few institutions such as the Museion that scientists received yearly stipends, but in a few places that collections of material and libraries were put at their disposal. The limited number of schools which came into being, and in which the members probably shared the expenses of living and research, were private foundations and not publicly supported. Unless a scholar was willing to seek association with a court — to become "a friend of a king" as the phrase went — he had to fall back on his own fortune or to practise a profession. Lucky was he who could practise one related to his studies, as a biologist might practise medicine.[1]

Society then having at first completely disregarded the scientist, did offer him some incentives of material advantage and prestige in the Hellenistic age, but they were few indeed and ineffective. For improvements were localized and sporadic. As little as in classical centuries was science a career many could afford to pursue. Kings sometimes tried to win the acclaim of the intellectuals by supporting science; it may also have happened that one or other prince was genuinely interested in scientific endeavours. But for the princes or the rich who could be induced to give their assistance, their patronage of science was I think more often than not a kind of showpiece or a matter of pragmatic considerations. Geographical exploration and the construction of war implements, which they mostly financed, were useful. Of support for long drawn out inquiries without practical results one hears nothing. The theoretical sciences certainly continued to be the concern of private individuals. And to say it once more, any help given was intermittent, from case to case; there was no consistent plan of promoting science.[2]

Why did science fail to secure more recognition and encouragement? The responsibility certainly does not lie with distrust of science, with political schemes of any class of society designed

[1] Contrary to the assumptions of nineteenth-century scholars (e.g. E. Curtius, "Die öffentliche Pflege von Wissenschaft und Kunst", *Alterthum und Gegenwart*, Berlin, 1877, p. 123), often repeated even nowadays, the Hellenistic age did not open up a new era in the social organization of science; see "Ancient science", pp. 598 ff.

[2] For the royal support of work on war engines see Philo of Byzantium, *Mechanics*, IV, 3, 5. The later stories about the help provided by Alexander the Great for research have been shown to be exaggerated ("Ancient science", p. 598, n. 62), and the same is probably true of the tradition concerning the first Ptolemies.

to prevent science from becoming a weapon in the fight for freedom and enlightenment. If fear was felt regarding the relationship of society and science, it was the scientists who were suspicious. For they were well aware of the fact that royal support or support from any outside quarters was potentially a danger to the objectivity of their research, because favours might be expected in return, favours that could necessitate distortions of the truth or actions irreconcilable with their ideals.[1] The true explanation for the reaction of society is I think to be found first of all in the scientific situation as it had taken shape by the time of Hellenism.

It was a situation not dissimilar to that of modern philosophy. Rival systems of science were competing with one another, rival systems which were in fact rival sciences. For there was nothing one could call science in the modern sense of the term, a body of knowledge valid everywhere, a system of principles, of rules of procedure and of theories, well defined and generally accepted. With the exception perhaps of mathematics, there were but "sciences", the adherence to which was optional. A science of mathematical astronomy faced a science of empirical astronomy. Empirical medicine, discarding anatomy and physiology, opposed dogmatic medicine based on anatomy and physiology. Descriptive geography rejecting quantitative analysis stood against a highly mathematized geography. Each of these sciences of course in the opinion of its proponents was true, but their claim to this effect clashed with counter-claims. This "dissension" as the ancients called it — a dissension not concerning particular results but concerning the basic presuppositions and aims of the scientific enterprise as such — made it almost impossible for anyone not a partisan to say what science was and what it was about, let alone to decide which of the existing systems of science should be encouraged and rewarded.[2]

That science in general or science as the Greeks knew it begins one day, and that, after the liberating word has been

[1] With regard to the scientists' fear of state subventions or court favours see "Ancient science", p. 593. On the other hand, although occasional persecutions of scientists occurred one cannot speak of political oppression, as is so often done nowadays (op. cit. pp. 589 ff.). The State was uninterested in science unless historians touched on particular political issues.

[2] That ancient science was in a state of dissension threatening its survival was a criticism made by scientists, not only by sceptical philosophers, e.g. Galen, *On Scientific Demonstration* (J. von Müller, *Abhandlung Akademie München*, XX, 1894, p. 419, quoted in "Ancient science", pp. 602 f.).

spoken, everyone knows the right course to follow, seems an ineradicable historical prejudice. In fact, the history of Greek science, in addition to being the story of the discovery of true and false data — true and false from the modern point of view — is also the story of the gradual discovery of the meaning of science. The concept of science itself has a history. It took almost eight hundred years to work out the implications of the enterprise on which the ancients had ventured and to create general agreement on it. *Tantae molis erat Romanam condere gentem.* The last step was only taken in the second century A.D., when largely through the work of Galen and of Ptolemy—theoreticians of science no less than scientists — a *scientia aeterna* began to be built up, science as it was to be understood from then on.[1]

When this happened, society took a greater interest in science than the classical and Hellenistic ages had done, and treated it with more respect and consideration. Universities were founded, professorships were endowed, schools multiplied. The unified Roman Empire had a unified science. Instruction became standardized; it taught one scientific truth, be the teaching given in Rome or Alexandria or Athens: "empirical" and "dogmatic" science were fused into what Galen called the teaching of "the best sect", the sect which stands above all sects. But the attempted cure was after all merely a palliative; it came too late. Soon political destruction made all constructive endeavour illusory. The ancients created science; they also developed it to the point where it could be assimilated into the social fabric. To carry out this assimilation effectively was left to other ages and other cultures.[2]

[1] E. Zilsel ("The genesis of the concept of scientific progress", *Journal of the History of Ideas*, VI, 1945, p. 327), who first compared the state of ancient science with that of modern philosophy, believed that such a comparison held for Antiquity as a whole. That this is not the case I have shown in "Ancient science" (pp. 602–4), where I have also pointed out that one therefore can hardly talk of a decay of science in late centuries. Granted that the late scientists furthered actual research to a lesser degree than their predecessors, the unification of science by which the earlier optional sciences were superseded was of decisive importance.

[2] That the stage at which dissension about the various possible approaches of science ended was reached under the Roman Empire, was I think not unconnected with the political circumstances. Galen prided himself on having unified medicine just as Trajan with his roads had unified Italy (*Opera omnia*, ed. C. G. Kühn, Leipzig, 1821–33, X, 623 f.). One might then well speak of an incentive provided for his work by the prevailing temper of the time. But this incentive worked only indirectly. The state did not participate in the efforts of Galen and the others. They proceeded as individuals acting on their own.

Yet, one may object, if men had been wiser, if they had recognized the value of science, if they had encouraged it as so many of the ancients themselves desired, the "dissension" of which I spoke could have been resolved earlier, and science would then have become integrated into civilization in Antiquity as it was later on. In such an objection there is I think a kernel of truth. The neglect of science on the part of society was undoubtedly due also to the predominance of other intellectual and emotional concerns.

Even those friendly to science often did not accept it altogether. The pre-Socratics and most of the classical philosophers to be sure were its fervent devotees. But among the minor Socratics emphasis on ethics began to grow, not to mention the fact that with Cynicism a conscious revolt of the civilized against civilization set in, which, though never spectacularly successful, left its mark on subsequent thought. Primitivism, the dream of a Golden Age of the past or future, a Rousseauesque admiration for the "noble savage" who has not eaten from the tree of knowledge, was the shadow of ancient rationalism and progressionism. Hellenistic philosophies, Stoicism as well as Epicureanism, were interested in science; in their last phases they even showed a strong appreciation of the significance of science. But they were given to the study of moral values at least as much as to the study of brute facts; if to them God was visible in nature, he was even more manifest in man and his actions. Rhetorical training, whose hold was probably greater than that of philosophical education, never included more than the rudiments of science, for everything beyond them was considered useless. The so-called liberal arts led to the threshold of science but no farther. And education in general, being a matter of the individual's free choice, continued to consist mainly in the study of poetry and music. Centuries after the eclipse of the sun had been proved to be a natural, recurrent phenomenon, such an event was still taken even by men in prominent positions as a divine omen, without their incurring the least censure except from the *avant garde* of intellectuals. For not everybody was willing to resign himself to the disenchantment of the world which followed from the attempt to comprehend nature in rational terms. Without the pressure of a general school system through which the results of science would be filtered down to the people, they did not feel obliged to believe in the results of science and preferred to cling to the mythos, to live in it, to think in its categories. Science never succeeded in breaking the power of mythology. No less an achievement than art and poetry, it was in contrast to them but a thin layer over ancient civilization and not at all as important to the Greeks and Romans as it was destined to become to the future.[1]

It goes without saying that the lack of institutionalization of ancient science accounts for many of its shortcomings. Without adequate prestige and recognition, without promise of financial security, it did not attract many people, not as many at any rate as could profitably have worked on securing the terrain which had been laid out. On the other hand, what was accomplished seems even more impressive because it was done with so little outside assistance. Considering why "men originally instituted a prize for competitions of the body, but none for wisdom", a pupil of Aristotle considers it a satisfactory answer to the puzzle that "the prize must be more desirable than the competition"; and he adds that though in the case of athletic contests such a prize can be found, "what prize could be better than wisdom?"[2] It would be carrying flattery to extremes if one believed that ancient society failed to pay scientists because kings and citizens admiringly realized that wisdom is its own reward. But one may fairly say, I think, that in a world in which science was not a career, the overwhelming majority of those who studied science must have done so for the sake of science. This is perhaps not the least of the reasons for the strength and the survival of the ideal of the theoretical life in all periods of ancient history. For motives rather than incentives, desire for the truth rather than outward allurement, had to persuade men to enter the service of science.[3]

[1] It seems unnecessary here to substantiate my description of the intellectual trends facing science. The facts I have mentioned are well known. I am concerned only to point out that they must be taken into account for an appreciation of the position of science in ancient society.

[2] *Problemata*, XXX, 11.

[3] In the opinion of the ancients, the political situation had great bearing on the progress of science. Pliny expresses his admiration for the scientists who accomplished so much despite constant warfare reigning in the Hellenistic period (*Natural History*, II, 45, 117). The *Pax Romana* was considered to create particularly favourable conditions for scientific work, and to impose a kind of obligation to make further strides (loc. cit.; also XIV, *praefatio*). According to Polybius (III, 59; XII, 28), science could make especially great progress in his time because after the rise of Roman power, men whose lives had so far been spent in the administration of their respective cities could now devote themselves to scientific pursuits. Such verdicts are reminiscent of the eighteenth-century evaluation of the great

V

In ancient moral theory, from Plato down to the end of Antiquity, the ethics of the good and virtuous man, the sage, is the main topic. But there is also, from the time of the Sophists, an undercurrent of ethical thought concerned with the morality of the judge, the lawyer, the physician, in short with professional ethics. To speak in Stoic categories, man in his life plays among other roles one which he assumes through his choice of work. In order to act well, he must be thoroughly acquainted with the character of his role, a character that varies with the various professions. What is fitting for the lawyer does not behove the judge; what becomes the soldier is unbecoming to the physician. And these demands of the role are objective demands imposed by the profession itself and have to be met by its adherents; the rules they state are as it were motive and incentive at the same time. It seems necessary therefore that in conclusion I should attempt at least to outline the professional ethics of the scientist. The direct testimony preserved on the topic is scarce. But it can be rounded out and made to speak more clearly by parallels from the professional ethics of the philosopher, with whom the scientist in Antiquity had so much in common.[1]

I take my departure from that statement of scientific ethics which seems to be among all that are extant the most explicit and the richest in implications. "Those who are altogether unaccustomed to research," says the Hellenistic physician Erasistratus,

monarchies as guarantors of peace and thus of the development of civilization, and certainly attribute to the state 'support' of science. But like the unifying influence of the Roman Empire toward the end of Antiquity (see above p. 30, n. 2), the preservation of peace made but an indirect, though certainly an essential, contribution to science.

[1] Concerning the influence of the Stoa on the development of professional ethics, cf. L. Edelstein, "The professional ethics of the Greek physician", *Bulletin of the History of Medicine*, XXX (1956) 411 ff. Medical ethics, of which most is known, shows that the profession was personified and thought of as making demands upon her followers, demands which operate in a sense as incentives, although they are, of course, but the expression of motives. Professional ethics includes also what might be called rules of performance, such as that a method must be adequate to the particular subject (e.g. Aristotle, *Metaphysics* II, 3, 995a 12 ff.), or that the authority of a writer matters little compared to the demands of truth (*Nicomachean Ethics*, I, 3, 1096a 15 ff.; cf. Plato, *Phaedrus*, 270C). Important as these rules are, I do not consider them in this context.

are at the first exercise of their intelligence befogged and blinded and quickly desist owing to fatigue and failure of intellectual power, like those who without training attempt a race. But one who is accustomed to investigation, worming his way through and turning in all directions, does not give up the search, I will not say day or night, but his whole life long. He will not rest, but will turn his attention to one thing after another which he considers relevant to the subject under investigation until he arrives at the solution of his problem.[1]

The thesis underlying Erasistratus's comments clearly is that scientific investigation presupposes training like that of an athlete. Without it the scientist will not be equal to the fight that is ahead of him. Neither art nor science can be conquered, says Democritus, if one is not willing to learn,[2] and the noble things of life one learns only through hard work[3] without it one cannot even learn how to read or to write, or to be a musician or an athlete.[4] A Platonic metaphor expresses the same thought in a different way. He who does not learn "to work like a slave" for the possession of the truth will never reach it.[5] Instead of being a slave to the body and its lusts, as man is by nature,[6] the philosopher or scientist must become a slave to knowledge. And it is not only hard work that is required, but also a tireless effort that withstands disappointments. Failure of an argument, Plato contends,[7] must not delude one into disdain of reason, into misology. One must persevere in the search, and fight the pessimism of the present with optimism regarding the future, with the hope that in the end one will win out. It does not matter after how long a time the truth will be reached.[8]

In such a stubborn and unrelenting contest all leads have to be explored, everything relevant has to be scrutinized. Small

[1] Galen, *Scripta minora*, ed. I. Müller (Leipzig, 1891) II, 17. I am quoting the translation of B. Farrington, *Greek Science* (2 vols., Pelican Books, Harmondsworth, 1949) II, 36. He as well as Heidel (*Heroic Age of Science*, pp. 53 f.) implies that Erasistratus's ethos is characteristic of 'the experimenter'. This, as will be seen, is not the case.

[2] 68B 59, Diels-Kranz. [3] Ibid. B 182. [4] Ibid. B 179.

[5] *Republic*, VI, 494D.

[6] *Phaedo*, 66D; cf. Gorgias, 82B 11a (15), Diels-Kranz.

[7] *Phaedo*, 89D ff.

[8] Cleanthes (apud Sextus Empiricus, *Adv. Mathem.*, IX, 90, Fr. I, 529, *Stoicorum veterum fragmenta* I, ed. H. von Arnim, 2nd ed., Leipzig, 1921) expressed similar ideas about the long struggle through which man attains virtue at the end of his life.

and great things have, or can have, equal importance. The dialectician is not allowed to honour the noble more than the mean and ridiculous,[1] and that is why the aged Parmenides tells the young Socrates that when he is older and more mature, he will not despise "cases that might be thought absurd, such as hair or mud or dirt or any other trivial and undignified objects".[2] Or as Aristotle expresses it in the introduction to his course on natural science, the student of nature

> will not leave out any one of [the animals] be it never so mean; for though there are animals which have no attractiveness for the senses, yet for the eye of science, for the student who is naturally of a philosophic spirit and can discern the causes of things, Nature which fashioned them provides joys which cannot be measured.[3]

Finally, in searching high and low and "turning in all directions", the scientist must make sacrifices of time, of comfort, of ease. He must risk health, even life. "Willingly would I burn to death like Phaëthon," exclaimed the astronomer Eudoxus, "were this the price for reaching the sun and learning its shape, its size and its substance."[4]

These are the main demands of the profession of science as the Greeks came to understand them. It cannot have been easy, for men who loved leisure and had no concept of the "nobility of toil", to turn their free time into hard labour, labour even of a slave. Nor can it have been less difficult for them to master that native pessimism and scepticism which made them so often complain that life is too short to arrive at wisdom.[5] One

[1] Plato, *Sophist*, 227B. [2] Plato, *Parmenides*, 130C; cf. E.

[3] *On Parts of Animals*, I, 5, 645a 7 ff.

[4] Plutarch, *Non posse suaviter vivi secundum Epicurum*, 1094A–B. These words were perhaps spoken in the famous debate on pleasure in which Eudoxus upheld against the Platonists the thesis that pleasure is the basic principle of human action (E. Frank, "Die Begründung der mathematischen Naturwissenschaft durch Eudoxus", *Knowledge, Will and Belief*, ed. L. Edelstein, Zürich and Stuttgart, 1955, pp. 154 f.). However that may be, the statement is made in the spirit in which Plato (*Republic*, II, 361E–362A; X, 613A) demands that the virtuous man uphold virtue unto death, even if crucified, a conviction shared by Stoics and Epicureans (see Cicero, *De finibus*, III, 13, 42 ff; IV, 12, 31; and *Tusculanae disputationes*, II, 7, 17 ff.).

[5] Cf., e.g., Protagoras, 80B 1, Diels-Kranz, and the first of the Hippocratic *Aphorisms*: "Art is long, life is short". For the contrast between the classical and the modern attitudes toward work, see, e.g., H. Michell, *The Economics of Ancient Greece* (Cambridge and New York, 1940), p. 14, and for changes in the Hellenistic evaluation of work in professions, Edelstein, "The professional ethics of the Greek physician", pp. 399 ff. The early reaction to exactness in science, "which seems to some people to be mean, no less

sometimes has the impression that they were themselves astonished at what they had achieved, and that this is the reason why they were fond of talking of peoples in their climate as by nature "lovers of wisdom", in contrast to other races that by nature were given to making money or indulging in the pleasures of the body.[1] And undoubtedly a native love of knowledge must have been a driving force in their quest for knowledge. But I am persuaded that there was another factor also, more elemental as it were than the love of any particular thing, however great and lovable. Every man of creative gifts, Aristotle asserts, "loves the work of his hands". "The cause of this", he adds,

> is that existence is to all men a thing to be chosen and loved . . . and that the handiwork *is* in a sense the producer in activity; he loves his handiwork, therefore, because he loves existence. And this is rooted in the nature of things: for what he is in potentiality, his handiwork manifests in activity.[2]

The knowledge of the scientist — expressed in definitions, classifications, empirical laws — is himself; it is his being, no longer as possibility but as reality, no longer as perishable existence of the hour but as eternal existence in the contemplation of the truth.[3]

Now, if the scientist lives up to the demands of his profession, if he plays his role as he should, he will be — as Galen says in his *Protreptic to the Sciences* which summarizes the long tradition of professional ethics — a worthy member of the "brotherhood" of those who have dedicated themselves to the pursuit of truth: geometers, arithmeticians, philosophers, physicians, astrono-

in an argument than in a business transaction" (Aristotle, *Metaphysics*, 985a 10 ff.; [Boll, "Vita contemplativa", p. 30]; see also Plato, *Theaetetus*, 184C), also betrays the originally aristocratic or rather gentleman's ethics of scholarship.

[1] Plato, *Republic*, IV, 435E.

[2] *Nicomachean Ethics*, IX, 7, 1167b 34 ff.

[3] *Nicomachean Ethics*, X, 1177a 27 ff. Aristotle (op. cit., IX) names as the outstanding case of love of one's "handicraft" the poet's love for his poems. Love of handicraft then may be asserted also of the scientist, whom he does not mention. Moreover, according to the Pythagoreans, "love for what is truly noble" manifests itself in practical pursuits and in the sciences (Aristoxenus, Diels-Kranz, I, pp. 478, 17 ff., and in general L. Edelstein, *The Hippocratic Oath*, Baltimore, 1943, p. 60). Xenophon in his *Oeconomicus* maintains too that without love for the object no worker can succeed. Perhaps not everyone would have agreed with Aristotle's contention that man through thought becomes immortal. But it was certainly the belief of most of the dogmatists, Platonists, Aristotelians and Stoics; see Ptolemy's epigram quoted above, p. 22.

mers and grammarians (Ch. 5). This brotherhood is presided over by the god Hermes, the "King of Reason" (Ch. 3) — while all ordinary men belong to the brotherhood over which blind Fortune rules (Ch. 3) — and it is not money (Ch. 6) or birth (Ch. 7) that here determines rank and dignity. The virtues of the father to be sure are "a fine treasure", but it is still better to be able to put against them the claim of Sthenelus: "We avow ourselves to be better men by far than our fathers were".[1] Thus it will be the son who gives glory to his ancestors and to his country (Ch. 7), not only through wisdom but also through his irreproachable life.

The followers of Hermes, Galen says, are "cheerful like their god", do not blame life as do the followers of Fortune, are steadfast and consistent in their actions (Ch. 3). Among them one finds no thieves, grave-robbers and murderers as in the rival brotherhood of common men (Ch. 4). Similarly, Euripides had praised him who contemplates the "ageless order of deathless Nature" as having "no care for deeds of shame" and "no impulse to his fellows' harm or unjust deeds".[2] And at the end of the Hellenistic era, when the possibility of the conflict of duties was better understood, Stoic philosophy had with intrepidity and forthrightness drawn the inevitable conclusion that "there are things so terrible and horrid that the wise man will not do them even to save his country".[3] For the sage, be he philosopher or scientist, lives in that *altera historia* which is not the history of a particular race or country or time, but the history of mankind.[4]

The true scientist, like the true poet or artist, one may say, chooses the role for which he is born. Granted that this is true, even the born actor has much to learn. Otherwise his natural talent may not be fully developed; it may even become spoiled

[1] *Iliad*, IV, v. 405.

[2] Fr. 910, Nauck.

[3] Posidonius apud Cicero, *De officiis*, I, 45, 159.

[4] For the conflict between the physician's obligations as citizen and as member of the medical profession see L. Edelstein, *Bull. Hist. Medicine*, XXX (1956) pp. 409 f. Despite the rare attestation, the problem must have been of great importance, for the role of the "patriot" is distinguished from other professional roles even in Horace's cursory treatment of the subject (*Ars poetica*, v. 312). That the scientist's fatherland is the world is stated by Seneca (*De otio*, 4, 1–2, and see above, p. 20). The sordid reality of what actually happened all too often, then as now, comes to the fore in Seneca's protestation that "the wise man will do even things of which he does not approve in order to accomplish in this manner greater ends" (Seneca apud Lactantius, *Institut. Div.* III, 15).

in course of time. Only the one who studies his role will be able to say at the end that he has performed well in the "comedy of life", and can justly ask for applause.[1] The discovery of the "personality" (*πρόσωπον*, *persona*) of the scientist, of his character traits, is not the least significant discovery in the history of ancient science. It revealed the objective duties and the true rewards of the scientific life, thus supplementing the force of personal motives and providing a strong incentive where none was provided by society. It created an ideal through which the inquiring mind, perhaps the most important piece of apparatus for scientific investigation, acquired a fixed and settled form.

The analysis I have given obviously does not exhaust the subject. Much more could and must be said about each topic in order to do justice to it. My analysis, however, is incomplete also in another sense. I have omitted from consideration a number of issues that might profitably have been taken up, because their discussion would have led me too far astray.

Not all that the Greeks and Romans regarded as scientific knowledge would nowadays be classified as such. It was a knowledge which included such 'pseudo-sciences' as astrology, Pythagorean number-symbolism, the Platonic scale of music, intrusions of the occult, and theories which the modern scientist calls superstitious or religious.[2] Although this very fact may indeed be indicative of an as yet incorrect understanding of science, it points more importantly to a different under-

[1] Suetonius, *Divus Augustus*, 99.

[2] That in Greek thought the 'scientific' and 'other' requests for knowledge are still undistinguished, has been noted by S. E. Toulmin, *The Place of Reason in Ethics* (Cambridge, 1960) 211. The tendency of recent historical studies to isolate within Greek science what seems scientific as judged by modern standards is justifiable and natural but it should not preclude an interpretation which takes as their science what the ancients labelled as such, or in other words takes science as part of the particular civilization, the particular historical situation in which it flourished ("Ancient science", pp. 576 ff.). The latter approach I think L. von Ranke also had in mind when, following French examples, he asserted that it was impossible to write the history of a nation without taking account of its scientific development (*Sämmtliche Werke*, Leipzig, 1888, LI–LII, 490, 552). In science as well as in art, man transcends the boundaries of nationality. And yet, there is even in art a national element; art tells something about the nation that made it (G. Dehio, *Geschichte der Deutschen Kunst*, Berlin and Leipzig, 1930, I, 1[4], p. 15). The history of ancient science can come to be understood more adequately only, I believe, if the objective and the subjective approach are combined.

standing of its meaning: science was thought to comprise both 'exact' and 'inexact' knowledge and consequently had a wider range of motives and incentives than modern science. Moreover, the ancient terms *epistemai*, *mathemata*, *scientiae* covered any methodical investigation by human reason of the data of human experience, and comprised the humanities as well as what is called science in modern times. An investigation of the subject here at stake should therefore take account also of historical studies, political theories, and ethics, so closely connected in Antiquity with the natural sciences that they were often the domain of one scholar. If this unity were stressed, it would become clearer I think why the truly practical sciences were the humanities — men thought they could remake themselves, as I put it before — and why the physical sciences remained largely theoretical, why, to use a famous phrase, the instinct of workmanship predominantly informed humanistic rather than so-called scientific studies.[1] Upon this central issue, a discussion of the ancient debate concerning the origin of science would throw further light. In certain periods two theories opposed each other, the one maintaining that all knowledge originated from practical interest, the other that it arose from theoretical concern. History was written and rewritten from each of these points of view. As far as the natural sciences are concerned, the upholders of the theoretical ideal were I think right. But the arguments used on both sides tell a good deal about the general evaluation of the scientific enterprise, which is decisive also for the reaction of society to science and the scientists.[2]

Finally, a distinction has to be drawn between the Greek and Roman contributions to the scientific movement. Though ancient science is fundamentally a Greek creation, the Romans had a share in it also. The Greek confidence in reason, their desire to penetrate the surface of phenomena in order to reach the essence of things, their striving to find the meaning of existence, which pervades even their dramatic art and in part their fine arts, gave to science its basic character. But the

[1] On the definition of science which I have here adopted see W. G. DeBurgh, *The Legacy of the Ancient World* (Pelican Books, Harmondsworth, 1953) II, 490, n. 2.

[2] For the two historical interpretations of the past, see W. Jaeger, "Über Ursprung und Kreislauf des philosophischen Lebensideals", *Sitzungsberichte der Preussischen Akademie der Wissenschaften*, Phil.-Hist. Klasse., XXV (1928) 390 ff.

Roman wish for comprehending results at one glance, for making them conveniently accessible — as evidenced in the Roman encyclopaedias — helped in bringing about unity of science. Nor is the Roman practicality and gift for organizing without influence on the integration of science into society and on the later strength of empiricism as well as on the development of a scholastic method.[1] And surely the Greek achievement ought to be compared with Oriental knowledge. The ancients, being the first idolaters of Eastern peoples, made this comparison themselves. They sometimes complained that if the Greeks would only learn to collect data as did the Babylonians, or to persevere in the tradition, to cling to what they have and know as did the Egyptians — their efforts might well amount to something. The revolutionary temper of the Greek race, their willingness to try something new every day and to try everything they could possibly think of, was held to be destructive rather than constructive. One wonders whether, had the Greeks been different, they would have invented science. Whatever the answer to this question, the origins of science would be set in sharper relief by a confrontation of Western and Oriental learning.[2]

Here I have been able in the main merely to try to trace the outlines of the ideal image of the scientist and of science that emerges from the testimony. This ideal, inherited by the Western world, remained supreme until Bacon put into words a new ideal that had gradually taken shape since the beginning of the Renaissance. To Bacon the scientist of Antiquity had ventured on a task reserved to God and the angels. He wanted to understand everything. Bacon preached greater humility than the pagan had with regard to knowledge, more concern for human ends, more love of man and more interest in his welfare here.[3] Bacon's criticism in some respects is well founded. The ancients were not distinguished for their sense of practical philanthropy, of social justice, or for caring for the poor. But

[1] In my characterization of the Greek spirit I have in the main followed H. D. F. Kitto, *The Greeks* (Pelican Books, Harmondsworth, 1951) 179, 181 f. For the Romans and science see, e.g. R. H. Barrow, *The Romans* (Pelican Books, Harmondsworth, 1951) 137 ff.

[2] Such comparisons of Oriental and Greek learning, from Plato's time on, became more and more the fashion. I mention here only those given by Diodorus (II, 29) and by Pliny (VII, 56, 191 ff.).

[3] On Bacon cf. M. E. Prior, "Bacon's Man of Science", in *Roots of Scientific Thought*, ed. Philip P. Wiener and A. Nolan (New York, 1957) 382 ff.

if Bacon derided the ancients' pride, they would I think have charged him with *hubris* on account of his daring to change the world that is and to rebuild it. They would I believe also have denied that their wish for understanding is but pride. Speaking about the theoretical life and pondering its outcome, Seneca avers that men try to comprehend the riddle of the universe in order that "God be not without witness"[1] — God, that is, reason. Indeed, one may well say that motives and incentives for science in Antiquity, for natural science, are in the last analysis derived from human eagerness to testify to the existence of reason in the world of nature.

[1] *De otio*, IV, 4.

LUDWIG EDELSTEIN

The Golden Chain of Homer

In his admirable work *The Great Chain of Being,* Professor Lovejoy has shown the importance which the concept of the Scale of Being and its figurative expression, the chain, had for Western thought from the early Middle Ages down to the nineteenth century. In an introductory chapter he has outlined the genesis of the idea itself in Greek philosophy. Yet, not primarily concerned with the Greek development, he has refrained from inquiring how far back in ancient literature one can trace the metaphor, and by what process it became a phrase identified with the Neo-Platonic theory of emanation. These questions I propose to discuss here, taking as my point of departure the passage in Macrobius' commentary on the *Somnium Scipionis* (I, 14, 15) through which, as Professor Lovejoy says, probably most medieval writers became acquainted with the simile of the chain.[1]

Speaking of the Supreme God, Mind, Soul and their creation, as well as of the creation of all subsequent things, Macrobius identifies " Homer's golden chain, which God, he says, bade hang down from heaven to earth " (*Homeri catena aurea, quam pendere de caelo in terras deum iussisse commemorat*) with the continuous succession of all things degenerating to the very bottom

[1] A. O. Lovejoy, *The Great Chain of Being*² (1942), 63.

of the series, "a connection of parts, from the Supreme God down to the last dregs of things, mutually linked together and without a break" (*a summo deo usque ad ultimam rerum faecem una mutuis se vinculis religans et nusquam interrupta connexio*).[2] The identification is made quite casually, and one can hardly believe that Macrobius should have been the first to offer it. In general, he follows Neo-Platonic writers, and it would therefore seem natural to believe that he took this metaphor from the same sources. However, it does not occur in Plotinus, who uses the other comparison which Macrobius adduces in his context, namely the series of mirrors (*e.g. Enneads*, I, 1, 8); nor is the chain of Homer mentioned with similar connotations in the extant writings of Porphyry, Iamblichus, or Julian. Consequently, scholars have suggested that Macrobius must have borrowed the simile from a Neo-Platonic work now lost.[3]

This supposition may well be correct. Yet, even if Macrobius depended on an earlier Neo-Platonic author, it is unwarranted to assume, as is usually done, that the metaphor was original with the Neo-Platonists.[4] It was in fact employed at least as early as the first half of the second century after Christ. The rhetor, Aristides, in his speech *On Zeus* contends that all gods are endowed with an emanation of the power of the highest deity, the creator of the world, and, he continues, "in the manner of the chain of Homer everything is fastened upon Him and everything is suspended from Him, a chain much more beautiful than that golden chain or any other chain one might

[2] The translation is Professor Lovejoy's (*loc. cit.*).

[3] M. Schedler, *Die Philosophie des Macrobius und ihr Einfluss auf die Wissenschaft des christlichen Mittelalters*, in *Beiträge z. Gesch. d. Philosophie d. Mittelalters*, XIII, 1 (1916), 12.

[4] E. g. W. Leaf, *The Iliad*, I[2] (1900), *ad* VIII, v. 19; L. Preller-C. Robert, *Griechische Mythologie*, I[4] (1894), 108, note 1; cf. also below, n. 33.

imagine" (*In Jovem*, 15).[5] Even granted that Macrobius gives a more elaborate picture of the chain, fundamentally the metaphor is used in the same sense by Macrobius as by Aristides. The latter, too, envisages a unity of unequal parts, a descending sequence of values (*ibid.*, 15–17). His description of the position of Zeus reflects the doctrine of Middle Platonism with its tendency to elevate the might of the one and supreme god and to unify the various realms of being under his leadership. At least to this eclectic system, then, one can trace the chain as a metaphor of the Scale of Being.[6]

Nor were the Middle Platonists the first to ascribe an exalted philosophical significance to the episode at the beginning of the eighth Book of the *Iliad* (vv. 1–40), where Zeus forbids the assembled gods and goddesses to meddle in the affairs of mortals, threatens them with dire punishment in case they disobey, and dares them to make trial of his strength in a rope-pulling contest, with a rope of gold to be suspended from heaven (v. 19);

[5] Ὥστε καὶ θεῶν ὅσα φῦλα ἀπορροὴν τῆς Διὸς τοῦ πάντων πατρὸς δυνάμεως ἕκαστα ἔχει καὶ ἀτεχνῶς κατὰ τὴν Ὁμήρου σειρὰν ἅπαντα εἰς αὐτὸν ἀνήρτηται καὶ πάντα ἐξ αὐτοῦ ἐξῆπται, πολὺ καλλίων ἄλυσις ἢ κατὰ χρυσῆν τε καὶ εἴ τινα ἄλλην τις ἐπινοήσειεν (43 Keil). For the date of the speech (around 142/3 A.D.), cf. J. Amann, *Die Zeusrede des Ailios Aristeides*, in *Tübinger Beiträge z. Altertumswissenschaft*, XII (1931), 36. Aristides' statement is adduced in explanation of the chains mentioned in Proclus' hymns by F. Jacobs, *Animadversiones in Epigrammata Anthologiae Graecae*, X (1801), 273; 277; cf. J. F. Boissonade, *Marini Vita Procli* (1814), 121. The passage is also quoted as an example of allegorical interpretation by C. G. Heyne, *Homeri Carmina* V (1802), 417. In the later discussion of the subject it has apparently been forgotten.

[6] For the doctrine of Middle Platonism, cf. F. Ueberweg-K. Praechter, *Die Philosophie des Altertums*[12] (1926), 524 ff.; R. E. Witt, *Albinus and the History of Middle Platonism* (1937). Amann, *op. cit.*, 24-27, speaks only of the influence of Plato and of the Stoa on Aristides; but cf. E. and L. Edelstein, *Asclepius*, II (1945), 107. Aristides' evaluation of the demiurge agrees with Albinus, *Didaskalikos*, ch. XII (p. 167, 18 ff.), on which see Witt, *op. cit.*, 133 f.

for in Homer surely it is a rope, not a chain, that is referred to, and it is called golden "to show its poetical character" (*Scholia A, ad loc.*).[7] From the fifth century B. C. this passage seems to have been of singular importance to all allegorizers; the earlier interpretations, I suggest, gradually led up to the meaning which the Middle Platonists later discovered in the words of Homer.

Plato's mention of the golden rope is the oldest philosophical testimony that has survived. In his opinion, the poet indicates by the rope "nothing other than the sun, and reveals that so long as the heavens and the sun keep moving, all things divine and human remain safe; but if this motion were halted, bound as it were, all things would be destroyed and everything, as the saying goes, turned upside down" (*Theaetetus*, 153 c-d). The allegory, as it is formulated here, probably is of Heraclitean origin, although it was hardly restricted to that school, and Plato adapts it to his own purposes.[8] In his ironic manner, he blends physical and metaphysical speculations. Like the sun, the rope maintains the existence of the cosmos and of all its parts. But the sun also symbolizes movement, and eternal movement, one might say, is considered the rope, the bond, that holds

[7] *Scholia Graeca in Homeri Iliadem*, ed. G. Dindorf, I (1875), 269. Cf. Leaf's comment on v. 19. Ps. Plutarch, *De vita et poesi Homeri*, 18, attributes to Homer an analogical use of the term, and so do some of the other scholia, but this surely is a later misunderstanding. The game referred to is described by Eusthatius, *Commentarii in Homeri Iliadem*, p. 1111.

[8] For the Heraclitean origin of the allegory, cf. e. g. L. Campbell, *The Theaetetus of Plato*[2] (1883), *ad loc.* Euripides (*Orestes*, v. 982) calls the sun a rock held in suspense between heaven and earth by golden "chains" (ἀλύσεσιν). The expression may be derived from Homer (cf. *e. g.* Leaf, on *Iliad*, VIII, v. 19); if so, this would be the earliest analogical interpretation of the Homeric *seira* which is attested; cf. below, n. 20. The explanation of the nature of the sun is that of Anaxagoras, as the scholia recall (*Scholia in Euripidem*, ed. E. Schwartz, I [1887], 193 f.), and he may have agreed with the allegorization of the Heracliteans. For Anaxagoras' interest in Homer, cf. F. Wehrli, *Zur Geschichte der allegorischen Deutung Homers im Altertum*, Diss. Basel (1928), 66; 84 f.

the phenomena in place. The student of the Platonic dialogues cannot fail to remember, in addition, that the sun is the offspring of the idea of the Good, the strongest of all bonds, and its analogue in the visible world (*Republic,* 508 b-c).[9] If the movement of the sun is tied up, then the appointed order of the world will be disturbed, just as Zeus threatens to pull all the gods up to heaven, along with the earth and the sea, and to bind the rope around Olympus, so that all things would be hanging in the air (vv. 23–26).

Both the physical and the metaphysical aspects of the Platonic explication were broadened by succeeding generations, and in some instances were merged again to such an extent that it is not always possible to distinguish them clearly. As for that interpretation in which the physical component predominates, some people continued to see in the golden rope an allegory of the sun (*Scholia A, ad* v. 19), or of its rays and the days (Palaephatus, *De incredibilibus,* XVIII; cf. Ps. Lucian, *De astrologia,* 22). The rope symbolized the chain of days of the Aeon, binding together the days of mankind up to that one on which everything will be destroyed, except god himself (Eusthatius, p. 695). Others held that the rope points to the orbits of the stars, which all great naturalists define as firebrands (Heraclitus, *Quaestiones Homericae,* ch. 36).[10] More particularly, it was taken to mean the orbits of the planets and their arrangement on the heaven (Eusthatius, p. 695, 10). Besides, the whole incident related by Homer was now exploited for its allegorical meaning. Zeus' boasting of what he might do to gods, earth, and sea (vv. 23–26) proved that in the poet's view the all-surrounding heaven could

[9] F. Boll, *Die Sonne im Glauben und in der Weltanschauung der alten Völker* (1922), 21. He seems the only one to stress this implication of the allegory within the context of the Platonic work.

[10] Heraclitus' book was probably composed in the first century A.D.; it is in the main indebted to Stoic sources.

justly be called the upper part of the spherical cosmos and the region of the earth the part below (Ps. Plutarch, *De vita et poesi Homeri*, ch. 94).[11] Zeus' threat to throw the rebellious gods down into Tartarus, as far below as heaven is high above earth (v. 16), indicated the central position of the earth (Heraclitus, *Quaestiones Homericae*, ch. 36). If Anatolius, the Peripatetic of the third century A. D., is to be trusted, already the "Pythagoreans" found this dogma confirmed by Zeus' words.[12] Finally, the metaphor of the rope was interpreted by the Stoics in two different ways. The rope could be a simile of the "chainlike intertwining," the interlacing of the elements whose nature was to be changed in the end through the general conflagration of the world (Eusthatius, p. 695). Or the rope signified the sun drying up the sea by which it is nourished; eventually, the sun will annihilate even the earth, and thus all that was below will be drawn above into "the heart" of the cosmos; Zeus alone, the personification of the ether, will not be absorbed into it (Eusthatius, p. 695, 10).[13] To put it differently, the altercations between the Olympians, properly understood, yielded the cosmology and cosmography of Homer.

[11] This work shows an eclectic-Pythagorean tendency; its date can perhaps be set at the beginning of the Roman Empire, cf. Wehrli, *op. cit.*, 21; 39.

[12] H. Diels-W. Kranz, *Die Fragmente der Vorsokratiker*, I[5] (1934), p. 225, 18 ff. (28A44). Aristarchus deleted the line (cf. K. Lehrs, *De Aristarchi Studiis Homericis*[2] [1865], 174), while Crates defended it (cf. H. J. Mette, *Sphairopoiia* [1936]. Fr. 39 b).

[13] Lucretius (II, 1153 f.) denies that men descended from heaven by the golden rope, and as Professor Louis A. MacKay, reminds me, the poet is usually understood to refer to a Stoic allegorization of the golden rope mentioned in *Iliad*, VIII. Moreover, Themistius (*Orat.* 32, 363d) is said to prove that the passage "was used in the way hinted at by Lucretius" (Lucretius, ed. H. A. J. Munro, I[3] [1873], *ad. loc.*). Yet, although Themistius speaks of a σειρά of eternal birth, the adjective ἄρρηκτος seems to make certain that what he has in mind is the δεσμὸς ἄρρηκτος with which Zeus fastened the hands of Hera (*Iliad*, XV, 19 f.). This bond actually was interpreted by the Stoics as the unbreakable unity of the elements (Ps. Heraclitus, ch. LX *finis*) that

On the other hand, the metaphysical side of the argument comes to the fore in a statement of Aristotle. Those who believe the origin of motion to be outside of motion, he says, should find appropriate Zeus' assertion (vv. 20–22) that the gods would be unable to overcome him and to drag him down from heaven to earth, even if they tried to do so with all their strength (*Movement of Animals*, 699 b 35 ff.).[14] And Theophrastus expresses a similar thought, claiming that the prime mover can be expected to be even stronger than the Homeric Zeus who boasts (v. 24) that he can do what his fellow gods are unable to accomplish (*Metaphysics*, II, 9, 5b15–17). While Aristotle and Theophrastus avail themselves of Homer's verses to illustrate the position of the transcendental prime mover, others were more realistic and thought that the poet in Zeus' menacing speech enigmatically suggested the merit of monarchy, for the rule of the many would be even worse in heaven than on earth (Eusthatius, p. 695, 10; *Scholia A, ad* vv. 25–26). Moreover, this Zeus, the Stoics claimed, is the personification of fate that holds sway over heaven and earth (v. 27; Eusthatius, p. 695). Homer, like all great philosophers, acknowledged one supreme deity. Does not Zeus end his warnings (v. 27) by affirming his superiority over men and gods alike? Does not Athena humbly answer the father of all, the supreme of lords (v. 31)? Does she not concede (v. 32): "We know only too well that your might

create animals and men (*ibid., init.*). The whole description of Hera's punishment through Zeus (XV, 18-21) symbolized the genesis of the cosmos (cf. J. Stern, *Homerstudien der Stoiker* [1893], 16). I should therefore suggest that Lucretius too was thinking of an interpretation of *Iliad*, XV rather than of *Iliad*, VIII (for *superne . . . de caelo*, cf. ὑψόθεν [XV, 18] and Ps. Heraclitus on this word).

[14] The genuineness of this treatise has been proved by W. Jaeger, *Hermes*, 48 (1913), 33, who has also pointed out that the use of the Homeric verses here agrees with Aristotle's general attitude as expressed in Book XII of the *Metaphysics*.

is dauntless" (Ps. Plutarch, *De vita et poesi Homeri*, 114)? Thus, he who challenged his peers to a tug of war emerged as the highest deity, an understanding of the Homeric account that apparently was quite commonly accepted. Lucian, in his Menippean dialogues, repeatedly pokes fun at the golden chain of Zeus and his pretense at being omnipotent, whereas Christian Apologists of approximately the same time concluded from the same evidence that Homer agreed with their own monotheistic teaching.[15]

From the testimony adduced it is clear, I think, that when the Middle Platonists expressed their concept of the structure of the universe through the metaphor of the golden chain, they merely followed an old-established procedure. At that time, the episode at the beginning of the Eighth Book of the *Iliad* had long been of central importance for philosophical allegorizers. To the modern reader, the Homeric tale has alternately appeared as a burlesque mockery of the divine, or as a poetical description of the gods' character that is imbued with tragic grandeur.[16] To the ancients, at least to those who wished to extract Homer's philosophy in agreement with their own predilections, it was fraught with deep meaning, a clue to Homer's physical and metaphysical beliefs. How this came about, it is difficult to determine. The love of etymologies may have provided the starting point for speculation. The rope, the *seira*, may have

[15] For Lucian, cf. e.g. *Juppiter confutatus*, 4; other passages have been collected by R. Helm, *Lucian und Menipp* (1906), 137. Even the *Scholia A*, *ad* vv. 25-26 raise the question, how Zeus can be the strongest, if once he was overcome by others (*Iliad*, I, 400). On the other hand, Vettius Valens, *Anthologiae*, IX, 8, p. 347, 7 ff. Kroll, sees in lines 19 ff. proof of Zeus' self-restraint and willingness not to overstep the law; this "mystic" interpretation unfortunately is mutilated by a lacuna. For the Christian view, cf. Ps. Justinus, *Cohortatio ad Graecos*, 24 (*Patrologia Graeca*, VI, p. 284 Migne).

[16] Cf. *e.g.* W. Nestle, *Anfänge einer Götterburleske bei Homer*, in *Griechische Studien* (1948), 14.

been brought together with the star, *Seirios*, or with Zeus *Seiren*, of whom the poet, Antimachus, affirms that he was named after *Sirius*, the dog-star rising in the month of the greatest summer heat.[17] Orphic poets referred to a golden rope which Zeus, "in accordance with the laws laid down by the goddess, Night, winds around all things." It is not certain that this statement formed part of the early Orphic doctrine, and consequently one cannot be sure that it helped in instigating the preoccupation of philosophers with the golden rope of Homer. But at one moment or other it must have provided at least an additional reason for the interest in the Homeric scene.

In the third century B.C., at any rate, the question could be asked, whether the Orphic rope may not be identical with that of Homer, for, as Philodemus attests, Cleanthes and Chrysippus tried to reconcile their own views with those of Homer and Orpheus and Musaeus.[18] Decisive perhaps was the fact that Zeus' threat to pull up earth, sea, and gods is indeed rather puzzling,

[17] M. Wohlrab, *Platonis Opera*, III^2,1 (1891), commenting on the *Theaetetus* passage, where the golden *seira* is identified with the sun, quotes a gloss of Suidas: *σειρ. σειρός: ὁ ἥλιος*; cf. also O. Apelt's note in his translation, *Platons Dialog Theätet*^{4} (1923), 161. For Antimachus, cf. B. Wyss, *Antimachi Colophonii Reliquiae* (1936), Fr. 31. Wyss interprets: *Juppiter torrens*; cf. A. B. Cook, *Zeus*, I (1914), 740. For the rôle which etymologies played in early interpretations, cf. the Platonic *Cratylus*, and in general Wehrli, *op. cit.*, 85 ff., who has also drawn attention to the fact that the allegorization of the golden chain is the oldest philosophical allegorization of a Homeric concept that has survived (88). Whether or not an ethical interpretation preceded the philosophical one, in this instance as perhaps in all others, I am not prepared to decide.

[18] For the Orphic references to a golden chain, cf. O. Kern, *Orphicorum Fragmenta* (1922), Fr. 166; for Cleanthes and Chrysippus, cf. I, 539 Arnim. W. Nestle, *Vom Mythos zum Logos* (1942), 129, apparently considers Fr. 166 part of the old Orphic theogony; he is even inclined to trace the beginning of all allegorization of Homer to the Orphics. But the only fact that can be established is that the goddess, Night, was regarded as the supreme deity in the older stratum of the Orphic tradition; cf. Fr. 28 Kern (Eudemus) and I. M. Linforth, *The Arts of Orpheus* (1941), 154 f.

and that hardly any other passage in the *Iliad* sketches so briefly and succinctly a scheme of the whole world. Zeus' words about Tartarus and its precise location in regard to Hades, as well as in regard to the distance between heaven and earth (v. 16), are spoken in the manner of a philosopher, as a late commentator remarks (Eusthatius, p. 694, 40); they recall an almost identical assertion in Hesiod's *Theogony* (v. 720). And surely, no scene in Homer gives a more vivid and unmistakable impression of the true distribution of power among the Olympians.[19]

Whatever the adequate cause of the allegorization, the Middle Platonists only did what all the philosophers on whose systems they based their own doctrine—Plato, Aristotle, the Stoics—had done before them. Moreover, allowing for certain changes made necessary by their own peculiar theories, their reading of the time-hallowed cipher was but the almost logical consequence of earlier interpretations. The theology that Aristides expounds in his speech *On Zeus* presupposes the dogma of Zeus' predominance; it takes it for granted that the golden rope has some cosmic significance. But Zeus is now regarded not only as a deity, incorporeal and comprehensible by reason alone (Ps. Plutarch, *De vita et poesi Homeri*, 114), or as fate (Eusthatius, p. 695); he is thought of as a personal god, as the creator of the world over which he rules, the one who unifies the diversity of being. Thus, while according to Homer Zeus is able, if he feels it necessary or if he so wishes, to pull up by a rope to his heavenly abode gods and sea and earth, according to Aristides he holds forever all things that he has created; in the manner of Homer's chain they are fastened upon and suspended from

[19] The similarity between *Iliad*, VIII, 16 and Hesiod, *Theogony*, 720, was noted by K. Ameis-C. Hentze, *Homers Ilias*, I[4] (1894), *ad loc.* Linguistic peculiarities of the lines and Hesiodic parallels are discussed by R. Mackrodt, *Der Olymp in Ilias und Odyssee*, Programm Eisenberg (1882), 9 f.

him. The epic picture of what might happen under certain circumstances is transformed—as is fitting for a symbol—into a description of what does happen from eternity to eternity. The rope is taken to mean a chain, the links of which are made up of the various parts of the cosmos connected and held together by Zeus.[20]

Moreover, this chain of Zeus Aristides finds worthy of praise in preference to "that golden chain or any other chain one might imagine." The binding power of Necessity, or Eros and Aphrodite had played a primary part in early cosmological theories; Necessity as the "concatenation of causes" and the golden chain of Aphrodite were familiar expressions in Aristides' time.[21] Yet these chains symbolized a force that works from without, that coerces matter into a unity alien to itself. Aristides subordinates them to Zeus. Eros and Ananke, he continues immediately following his pronouncement on Zeus, are themselves children of the king of gods, begotten by him at the beginning

[20] My interpretation of Aristides' understanding of the Homeric description presupposes that he did not read vv. 25-26, according to which Zeus intends to bind the rope around Olympus, so that all things will be hanging in the air. These lines were deleted by Zenodotus, because they seemed to contradict a statement previously made by Homer about Mount Olympus; cf. Lehrs, *op. cit.*, 168. They are also omitted in another speech of Aristides (28, Par. 45 Keil), where he quotes *Iliad*, VIII, 17-27. *Scholia A, ad* vv. 25-26, however, give the impression that it was just these lines which were taken to mean that everything is dependent on god. The Middle Platonic commentary on the *Theaetetus*, *Berliner Klassikertexte*, II (1905), 49, explains only Plato's statement on the golden rope and does not help to clarify Aristides' views. I should note that Aristides paraphrases σειρά by ἅλυσις; to him, then, as to all later philosophers, the "rope" definitely was a "chain." Whether or not the two terms were used interchangeably before him, cannot be ascertained. Some of the Stoic allegorizations (cf. above p. 52) seem to indicate such a usage, especially the identification of the rope with Fate.

[21] For Aristides' polemic against older cosmogonies, cf. Amann, *op. cit.*, 76 ff. The chain of Aphrodite is mentioned *e.g.* by Lucian, *Demosthenis Encomium*, 13. For Fate as the concatenation of causes, cf. *St. V. Fr.*, II, 917 Arnim, and Ps. Plutarch, *De fato*, 570 b; also 574 c: ὁ τῆς ἁλύσεως λόγος.

of the world "so that they should bind the universe together for him" (*In Jovem*, 15). In this way, the work of Eros and Ananke becomes an effluence of Zeus' own power. Their chains, as well as that of Zeus himself, are taken to symbolize a unity that resides within, for all creation is itself part of the creator to whom it owes its existence.

Thus the *aurea catena Homeri* was established by the Middle Platonists as a figurative expression of the Scale of Being. A poetical phrase became a philosophical catchword; the implement of an athletic contest became a metaphor of the innermost essence of the universe. Could it be that behind Homer's own fancy a symbol was hidden which he playfully transformed, and that later philosophers in their attempts to find an allegorical meaning in his story only reverted to its original significance? The romanticists among the nineteenth century writers on mythology were prone to call the golden chain a mythical or religious *Ursymbol*, clearly expressed in Hindu sacred literature by Vishnu, who speaks of the cosmos as suspended from himself "like a row of pearls on a string." Such an opinion will nowadays hardly be acceptable to anyone.[22] Nor does the more recent interpretation of the chain as an astronomical *Ursymbol* seem any more satisfactory. In the view of certain peoples, the Milky Way was thought to be an immense rope, and the golden rope hung from heaven, it has therefore been said, may have been suggested to Homer by a popular conception of the galaxy. But no remnant of such a belief on the part of the Greeks has survived, and what may be true of other times and other countries need not necessarily be true of them.[23]

[22] F. Creuzer, *Symbolik und Mythologie der alten Völker*, I (1810), 116 ff., quoting from Fr. Schlegel, *Über die Sprache und Weisheit der Inder*, 303.

[23] The astronomical interpretation has been proposed by A. B. Cook, *Zeus*, II, 2 (1925), 1211, with reference to W. Gundel, *Sterne und Sternbilder im Glauben des Altertums und der Neuzeit* (1922), 46. Concerning the Milky

In Greek popular tradition the rope is of some importance. In the fantasy of the people it is connected with the figure of death. It occurs in magic beliefs and rituals. Binding by a rope is a means of sorcery. Closely related to such ideas is the simile of the thread of life which the Fates spin on their distaff, and which in Germanic mythology reappears as the rope of Fate. These views apparently were widely current. Even Homer takes notice of some of them. He frequently speaks of the thread of life. Once, the gods attempted to bind their king and father (*Iliad*, I, 400), a fact that ancient interpreters found it hard to reconcile with the strength of Zeus, as it is pictured in the Eighth Book of the *Iliad* (*Scholia A, ad* vv. 25–26). Zeus himself fastened around Hera's hands a golden bond "that might not be broken" (*Iliad,* XV, vv. 19–20). That he threatens to fasten the golden rope around Olympus and thus to hold earth and sea in mid air, could be another reminiscence of such popular beliefs in the power of the rope. Still, in this way one may explain a detail of the story, but it can scarcely be the explanation of the whole tale.[24]

Among the divine figures it seems that Hecate, and she alone,

Way as a rope in Babylonian mythology, cf. R. Eisler, *Weltenmantel und Himmelszelt*, I (1910), 98. The philosophical use of such a simile, as for instance in the myth of the Platonic *Republic* (616 b-c), is of course quite a different matter.

[24] The testimony on Greek popular beliefs has been collected by J. Heckenbach, *De nuditate sacra sacrisque vinculis, R. G. V. V.*, XI, 3 (1911), esp. 87 ff., and J. Scheftelowitz, *Das Schlingen- und Netzmotiv im Glauben und Brauch der Völker, R. G. V. V.*, XII (1912-13), Heft 2, *passim*. For folktales in Homer, cf. G. M. Calhoun, Homer's Gods, *T. A. P. A.*, LXVIII (1937), 17, and *A. J. P.*, LVIII (1937), 267. For the thread of life in Homer, cf. *Iliad*, XX, 128; XXIV, 210; *Odyssey*, VII, 198. The reference to the rope of Fate in Germanic mythology I found in J. J. Bachofen, *Versuch über die Gräbersymbolik der Alten*[2] (1925), 315; cf. W. Mannhardt, *Germanische Mythen* (1858). Bachofen interprets the rope of Ocnus, the plaiter, as the rope of life; even if this interpretation were correct, it would not help to explain Homer, since the story seems to be of much later origin.

appears on late monuments with a key and a rope as her attributes. They are commonly understood to be identical in meaning and to indicate her power to open and close the gates of Hades, the rope being the older means by which to fasten a door. But originally, Hecate was not a goddess of the nether world. She was one of the great mother goddesses, one of the most highly revered deities of Asia Minor. Hesiod's *Theogony* describes her might, the privileges granted to her by Zeus "in earth and in heaven and in sea" (v. 427).[25] Homer never mentions Hecate. She belongs to a world that was superseded by the Olympian religion and mythology. Could the rope have been an ancient attribute of Hecate, who was sovereign over the three realms of the cosmos, signifying her all-pervading power? Could Homer have thought of this attribute when he let Zeus challenge his peers to a rope-pulling contest in which the king of gods threatens to pull up gods and earth and sea? Did he smile deprecatingly at another, a defeated mythology? Or does Homer's account betray the faint memory of a fight between some opposing powers? In Germanic mythology, Thor, the god of thunder and lightning, is said to have pulled up by a chain the Midgard serpent, a monster that surrounded the whole earth. The similarity of the Homeric account and the Nordic saga does not suffice to assume a common source of the two, or to aver that there must have been a deeper significance behind the Homeric tale. But the parallel is striking, and it

[25] The Hecate monuments are surveyed by E. Petersen, *Die dreigestaltige Hekate, Archaeol.-epigraph. Mitt. aus Oesterreich,* IV (1880), 140-74; V (1881), 1-84, esp. 80; cf. also W. H. Roscher, *Lexikon der griech. u. röm. Mythologie, s.v. Hekate,* I, 2 (1886-90), *col.* 1906. For key and rope, cf. Eusthatius, *In Odysseam,* p. 1923, 50. For Hecate and her original power, cf. O. Kern, *Die Religion der Griechen,* I (1926), 45 ff., who has also shown, *op. cit.*, 245 ff., that one cannot eliminate the hymn on Hecate as an "Orphic" interpolation and that the lines form an intrinsic part of the *Theogony.*

emphasizes the possibility that Homer may not merely have given free rein to his fantasy.[26]

Which one of these speculations comes nearest to the truth, or whether it is legitimate at all to ask if the Homeric story originally had a symbolic meaning, will probably never be known for certain. To the Greeks, at any rate, Zeus' warnings addressed to the assembled gods and goddesses revealed nothing more than the thought of Homer. The Middle Platonists, like all earlier philosophers, turned to Homer not as a writer of hieratic poetry, but as the father of philosophy, whose ideas, expressed in mythological language, needed and demanded translation into rational concepts.

Once they had found in the chain a metaphor of the Scale of Being, one would almost expect Plotinus to have adopted the simile for his intellectual vision of the One and the Many and their interrelation. He himself is inclined to speak, in terms similar to those used by Aristotle and by the Middle Platonists, of things as fastened upon the Good (*e.g. Enneads*, V, 5, 9); in the same context he refers to a hand grasping the universe at its extremity (VI, 4, 7). Yet his favorite illustrations of the process of emanation are heat emanating from fire, cold originating from snow, rays sent forth by the sun, light reflected by a mirror, a stream that issues from its source, sap that ascends from the root. In other words, Plotinus usually selects physical or biological processes for his comparisons. His highest transcendent being is above will and intellect, as it is above the activity of the demiurge. Besides, his allegorizations are few and cautious. He pays scant attention to the gods of mythology.[27]

[26] The comparison between the episode in Homer and the Thor story has been made by L. Radermacher, *Mythos und Sage bei den Griechen* (1938), 110. I should mention that Kern, *op. cit.*, 202; 209, considers the Homeric lines a remnant of hieratic poetry.

[27] Cf. *Enneads*, V, 4, 1, and E. Bréhier, *Plotin, Ennéades*, V (1931), *ad*

Who then introduced the metaphor of the chain into Neo-Platonism and transmitted it to Macrobius? Porphyry and Iamblichus are the two philosophers to whom Macrobius is indebted for his understanding of the Plotinian teaching, and Porphyry has been suggested as the one to whom he may owe the concept of the *aurea catena Homeri*.[28] However, reflecting on the general attitude of Porphyry one wonders whether this disciple of the master could really have added the metaphor in question. Much as he was given to allegorizations of Homer and to a belief in the traditional religion before he became a Neo-Platonist, after his conversion he closely followed in the footsteps of Plotinus; he interpreted religion and mythology in an ethical, rather than in a metaphysical sense. With Iamblichus, a change set in. The value of the religious inheritance was reaffirmed. Allegorization was now extended to be all-inclusive, it became systematic and was concerned with the transcendental significance of religion. The will of the gods, their power, was strongly emphasized. Within the context of such an interpretation of the world, the chain of Zeus, who possesses all the qualities which he creates, seems to have its proper place, and it therefore appears likely that Iamblichus or one of his followers, rather than Porphyry, was the source of Macrobius.[29]

loc.; also Witt, *op. cit.*, 135, whose formulation I have followed. E. Zeller, *Die Philosophie der Griechen*[3], III, 2 (1881), 499, note 2, has noted the agreement between Plotinus and Aristotle. For Plotinus' concept of the highest being, cf. Zeller, *op. cit.*, III, 2, p. 496; for his attitude toward mythology, cf. C. H. Kirchner, *Die Philosophie des Plotin* (1854), 190 ff.

[28] Cf. Schedler, *op. cit.*, 12. For Macrobius' sources in general, cf. Ueberweg-Praechter, *op. cit.*, 651 f.

[29] For Porphyry, cf. J. Bidez, *Vie de Porphyre* (1913); his method of allegorization, esp. 108 f. For Iamblichus and his position, cf. K. Praechter, *Genethliakon für C. Robert* (1910), 128 ff.; Ueberweg-Praechter, *op. cit.*, 615 f. The contrast between the two leading Neo-Platonists has recently been accentuated by N. H. Baynes, *The Hellenistic Civilization and East Rome* (The James Bryce Memorial Lecture, 1946), 27 f.

One other fact should be noted. Among the later Neo-Platonists—all of them deeply influenced by the teaching of the "divine Iamblichus"—Proclus is the first to have glorified the golden chain of Homer as a cosmic symbol. He identifies it with the golden chain of Orpheus and with the Platonic *desmos*, "the fairest of all bonds." The concept of the chain, or series, is basic for his whole explanation of the universe.[30] But he also speaks of chains linking men to specific gods, their patrons or patronymic deities, as it were, and taken in this sense, the metaphor of the chain is part and parcel of its usage as a figurative expression of the Scale of Being. Now, the chain symbol of spiritual lineage can be traced to earlier writers, to the generation preceding Macrobius or contemporary with him. Thus, to Eunapius, Julian's claim to being descended from the sun is not comparable to Olympia's assertion that her son, Alexander, was the offspring of Zeus; Julian's statement rather implies the belief that he was bound to the solar kingdom by a "golden chain," in the same way in which the Platonic Socrates affirms: we are the followers of Zeus; others are the followers of other gods.[31] The theoretical exegesis is derived from Plato, as Eunapius himself states; the language in which it is couched is not. In the passage of the *Phaedrus* (250 b) to which Eunapius refers, Plato does not speak of a chain. Even in the *Ion*, where poets and

[30] Concerning the golden chain of Homer, cf. especially Proclus, *In Timaeum*, 28 c (I, p. 314, 17 ff. Diehl); also Fr. 166 Kern (cf. above, note 18). For σειρά in a general sense, cf. *e.g. The Elements of Theology*, ed. E. R. Dodds (1933), *Propositio* 21, and Dodds' note *ad loc.* The hymns of Proclus provide numerous instances of the chain connecting gods and men. After Proclus, Damascius, *Dubitationes et Solutiones*, ed. C. A. Ruelle, I (1889), esp. 154, is most explicit about the meaning of the chain.

[31] Cf. *Fragmenta Historicorum Graecorum*, ed. C. Müller, IV (1868), 24 (Fr. 24). The passage is referred to by F. Creuzer, *Plotini Opera Omnia*, III (1835), 323, *ad Enn.* VI, 1, 3. Eunapius uses the simile of the chain also in his *Vita Porphyrii*, 457 Boissonade.

rhapsodes are said to be suspended from the Muses, while from them a cluster or chain "of other persons is suspended to take over the inspiration" (533 e), he bases his simile not on the example of the chain, but on that of the magnet and the iron rings which it attracts. Obviously, then, Eunapius, the historian of the school of Iamblichus, has replaced the terminology of Plato by that of Homer. For him, the Homeric chain must have been an established symbol of the connection between god and man, between the divine and part of the cosmos.[32] The same figure of speech repeatedly occurs in the hymns of Synesius, another follower of Iamblichus and a contemporary of Macrobius. This, I think, is additional reason to hold that it was Iamblichus, or the circle around him, who considered the chain a figurative expression applicable to Plotinus' theory of the Scale of Being; in other instances, too, they were not averse to accepting pre-Plotinian concepts.[33]

[32] In this context it is interesting to recall that Lucian, whose writings Eunapius must have known quite well (*Vita Sophistorum, Prooemium,* 454 Boissonade), describes a statue of the Celtic Heracles, the god of eloquence, from whose tongue chains of gold and amber are suspended, by which in turn the god's worshippers are fettered (*Hercules,* 3; cf. F. Koepp, *Ognios,* in *Bonner Jahrbücher,* Heft 125 [1919], 38 ff.). Whether or not such a statue actually existed, the description, which was to have great influence on Renaissance art, certainly agrees with Lucian's own views, for he says that the teacher "lets down his words, just as the Homeric Zeus lets down his golden chain," thus pulling up his pupils (*Hermotimus,* 3); he applies the picture of the chain also to his own speech (*Hercules,* 8). Lucian, then, sees in the chain a simile of inspiration through oratory, and such a figure of speech may be a contamination of the Homeric language with the theory of the *Ion*—a similar contamination occurs in alchemistic literature, where the "Platonic rings" and the "Homeric chain" are used interchangeably; cf. F. Hoefer, *Histoire de la chimie,* II (1866) 245 f.; H. Kopp, *Aurea Catena Homeri* (1880). On the other hand, Eusthatius, p. 695, 60, maintains that the golden chain and the whole passage in which it occurs formed a *topos* for the encomiastic literature on kingship. Even if Eunapius knew of such a rhetorical theory, he transformed it into a philosophical doctrine.

[33] Wilamowitz, *Sitzungsber. Berlin Akad.* (1907), 272 ff., has shown that,

Through the works of Macrobius and Proclus above all, the metaphor of the chain then came to be a phrase typical of Neo-Platonic teaching. Later generations forgot that the *aurea catena Homeri* had been interpreted and reinterpreted by writers preceding the Neo-Platonists, that in fact it had been a concept highly important in all Greek philosophy and literature, just as, in Professor Lovejoy's words, it was to be "one of the most famous in the vocabulary of Occidental philosophy, science, and reflective poetry." [84]

before Proclus, the chain as a symbol of human descent occurs in Synesius. As the ultimate source of the simile he names Homer and Orpheus (cf. also Dodds, *op .cit.*, 208 f.), and he points out the necessity of determining the intermediate steps in the history of the metaphor. For other examples of a "harking back to pre-Plotinian sources . . . in later Neo-Platonism," cf. Dodds, *op. cit.*, 258.

[84] *The Great Chain of Being*, p. vii. Cf. now also E. Wolff, *Die goldene Kette* (Die Aurea Catena Homeri in der englischen Literatur von Chaucer bis Wordsworth) [1947].

BULLETIN OF THE HISTORY OF MEDICINE

ORGAN OF THE AMERICAN ASSOCIATION OF THE HISTORY OF MEDICINE
AND THE JOHNS HOPKINS INSTITUTE OF THE HISTORY OF MEDICINE

Founded by Henry E. Sigerist

Editor—Owsei Temkin

VOLUME XXVI | JULY–AUGUST, 1952 | NUMBER 4

THE RELATION OF ANCIENT PHILOSOPHY TO MEDICINE *

LUDWIG EDELSTEIN

I realize that the subject which I propose to discuss is somewhat alien to the topics to which your studies are devoted. Yet I venture to believe, and I hope not gratuitously, that my subject will seem to you meaningful at least and worth discussing. In our day it has become a commonplace to say that philosophy, the science of man, is to be based on physical science, especially on biology, physiology, medicine, and anthropology, that " the facts of man [are] continuous with those of the rest of nature." [1] Thus, understanding and conduct are to attain a firm foundation, and we flatter ourselves with the belief that in giving so much credence to medicine in the widest sense of the term we are developing tendencies inherent in ancient, in pagan thought. Did not the Greeks who worshipped the body consider man part of nature, different to be sure from animals and the world around him, but still, like all products of nature, obedient to the eternal laws of the cosmos?

At first glance, Greek philosophy seems to bear out the correctness of

* This paper was read in 1945 before the General Seminar of the New School for Social Research in New York. Preparing it for publication I have added some references to ancient sources and modern literature and have made a number of changes; but the argument has remained substantially the same.

[1] J. Dewey, *Human Nature and Conduct* [The Modern Library], 1930, p. 12; cf. p. 324.

such a thesis. Whether we study the fragments of the Presocratics, or the writings of Plato, Aristotle, the Stoics, or the Epicureans, all these philosophers, idealistic and materialistic alike, discuss the structure of the human frame. Everywhere is man's mind seen in close relationship to his body. Various temperaments are differentiated in accordance with the variety of bodily constitutions. Shakespeare's words about Brutus, "His life was gentle, and the elements/ So mix'd in him that Nature might stand up/ And say to all the world, 'This was a man!'",[2] seem well to express the Greek view. Moreover, philosophical books are full of physiognomic observations. The physical appearance of the human being is used to diagnose his character. The diversity of races, their achievements in art and culture are traced to physical environment. By nature, says Plato, are the Greeks fond of learning, the Thracians and Scythians high-spirited, the Phoenicians and Egyptians lovers of money.[3] And later philosophers make similar statements. Do such views not clearly indicate that Greek philosophy must have learned from Greek medicine? For from what source other than medicine can its noted naturalism stem?

Indeed, modern interpreters are inclined to speak of an influence of Greek medicine on ancient philosophical thought. I doubt the historical adequacy of such an assumption. I think that in antiquity, philosophy influenced medicine rather than being influenced by it. Philosophical insight guided the physicians in their biological, physiological, and anthropological studies. And while in this respect, philosophers were the teachers of physicians, they even were their antagonists in the struggle for leadership in the conduct of life, sternly rebuking the physicians' ambition to prescribe to man what he ought to do. The true contribution of medicine to philosophy, I venture to suggest, lies in the fact that philosophers found in medical treatment and in the physician's task a simile of their own endeavor. The healing of diseases, as well as the preservation of health, provided an analogy which served to emphasize the validity of certain significant ethical concepts and thus helped to establish the truth of philosophy; therein consisted the most fruitful relationship between ancient medicine and ancient philosophy.

Now, as regards the alleged scientific influence of medical research on philosophical studies, one must first of all beware of imagining ancient

[2] *Julius Caesar*, V, 5, 73-75.

[3] *Republic*, IV, 435 e-436 a; cf. *Laws*, 747 d-e.

medicine in the likeness of modern medicine and must remember that medicine in antiquity was primarily a craft. The Homeric poems group the physician together with the singer and the builder among those craftsmen whom everybody welcomes, although "a leech is of the worth of many other men for the cutting out of arrows and the spreading of soothing simples." [4] Fundamentally the same situation prevailed throughout all periods of ancient history. The average physician had a certain technical proficiency; he knew medicine, as the phrase goes. He acquired his skill through apprenticeship with another physician, and when he became a master in his own right, he practiced his craft, or art, as crafts and arts are always practiced, namely, in accordance with traditional views and usages. He prescribed remedies which had proved helpful before; he took care of wounds and other surgical cases in the way in which previous generations had taken care of them. While learning his trade he was not a "student of medicine"; while carrying on his business he was not a "scientist" applying theoretical knowledge to the case at hand. On the level of common medical practice biological and physiological inquiries were neither presupposed, nor were they actually made. There was not even an obligation to get any kind of training or to study at all; anybody could set himself up as a doctor without acquiring a licence or undergoing an examination. It is therefore not astonishing that even in the second century A. D. there were physicians, at least in the country, who were unfamiliar with the difference between arteries and veins,[5] a difference that had been recognized five hundred years before. Yet they could well be successful and respected practitioners, for they relied upon experience, adroitness, and manual perfection, rather than on study or research.

It is in contrast to these craftsmen—the majority of physicians throughout Graeco-Roman civilization—that a relatively small number of medical men aspired to overcome the narrow limits of their craft. If it is characteristic of all Greek scientific achievement that it was the feat of individuals following the bent of their own minds, these doctors certainly were among the finest examples of unsolicited curiosity and delight in learning. Living mainly in the big cities of the ancient world, in the centers of culture, it was they who established the science of medicine as a thin layer over the vast body of merely technical and empirical skill. They patiently observed the courses of diseases, differentiated their various

[4] *Iliad*, XI, 514 f.; cf. *Odyssey*, XVII, 382-86.
[5] Gellius, *Attic Nights*, XVIII, 10.

types, gave aetiologies, elaborated a theory of prognostics, formulated methodical rules of treatment. Doing all this, and much more than I can mention here, some of them also realized that the study of the human body must form the basis of medicine.

I have advisedly said that only some physicians acknowledged the need for such studies, for it was not until the very end of antiquity that biology and physiology were generally considered indispensable for medicine. And whether one peruses early or late medical authors concerned with these subjects, he immediately becomes aware of the fact that they were inspired by philosophy.

Even among the so-called Hippocratic writings of the fifth and fourth centuries B. C., the oldest surviving medical books, there are some treatises which deal with the nature of the human body. The doctrines here propounded clearly are adaptations of Presocratic theories, of Heraclitus, of Diogenes of Apollonia, and of others. The "Sicilian" physicians were adherents of Empedocles and of his doctrine of the four elements. Diocles, the "second Hippocrates", was an Aristotelian. In Hellenistic times, the medical sect of the Dogmatists, emphasizing the value of anatomy and biology, defended its position by reference to the doctrines of the Dogmatic philosophers and proceeded to explain the phenomena under investigation in accordance with their systems, Platonic or Aristotelian, Stoic or even Epicurean. In the same way the Empiricists, who denied that one can detect the hidden causes of the functions of the body or that such an understanding is useful for medicine, relied on philosophical arguments. They were followers of the Academic Scepsis. When subsequent to Galen, and largely through his influence, Dogmatic medicine became the representative medical system, and knowledge of biology and physiology was at last required of all scientists, a Platonizing Aristotelianism, modified by Stoic natural philosophy, became predominant in medical theory.

Only in one instance, as far as I am aware, was the assertion made that a true understanding of the nature of man can be gained not from philosophy, but from medicine alone. Yet to the Hippocratic author of *On Ancient Medicine*, who proffered this suggestion and who was perhaps himself influenced by the scepticism of the Sophistic movement, man's nature consists in his individuality; it is the sum-total of his particular reactions to food and drink; it is that which is incomparable and varies from case to case. Like later physicians in whose discussions the principle *individuum est ineffabile* was clearly formulated,[6] the Hippocratic writer was troubled by the problem of how the uniqueness of existing phenomena can ever be comprehended by any general theory, and he therefore rejected generalizations altogether. The doctor's insistence that the object of medicine is the individual patient, that the individuality of the phenomena constitutes their only reality, led to the formation of the Methodist school of medicine, the third of the Hellenistic sects, which, affiliating itself with the newly revived philosophy of Pyrrho, renounced the possibility of all general knowledge and professed to be guided only by the Now and Here. Physicians of a similar hue in the first century B. C. had been influential in the restoration of Pyrrho's philosophy. Thus medicine to a certain extent counteracted the Greek predilection for the typical, the negligence of the particular. From the modern point of view, this may well seem to be its most outstanding contribution to Greek thought. But medical scepticism, consistently opposing any attempt at generalizing, also made the establishment of biology or physiology as a science illusory.[7]

It is fair to say, then, that only where medicine became allied with Dogmatic philosophy, did physicians actually engage in scientific research concerning the questions of life and death, of health and disease, and that they derived the principles of their biological and physiological investigations from a more comprehensive view of the universe. Of course, I do not wish to imply that all Greek medical scientists were entirely unoriginal. Men like Herophilus or Erasistratus or Galen did not hesitate to interpret the nature of the human body in accordance with their own observations. They felt free to contradict specific philosophical doctrines and in some instances to evolve new theories. But in doing so, they philosophized, they were themselves philosophers, as in Galen's opinion the true physician should be. Even the change from animal anatomy to human anatomy, which certainly was brought about by physicians, was based by them on philosophical rather than medical argumentations.[8] Moreover, once it was admitted that the doctor must be an expert in matters concerning the structure of the human body, medical research led to the

[6] Cf. K. Deichgräber, *Die griechische Empirikerschule*, Berlin, 1930, p. 311.

[7] For the development here sketched, cf. L. Edelstein, "Empirie und Skepsis in der Lehre der griechischen Empirikerschule," *Quellen u. Studien z. Geschichte d. Naturwissenschaften u. d. Medizin*, III, 4, 1933, pp. 253 ff.

[8] Cf. L. Edelstein, "The Development of Greek Anatomy," *Bulletin of the Inst. of the History of Medicine*, III, 1935, pp. 241 ff.

discovery of many new data. Dissections and experiments performed by physicians enriched biological and physiological knowledge and made it more precise, as well as more detailed. Yet it is not amiss to recall the fact mentioned before that up until Galen's time not all physicians were interested in inquiries of this kind. And even Galen himself did not believe a study of the entire body to be necessary for medical purposes. Nor did his medical writings impart to physicians more than a description of facts. Their explanation, the scrutiny of the organism as a whole, he put into his philosophical books, which he wrote as a philosopher for philosophers.

Under these circumstances, what Aristotle says of his own time seems indeed true of the entire history of Greek philosophy and of Greek medicine: physicians concerned with biology and physiology—that is, the ingenious and subtle ones, or the more philosophical ones, as Aristotle calls them in distinction to the great mass of doctors—took their departure from philosophy, just as truly systematic natural philosophy ended in a consideration of the principles of life, of health and disease, and of the constituents of the body.[9] Consequently the assumption of an influence of Greek medicine on Greek philosophy must be regarded, I think, as historically incorrect; modern naturalism and ancient naturalism are not identical. To call the Presocratics physicians and scientists rather than philosophers, as has become fashionable, or to say that from Empedocles on "it is impossible . . . to understand the development of philosophy without keeping the development of medicine constantly in view,"[10] is, I am afraid, a misrepresentation of the actual situation. It was as philosophers that the Presocratics embarked on the quest for the nature of things, and trying to detect the causes of all physical phenomena they also dealt with the human body. Nor is it meaningful to assume that Socrates, granted that he was an empiricist, learned the empirical method from medicine. The empiricism of the Hippocratics, as far as it was a conscious method, was itself derived from philosophy, as were their hypotheses concerning the nature of man. If one points to Plato's relation to contemporary physicians, one must at the same time admit that the physicians whom he may have followed were themselves imbued with philosophy. If one holds that biological research culminated in Aristotle's philosophy, one must realize that the concept of the organism which acts

[9] Aristotle, *De Respiratione*, 480 b 26 ff.; *De Sensu*, 436 a 19 ff.

[10] J. Burnet, *Early Greek Philosophy*, 4th ed., London, 1945, p. 201, n. 4.

according to purpose was the discovery of the philosopher Aristotle. The doctors of his generation had no inkling of this and understood the body in terms of those early philosophies which the Platonic *Phaedo* and the Platonic *Laws* tried to combat for the first time. Nor does Stoic philosophy, as outlined in Cicero's *De Natura Deorum*, or Epicurean physiology, as described by Lucretius, indicate a preoccupation with medicine. Like physics, such studies in antiquity were the legitimate concern of philosophers and remained, even when taken over by physicians, philosophical rather than scientific inquiries. While astronomy and mathematics no doubt largely determined the course of ancient philosophy, medicine on the whole stayed within the boundaries laid down by philosophy. In its biological and physiological theories it reflects the history of philosophy, but it does not explain it.

The same dependence of medical investigations on philosophical presuppositions is evident in the rare cases in which a medical treatise touches upon anthropological and ethical problems.[11] The famous Hippocratic book *On Airs, Waters, and Places* derives the human character from climatic conditions. The Asiatics are feeble, not war-like, but gentle, it contends, because in Asia the seasons are uniform and do not change either toward extreme heat, or toward extreme cold. Yet unlike Montesquieu, of whom this claim is reminiscent, the Hippocratic author does not believe that the form of the state also corresponds to natural conditions, such as the size of the country or the climate. To him laws, civic institutions, are an independent creation of the human mind, they have a causality of their own, they themselves create in man a second nature, as it were, so that in a monarchy even naturally brave and spirited people degenerate into cowards. It is Democritus who speaks through the mouth of the Hippocratic writer. Or again, Galen holds that all philosophers and all physicians are unanimous in assuming that the faculties of the soul depend upon the mixture of the elements of the body. Yet he warns his reader not to forget "the creative power of nature which shapes parts according to the traits of the mind," he reminds him that "Aristotle dealing with this very subject wondered whether there was not a beginning more divine, something greater than just heat and

[11] How seldom medical writers dealt with the subject becomes clear from a perusal of the survey given by A. Rivaud, "Recherches sur l'anthropologie grecque," *Revue Anthropologique*, XXI, 1911, pp. 157 ff.; 457 ff.; XXII, 1912, pp. 20 ff. I should mention that physiognomic observations are to be found in Greek medical writings, but they are related to the state of the body rather than to that of the mind.

cold and moist and dry. Wherefore I think it wrong of man to draw such rash conclusions in matters so great and assign to the qualities alone the power of shaping the parts. It is possible that these are nothing more than the instruments and something else the masterhand."[12] Moreover, Galen states, by chosing the right food and drink, by regulating his life correctly, man is able to attain virtue. And he is free to choose what is right; it lies within him to welcome the good, to admit and love it, to shun, to hate, and to flee the evil. To be sure, in Galen's opinion, Chrysippus, the great Stoic philosopher, owed his right understanding of the world to the right mixture of the elements in his body. Nevertheless, he would not detract from Chrysippus' merit; for it was Chrysippus who by building up his body in the right way made himself understand the truth. Unlike Shakespeare, whose lines immortalizing the fatalism of a naturalistic view I have quoted in the beginning, Galen would not allow Nature to lay claim on Brutus' greatness. For the Greek physician agrees with Plato who, though he emphasizes the fact that man's character is shaped by climatic factors, does not on that account dream of absolving him from the responsibility for his actions; or with Aristotle and other philosophers who, much as they stress the importance of natural gifts, of habits and education, do not hesitate to proclaim man's freedom. He expressly denies the validity of the conclusion that the dependence of the faculties of the soul on the faculties of the body makes praise or blame of human actions unjustifiable.

At this point I beg your leave to make a digression. We are prone to quote the maxim *mens sana in corpore sano*, taking it to epitomize the ancients' conviction that only in a sound body can and will there dwell a sound mind. Actually Juvenal, whom we are quoting, says: "Let us pray that there be a sound mind in a sound body."[13] No ancient physician or philosopher, I think, would have believed that a sound body would or could so to say automatically produce a sound intellect and sound emotions. Galen's pronouncement on man's character, to which I have just referred, is, as he himself implies, typical of medical and philosophical thinking. It presupposes the acceptance of the Dogmatic concept of the soul, which through some of its faculties is the organ of

[12] *De Temperamentis*, II, ch. VI [I, pp. 635 f. Kuehn]; I am quoting the translation of the passage given by M. Greenwood, *The Medical Dictator*, London, 1936, p. 33. For the following reference to Galen, cf. *De Sequela*, ch. XI [IV, pp. 814 ff. Kuehn]; cf. also ch. IV [IV, p. 784 Kuehn].

[13] Juvenal, *Sat.*, X, 356: *orandum est ut sit mens sana in corpore sano.*

emotions and mind, while through others it regulates the physical functions. The soul, moreover, or at any rate the mind, is considered a substance different from the body, even if modifiable by it. Philosophers more materialistic than Galen, denying the existence of spiritual substances, assumed at least the autonomy of man. Epicurus more vehemently than Plato or any idealistic philosopher defended human freedom. Stoic fatalism questioned man's freedom of action, not his responsibility for his character. It remained for Descartes to claim that the body was a machine, a mechanism that took care of all bodily movements and also produced emotions. It remained for Spinoza, elaborating on Descartes, to claim that "he, who possesses a body capable of the greatest number of activities, possesses a mind whereof the greatest part is eternal." [14] Descartes saw quite clearly that his concept of the working of the body contradicted the ancient concept of the soul. His new theory was based on Harvey's discovery of the circulation of the blood, from which it seemed to follow that the bodily functions went far beyond anything man had imagined before.[15] Later physicians continuing research along the lines suggested by Harvey, Descartes, and Spinoza, began to uncover the marvels of the body-machine. Medical insight began more and more to change the direction of philosophical thought. Ethics became allied with biology; the mind could now be considered an epiphenomenon of the body.

I am not asking who is right and who is wrong. I have made this digression only in order to accentuate the difference between the ancient and the modern situation. Ancient medicine neither in scientific nor in ethical matters made startling discoveries that heralded a new era; it voluntarily submitted itself to philosophy. This is perhaps one of the reasons for its failure as a science, great as it was as an art. On the other hand, the submission of medicine to philosophy may also in part account for the fact that in all investigations concerning an understanding of the body, as well as of the mind, the leadership rested unchallenged with philosophers.

But it is time for me to dismiss the consideration of these problems and to explain why, in spite of the affinity between medicine and philosophy stressed so far, the two could, as I stated at the very outset, have been opposed to one another in the controversy about the goal of

[14] Spinoza, *Ethics*, V, 39 (transl. by R. H. M. Elwes, *Philosophy of Benedict Spinoza*, p. 274).

[15] *Traité des passions*, I, article 1; 7; cf. *Discours de la méthode*, part V, 7 ff.

life. To make this understandable, I must first of all remind you of the truism that to the ancients, health certainly was one of the highest goods. Indeed, the Sceptic philosopher Sextus does not hesitate to say that to the common people, the men of practical life, health was the *summum bonum* at all times.[16] From post-Homeric centuries onward even poets and writers in ever-increasing numbers contended that without health nothing in this world has any value. To take such an attitude was well in accord with the inborn pessimism of the Greeks, their sceptical doubts as to the chances for happiness, their clear awareness of the tragic aspect of human life. Physicians generally sided with the many, with the pessimists and sceptics. Since the fifth century B. C. they consistently proclaimed that, as Herophilus phrased it, "when health is absent, wisdom cannot reveal itself, art cannot become manifest, strength cannot fight, wealth becomes useless, and intelligence cannot be made use of." [17] And they urged that not only those who were ill, but also those who were healthy should follow the dictates of medicine, in order to remain healthy.

Their demand at first glance may sound reasonable enough. Yet it seems less convincing as soon as one begins to realize its implications. Since health was considered a balance of the various constituents of the human body, at every moment upset by man's actions, by his taking any food or drink, it had at every moment to be restored consciously. Consequently, a healthy person had to watch himself continuously, he had to subject himself to minute rules, he had to guard against any deviation from the prescribed regimen. Only thus could he be healthy and live long, he was told. An odd way of achieving health and longevity! One might well characterize it in the words in which Macaulay describes how oligarchical government achieves its stability, words which in fact are inspired by Plato's description of ancient dietetics. Oligarchical government, Macaulay says, "has a sort of valetudinarian longevity; it lives in the balance of Sanctorius; it takes no exercise; it exposes itself to no accident; it is seized with a hypochondriac alarm at every new sensation; it trembles at every breath; it lets blood for every inflammation; and thus, without ever enjoying a day of health or pleasure, drags out its existence to a doting and debilitated old age." [18]

[16] Sextus Empiricus, *Adv. Mathem.*, XI, 49.

[17] Herophilus *apud* Sext. Empiricum, *Adv. Mathem.*, XI, 50. For details of the medical theories here referred to, cf. L. Edelstein, "Antike Diätetik," *Die Antike*, VII, 1931, pp. 255 ff.

[18] I am quoting Macaulay's remark from P. Shorey's note on the *Republic*, 406 b [Loeb].

But obeisance to such an ideal does not merely stifle enjoyment and pleasure; it makes man unfit for life. It makes him the slave of his body. He loses all freedom of action and decision; he cannot fulfill his duties as a citizen. Plato was not slow in pointing out all these dangers, nor did the Romans overlook them; their initial resistance to Greek medicine was to a large measure due to their opposition to doctrines which threatened to destroy normal political and civic life. Besides, such a regimen of precaution and concern with the body, as again Plato reproachfully remarked, can be followed by the wealthy alone, by those who are not forced to earn a living. Physicians did not deny the correctness of this charge, but they dismissed the case of the poor as beyond repair and turned all their attention to the rich, the only ones who in their opinion could live a worth-while life. And there is little doubt that many among the great and the wealthy heeded the advice of the physicians, especially in those centuries in which the city state began to lose in importance, or in which the political activity of the individual was diminishing, that is, in the Hellenistic period and in the time of the Roman emperors. Desiring health as they did, unhampered by any professional obligation, uninterested in being busy for the sake of being busy, the upper classes were free to live for their health, to indulge in the idolatry of the body endorsed by the physicians.

It was inevitable therefore that philosophers passionately fought against medicine and its glorification of health, just as they had opposed the agonistic ideal and the glorification of the athlete. More consequential even than their criticism of the political and social dangers which the teaching of medical dietetics promoted was their vigorous denial that health was the *summum bonum*, that it was identical with happiness, the aim toward which all human endeavor should be directed. Naturally, it is not my intention to contend that Plato, Aristotle, the Cynics, the Stoics, the Epicureans were altogether contemptuous of health. Before the slow disintegration of ancient culture set in, no Greek would have gone to that extreme; health remained a good to be at least preferred, as the Stoics put it. But philosophers were unanimous in their judgment that values other than health are superior. To give more emphasis to their point of view they even laid down their own rules for a proper regimen. What Plato in the *Republic* and in the *Laws* says about gymnastics, the education of children, the daily routine of men and women, what Plutarch sets forth in his charming little book *Advice on How to Keep Well*, serves to teach all and sundry how to live healthily without putting oneself into a strait jacket and without neglecting one's social and moral obligations.

To repress the dangers threatening from the leadership of physicians in society, Samuel Butler in his *Erewhon* made it a crime to be sick and therefore to be in need of medical care. Otherwise, the judge in the Erewhonian trial says, "the doctors should be the only depositaries of power in the nation, and have all that we hold precious at their mercy. A time of universal dephysicalization would ensue." [19] Butler's solution of the difficulty as he saw it may be ingenious, but it is hardly practicable. The problem was solved more reasonably and adroitly by Greek philosophers. Even Plato did not go beyond restricting the physician's practice to cases of emergency. However, he and Aristotle and all subsequent philosophers raised the question of who should determine what is valuable and what is not. The physician decides whether his patient ought to take walking exercise or not; he does not and cannot tell him whether he ought to be healthy or not, whether his life should be saved at all cost. In other words, the positing of aims lies with philosophy, not with the art of medicine, or with any other art or science, for that matter.[20] The physician therefore must mind his own business and not interfere with things that are beyond his reach. He may excel in preserving the health of those who wish to be healthy, in healing the diseases of those who wish to get well; but he cannot tell men what they should wish. In modern times, the physician has become the confidant of the healthy and of the sick, the expert of social agencies, the counselor of the judge, the authority to whom even the planners of foreign and domestic policies look up. To the Greek philosophers, he was no advisor on morals, justice, or politics. To them, medicine was not another form of education or philosophy. They clung to their prerogatives and insisted on their absolute sovereignty.[21]

Nevertheless—and this brings up the last aspect of my subject which I wish to discuss—whenever philosophers tried to interpret for the benefit of others the significance and meaning of their own endeavors, they could not find any parallel more illuminating than that of philosophy and

[19] Ch. XI (Some Erewhonian Trials).

[20] Cf. *Ethica Eudemia*, II, 2, 1227 b 25 ff.; cf. also *Ethica Nicomachea*, III, 3, 1112 b 12-16; *Magna Moralia*, I, 1, 1182 b 28-30. Cf. also Plato, *Laches*, 195 c-d.

[21] The dissension between physicians and philosophers is not taken into account by W. Jaeger, *Paideia: The Ideals of Greek Culture*, New York, III, 1944, pp. 3 ff.; this is one of the main reasons why I cannot agree with his evaluation of the role of medicine, cf. especially pp. 44 f.

medicine. Writers of all philosophical creeds gave a prominent place to the analogy of body and soul, to the similarity between the training of the body and the discipline of the soul, to the consideration of medicine as a counterpart of ethics, and, as I suggested before, it was perhaps in the usefulness of this comparison for the philosophical argument that lay the greatest debt of philosophy to medicine. What were the reasons for this peculiar predilection which philosophers showed for the medical simile? The frequency of references to medicine in philosophical books has, of course, often been noticed, but so far it has not found a satisfactory explanation.

Now, the starting point of all the comparisons between body and soul is perhaps not too difficult to understand. The philosopher, insisting on the value of the soul and proclaiming its superiority over the body, was faced with man's natural partiality to his body. He was therefore driven to contrast the two; he had to try to turn man's thought from his body and its interests to his soul and its concerns. In this attempt the Greek philosopher, while on the one hand finding his task especially difficult due to the Greeks' love of the body, gained on the other hand a specific advantage. From the fifth century B. C., that is, from the time when the discussion of ethical problems became an integral part of philosophy, medicine propounded the doctrine that the body needs conscientious care if it is to perform its functions properly. Philosophy therefore found in medicine a basis for exhortation which appealed strongly to the Greeks. Was it not obvious to conclude that what is true of the body must also be true of the soul, since body and soul are both parts of our being? That in fact it must be true to an even higher degree in regard to the soul which is so infinitely more precious?

Yet the protreptic appeal to the body and its medical needs, intended to enforce the dogma that the soul likewise needs care, was not merely emotional, it implied at the same time another purpose. In the beginning of the *Nicomachean Ethics*, Aristotle parallels his teaching concerning moral qualities with the teaching concerning health, because, he says, it is necessary to explain what is invisible by means of visible illustration.[22] The soul is invisible; knowledge about it is elusive. By comparing the soul to the body, that which is seemingly unreal is translated into comprehensible language. And if one remembers that in antiquity everybody was familiar with medicine—it was the only art or science about

[22] II, 2, 1104 a 13-14.

which everybody knew something; physicians wrote books for the general public; laymen discussed medical problems with their physicians; in short, medical knowledge was perhaps diffused more widely in Greek and Roman times than in any other period of history—one immediately realizes the particular forcefulness of such medical illustrations. In referring to medical insight the philosopher speaks of something that people can be expected to possess and that will help them to grasp the new kind of insight that they are expected to acquire through philosophy.

At this point, however, you may ask: how can medical knowledge, knowledge of the body, be helpful toward an adequate understanding of the soul? Are not body and soul essentially different? Is it not just the difference between the two which the philosopher tries to point out? My answer is that it is characteristic of Greek ethics that it conceives of the soul in the likeness of the body, that it visualizes the soul in very much the same way in which the body was understood, not on a highly technical level, to be sure, but rather in terms of that medical doctrine which was basic and almost universally accepted. The body has its desires, it strives to be filled, to be satiated. These bodily appetites in themselves tend to be extreme; they have no self-restricting limits. In order to prevent disease, to attain health, it is necessary to check the natural tendencies, to introduce measure, a standard by which to curtail the unlimited appetites. The desires of the soul, in the view of the Pythagoreans, of Plato, and of Aristotle, likewise tend to extremes; they strive unceasingly to be satisfied. Pythagorean ethics, Platonic justice, the Aristotelian doctrine of the mean, teach the measure, the standard by which the extremes of our passions are to be reduced to their right proportion. Nor did the body fail to provide an example when Cynics, Stoics, and Epicureans considered all natural activities of the soul, all natural emotions as bad, or even diseased. Does not language itself indicate the similarity of body and soul? Are not the emotions called by the same name, *pathe*, that denotes the sickness of the body? Is it not true—to use Lucretius' words—that "our soul itself has a flaw and that by this flaw an inward corruption taints all that comes from without, even though it were a blessing"? [23] And is it not equally true that the body and its natural functions are diseased? If man is not constantly on the lookout, he continually falls into disease, he is continually sick. This was exactly the theory on the basis of which the dietetics for the healthy

[23] *De Rerum Natura*, VI, 17-19 [Loeb translation, adapted].

was developed, as I have pointed out before. Like the body then, which must be made healthy, so the soul, sick by nature, needs purging, as Lucretius says, or treatment, as the Stoics contend, in order to be healthy.[24] Only in this manner can virtue be achieved, that state of eudaemonia which philosophers never tired of celebrating as "the health of the soul."

Important as the medical simile proved to be in all these respects, its deepest significance becomes apparent only in the consequences drawn from the analogies I have mentioned so far. To understand their full bearing it is necessary to recall one feature of Greek medicine that was obvious to the ancients, yet is rarely appreciated by modern interpreters. Greek medicine reversed man's natural beliefs; it had something paradoxical about it. It seems natural to suppose that we are healthy as long as we are not sick, that if we follow the instincts of our body we will be well. The teaching of Greek dietetics, the doctrine according to which every one, even the healthy person, must care for his body, ran counter to man's natural feelings. Moreover, it always remained strange to the ancients that man should renounce his rights over himself and should obey the physician, who reigns over him as the king reigns over his subjects, to borrow a phrase of Galen.[25] To accept such a rule again seemed unnatural, for the body is our own; we are its masters, and no one else. The irritation felt was aggravated by the fact that the free citizen, the rich man, had to follow the commands of a craftsman who often was a slave. Finally, the Greeks and Romans never ceased wondering about the paradox that by cauterizing and cutting, by doing violence to his body, man should achieve health, that good should come of something that in itself is painful and causes suffering.

It was precisely this paradoxical truth that reason and experience had taught man to accept in medical matters, on which philosophers seized for their purposes. You find the philosophers' teaching paradoxical, Epictetus asks. And he answers his own question by saying: "But are there not paradoxes in the other arts? And what is more paradoxical than to lance a man in the eye in order that he may see? If anyone said this to a man who was inexperienced in the art of surgery, would he not laugh at the speaker? What is there to be surprised at, then, if in philosophy also many things which are true appear paradoxical to the inexperi-

[24] *De Rerum Natura*, VI, 24; Chrysippus, Fr. 471 Arnim.
[25] *De Methodo Medendi*, I, 1 [X, p. 4 Kuehn].

enced?" [26] Indeed the whole range of the transvaluation of values that was brought about by philosophical ethics, could best be illustrated by the medical example.

The paradoxical quality of Cynic and Stoic teaching concerning natural feelings and emotions needs no emphasis. Their notion of the "health of the soul" was as shocking, the very antithesis of the natural, as was the medical teaching about the health of the body. Nor did Lucretius deny that Epicurus' doctrine of "the healthy soul" seemed "somewhat harsh to those who have not used it, and the people shrink back from it." [27] By pleasure they understood something quite different from that which Epicurus considered pleasure. But did Plato's philosophy contribute less toward changing common beliefs? To be sure, he still upheld the old values; but did he understand them in the same way? Is it natural to believe that it is better for man to suffer injustice than to do injustice, if he must choose between the two? Plato found it necessary to turn man's neck, so as to make him see the light of truth.[28] Or is Aristotle's ethical theory opposed to a lesser degree to man's instinctive feelings? Can one immediately understand his contention that matters of conduct and expediency have nothing fixed or invariable about them, that moral qualities are so constituted as to be destroyed by excess no less than by deficiency? [29] Aristotle at any rate did not think this to be self-evident and took great pains to prove it.

Moreover, if man must acquire the knowledge needed to regulate his physical life from the physician, the expert, who has found it, if he must submit himself to his judgment, to his guidance, the same demand was made by the philosopher, and again it was upheld regardless of the social position of the expert, of the ruler, and of the ruled. It is true, Plato still believed that the individual by himself should and could find the truth. Socrates, to him, was not a physician; his help in finding the right answer was comparable to the assistance given by the midwife; man's knowledge is his own child, as it were. But wherever Plato tries to solve ethical questions within the framework of political theory, he finds no more cogent parallel to the position which the true statesman ought to occupy than that of the physician. Statesmen must rule, he says, "whether they are rich or poor, over willing and unwilling subjects alike, with or

[26] Epictetus, *Dissertationes*, I, 25, 32-33 [Loeb].
[27] *De Rerum Natura*, IV, 18-20 [Loeb].
[28] *Republic*, VII, 515 c.
[29] *Ethica Nicomachea*, II, 2, 1104 a 11 ff.

without written laws, just as physicians must prescribe cures with or without the patient's consent, and whether they do so on the basis of written laws or without them, and whatever they do, whoever they are, we call them physicians." [30] Aristotle, on the other hand, bids us to be our own doctors, hitting the right mark through our own insight. With the Cynics and Stoics the philosopher himself became a doctor, the expert who diagnosed the disease of man. For the diagnosis of our passions, says Galen, cannot be entrusted to ourselves; it must be entrusted to other people, and " it is not just any chance person to whom this oversight can be given." [31] Ethics thus became *medicina mentis*, medicine of the soul; the philosopher came to rule over his client with absolute power.

Nor was the final point of comparison overlooked: the treatment cannot be soft and in accordance with our wishes; it must be painful, it must hurt. Plato insisted that the true statesman must be allowed to kill or to banish people, just as the physician is allowed to heal by cutting us, or burning us, or by causing us pain in any other way.[32] And while Lucretius was intent on lessening the bitterness of the remedy by adding " the delicious honey of the Muses," [33] the Stoics delighted in emphasizing the harshness of the treatment. It may suffice to quote Epictetus: " Men, the lecture room of the philosopher is a hospital; you ought not to walk out of it in pleasure, but in pain. For you are not well when you come; one man has a dislocated shoulder, another an abscess, another a fistula, another a headache. And then am I to sit down and recite to you dainty little notions and clever little mottoes, so that you will go out with words of praise on your lips, one man carrying away his shoulder just as it was when he came in, another his head in the same state, another his fistula, another his abscess? And so it's for this, is it, that young men are to travel from home, and leave their parents, their friends, their relatives, and their bit of property, merely to cry 'Bravo!' as you recite your clever little mottoes? Was this what Socrates used to do, or Zeno, or Cleanthes? " [34] It is indeed true that this paradox, like all others, could best be made clear by the paradox of medicine, as Epictetus says.

[30] *Politicus*, 293 a-b. For Plato and the simile of medicine, cf. also L. Edelstein, " The Role of Eryximachus in Plato's Symposium," *Transactions of the Amer. Philol. Assoc.*, LXXVI, 1945, pp. 98 ff.

[31] *De Animae Perturbationibus*, I, ch. vi [V, p. 30 Kuehn] transl. by A. J. Brock, *Greek Medicine* [The Library of Greek Thought], 1929, p. 170.

[32] *Politicus*, 293 b.

[33] *De Rerum Natura*, IV, 22.

[34] *Dissertationes*, III, 23, 30-32 [Loeb].

I have come to the end of my analysis of the relation between Greek philosophy and medicine. Many intricate questions I could only touch upon. Many difficult problems I could discuss only in a general way. Details have still to be worked out. The characteristic differences prevailing in the various centuries must be marked more clearly. But this much, I think, can be stated safely: medicine did not influence philosophy by giving to it scientific information, nor did it help philosophy to find a solution of ethical questions. But medicine did serve philosophy as a means of explaining and of making acceptable to men that conclusion which philosophy itself had reached, that man can live without philosophy as little as he can live without medicine.

quite as well as the somewhat colorless recapitulation of the MSS: εἰ δ[ὲ θεός σοι] ἔδωκεν [ἔπος νημερτὲς ἐνισπεῖν].

In editing the complete text of 540 it might have been well to indicate in the *apparatus* the correct readings (like Ἑλλάδα for Αλλαδ[α] in 683) even though these corrections had been made by Milne in the earlier publication; and this has been done in the edition of the prose summary.

A few relatively unimportant shreds from extant texts of Euripides, Thucydides, Xenophon, Pseudo-Demosthenes, and Lycurgus bring one to the elaborate indices and the plates.

In general the book is beautifully and accurately printed (two or three trifling blemishes that will disturb no one are all that I have noted). The editorial workmanship maintains in erudition, ingenuity, and judgment the very highest standards of performance by the author's celebrated fellow-countrymen, and may well be viewed with pride by that distinguished scholar, Wilhelm Schubart, to whom, as teacher and friend, the volume has been dedicated.

W. A. Oldfather.

University of Illinois.

M. Pohlenz. Hippokrates und die Begründung der wissenschaftlichen Medizin. Berlin, de Gruyter, 1938. Pp. 120. RM. 6.

This book is a new vindication of the doctrine of Hippocrates and his work in opposition to recent and earlier scepticism. The system of the founder of scientific medicine is reconstructed from the two Pre-Alexandrian testimonies still available (pp. 63-79) and then identified with theories of a few of the so-called Hippocratic writings (pp. 79-80), especially with those of *Airs Waters Places* and *Sacred Disease*; the latter treatises are analyzed at great length in the first part of Pohlenz' book (pp. 3-62). Finally Hippocrates' importance for later generations and his influence on them are evaluated (pp. 81-96). An appendix containing the footnotes and a short survey of recent literature (pp. 97-120) complete the work.[1]

Pohlenz' main problem is the determination of Hippocrates' system; all the other inquiries made are either supplementary to this or based on its solution. The question as to how the testimonies of Plato (*Phaedrus* 270 C) and of Aristotle's pupil Meno (V, 35 ff.)[2] are to be interpreted, therefore, must be the chief topic of this review also. Like Pohlenz, I shall deal first with the later testimony of Meno who relates the Hippocratic ex-

[1] In the meantime Pohlenz has given a summary of his views in *Die Antike*, XV (1939), pp. 1 ff.

[2] *Anonymi Londinensis ex Aristotelis Iatricis Menoniis et aliis Medicis Eclogae*, ed. H. Diels, *Supplementum Aristotelicum*, III, 1 (1893).

planation of diseases and then consider that of Plato, the earlier witness, who describes the Hippocratic method only (cf. Pohlenz, p. 75).

Pohlenz claims that the account given in the Meno-Papyrus has never been analyzed before as it should have been; for the original words of Meno have not been clearly distinguished from later additions on the part of the doxographer who made the excerpts from Meno's history of medicine (p. 65). The text, as it stands, so Pohlenz says himself, unmistakably attributes to Hippocrates an explanation of diseases by the φῦσαι ἐκ τῶν περιττωμάτων, "Gase, die sich aus den Perittomata entwickeln" (p. 66). Yet, according to Meno, Pohlenz maintains, Hippocrates spoke of φῦσαι alone (p. 67) and explained diseases through the air taken into the body with nutrition (p. 68). The concept of the air excreted from the remnants of food is an interpolation of the doxographer (p. 67) which must be eliminated so as to make the text intelligible and consistent (p. 68).

It seems strange that Pohlenz should charge the doxographer with having altered Meno's words. For the report in question, at the beginning (V, 36-37) and at the end (VI, 42), is expressly characterized as the opinion of Aristotle, i. e. of Meno. The doxographer disagrees with this opinion, so much so that he adds his own views concerning Hippocrates' doctrine which he outlines in accordance with some of the so-called Hippocratic writings (VI, 43 ff.). Why, then, should he have changed Meno's account? And if he did, why has he interpolated a concept which he himself later on does not ascribe to Hippocrates? Or has the later description of the Hippocratic theory, so utterly at variance with the previous one, been added by somebody else? Pohlenz, who does not enter into these questions at all, seems to believe that not only the doxographer but also a third person may have participated in the preparation of the excerpts as they are preserved (p. 65).

However these difficulties may be accounted for, Pohlenz thinks that he can prove the probability of the assumed alteration by two facts: the doxographer, he says, has classified all the theories with which the Hippocratic doctrine is grouped under a term originally foreign to them, namely that of περιττώματα (p. 65); besides, he has introduced into the summary of the Platonic theories a concept which is not to be found in the Platonic text (p. 66). I am not prepared to decide whether Hippocrates himself could use the word περιττώματα. That, in the sense of remnants of food, it occurs for the first time in Diocles' fragments does not prove that it was not used before (contrary to Pohlenz, pp. 65-66); the material preserved from earlier writings is too scanty to allow such a conclusion.[8] It is, however, the less

[8] I note that Ilberg, in his copy of Diels' edition of the Meno-Papyrus, now in the Institute of the History of Medicine at the Johns Hopkins

necessary to discuss this question since Pohlenz himself in his argumentation puts all emphasis on the alleged misrepresentation of Plato's views: ". . . wie unbekümmert . . . der Doxograph nicht nur formal umstilisiert, sondern auch sachlich umgestaltet, können wir in einem Fall (*scil.* in the Plato-report) noch mit Händen greifen," he says (p. 66).[4]

I shall not insist that the doxographer, if he is not correct in his description of the Platonic doctrine, need not necessarily be incorrect in his representation of the Hippocratic dogma. I rather ask whether he really misrepresents Plato's theory. Pohlenz claims that the doxographer ascribes to Plato, as he does to Hippocrates, an explanation of diseases by the φῦσαι ἐκ τῶν περιττωμάτων (XVII, 46-47); this term, however, does not occur in the *Timaeus* on which the résumé is obviously based; the doxographer, then, has falsified his source (cf. Pohlenz, p. 66). But the text of the Plato-report reads thus (XVII, 44-47):

παρὰ [δὲ]
τὰ περιττώματα συνίστα[νται τριχῶς]
αἱ νόσοι, ἢ π[α]ρ[ὰ τὰς] φύσας [τὰς ἐκ τ(ῶν)] πε-
ριττωμ[άτ(ων) ἢ παρὰ] χολὴν ἢ φλέγμα·

It is then, first of all, not the doxographer who, as Pohlenz says, speaks of air excreted from the περιττώματα. The concept of the φῦσαι ἐκ τῶν περιττωμάτων is a conjecture of the editor of the papyrus. If the words, as restored, do not correspond to the Platonic text, the editor has erred, not the doxographer.[5]

But one may object: even if φῦσαι ἐκ τῶν περιττωμάτων is a conjecture, the words φῦσαι and περιττώματα (cf. also XVII, 14) are preserved in the papyrus, and yet neither of them is to be found in the *Timaeus* (cf. Pohlenz, p. 66). Does this difference not suffice to prove a misunderstanding of Plato's views and, consequently, to cast suspicion upon the correctness of the representation of Hippocrates' views? To be sure, Meno speaks of φῦσαι, whereas Plato speaks of πνεῦμα (*Timaeus* 84 D). But it is

University, refers (Index *s. v.* περισσώματα) to E. Howald, *Hermes*, LIV (1919), pp. 187 ff. and G. Méautis, *Philologische Wochenschrift*, XLV (1925), pp. 184 ff.; both authors endeavour to prove the early occurrence of κάθαρσις and περιττώματα.

[4] K. Deichgräber (*Abhandlungen der Preussischen Akademie der Wissenschaften*, Phil.-Hist. Klasse [1933], Nr. 3, p. 153) was the first to assume this inaccuracy of the report on Plato. Diels (*Hermes*, XXVIII [1893], p. 425), however, had already asserted the methodological value of the Plato-account, because it affords a check on Meno's reliability. For other minor divergencies cf. A. Rivaud, *Platon, Œuvres Complètes*, X (1925), p. 115, n. 4. Cf. note 13 *infra*.

[5] It is misleading, it seems to me, for Pohlenz in quoting the papyrus (p. 66, n. 2) not to indicate the lacunae and emendations. Especially if an argument is based on such a text, the reader is entitled to be informed about what is preserved in the original and what is modern conjecture.

the air that has entered the human body with which Plato is concerned, and this air is commonly called φῦσα or φῦσαι by physicians.[6] Plato himself was aware that the term which he uses was antiquated and that, already in his time, φῦσα was the more common medical expression (cf. *Republic* 405 D).[7] The change in terminology made by the doxographer is, then, certainly no falsification of Plato's opinion. Moreover, it is true that Plato does not use the expression περιττώματα. Yet, the second cause of illness which he mentions is phlegm, the third bile (Meno, XVII, 47; *Timaeus* 85 A ff.). These qualities, in Aristotelian language are named περιττώματα.[8] The third class of diseases (*Timaeus* 84 C) which Meno is paraphrasing comprises then two species which are correctly referred to by the term which Meno introduces.

But what about the φῦσαι ἐκ τῶν περιττωμάτων, if this is the correct restoration of the lacuna? Pohlenz is right in pointing out that in *Timaeus* 84 D Plato is discussing the air which the human being breathes (p. 66). Yet, in *Timaeus* 84 E, a passage which, strangely enough, is not quoted by Diels, who in his notes refers only to *Timaeus* 84 C-D, the first way in which illness arises is characterized thus: πολλάκις δ' ἐν τῷ σώματι διακριθείσης σαρκὸς πνεῦμα ἐγγενόμενον καὶ ἀδυνατοῦν ἔξω πορευθῆναι . . . . This Martin takes to mean: "Souvent aussi, la chair se trouvant raréfiée dans quelque partie du corps, il s'y engendre de l'air, qui, n'en pouvant sortir . . ."[9] Such a sense, however, could well be epitomized by φῦσαι ἐκ τῶν περιττωμάτων. For disintegrated flesh is the material from which, according to Plato, bile, phlegm, etc. are produced.[10] Moreover, Meno, in consequence of the importance of the περιττώματα in all three cases, would with some justification have subordinated them to the general heading νόσοι παρὰ τὰ περιττώματα (XVII, 45).

Of course, one cannot decide whether Meno understood the

[6] Cf. *Breaths*, chap. 3 (*Hippokrates*, ed. J. L. Heiberg, *Corpus Medicorum Graecorum*, I, 1 [1927], pp. 92, 20; 95, 15, etc.); cf. Pohlenz, p. 67, n. 2, and p. 67 where he himself understands φῦσα as air breathed in by the human being.

[7] I was reminded of this passage by H. Cherniss.

[8] Cf. Aristotle, *Historia Animalium* 511 b 9; Pohlenz (p. 66, n. 2) also refers to this passage, yet, in his interpretation of the Plato passage, takes the word to mean remnants of food, a meaning which it cannot have either here (XVII, 45) or before (XVII, 14), although in the Hippocrates-account it is used in the limited sense of remnants of food (cf. Aristotle, *De Generatione Animalium* 724 b 26; Pohlenz, p. 65, n. 3).

[9] Th. H. Martin, *Études sur le Timée de Platon*, I (1841), p. 225. Already Marsilius Ficinus translates: Saepe etiam intra corpus discreta et rarefacta carne innascitur spiritus: qui cum foras egredi nequeat . . . (quoted from Plato, ed. I. Bekker, III, 2 [1817], p. 126). With Martin's translation agree R. D. Archer-Hind, *The Timaeus of Plato* (1888), and F. M. Cornford, *Plato's Cosmology* (1937).

[10] Cf. *Timaeus* 82 C, and A. E. Taylor, *A Commentary on Plato's Timaeus* (1928), p. 591.

Plato passage as do Martin and others. It is also possible to translate the words in question differently: "And often, when the flesh is disintegrated, air which is enclosed in the body and is unable to pass out. . . ." [11] Such an interpretation is suggested as the right one by the fact that in 84 D, too, it is not air alone which, according to Plato, brings about illness; it is air combined with some other substance, with *ῥεύματα* which are produced from phlegm (cf. *Timaeus* 85 B, and for the expression *ῥεύματα* again *Republic* 405 D). If the lungs are filled with these rheums, the usual passage of the air is hindered, and it is for that reason that diseases are caused. If in 84 E Plato is also referring to the air coming from outside, the discussion of air as cause of diseases would be uniform. In both cases, as distinguished by Plato, air would be harmful only together with some other substance, with rheums or with disintegrated flesh in Platonic terms, with phlegm or bile, or in Aristotelian categories with *περιττώματα*. Meno, then, may have spoken of *φῦσαι μετὰ περιττωμάτων* [12] and he would have been equally justified in calling the third class of diseases *νόσοι παρὰ τὰ περιττώματα*. The advantage of such an emendation is that in his summary, then, he does not omit the explanation of diseases brought about by air from outside (84 D), although one must not forget that his résumé as a whole is not exhaustive and that he leaves out other points also.

At any rate, whatever restoration is adopted, the trustworthiness of the Hippocrates report cannot be disproved on the evidence adduced by Pohlenz. Many other instances, moreover, confirm the correctness of the data given in the papyrus (cf. Deichgräber, *op. cit.*, p. 159). It is true that sometimes the account is enlarged by the addition of similes [13] and that the language is colored by later terminology, but the basic facts, it seems, are authentic. What Meno relates about Hippocrates,

[11] Plato, *Timaeus etc., with an English translation* by R. G. Bury (The Loeb Classical Library), p. 229; cf. Taylor (*op. cit.*, p. 601) who interprets: ". . . whenever an abnormal 'division' or cavity is formed within the flesh, wind collects to fill it, and is unable to find a proper outlet." Cf. also A. Rivaud, *op. cit.*, p. 217: "Souvent aussi, la chair se disjoint à l'intérieur du corps; de l'air s'y enferme et, ne pouvant pas en sortir. . . ."

[12] Cf. *Timaeus* 83 E *μετὰ πνεύματος αἷμα*; 83 B *ξανθὸν χρῶμα μετὰ τῆς πικρότητος*. According to the above interpretation I propose to read in the papyrus:

παρὰ [δὲ]
τὰ περιττώματα συνίστα[νται τριχῶς]
αἱ νόσοι, ἢ π[α]ρ[ὰ τὰς] φύσας [τὰς μετὰ] πε-
ριττωμ[άτ(ων) ἢ παρὰ] χολὴν ἢ φλέγμα·

[13] For instance in the Plato report (XVI, 24 ff.); cf. Diels, *Hermes*, *loc. cit.*, and note 4 *supra*. That the simile given in the Hippocrates passage can be original (Pohlenz, p. 67) I do not deny (cf. *R.-E.*, Supplement VI [1936], 1323). The probability, however, is not increased by the observation that similes are added in other places.

therefore, has to be accepted as it stands; it cannot be reinterpreted as Pohlenz proposes to do. Hippocrates, according to Meno at least, has explained diseases by the air excreted from the remnants of food, and well he may; there is no reason either to assume that Meno was mistaken in his description of the Hippocratic dogma.[14] For similar theories are known from other great physicians of Hippocrates' time; the importance of food for the development of diseases, the influence of digestion is stressed over and over again in the *Corpus Hippocraticum*. The doctrine that it is air, not a liquid which is excreted from the remnants of food (cf. e. g. Meno, V, 12 ff.) would be the specifically Hippocratic modification of a more common dogma.

As I cannot agree, then, with Pohlenz' interpretation of the Meno-Papyrus, I cannot follow him in his interpretation of the *Phaedrus* either. This second and most important testimony on Hippocrates Pohlenz takes to mean that, according to Plato, Hippocrates found it impossible to understand the nature of the body without the nature of the cosmos (ἄνευ τῆς τοῦ ὅλου φύσεως 270 C), and, consequently he ascribes to Hippocrates a thorough observation of the seasons, of the air, etc. (p. 78; cf. pp. 4-5). That in Plato as well as in other writers τὸ ὅλον may mean "cosmos" is certain; Pohlenz (p. 75, n. 1) gives additional proof for such a sense. It is equally certain, however, that the word, especially in the Platonic dialogues, signifies the whole, the logical or organic unity, a usage for which Pohlenz does not cite any parallel. The problem is not whether τὸ ὅλον can be understood only in the one way or in the other, it is rather which of the two meanings of the word is implied in the passage in question.[15]

[14] This was, for instance, the belief of Diels, *loc. cit.*, pp. 424-434; cf. the introduction to the edition of Meno, p. xvi. That Meno had an adequate knowledge of ancient medicine seems now generally assumed. That his account of Hippocratic views is consistent (contrary to Pohlenz, p. 68) has been shown *R.-E.*, *loc. cit.*

[15] Already in antiquity the opinion of the interpreters was apparently divided; Galen (*Corpus Medicorum Graecorum*, V, 9, 1 [1914], p. 55, 16; cf. p. 53, 26) understands τὸ ὅλον as cosmos; Hermias (*In Platonis Phaedrum Scholia*, ed. P. Couvreur [1901], p. 245, 5) takes it to mean the whole body (cf. *R.-E.*, *loc. cit.*, 1319). Of modern interpreters L. Robin (*Platon, Œuvres Complètes* [Collection Budé], IV, 3 [1933]) sides with Galen; cf. also Wilamowitz, *Platon* (1929)², p. 462, and W. H. S. Jones, *Hippocrates with an English Translation* (The Loeb Classical Library), I, p. xxxiii. Hermias' interpretation is upheld by B. Jowett, *The Dialogues of Plato translated into English*, I³ (1892), p. 479, but already proposed as the only satisfactory solution by W. H. Thompson, *The Phaedrus of Plato* (1868), p. 124. Cf. L. Edelstein, *Περὶ ἀέρων und die Sammlung der Hippokratischen Schriften*, *Problemata*, IV (1931), pp. 129-135; G. M. A. Grube, *Plato's Thought* (1935), p. 213, n. 1. P. Shorey (*What Plato said* [1933], p. 205) refers to *Lysis* 214 B and *Charmides* 156 B ff.; he seems to understand τὸ ὅλον as cosmos and as the whole of the body; so does W. Nestle, *Hermes*, LXXIII (1938), p. 18.

Socrates claims that the procedure of medicine and that of rhetoric are identical; in both arts it is necessary to give a diaeresis of the object concerned (*διελέσθαι φύσιν* 270 B).[16] He, then, asks whether it is possible to understand the nature of the soul, the object of rhetoric, without the nature of the whole (270 C). Phaedrus answers with a reference to Hippocrates who holds it impossible to acquire even medical knowledge without such a method (*ἄνευ τῆς μεθόδου ταύτης ibid.*). Whereupon Socrates, who is not satisfied with Hippocrates' authority before inquiring into the validity of the argument, tries to explain what kind of investigation Hippocrates and right reason demand concerning nature (*περὶ φύσεως ibid.*). They demand, he says, for the understanding of every nature (*περὶ ὁτουοῦν φύσεως* 270 D) two things: first an investigation as to whether the object is simple or multiform, and then a division of the object into its parts together with a determination of the relation of these parts to each other and to the factors influencing them (*ibid.*). In other words, they demand definition and diaeresis; that these two processes are inseparable has been stressed even before (e. g. 265 D-266 B); each diaeresis involves a conception of the whole which is to be divided into its parts. The nature of the whole, then, which, as Socrates says, is presupposed by every right understanding, must be the comprehension of the particulars into one idea;[17] the method which Hippocrates follows also in medicine must be the general definition of its object, the human body.

Socrates discusses the identity of the methods used in rhetoric and medicine so as to explain what he said before and what Phaedrus did not understand. *Πᾶσαι ὅσαι μεγάλαι τῶν τεχνῶν προσδέονται ἀδολεσχίας καὶ μετεωρολογίας φύσεως πέρι· τὸ γὰρ ὑψηλόνουν τοῦτο καὶ πάντῃ τελεσιουργὸν ἔοικεν ἐντεῦθέν ποθεν εἰσιέναι* (269 E-270 A), Socrates claimed and then exemplified his statement by the relation of Pericles to Anaxagoras. Does Socrates, by speaking of *μετεωρολογία φύσεως πέρι*, refer to "Meteorologie" or "Himmelsspekulation," that is astronomy and mathematics, and is the word chosen by Plato in order to indicate his agreement with Hippocrates who by the same term expressed the belief

[16] I doubt that *Laws* 946 B *κλήρῳ διελόντας τὸν νικῶντα*, the passage to which Pohlenz refers (p. 75, n. 1) has the same meaning as *διελέσθαι* in the *Phaedrus*. At any rate, the division of the soul has its analogy in medicine as Pohlenz himself, in spite of his qualifying interpretation of *διελέσθαι* in the notes (p. 75, n. 1), admits in his text (p. 76). For the identity of the dialectical procedure of the *Phaedrus* with that of the late dialogues, the *Sophist* and the *Politicus* cf. J. Stenzel, *Studien zur Entwicklung der platonischen Dialektik von Sokrates zu Aristoteles* (1907), p. 62.

[17] For this use of *τὸ ὅλον* cf. e. g. Stenzel, *op. cit.*, p. 66 and *R.-E.*, *loc. cit.*, 1318-1320. *Symposium* 205 B and D give a particularly good example of this sense of *τὸ ὅλον* and *εἴδη* (the whole and the parts of a concept) even in a context which is not strictly dialectical.

that astronomy is necessary for medicine (Pohlenz, p. 78)? In the *Republic* (529 A) Glaucon praises the study of astronomy because "it compels the soul to look upwards (εἰς τὰ ἄνω ὁρᾶν) and leads it away from the things here to those higher things," but Socrates answers (529 A-530 C): "You seem to me in your thought to put a most liberal interpretation on the study of higher things (τὴν περὶ τὰ ἄνω μάθησιν); for apparently, if anyone with back-thrown head should learn something by staring at decorations on a ceiling, you would regard him as contemplating them with the higher reason (νοήσει) and not with the eyes. Perhaps you are right, and I am a simpleton. For I, for my part, am unable to suppose that any other study turns the soul's gaze upward (ἄνω ποιοῦν ψυχὴν βλέπειν) than that which deals with being and the invisible . . . It is by means of problems, then, . . . as in the study of geometry, that we will pursue astronomy, too, and we will let be the things in the heavens, if we are to have a part in the true science of astronomy and so convert to right use from uselessness that natural indwelling intelligence of the soul." [18] It is, then, certainly not observation of the heavens, not even the usual form of astronomy which Socrates acknowledges as propaedeutics to higher knowledge. What he alludes to in demanding for all great arts ἀδολεσχία καὶ μετεωρολογία φύσεως πέρι can only be a study detached from the visible world, "discussion and high speculation about the truth of nature," [19] of the nature of the object (cf. περὶ φύσεως 270 C; φύσις 270 B-D), as he says here, of generalisation and diaeresis, as he states later on (270 B ff.). One can hardly conclude from this passage that Plato agreed with Hippocrates who held it necessary that the physician know the influence of the seasons on the development of diseases. The words, understood in their Platonic sense, only confirm that Hippocrates recommended definition and division of the object of medicine, of the human body.

Finally, Plato always regards it as the task of the good craftsman to apprehend the whole of his object, and in particular, as that of the physician, to study the whole of the body and not only its parts. So he says in the *Charmides* (156 C) as well as in the *Laws* (902 D-E; 903 C). Should the great Hippocrates, whom Plato admires, not fulfill the conditions set up by Plato for good craftsmanship? Should he, on the contrary, be inclined to speculations or studies of which Plato himself does not approve? Neither the procedure of diaeresis nor the terminology

[18] Plato, *The Republic with an English Translation* by P. Shorey (The Loeb Classical Library), II, pp. 181-183; 187-189. For a more detailed interpretation of the passage cf. E. Hoffman, *Vorträge der Bibliothek Warburg* (1923-24), pp. 34 ff., and Shorey in the notes to his edition.

[19] I am using Jowett's translation (*loc. cit.*, p. 478). That μετεωρολογία may have such a meaning is shown by Edelstein, *loc. cit.* The Platonic doctrine of the ἄνω and κάτω is outlined by G. Teichmüller, *Studien zur Geschichte der Begriffe* (1874), p. 391.

used in it are inventions of Plato; they are known to earlier generations. There are no valid historical objections, then, to the assumption that Hippocrates actually demanded definition and division; because he did so, he need not be a Platonist, nor a believer in the Platonic idea (contrary to Pohlenz, p. 75, n. 1). On the other hand, Diocles, the follower of Hippocrates, maintained that it is the whole nature of the body which is responsible for diseases. Moreover the method of diaeresis, Galen says, was an integral part of later medical theories which depended on Hippocrates' system.[20]

To be sure, if the testimonies of Meno and Plato are interpreted as I think they have to be, Hippocrates is not the founder of the πνεῦμα theory (cf. Pohlenz, pp. 73 ff.; 92 ff.) but of scientific medicine in the Platonic sense of the word science (cf. *Philebus* 16 C). Moreover, there is no book among the so-called Hippocratic writings which can be ascribed to Hippocrates himself. That even from Pohlenz' point of view this could not be done, I believe, is certain.[21] But I do not discuss this question, since I think that the interpretation on which Pohlenz relies in his attempt to establish the authenticity of certain books is not convincing. It is true that after a hundred years of research it is still impossible to claim that the genuine works of Hippocrates have been ascertained.[22] But Hippocrates' method, his doctrine are known, though his books are lost. The writings of many great scientists and philosophers have been destroyed, only testimonies concerning their achievements are left. To acknowledge that is no verdict, no negativism; it is a statement of fact.

LUDWIG EDELSTEIN.

THE JOHNS HOPKINS UNIVERSITY.

Harvard Studies in Classical Philology, Vol. XLIX. Cambridge, Harvard University Press, 1938. Pp. 281.

The forty-ninth volume of the *Harvard Studies* opens with a full account by Professor Carl N. Jackson of the scholarly career of the late Professor Herbert Weir Smyth of Harvard University to whom the book is dedicated. The tribute to Professor Smyth

[20] Concerning the diaeresis before Plato cf. A. E. Taylor, *Varia Socratica* (1911), pp. 212-246; E. Hoffman, *Anhang zu Zeller, Philosophie der Griechen*, II, 1 (1922), p. 1073. For Diocles (ἡ ὅλη φύσις) cf. Fragment 112 (p. 163, line 2 Wellmann and W. Jaeger, *Diokles von Karystos* [1938], p. 29). The Hippocratic diaeresis was taken over by Mnesitheus and Diocles, cf. Galen XI, p. 3 (Kühn) = Mnesitheus, Fragment 3 (H. Hohenstein, *Der Arzt Mnesitheos aus Athen*, Diss. Berlin [1935]).

[21] Cf. L. Edelstein, "The Genuine Works of Hippocrates," *Bulletin of the History of Medicine*, VII (1939), pp. 236 ff.

[22] Cf. W. Jaeger, *op. cit.*, p. vi.

VOLUME X, NUMBER 4 OCTOBER, 1949

THE FUNCTION OF THE MYTH IN PLATO'S PHILOSOPHY*

BY LUDWIG EDELSTEIN

Every reader of Plato's works, even the casual reader, must be aware of the fact that this master of subtle logical disputation is also an adept of myth. To be sure, dialectics for Plato always remains the central topic of philosophy. The early dialogues, with the exception of the *Protagoras*, do not contain any mythical tale at all. In the later writings—the *Phaedo*, the *Gorgias*, the *Symposium*, the *Republic*, the *Timaeus*, the *Politicus*—they are introduced on rare occasions and with specific motivations. Nevertheless, at least starting with the middle period of Plato's literary activity, these wondrous stories seem to occupy a fixed and allotted place within the cosmos of his philosophy. And on their embellishment he has bestowed no less exertion, no less diligence than on the elaboration of definitions and divisions. The unfathomable profoundness of the dialectician is equalled if not surpassed by the captivating grace of the story teller. Nowhere, perhaps, does Plato show as clearly as in the recounting of a myth that to him indeed "speech is more plastic than wax and other such media" (*Republic* IX, 588 D). Listening to his tales, one is spellbound, one is bewitched as it were, one believes in the reality of worlds which no mortal eye has ever seen or will ever penetrate.

Yet is it not precisely the artistic charm, the appeal to the emotional, that disqualify the myth from being used by the philosopher? Are mythology and philosophy not enemies, the one seeking pleasant fancies, the other seeking stern truth? Hegel, speaking of Plato's myths, claims that such stories are appropriate only for the childhood of mankind; when reason has grown up and has matured, they become obsolete. The ancient rationalists did not judge differently. To them, Plato's fondness for mythology was but additional proof that he was willing to revert to old superstitions; for long before Plato, Greek philosophers had discarded the myth as unworthy of him who searches for

* This and the following article were read before the Johns Hopkins Philological Association in 1947.

knowledge. To counter such charges, the Neo-Platonists of antiquity and of later centuries insisted that the Platonic tales were meant to be taken allegorically, that a truly philosophical significance was hidden in them.

On the other hand, it has been maintained by many interpreters of Plato's works, modern and ancient alike, that he attributed to the myth a validity of its own. He was aware, it has been claimed, of the limitations of reason; about certain problems, the soul and the cosmos, one can discourse only in pictures of imagination. Those who are themselves Kantians see in the Platonic myth an instrument by which transcendental feeling is roused and regulated. Man is likely to transgress the limits set to his understanding; the myth directs the licentiousness of human reason into proper channels. The Romanticists go even further. According to them, Plato was not only conscious of the limits of rational thought, he also knew that in mythical fantasy, in inspiration which the philosopher shares with the poet, man experiences the revelation of a higher truth, of the suprarational or the divine. It is in a soberer mood that philosophers, historians and philologists motivated by modern pragmatism or existentialism consider the myth a device by which Plato intended to call men to action or to express in words that part of his being which defies the rigidity of conceptual knowledge.

Divergent as these interpretations are, all of them acknowledge one fact: the question of the significance of the Platonic myth is linked up with the problem of the relationship between reason and imagination, between philosophy and poetry. Plato himself spoke of a controversy between the philosopher and the poet in regard to mythology. Even to him, the quarrel between the two was one of old standing (*Republic* X, 607 B), nor did the fight cease in the following generations, each of which turned to Plato in agreement or disagreement with his views. Both these aspects of the issue, the philosophical and the aesthetic, I have in mind when I attempt once more to determine what instigated Plato's interest in the myth. In my investigation I shall pay attention not so much to the modern theories—only from time to time shall I pause to consider them—as I shall try to follow Plato's lead, even Plato's words, in order to characterize his position in his own terms. And since his myth is not an entirely artificial creation but is set against the background of common Greek mythology and determined by it, I shall begin by analyzing Plato's attitude toward the current beliefs.

In Plato's time, mythology was still a living power. It was the traditional religion of the Greeks, their "theology" as Plato says (*Republic* II, 379 A), that had been fashioned mainly by Homer and Hesiod. It dealt with gods and daemons and heroes, with the world's coming into being and the future life in Hades (*Republic* III, 392 A). As the accepted religion of the day it pervaded the whole existence of the people. To this popular mythology, Plato like many an earlier philosopher or poet, was bitterly opposed, for in his opinion it was impious and full of error. Not even in education was he willing to give it its traditional place. Discussing the training of the guardian of his ideal state, he considers for a moment whether it would be possible to retain the ancient saga, that is, the old kind of poetry, and to purge it of its objectionable features by submitting it to allegorical interpretation. But he decides that the young would be unable to distinguish between what is and what is not allegory (*Republic* II, 378 D). Mythology, he concludes, ought to be reformed altogether.

Plato did not feel it incumbent upon himself to compose this new kind of mythological stories. He only lays down the patterns after which they should be written (*Republic* II, 379 A ff.). Philosophy proves that God is good, that he never deceives. Consequently, every myth that tells of gods who cheat men or cheat each other, has to be discarded. Likewise, tales, according to which the gods fall prey to emotions, will be deleted. For the deity is free of passions; envy has no place among the gods. The entire vocabulary of terror and fear is to be expunged from the description of Hades. Death is nothing to be feared. The myth, thus, must be made to conform to the results of philosophy. Such stories alone are to be told to the child as reflect the truth of dialectics.

This, in brief, is Plato's program for a new mythology that may be used in education. And thus far one should expect the philosopher Plato to go. At best one would anticipate that he might allegorize the myth for philosophical purposes; for the philosopher, to be sure, must be capable of distinguishing between what is and what is not allegory. Plato occasionally plays with the allegorical interpretation, a means by which philosophers and rhapsodists of his day were wont to reconcile the thought of previous centuries with the findings of progressing knowledge. Thus he mentions Homer together with those who hold "that all things are the offspring of flow and motion," since the myth of the marriage of Oceanus and Tethys (*Iliad* XIV, 201; 302) apparently is meant to express such a philosophical explanation of the universe (*Theaetetus* 152 E). But when Socrates is asked in plain language whether he believes in the truth of fables, he declines even to take them as allegories. Allegorical interpretation of the myth, in his opinion, is "a rustic kind of wisdom" that leads nowhere; it can hardly ever be brought to completion (*Phaedrus* 229 B–230 A).

Instead, Plato creates a mythology of his own. That in doing so he draws heavily on the common mythology is obvious. The framework, the basic symbols, the main figures of the Platonic myths have their counterpart in the old familiar sagas, and those who recount the tales, be they Socrates or any other of the interlocutors, usually give their report on the authority of other people. It is equally obvious that Plato composes his philosophical myth in accordance with that insight which he has gained through dialectical analysis. The myth to him is a story shaped at will. As such it is not the antithesis to reason. Introducing one of his descriptions of the nether world, Socrates can say to his partner in the dialogue (*Gorgias* 523 A): you will regard my account as a fable (*mythos*), I regard it as a reasonable story (*logos*). The myth, in his hands, is truly an instrument of the human intellect. Nevertheless, the myth is not presented with the certainty that inheres in dialectical knowledge. Of a myth one can only be persuaded. It would be unfitting for a man of sense to maintain that things actually are as the myth describes them; this is at most likely or probable (*Phaedo* 114 D). The myth, "taken as a whole, is false, but there is truth in it also," affirms Socrates of the fables of the poets (*Republic* II, 377 A). The same is valid of the Platonic myth. And yet, the philosopher must venture to believe in it; he will gladly listen to these tales (*Phaedo* 114 D; *Timaeus* 29 D). Without the addition of a myth, some of the philosophical investigations would certainly not reach their goal (*Republic* X, 614 A).

Why is this so? Why is philosophy in need of mythology which, as Plato admits, does not convey pure truth even if truth is contained therein? These questions can be answered only by an evaluation of the philosophical myths themselves. But before I venture to scrutinize them it is appropriate, I think, to emphasize two results that can already be established. Whoever takes the Platonic myth as allegory is hardly right. Ancient and modern Neo-Platonists are refuted by Plato's own words. He refused to apply allegorical interpretation to the myths of others; he certainly did not wish to have this "rustic kind of wisdom" applied to his own mythology. But whoever finds in the Platonic myths the revelation of a higher knowledge is not right either. Reason to Plato is supreme; myth is subservient to reason. For him, the myth has nothing solemn or mysterious, as the Romanticists are prone to imagine. Plato's philosophical fable is the fable of the philosopher.

Now there are two groups of stories in the dialogues that in Platonic terminology can be classified as myths: those dealing with an account of the creation of the world and with an account of the early history of mankind, and those that deal with the fate of the soul before and after this life and have a bearing not on metaphysics or science but rather on ethics. The *Timaeus*, the *Critias* and parts of the *Politicus* provide the tales concerned with an understanding of the world in which man lives and of his past; the *Phaedo*, the *Gorgias*, the *Phaedrus* and the *Republic* provide those concerned with the destiny of man in the world above the heavens from which he comes and to which he may return.

The presuppositions of the first group of these myths are clearly set forth by Plato. Human reason can grasp only that which always is and never changes; it can grasp only the eternal forms or ideas. Concepts, that is, express the universal, and thus contain truth and certainty, though by their very nature they are unable to give any information of the individual, of that which changes and becomes. If one wishes to speak of change and becoming, as it is characteristic of the history of the world, one can do so only by relating a story, a myth, the consecutive parts of which reflect and imitate change. And since the links in this story, themselves belonging to change and becoming, are not to be grasped by reason either, still less by experiment, such stories remain guesswork. They will be neither self-consistent nor exact (*Timaeus* 29 C–D). The occurrences of early history, of "antiquity," likewise are beyond human knowledge; in regard to them too one can supply only imagined probabilities instead of ascertained facts (*Republic* II, 382 D). The investigation of the beginnings of history is mythology (*Critias* 110 A).

But what then is true, what is false in these stories? It seems as if such tales about nature and history could not have any truth whatever. Such an assumption, or conclusion, would be erroneous. If one constructs nature in such a way that the story shows how God created the world so as to make it as perfect as possible; if one constructs history in such a way that the story shows how God is present in history, how the various periods of the development of mankind were nearer to God or farther removed from Him—under this condition and to this extent is the account truthful. For time and temporal events came into being so that they might be as like to the patterns of eternal nature as possible (*Timaeus* 38 B–C). If taken as a symbol of eternity, the world is understood correctly. An accurate historical account is the transposition of an ideal drawing,—outlined as it were in a fable,—into the realm of fact (*Timaeus* 26 B; cf. *Republic* II, 382 D). On the other hand, the manner in which the eternal is embedded in natural phenomena and human deeds, can only be surmised by man. Certainly, one account may be more likely than another, yet to give the most likely account is all that human nature permits (*Timaeus* 29 C–D; cf. *Republic* II, 382 D). The details with which the story is embellished, in the last analysis, remain uncertain. Plato would not stake his reputation on the theory that divine providence stationed the liver in the lower region of the body so that this organ, being the seat of the vegetative soul, will not disturb the divine intellect residing in the head (*Timaeus* 70 D ff.). Nor would he be willing to wager his good name on the claim that in the Golden Age all men used to discourse all day long with one another and with the animals (*Politicus* 272 B–C). The "facts" of nature and of history, which ancient and modern commentators have tried to sift out of the myths of the *Timaeus* and the *Critias* and the *Politicus*, these "facts," however likely, remain guesswork. Certain is only this much, that God, looking up to ideas, created the cosmos, that there was divine guidance of mankind in the past and that some day it will be restored.

Yet, if this is so, if no more certainty can be obtained, must one not ask why these elaborate stories are told at all? Can the philosopher not do without them? He really does not gain more from listening to them, or from composing them, than he might express in one sentence, namely that the world is the work of God's handicraft and that His providence pervades human history. As for the rest, opinions, even those that approximate truth, are not truth, and to philosophize, Plato teaches, means to aim at knowing rather than at opining. To be sure, it is inherent in the nature of human understanding that truth and falsehood are forever closely interwoven. Altogether free from falsehood, altogether simple and true in word and deed, are the divine and the daemonic alone (*Republic* II, 382 E). But then one should think that the philosopher should try to become like God not only in his deeds so far as this is possible for him (*Theaetetus* 176 B), but also in his words; at least he should refrain from uttering falsehood. He should show his responsibility and his judgment by not going further than his knowledge will carry him. With such considerations or objections Plato, it seems, is nowhere concerned. In passing he mentions that the historical tale may serve for the clarification of logical difficulties (*Politicus* 274 E); the cosmological myth "beginning with the origin of the cosmos and ending with the generation of mankind," allows the historian to take over mankind "already, as it were, created by speech" (*Timaeus* 27 A). But even where Plato refers to the usefulness of the historical myth, it is a usefulness that at the same time offers some amusement (*Politicus* 268 D). The search for the history of old and mythology "are visitants that come to the city in company with leisure" (*Critias* 110 A). And of cosmology Plato simply states: "Whenever for the sake of recreation a man lays aside arguments concerning eternal realities and considers probable accounts of becoming, gaining thereby a pleasure not to be repented of, he provides for his life a pastime that is both moderate and sensible" (*Timaeus* 59 C–D).

The myths concerning nature and history, then, are a pastime, an amusement, a playful game (*paidia*), a recreation from arguments concerning ideas, a means by which to while away our leisure (*schole*). To understand the full impact of these words, one would have to be able to penetrate the deepest depths of Platonic philosophy. To outline briefly what the terms seem to imply, I hazard only with diffidence. Nothing in this world, Plato teaches, exists without its opposite (*Phaedo* 60 B). Pleasure is inextricably connected with pain, pain with pleasure. In ethics, the hedonistic calculus, therefore, will never work out. Evil can never be done away with; for there must always be something opposed to the good (*Theaetetus* 176 A). It is impossible to strive for the one without accepting the other. In the same way, seriousness would defeat its own purpose if it were not willing to admit playfulness. Thus the philosopher knows that one can teach philosophy only by discussing its problems with the individual, by delivering the thoughts which reside in the pupil's soul, and it is this living dialogue with others that is the serious task of the philosopher. Nevertheless, he will put down his views, and "plant the garden of letters." Doing this is a pastime, an amusement in which he passes his leisure as others pass it, refreshing themselves with banquets and kindred entertainments (*Phaedrus* 276 D–E). Moreover, there can be perfection even in playfulness. Just as the works of the philosopher which he composes for his own amusement, the written dialogues, are composed with infinite care, encompassing a cosmos of men and arguments, endeavoring to capture the best, the most convincing *logos*, so the myths are composed with infinite care, selecting the best, embodying all findings of men, so as to make the tale the most likely account. Finally, to play may indeed be an imitation of the divine. Is it not difficult to say whether men, the ingenuous puppets of the gods, were contrived as playthings of theirs, or rather for some serious purposes (*Laws* I, 644 C)? And should man not live playing at peaceful pastimes, —the really serious business of life,—sacrificing, singing, dancing, so that he be able to win heaven's favor (*Laws* VII, 803 E)? Certainly one partakes of immortality by serious philosophizing, by "thinking thoughts that are immortal and divine" (*Timaeus* 90 B–C). Yet stories dealing with the world and with mankind are also admirably suited for celebrating the deity. It is at the festival of Athena that the myths of the *Timaeus* and the *Critias* are recited (*Timaeus* 26 E). Thus, the terms seriousness and playfulness are imbued with the peculiar ambiguity of Platonic irony, and in the twilight of this realm only this much remains certain: they are the two aspects of the one indissoluble unity of human and maybe even of divine life.

Whether or not I have succeeded in suggesting the implications of Plato's thought, and even though its final significance may remain inscrutable, one must accept Plato's verdict that the cosmological and historical myth is a play, an entertaining story that is likely, though by no means entirely trustworthy. I need hardly stress the fact that by taking such an attitude toward the problems of natural science and history, Plato was utterly at variance with the great natural philosophers and critical historians of the fifth and fourth centuries B.C. The former,—and among them Democritus was perhaps the foremost—had propounded a rational analysis of nature; experience had been given its share in this undertaking. Thucydides had separated history from mythology; even prehistory, to him, was a realm to be penetrated by critical conjectures based on factual evidence. Plato, one might say, sided with the metaphysician Parmenides and with Herodotus, who admitted the myth into the field of history. Plato holds indeed that human reason is limited. The important point is that he finds the limitations of reason where ancient rationalism, as well as modern rationalism, detects the strength of reason if allied with experience: in the detailed understanding of the phenomena of nature and of history. On the other hand, Plato takes it for granted that reason is capable of proving the principles of an interpretation of both natural and historical facts. What Kant introduces as an hypothesis, the teleology of nature and of history, as an "as if" in his famous phrase, Plato holds to be beyond doubt. It seems to me that those who interpret Plato in categories of Kant are inclined to overlook, or to minimize, this fundamental difference between the two. And yet, it is precisely this disagreement that speaks against their attempt to define the Platonic myth as a means of rousing and regulating transcendental feeling. That which to Kant is transcendental feeling or licentiousness of reason, to Plato is the very task of reason, and mythical fantasy or feeling holds sway where Kant's rational causality reigns supreme. Again, since it is the world and history that withstand the rigidity of conceptual thinking, it would hardly do to restrict the use of the myth to questions concerning the cosmos and the soul, nor would it be sufficient to say that the myth expresses the inner existence of man or appeals to his practical nature. Though the historical tale according to the educational theory of the *Republic* (II, 382 D; cf. *Politicus* 274 E) is of practical value, the philosophical myth, the imaginative picture of the perishable, is an intellectual amusement.

Yet it is time to leave these discriminations aside and to turn to the second group of myths which I have to consider, those that deal with the fate of the soul before and after this life, those that is which have a bearing on ethics. In regard to them Plato's presuppositions are not expressed as clearly as they are in regard to the first group of myths; still, they can be comprehended with a fair degree of assurance. In his ethical research the philosopher is able to establish with certainty the rules of conduct; it can be proved that to suffer injustice is better than to do injustice. Socrates succeeds even in establishing the immortality of the soul, at least to his own satisfaction and to that of his friends. He has never met anybody who, trying to defend amorality, could not be refuted (*Gorgias* 527 A–B); he is convinced that no argument can be brought against his thesis that the soul is immortal which he would not be capable of countering or of showing to be erroneous. In ethics, then, the case stands differently than in natural science and history: human reason is able to cope with its task, it provides knowledge. To be sure, Plato is willing to admit that the dialectical argument may run into difficulties; objections may be raised, nor is it easy to distinguish between good and bad arguments. But on that account one ought not to despair of the intellect; the disappointment should not make a man a hater of reason, a misologist; it should not cajole him into adherence to mere belief, or into scepticism, or worst of all, into acquiescence. One must blame one's own lack of skill, one must go on investigating, and in the end the right argument will emerge victorious (*Phaedo* 89 B ff.). And yet after having proved the rules of right conduct, the immortality of man, Socrates adds a myth, depicting the life of the soul in Hades (*Gorgias* 523 A ff.), or picturing the rewards and punishments that await the soul in the Beyond (*Phaedo* 107 B ff.). Otherwise, he says, the argument would not be complete (*Republic* X, 614 A).

The ethical myth, then, is an addition to rational knowledge; it does not take the place of rational knowledge, as do the historical and scientific myths. It is a superfluity of riches, as it were. On the other hand, it is true, the ethical myth, too, transcends knowledge. That the souls are born many times, that from Hades they rise in the ninth year to the upper sun (*Meno* 81 B–D), that there is a heaven where at the banquets of the gods divine intelligence feasts on ideas and where the horses of the deities are given ambrosia and nectar (*Phaedrus* 247 A–E)—how unlike the banquets of the Homeric gods!—all such things of course cannot be really affirmed or established with certainty. And even if the most elaborate results of contemporaneous learning are integrated into a story (*Phaedo* 108 E ff.), as is perhaps Democritean science into the cosmological myth, the details remain guesswork. The picture of the cosmos, of the earth changes; the representations of Hades in the *Gorgias* and in the *Phaedo* are not identical, and the historical myths of the *Politicus* and the *Critias* agree with each other just as little. Here fantasy holds sway. It would not be fitting for a man of sense to assert that all this is exactly as it has been described (*Phaedo* 114 D). What is certain is again but the pattern of construction: that there is life after death and previous to life.

But why should it be necessary to resort to surmise that cannot stand the test of logical criticism? Is not the ethical myth even more superfluous than the cosmological and historical tales, since ethical knowledge is self-sufficient? In addition, reward in this world or in the Hereafter should not influence the actions of the righteous. He must follow the moral law whatever the consequences. Plato is aware of this objection. He proves that justice itself is best, even if stripped of all rewards that may be bestowed upon it by men or gods, whether it possesses the ring of Gyges or the helmet of Hades to boot (*Republic* X, 612 B; cf. II, 367 D–E). Nevertheless, having ended the inquiry "which indeed is no easy one but calls for keen vision" (*ibid.* II, 368 C), he grants to the just not only all the rewards that virtue brings men among men but also those which it receives from the gods (*ibid.* X, 612 D). His reason is that "the tale was saved as the saying is, and was not lost, and it will save us if we believe it" (*ibid.* X, 621 B–C). If the philosopher ventures to believe that the gods are not indifferent to the fate of men, neither here nor there, he will find the venture worth while, for he will be of good cheer, he will gain courage (*Phaedo* 114 D). He will exert all his strength in acquiring virtue and wisdom in life, "for the prize is fair and the hope great" (*ibid.* 114 C); he will endure in the moral contest of life that is worth all other contests on this earth (*Gorgias* 526 E). In other words, the ethical myth speaks to man's passions; it rouses and confirms hopes; it enhances courage and allays fears. It is like a charm that one must sing to oneself (*Phaedo* 114 D). And since the song is directed toward the emotional part of the soul, since it is meant to have a psychological effect—if I may use this phrase—it gains in power, if it is repeated and drawn out (*ibid.* 114 D). Man's reason may be convinced by an argument that is given once; fear and hope take time in being moulded aright, they need ceaseless training.

Whereas the cosmological and the historical myths are a pastime of the intellect, the ethical myth is rooted in man's irrational nature, and it cannot be banished from philosophy because both these parts of the human soul must be equally tended by the philosopher. Inasmuch as man thinks, "inasmuch as he is for ever tending his divine part and duly magnifying that daemon who dwells along with him, he must be supremely blessed. But the way of tendance of every part by every man is one—namely, to supply each with its own congenial food and motion" (*Timaeus* 90 C). Nor is it merely a question of giving to each part its own deserved due for the sake of fairness and justice. Pleasure and fear can influence the intellect; they bewitch reason and destroy insight. Just as men have their opinions stolen from them by time which "strips them unawares of their beliefs," or by arguments that overpower them with their seeming strength, just as men change their minds compelled by some physical pain or suffering, so they alter their views "under the spell of pleasure or terrified by some fear" (*Republic* III, 413 A–C). Pleasure and fear therefore may at any moment put the intellect to shame unless they are properly guided. Moreover, in addition to the two foolish and antagonistic counsellors whom everybody possesses within himself, Plato says at the end of his life, calling them by the name of pleasure and pain, everybody possesses opinions about the future, "which go by the general name of 'expectations'; and of these, that which precedes pain bears the special name of 'fear,' and that which precedes pleasure the special name of 'confidence' " (*Laws* I, 644 C). Whatever man knows, whatever he grasps by reason, whatever he decides about right and wrong, he also anticipates his coming fate, he fears and hopes for his future in this world no less than in the other, and he will persevere in the truth which philosophy teaches only if his hopes and fears are in accordance with his knowledge. That is why one must counteract sorcery by sorcery (cp. *Republic* III, 413 C with *Phaedo* 114 D).

In the beginning of my discussion I have drawn attention to the fact that the myth, important as it is for Plato, does not have a place in all his dialogues, that in fact it comes to play its rôle in his later works alone. Perhaps I can now explain this circumstance and in doing so summarize my results and clarify them to some extent. The scientific and historical myths are propounded above all in the *Timaeus* and in the *Critias,* which were certainly written after the *Republic.* In the latter work the ideas or forms are for the first time clearly viewed as the source of the existence of things as well as of their essence, that is, of their being in the full meaning of the term. Thereby the problem was raised how the creation of the world of phenomena, of nature and of history, should be understood in detail, provided that the idea of the good is the cause of all existence. The *Timaeus* and the *Critias* undertake to give the answer. On the other hand, the ethical myth is found in the *Gorgias,* the *Phaedo,* the *Phaedrus,* the *Republic.* In the *Gorgias* Plato hints at his conviction that man's reason is not omnipotent (525 B–C). While in his early dialogues he gave the impression that to know the good means to be able to do the good, he now begins to acknowledge that in man's soul there are powers capable of thwarting the decisions of reason. The *Phaedo* speaks of the conflict between man's soul and his passions (94 D–E). The *Phaedrus* and the *Republic* develop the dogma of the tripartite soul in which reason holds but a precarious supremacy. Justice, the highest virtue, now is that attitude of man which makes the parts of his soul function in their native way. Reason is to lead; the passions are to be led, and they are to be controlled mainly by habituation. The ethical myth could indeed hardly be introduced in any dialogue that antedates the *Gorgias.* (The *Protagoras* which I have mentioned as the only exception from the rule, really is not an exception; for the myth told there, even though it may be tinged by Platonic concepts, is a more or less historical reproduction of the views of Protagoras).

Proposing such an explanation I do not wish to identify myself with those theories which suggest a development of Plato's philosophy. Even if Plato has established the ideas as the causes of existence for the first time in the *Republic,* even if he has brought out the importance of the irrational factor for the first time in the *Gorgias,* his thought may have proceeded along similar lines long before. His written work, the earlier dialogues, centered on different subjects. Besides, even in his latest work, the *Laws,* Plato insists on the dogma that virtue is knowledge, and tries to reconcile this theory with his insight into the independence of passions; he does not entirely discard his ethical rationalism. Whether Plato's turning to mythology resulted from a change of heart, or whether it was the natural outgrowth of convictions that he always cherished, the significant fact remains that he dared to integrate, or re-integrate, the myth into philosophy. By this venture he succeeded in reconciling the irrational and the rational aspects of human nature. It is the saving grace of Plato's intellectualism that it can do justice to the emotions without infringing upon the prerogatives of reason, which to be sure is man's most precious possession, for it is divine. Just as the intellect is allowed, nay obliged, to play no less than to obey the strict laws of dialectics, to imagine no less than to define and to divide, so the intellect is enjoined to be intelligent as well as kind and understanding in its relation to that man within man, or to the "child within us" (*Phaedo* 77 E) who fears and hopes and who must be persuaded until his fears are charmed away and a spell of hope has been cast upon him. Plato is not a Stoic for whom passions are but mistaken judgments. The rigid dignity of the wise man, superior to pain and pleasure because he has made himself insensible to passions, is as foreign to Plato as is the stern pathos of doing one's duty in the course of human affairs, of the business of the day. On the other hand, Plato's rationalism is a far cry from that of the Kantian. God and immortality, to Plato, are not transcendental objects, postulates of practical reason but never to be grasped by theoretical reason. He knows that God exists, that man is immortal. He can indulge in metaphysical dreams with a good conscience; these reveries are a permissible, nay a necessary, pastime of the intellect. Moreover, Plato is willing to hope for reward, to believe in eudaemonia, in the eudaemonia of the righteous in thought and deed, for in this hope, in this belief, he feels more certain of his moral existence. But never does he acknowledge a truth that reason cannot grasp, that lies beyond its reach, because reason is "fragmentary." The myth, shaped in accordance with reason, brings to the realm of the passions the light of the intellect; it instigates man to act with hope and confidence toward the goal which reason has set before him. Through the myth the inner core of man's existence receives the commands of the intellect in terms that are adequate to its irrational nature. Thus man in his entirety is put under the guidance of philosophy, and Plato has fulfilled the demand which he himself made even upon the student of the world of physical phenomena: "in all things to seek after the divine for the sake of gaining a life of blessedness, so far as our nature admits thereof, and to seek the necessary for the sake of the divine, reckoning that without the former it is impossible to discern by themselves alone the divine objects after which we strive, or to apprehend them or in any way partake thereof" (*Timaeus* 68 E–69 A).

Mythology, then, is an intrinsic part of Platonic philosophy. It is for good reasons that it has its place within the cosmos of Plato's thought. It was not Plato's reactionary temper, it was not anti-rationalism that caused him to revert to the myth. This much I trust to have shown through my brief analysis of the subject. In bare outlines I hope to have made clear the indispensable function of the myth within the framework of subtle dialectics. Supposing that the main points of my discussion are correct, it would still be necessary to work out the details of my thesis. For that purpose one would have to consider not only the most important mythical tales but even those which Plato tells in passing, such as the fables referred to in the *Phaedrus* (274 C ff.), or in the *Meno* (81 A ff.). In addition, one would have to connect the study of the myths with that of the several dialogues in which they appear and then again to relate the use of mythology to the specific philosophical problems which Plato tries to unravel in his various works. All this I cannot do here. But if I wish not to be remiss even in answering those questions which I myself have raised here,

I must go at least one step further and show in which way Plato's attitude toward mythology affects his judgment on poetry.

That it is the task of the poet to compose myths, Plato himself acknowledges (*Republic* II, 378 E), and one might therefore claim that the myths which he has woven into his dialogues are the work of the poet Plato. Yet he has deigned to write only such myths as are fit for the accomplished philosopher. As I have pointed out before, he refrained even from composing those stories which were to be used in the education of the future guardians of his ideal state; rather did he restrict himself to laying down the patterns according to which they were to be fashioned (*Republic* II, 379 A ff.). Surely, it was not his intention that his own philosophical myths should be read by children, in a school edition, as it were. Beautiful and poetical as they are, they would be beyond the grasp of the young. They are, moreover, prose compositions, not poetry in the strict sense of the word, and it is poetry, music, that is needed for the education of the soul (*Republic* II, 376 E). Nor would Plato have imagined that on the basis of his philosophical myths religion could be taught to the many. And yet, he was of opinion that for the multitude mythology embodies all that they will ever be able to learn about the divine. Philosophy, he held, is but for the few. Even royal statesmanship guides the people in unison with rhetoric, persuading them "by telling stories" (*Politicus* 304 C). In his *Laws,* therefore, he bases the life of the city not on philosophy—an impossibility in the world of reality with which this dialogue deals—but on mythology. However, it is a reformed mythology and by no means the objectionable old inherited religious legend which he wishes to enthrone. Hermes is not to be the Hermes of the poets or "perverse myth mongers" (*Laws* XII, 941 A–B). The masses are not to be deceived or swayed by mere fiction. What they are deprived of is the philosophical understanding of the truth; they are limited to the imaginative reflections of dialectical knowledge. Unlike the Stoics, or modern Machiavellian statesmen, Plato was not willing to let the people live under the domination of a religion which he himself despised, while he reserved for the philosopher the right to apply his own thought to the common religion, thereby giving it a different meaning. And who other than the poet could be charged with composing the myths needed for the education of the citizens of the "ideal state" or for that of the masses in the "second best state"?

Still, it seems as if Plato had refused forever to poetry a place among the goods to be enjoyed by men. He has driven out of his city, the pattern of which is "laid up in heaven" (*Republic* IX, 595 B), the "honeyed muse in lyric or epic," Homer "the most poetic of poets and the first of tragedians"; no poetry is admitted "save only hymns to the gods and the praises of good men" (*Republic* X, 607 A). But it is the poetry of the past alone and of his own day which he thus condemns almost without exception, even though he is conscious of her spell and seems to hope against hope that her advocates may be able to plead her cause and show "any reason for her existence in a well-governed state." For "reason constrained us" to dismiss her from the state (*ibid.* X, 607 B–C). If poetry is "not only delightful but beneficial to orderly government and all the life of man," if she "bestows not only pleasure but benefit," it will be clear gain to listen to her, she may justly return from her exile (*ibid.* 607 D–E). There is no real quarrel between poetry and philosophy, as long as poetry will bow to censorship (*ibid.* II, 377 C; cf. Laws II, 658 E ff.). This censorship is not to be exercised by any chance person, or by the arbitrary decision of aesthetic or philosophical criticism, nor is the usefulness of poetry to be understood in terms of narrow and passing political or moral ideas. The poet, to use a phrase of Goethe's, must take "the veil of poetry from the hands of truth." Just as Plato has refused entrance to the old kind of poetry because "it would be impious to betray what we believe to be the truth" (*Republic* X, 607 C), so he imposes upon poetry the censorship of truth, of true usefulness. She must learn to represent God in His true quality (*Republic* II, 379 A ff.), to picture man not as he may actually live, but as he ought to live in accordance with the destination of his higher nature (*Republic* X, 604 B ff.; cf. *Laws* II, 660 E ff.).

The fact that poetry, if it conforms to such standards, will in some respects be the loser, is fully realized by Plato. He says himself: "The fretful part of us presents many and varied occasions for imitation, while the intelligent and temperate disposition, always remaining approximately the same, is neither easy to imitate nor to be understood when imitated, especially by a non-descript mob assembled in the theater" (*Republic* X, 604 E). Poetry which submits to Plato's ideal is a thing difficult to accomplish; it is in danger of becoming boring; its popular appeal is diminished, and this, to be sure, holds equally good in regard to the description of man and gods. The myth, as Plato imagines it, cannot compete with the poetical charm or attractiveness of Homer's stories, or with the overpowering greatness of the tragic fate that pervades the tales of Aeschylus or Sophocles. Nevertheless, the task can be achieved by him who believes that truth is the goddess supreme. In subject matter poetry in fact would not differ from Homer's and Hesiod's and Aeschylus' poems, for they too wrote about the heavens and the realm of the dead, about the genesis of the world, about the Golden Age, about gods and men, and Thersites has his place in Homer as well as Achilles. How grandiose an epic that sings of the creation of the world and the judgment in Hades, as the *Gorgias* and *Phaedo* picture them, of the heavens, the gods and the souls in their chariots, as the *Phaedrus* describes them, of the Golden Age, as the *Politicus* visualizes it! How stirring a tragedy the death of Socrates! How comic a figure that mannikin, the philosophical pretender who looks like "a bald-headed tinker, who has made money and just been freed from bonds and had a bath and is wearing a new garment and has got himself up like a bridegroom and is about to marry his master's daughter who has fallen into poverty and abandonment" (*Republic* VI, 495 E)!

The possibility of a new poetry on Plato's terms one can readily conceive, and for such a new poetry that would fulfill his demands, Plato, I think, was hoping. His dialogues gave to the philosopher a new mythology, and in this sense they constituted a new poetry. But he was waiting for poets who would do fresh work, who would replace the prose myth which he had composed by a truly poetical myth embodied in epics and tragedies and comedies as well as in hymns to the gods and in praises of good men. These poets he would have admitted not only to the "second best state," as he actually did, where the polity is framed "as a representation of the fairest and best life, which is in reality, as we assert, the truest tragedy," where men themselves are "the authors of a tragedy at once superlatively fair and good" and thus rivals of the poets "as artists and actors of the fairest drama" (*Laws* VII, 817 A ff.); he would have admitted them even to his "ideal state," in regard to which "it makes no difference whether it exists now or ever will come into being," which is there for him "who wishes to contemplate it and so beholding to constitute himself its citizen" (*Republic* IX, 595 B). To their poetry, even the philosopher

Plato would gladly have listened, for to him, rhythm and harmony more than anything else find their way to the inmost soul and take strongest hold upon it, "bringing with them and imparting grace" if they are rightly chosen (*Republic* III, 401 D). Poetry does not, as Aristotle would have it, free men from passions, but by representing them implants them in man's heart (*ibid.* X, 606 A–B; cf. 605 B). Where could Plato find a stronger ally for that aim which he attributed to the telling of a myth than in poetry, that is, in the right kind of poetry?

The ancient poets did not heed Plato's call. The epic, as far as it dealt with nature and history, became didactic poetry, versified science. The natural phenomena were not viewed as a simile of the eternal; they were interpreted and explained in a rational way. The mechanistic universe which Lucretius celebrates is the antithesis of the world created by the Platonic god. Even the poem of Manilius, though it knows of providence, does not know of the Beyond. History, too, became rationalized. Lucanus, to be sure, is aware of the divine fate that governs human events. But the Fate in which the Stoic believed is not the deity to which the Platonist paid his respect. Vergil's epic comes perhaps closer to Plato's wishes; still, it hardly is all that he was anxious to have. As for tragic poetry, wherever it did not rework the themes of old mythology, or in Roman times, simply translate the classic and Hellenistic Greek drama, it even resorted to the description of contemporary life. The philosophical plays of the Cynics or Stoics were moral exercises; the triumph of man over fear and hope, over fate, was glorified. The comedy reviled the gods in the style of Aristophanes. Man was shown in his most human aspects; fun was poked at him as he lives his daily life, concerned with the petty worries and pleasures of his individual existence.

Ancient poetry did not fulfill the expectations of Plato. Or perhaps I should say it could not fulfill his expectations. Plato was the only one who believed in the cleavage between idea and reality; he was the last one to believe in the truth contained in the myth. After him, the myth became allegory, it was no longer religion; it was merely an embellishment, a poetical adornment. Whether any poet of later ages, living in a world of new beliefs and new hopes, ever rose to the height of Plato's vision of a new poetry, this is not for me to decide.

University of California at Berkeley.

AMERICAN
JOURNAL OF PHILOLOGY

VOL. LXXXIII, 1 WHOLE No. 329

PLATONIC ANONYMITY.

FOR GEORGE BOAS

August 28, 1961

Of the many problems raised by the dialogue form which Plato chose as his medium of writing, perhaps none is more vexing than that he never speaks in his own name. Refusing to assume responsibility for any of the views which he proposes, he gives the impression that the story he is telling is not his. What is the reason for this self-effacement, this anonymity, which he maintains throughout his literary work and which is in striking contrast with the emphasis on personal convictions, the love of originality, prevailing in Preplatonic philosophy, as well as in contemporaneous and in even earlier Greek literature?[1] It is no wonder that this question has exercised the interpreters of Plato. To discover its answer is surely prerequisite to an understanding of Plato's work, to an appreciation of the specific form in which he presents his philosophy. And yet one may almost despair of ever finding the solution of the puzzle since the dialogues, just as they are silent about Plato, refrain from disclosing why he is not a participant in the debates which the dialogues he composed all his life pretend to record.[2]

But in saying this I may seem to have exaggerated the difficulty of the problem. After all, in the letters, which nowadays are usually considered genuine, and in which Plato speaks in his

[1] Cf. P. Friedländer, *Platon*, I² (1954), pp. 133 f.

[2] For the recent literature on the problem here under discussion, see Ph. Merlan, "Form and Content in Plato's Philosophy," *Journal of the History of Ideas*, VIII (1947), p. 407.

own name, he does talk about his literary work, its character and purport. Here, then, the interpreter appears to have at his disposal objective evidence which should provide Plato's own answer to the issue in question, and, therefore, it will first be necessary to scrutinize the content of these assertions.

As the second of the letters avers: "The greatest safeguard (*sc.* against divulging the truth improperly) is to avoid writing and to learn by heart; for it is not possible that what is written down should not get divulged. For this reason I myself have never yet written anything on these subjects (*sc.* the doctrine concerning the nature of the 'First'), and no treatise by Plato exists or will exist, but those which now bear his name belong to a Socrates become fair and new" (314 B-C).[3] Again, the seventh letter claims: "Thus much I can certainly declare concerning all these writers, or prospective writers, who claim to know the subjects which I seriously study (*sc.* the highest and first truth of Nature [344 D]), whether as hearers of mine or of other teachers, or from their own discoveries; it is impossible, in my judgment at least, that these men should understand anything about this subject. There does not exist, nor will there ever exist, any treatise of mine dealing therewith. For it does not at all admit of verbal expression like other studies. . ." (341 B-C).

These startling sentences have recently been taken to mean that Plato "is to a certain extent disowning his writings. They are for him but presentations of a possible philosophical standpoint; of a standpoint the truth of which he acknowledges conditionally."[4] Or, to put it differently, all the figures of the dialogues, including that of Socrates, are pseudonyms of Plato.

[3] This translation (as the one immediately following) is taken from R. G. Bury, *Plato*, VII (The Loeb Classical Library, 1929). I have, however, rendered the phrase *καλοῦ καὶ νέου γεγονότος* (314 C) as "fair and new" rather than as "fair and young." According to tradition, Gorgias, greeted by Plato with the words "there comes our noble and golden Gorgias," replied: "Noble (*καλόν*) indeed and new (*νέον*) is this Archilochus that Athens has produced" (*Athenaeus*, XI, 505 D). Gorgias means to say that Plato is a new Archilochus who, in his writings which caricature the personalities represented, has revived the invective of the great iambic poet of old. A similar thought is I think expressed in the second epistle; cf. below, p. 3.

[4] Merlan, *op. cit.*, p. 415.

The opinions expressed by the leading characters are of his making to be sure, but he has voiced them only in order to abandon them. For there is no objective philosophical truth; one's whole life-work must be denied; there is only something like "existential" uncertainty. And this is the concept of truth which in fact pervades the dialogues themselves and inspires also Plato's political theories and activities.[5]

That Plato held such a concept of truth, I doubt. Even granted that he did, however, the passages quoted from the letters would not justify what is claimed for them.[6] For in the one statement (*Epistulae* II) Plato not only disowns his writings to a certain extent, he dissociates himself from them altogether and attributes them to someone else. Their real author is Socrates, not Plato; it is his teacher who speaks here.[7] In the other statement (*Epistulae* VII) Plato denies that he has ever written, or will ever write, a book on what he "seriously" studies. And as the letter expressly says later, "whenever one sees a man's written compositions—whether they be laws of a legislator or anything else in any other form—these are not his most serious works, if so be that the writer himself is serious" (344 C). The dialogues in Plato's opinion, then, are not his "most serious works," and can hardly be taken to contain his philosophy of "existential" uncertainty, or to demonstrate his conviction that all philosophical discourse is, so to say, preliminary and transitory, undoubtedly a most important and "serious" philosophical truth.[8]

[5] Merlan, *op. cit.*, pp. 424 f. (pseudonymity); 415-24 (concept of truth; Plato's political intentions); 425-7 (Plato's oral teaching).

[6] On Plato's concept of philosophical truth, cf. below, pp. 17 f.

[7] Friedländer finds in *Epistulae* II, 314 B-C merely the admission that Plato in all his writings always spoke through a mask, that he always made Socrates speak or listen (I[1] [1928], p. 152; I[2], pp. 120 f., the passage is taken in a different sense, cf. below, note 10). This interpretation seems to me to overlook the important fact that according to the letter no book of Plato's exists and that a *caveat* against all writing is entered; see below, p. 4.

[8] Merlan (cf. above, pp. 2 f.) assumes that the two letters give a consistent view of Plato's writings, and this is true in so far as both deny the existence of any book that can be called Platonic in the strict sense of the term. It should be noted, however, that while the second letter attributes the dialogues to Socrates, the seventh letter says nothing about their "authorship," nor does it define their purpose and meaning.

As far as Plato's silence about himself is concerned, one can conclude from the letters only that he does not speak in his own name because the dialogues have nothing in common with his philosophy. His written work is intended to represent if not the letter, then the spirit of Socrates' teaching. Here Socrates has been reborn and come to life again, and therefore the dialogues "belong to a Socrates become fair and new" (*Epistulae* II, 314 C).[9] To search in these writings for Plato's philosophy is vain. Moreover, it is clear that this philosophy was not, and could not be, put in writing. According to the seventh letter, the truth about "the highest things of nature" does not at all "admit of verbal expression like other studies" (341 C). Avoidance of writing is "the greatest safeguard"; it is not right to divulge the truth improperly, the second letter holds (314 B). Plato's own teaching consisted in oral instruction; it was esoteric.[10] Or, as some modern scholars have put it—the Platonic writings give an impersonal picture of reality, past and present, an historical record, so to say. Socrates' philosophy is represented in the conversations in which he is the main interlocutor, while in the later works, where Socrates is silent or is absent, Plato gives his judgment on earlier and on contemporary philosophical systems, or on what he thought fit to communicate to a larger public. His own philosophy must be reconstructed from testimonies outside the Platonic dialogues.[11]

[9] For the words "Socrates fair and new," cf. above, note 3. Whether or not the letter suggests that the dialogues give an historical or an idealized picture of Socrates (as held by J. Harward, *The Platonic Epistles* [1932], *ad* 314 c 1), can hardly be ascertained.

[10] H. F. Cherniss, *The Riddle of the Early Academy* (1945), p. 13, has insisted on this conclusion with reference to the seventh letter. It is equally valid in my opinion with reference to the second letter. According to Friedländer (I[2], pp. 120 f.) who believes that the letters agree with what Socrates says in the *Phaedrus* about the relative value of talking and writing, the "mystische Reich" and the "persönliche Heilsweg," perhaps implied in the seventh letter (p. 65), are not irreconcilable; the dichotomy between oral teaching and written work explains the unsystematic and fragmentary character of the dialogues (p. 64). But as I have tried to show, according to the letters the dialogues cannot be considered at all as a representation of Platonic philosophy; see also note 15.

[11] Cf. J. Burnet, *Greek Philosophy*, I (1914), pp. 178, 214; and A. E. Taylor, *Plato* (1936[2]), p. 10.

Yet, if it were true that he who wishes to learn about Plato's thought must discount the written work, it would indeed be strange that all Plato's associates—men like Aristotle, Speusippus, Xenocrates, and Crantor—often based their interpretation of Plato's philosophy on statements made in the dialogues, and were apparently unaware of the opinion pronounced in his letters. That they misunderstood some, or even many, of Plato's theories is conceivable; that they differed in the exegesis of particular passages is not surprising.[12] One cannot imagine, however, that none of them should have grasped a clearly avowed injunction that the endeavor to study his writings for the purpose of finding out about his "serious" teaching would be futile, nay, against his wishes. Moreover, there is positive evidence that the theory of Ideas proposed by the Platonic Socrates —the pivotal doctrine of the dialogues—is Plato's distinctive contribution to philosophy.[13] Historical data are undoubtedly integrated into Plato's oeuvre. Such writings as the *Apology* and the *Crito* may be meant to recall the "historical" Socrates. But on the whole, all appearances notwithstanding, the arguments elaborated, whether positive or negative, must be considered Plato's and the results arrived at have to be regarded as his conclusions.[14] For this reason, contrary to the now prevailing view, the statements in the two letters, which give the verdict on Plato's writings and attribute to him a philosophy different from that of the dialogues, cannot be genuine. There is no source from which an authentic explanation of Plato's anonymity could be derived.[15]

[12] For these differences of opinion, see Cherniss, *op. cit.*, chap. III, especially pp. 72 ff.

[13] Cf. Cherniss, *op. cit.*, p. 10.

[14] Recent writers tend to consider even the *Apology* and the *Crito* as fundamentally Platonic (cf. e.g. Friedländer, *Platon*, II[2] [1957], pp. 143 ff.), but, in my opinion, the thesis that these two writings are mainly dedicated to a portrayal of the "historical" Socrates has not been disproved. Whether Plato's first dialogues were historical and he later turned to writing others in which Socrates was but the mouthpiece of his opinions, or whether the composition of "historical" dialogues was an interlude in his career, is a question I shall not presume to discuss here, where I am concerned only with Platonic anonymity in the works giving Plato's own views. See also below, note 48.

[15] The question of the genuineness of the Platonic letters is still *sub judice*. The seventh is considered Plato's by the majority of modern

I add in passing that no assistance is to be had from ancient critics either. Their practice was to seek out in the dialogues the figures through which Plato expounds his doctrine and to separate them from those through which he refutes false opinions; they distinguished between historical and imaginary characters.[16] Such a procedure was of course the result of their awareness of the problem of Platonic anonymity. However, in antiquity the question of the motives for Plato's silence was, it seems, never raised explicitly. At any rate, no testimony to

critics, while the second is attributed to him only by a minority (cf. G. Boas, "Fact and Legend in the Biography of Plato," *The Philosophical Review*, LVII [1948], pp. 439 ff., and for the later discussion, Friedländer, I², chap. XIII, pp. 249 ff.). Yet, as has already been stated by E. Zeller, *Die Philosophie d. Griechen*, II, I⁴ (1889), pp. 486 f., the assumption made in the letters of an oral teaching different from that of the dialogues is untenable in view of Aristotle's attitude toward Plato's writings. Reasons for the spuriousness of the letters in their entirety I hope to give in a forthcoming analysis of the seventh letter. A. E. Taylor (*Mind*, XLVIII [1909], p. 124, note) claims that what is said in the second letter is "both possible and natural in Plato's own mouth at a time when the *Philebus*, *Timaeus*, and *Laws*, and possibly the great 'dialectical' dialogues were unwritten. It is much more unlikely that a forger, with the whole series of Plato's works before him, should have thought of making such a remark" (cf. Harward, *op. cit.*, *ad* II, 314 c 1). But modern writers too, with the whole series of Plato's works before them, sometimes speak of his Socratic dialogues; concerning Aristotle who has done so, cf. below, note 37.

[16] According to Diogenes Laertius (III, 52), Plato's views are expounded by Socrates, Timaeus, the Athenian and the Eleatic Stranger, while false opinions are represented by Thrasymachus, Callicles, and other Sophists. Diogenes' discussion starts (51) with the problem of whether Plato is a dogmatist or a sceptic, that is, whether he writes to establish any positive teaching or merely refutes all opinions (cf. Sextus Empiricus, *Pyrrh. Hyp.*, I, 221, and Cicero, *Acad. Post.*, II, 74; also I, 16; 46). (Some held that Plato "employed a variety of terms in order to make his system less intelligible to the ignorant" [Diogenes Laertius, III, 63].) Quintilian (II, 15, 26) notes that Plato in the *Gorgias* "seems to indicate" (*videtur . . . significare*) through the mask of Socrates what he himself thinks. This sounds as if some critics, denying that Socrates was speaking for Plato, regarded the dialogues as historical. (Concerning specific identifications by the scholia, cf. below, note 37.) These are the testimonies with which I happen to be familiar; so far as I know, the evidence has never been systematically collected.

this effect is extant.[17] The solution of the riddle must be found without any authoritative guidance. One can aim only at a conjecture, the most likely hypothesis which one can derive from the Platonic work itself.

Now if one reads the dialogues with a view to the issue at stake, the most striking fact certainly is Plato's predilection for the use of the Socratic mask. In the greater number of his writings Socrates is the protagonist of the argument. It is therefore commonly held that gratitude for what he learned from his master made Plato attribute to Socrates the truth he himself had found. The dialogues are an offering to him who through his teaching and the example of his life and death had, to use Homer's words, removed the cloud from Plato's vision that he might clearly distinguish men and gods (*Iliad*, V, 127 f.; cf. *Alcibiades*, II, 150 D). That is why Socrates is time and again given the leading role; why the illusion is created that the philosophy taught is Socratic rather than Platonic; why he who had refrained from writing was enshrined in words that were to be read and re-read and thus was made the foremost teacher of all who strive for philosophical knowledge.[18]

In addition to this motive of personal gratitude, artistic reasons, one says, determined Plato's choice of Socrates as his

[17] Such an assumption appears to be contradicted by a scholion on *Epistulae* II, 314 B-C, printed in C. F. Hermann, *Platonis Dialogi*, VI (1902), p. 390, which says: "From this statement it becomes clear why Plato does not have any share in his dialogues" (cf. Friedländer, I[1], p. 152, note 2; the scholion is no longer quoted in this context at I[2], p. 39, but see I[2], p. 121, note 9). The scholion is not contained in G. C. Greene's edition of the *Scholia Platonica* (1938) based on the early manuscript tradition. It is taken from *e*, a codex of the 15th century (cf. Hermann, *Praefatio*, VI, pp. xxx ff.; also Bekker's *Praefatio* to his edition of Plato, IX [1826], p. 121; I, p. CII [Parisinus 2012]), as Professor Greene has pointed out to me. Since it is missing from Parisinus A (9th century) and O (Vaticanus I, 9th-10th century) to which *e* indirectly goes back—and Professor Greene was good enough to confirm this by checking the facsimiles of these manuscripts—it must be an interpolation in *e* itself (or in Laurentianus O, its immediate source, and in Professor Greene's opinion a 14th or 15th century manuscript). The view it represents, therefore, is definitely post-classical. I am much indebted to Professor Greene for clarifying the problem of the origin of the scholion.

[18] Cf. Zeller, *op. cit.*, II, 1[4], p. 578; also Friedländer, I[2], pp. 138 f., and Merlan, *op. cit.*, p. 425.

mouthpiece. If philosophy was to be represented as a dialogue, if there was to be one man to give unity to the disjointed arguments on various topics, Socrates was cast for such a role. He could well portray the philosopher superior to everyone else, the constant proponent of the right argument. He could be the ideal philosopher who represents the consistency of life and teaching, the identity of theory and practice, which the dialogues advocate. It would hardly have been gracious or fitting for Plato to invest himself with all the virtues—intellectual and moral—with which the protagonist of his conversations must be endowed if the desired effect of the dialogic movement of thought is to be produced, and the impact of a life lived in accordance with truth is to be conveyed to others.[19]

One cannot deny the weight of this argument. Plato's indebtedness to his teacher was certainly a decisive factor in his willingness to renounce his claims to the personal fame and recognition that would have been his had he declared himself to be the author of the truth. Once this basic decision was made —admittedly, the aesthetic considerations mentioned could come into play only afterwards—self-effacement before Socrates was natural. But one wonders whether such self-effacement does not presuppose a stronger emotional bond between him and Socrates than gratitude.[20] Mere gratitude for what he learned from Socrates, one feels, does not fully account for the fact that so great a philosopher as Plato should pretend to be merely transcribing the thoughts of another. Some interpreters, therefore, have compared Plato's relationship to Socrates with the discipleship of the Apostles for whom the Word had become flesh in their Master and who dedicated their lives to proclaiming His truth. Some have spoken of Plato's self-identification with Socrates.[21] Or as one has said—in a language more adequate

[19] Zeller, *op. cit.*, p. 579. In practice, if not in theory, such reasons as advanced by Zeller are taken into account by all interpreters, but he has emphasized them most strongly.

[20] The insufficiency of the motive of gratitude has been stressed by Friedländer, I[2], p. 139, cf. pp. 134 f.

[21] For the comparison of Plato with the Apostles cf. e.g. R. H. S. Crossman, *Plato Today* (1958), p. 73. It is stated by F. C. Baur, in his famous "Sokrates und Christus" (*Drei Abhandl. z. Gesch. d. alten Philosophie* [1876], pp. 321 ff.), in the following way: just as the Apostles recognized in Jesus' coming a turning point in the history of

perhaps to the world in which Plato lived—it was *eros* that bound him to Socrates, not merely the community of teaching and learning. Plato's yearning to see the ideal in bodily presence, so that he could more easily submit to it, found its fulfillment in the greatness of Socrates.[22]

That guidance toward knowledge is an essential part of Plato's theory of learning is true even though he is not unaware of the fact that man can also find his way by himself (*Symposium*, 211 B). But this initiation by an individual whom one loves would not, I think, make Plato's silence about himself more understandable. For, as he sees it, the true *eros*, kindled by the love of one person beautiful in body and in soul, does not end in such an experience and rest satisfied with it. The encounter with the other remains a decisive moment in one's life, a moment to be remembered, yet it is only a turning point, a point of passage on the road to be pursued. Rightly taught, man "will abate his violent love of the one, which he will despise and deem a small thing (σμικρὸν ἡγησάμενον), and will become a lover of all beautiful forms" (*Symposium*, 210 B); he will become a lover of institutions, laws, and all the sciences, contemplating "the vast sea of beauty" (D). The true order "of going, or being led by another, to the things of love, is to begin from the beauties of earth and mount upwards for the sake of that other beauty, using these as steps only" (211 B-C). Such are "the greater mysteries" of *eros* that follow upon "the lesser mysteries" (209 E-210 A).[23] For Plato there is no human being in whom the

mankind, so Plato recognized that with Socrates a new period in the history of human thought had begun and, again like the Apostles, dedicated his life to recording the unique and decisive event that he had witnessed. A self-identification of Plato with Socrates is assumed by A. Diès, *Autour de Platon*, I (1927), pp. 180 f. Sometimes Plato's attitude is likened to Dante's relationship to Beatrice (Friedländer, I[1], p. 159 [I[2], p. 144, the reference to Dante is omitted]); Goethe's "Marienbader Elegie" has also been compared (U. v. Wilamowitz, *Platon*, I [1919], p. 386).

[22] Cf. Friedländer, I[2], pp. 135-7; 139.

[23] Socrates, rejecting the *eros* of Alcibiades (216 C ff., cf. 222 A-B), is indirectly shown to adhere to the "greater mysteries" of Diotima. For this "Es-Dimension" of *eros*, see also Friedländer, I[2], p. 55. He insists on the importance of guidance even in Diotima's speech (p. 72). Yet in addition to *Symposium* 211 B already quoted (the alternative of "going or being led by another") cf. also 210 D: φαῦλος . . καὶ σμικρολόγος,

truth has become flesh, no one to whom one must or should surrender one's individuality. He does not know of any self-effacement before a master, or of any self-identification with him, that would issue in the proclamation of a faith. The Platonic *eros* requires that man reach out for a goal that lies far beyond what an individual can give him, or what can be found in him.[24]

I see no reason to think that Plato's was not such an *eros*. That he believed he owed much to Socrates, that he was convinced he had found the truth with his help, one will readily assume.[25] That his admiration for his teacher was rooted in an erotic friendship, one can neither deny nor affirm. Plato maintains silence also about his coming under the influence of Socrates, the event which probably marked his conversion to philosophy.[26] But this much is certain: love for his teacher in

and cf. *Symposium* 210 B with *Phaedo* 91 C: σμικρὸν φροντίσαντες (referred to below, p. 17).

[24] The same conclusion follows from a consideration of Plato's attitude toward truth and authority; cf. below, pp. 16 f. That those Platonists of the Renaissance who imagined "a love which reaches the divine without abandoning the human" were reading into Plato's *Symposium* the tradition which originated in the later middle ages, has been pointed out by C. S. Lewis, *The Allegory of Love* (1958), chap. I, p. 5.

[25] I refrain from arguing about Friedländer's intimation that there was a feeling of insufficiency in Plato, a belief that in his generation Socrates' greatness was no longer equalled (I^1, p. 149; the assertion is more cautiously phrased at I^2, pp. 135 f., 338, note 4). Others have found in the *Phaedo* (78 A) an indication of Plato's conviction that he was destined to carry out Socrates' philosophical dreams; cf. also Crossman, *op. cit.*, p. 78, cf. 72.

[26] Plato's name is mentioned in the *Apology* (34 A; 38 B) and in the *Phaedo* (59 B). None of these passages betrays his feelings about Socrates (for the statement in the *Phaedo*, cf. J. Burnet, *Plato's Phaedo* [1937], *ad loc.*). That the same is true of the reference to Socrates in the seventh letter (324 E), Friedländer has noted (I^2, p. 138). His interpretation of Plato's relationship to Socrates is therefore based on Alcibiades' speech in the *Symposium* and on the *Theages* (pp. 137 f.) which Plato, in his opinion, could not have written had he not experienced this *eros*. Friedländer adds that in the Athens of the fifth century every friendship between men involved "the power of the great Daimon" (p. 137). The latter assumption I shall not venture to argue. But it seems certain to me that so great a writer and poet as Plato could understand and depict also what he had not experienced. Recent authors often state it as a fact that Plato shared the preference for homosexual relations (e.g. A. D. Winspear, *The Genesis of Plato's*

whatever form it manifested itself does not on Plato's terms account for what it is supposed to explain.

More important still, it appears to follow from what has been said that the usual interpretation of Platonic anonymity lays too much stress on personal feelings of gratitude and affection. Alone, they hardly provide a secure basis for the hypothesis sought. Other considerations seem to confirm such a conclusion. How would Plato have justified the fact that he felt at liberty to impute to Socrates a philosophy entirely alien to him? As tradition has it, Socrates, on hearing Plato read the *Lysis*, exclaimed: "By Heracles, what a number of lies this young man is telling about me," for, as Diogenes Laertius adds (III, 35), "he has included in the dialogue much that Socrates never said." The anecdote most likely is apocryphal, yet the charge it makes is warranted. Against the objection that he is distorting reality, Plato could hardly have defended himself by pleading gratitude, and adding that he was writing with the license of a poet. No doubt, his dialogues are a kind of poetry.[27] But if he had no better answer, one might venture to think that those Socratics showed their gratitude in a more convincing and more humble manner who made it their business to put down for posterity the actual words and deeds of Socrates.

Perhaps the riddle can be brought nearer its solution by an historical parallel that so far has not been considered in the debate on Plato's anonymity. For although, as I pointed out at the very beginning, an insistence on one's originality, on one's own opinions, is prevalent in Preplatonic philosophy, the masking of one's thought is certainly not to be found in Plato alone.

Thought [1956[2]], p. 243, quoting as evidence *Symposium* 184 C, the speech of Pausanias). Plato of course speaks of homosexuality quite openly, as a Greek would; he sometimes praises and sometimes condemns it (the passages have been collected by Zeller, *op. cit.*, II, 1[4], pp. 887 f.). I do not see how one can draw any conclusions concerning Plato himself from the evidence preserved, or that it would be of any importance if one could, except perhaps for the biography of Plato. Even for this purpose, however, it would be necessary to know how he reacted to his feelings. Socrates, it is said, had overcome through reason the passions one was able to read in his face (e.g. Cicero, *Tusc. Disput.*, IV, 37, 80).

[27] Cf. e.g. Aristotle, *Poetics*, 1447 b 11, and for the ancient testimony, A. Brandis, *Handb. d. Gesch. d. Griech.-Röm. Philos.*, II, 1 (1844), pp. 154 ff.

The so-called Pythagoreans, too, attributed their own truth to their master, Pythagoras, and set aside their own aspirations to glory, regarding it as right to do so. According to Aristoxenus (Iamblichus, *De Vita Pythagorica*, 198—58 [45] D6 [Diels-Kranz]), it was held to be "fair" (καλόν) among them "to dedicate everything to Pythagoras and to ascribe it to him (cf. *op. cit.*, 158), and to claim no fame of one's own (δόξαν ἰδίαν) for one's discoveries, or at any rate rarely." And the same practice is presupposed in another testimony concerning the members of the school (*De Vita Pythagorica*, 87) which seems to go back to Aristotle's lost essay *On the Pythagoreans*.[28]

That Plato may have been influenced by the Pythagorean example is not improbable. He was familiar with their "manner of life" (*Republic*, X, 600 B) and favorably disposed toward Pythagoreanism. This one may assert, without reopening the much disputed question of Plato's relation to the Pythagoreans. It seems, therefore, worthwhile to inquire how they justified their "fair" deception, their disclaimer of fame, and whether their justification could not also be Plato's.[29]

As Aristotle states, the Pythagoreans affirmed that "what they say is true" (καὶ ἃ λέγουσιν αὐτοί, ἀληθῆ εἶναι [*De Vita Pythagorica*, 87]). In other words, they held that since Pythagoras too had been concerned with discovering the truth, it seemed to them permissible to make him the spokesman of their truth, a truth they had found by carrying out his intentions and by following his approach to the study of philosophical problems. For, in their opinion, Pythagoras had been the first mathematician and the first to develop the mathematical method which they considered fundamental for all philosophizing.[30] Again, Aristoxenus, before mentioning that the Pythagoreans considered it fair to remain anonymous, states that neither wish for gain nor love of honor (φιλοτιμίαν) "should become the cause

[28] Cf. E. Frank, *Aristotle's Testimony on Pythagoras and the Pythagoreans*, ed. by Emma J. Edelstein (to be published 1962), Commentary on Fr. XI.

[29] Even those who are critical of the tendency to link too closely Platonism and Pythagoreanism (cf. e. g. G. M. A. Grube, *Plato's Thought* [1958], Appendix I), do not deny a Pythagorean influence on Plato's philosophy (p. 4). In the interpretation of the Pythagorean testimony here to be considered, I follow E. Frank, *op. cit.*

[30] Cf. E. Frank, *Plato u. d. sogen. Pythagoreer* (1923), *passim*.

for dissension; rather should all Pythagoreans behave toward one another as a good father behaves toward his children" (*De Vita Pythagorica*, 198). Another piece of evidence that cannot be dated exactly, but which is quite in agreement with the sentiment underlying the testimony of Aristoxenus, puts the matter thus: "The Pythagoreans set friendship and an harmonious life as the aim of their whole philosophy . . . they welcomed sharing the discovery of their teaching, and the writings of one of them (ἑνός) were considered to be the common property of all (κοινὰ πάντων [Proclus, *In Timaeum*, I, p. 15, 26 ff., Diehl])."[31]

It is, then, an ethos of research that caused the Pythagoreans not to speak in their own name. Those engaged in the intellectual venture form a community—they cooperate with one another; only thus can the envisaged goal be reached. In view of this fact the individual who makes a particular discovery is insignificant. The common cause of finding the truth is far more important than any personal feeling of vainglory. On the other hand, it would seem almost necessary that the Pythagoreans attribute their results to him who had opened for them the road to knowledge. Certainly, they could not exclude their teacher from the truth all men of learning have in common. The resulting distortion of historical reality is a "fair" deception because it expresses an ideal reality. In addition, it attests the Pythagoreans' gratitude to their master and also their allegiance to the philosopher whose pupils and successors they are proud to be.[32]

Now it goes without saying that Plato would feel at one with Socrates in the desire for truth, and one does not have to give elaborate proof of the fact that in his philosophical endeavor he thought he was continuing the method of Socratic investigation. Besides, the dialogues cry out against man's self-seeking, against the longing of the human heart for self-gratification and self-assertion. The lover of honor and distinction (τὸν φιλόνικόν τε καὶ φιλότιμον) is the first of "the inferior types" of men

[31] The comparison of the teacher with the father is characteristic of Pythagorean doctrine, cf. L. Edelstein, *The Hippocratic Oath*, *Supplements to the Bulletin of the History of Medicine*, I (1943), pp. 43 f.

[32] It is perhaps not without significance that in the *Phaedo*, where one has always found traces of a Pythagorean influence, Socrates is once named the father of his pupils (116 A) and insight is called "a good which belongs in common" (63 D).

(*Republic,* VIII, 545 A). To stamp out self-love, not to seek one's own, to share everything with others, to make all things common property, is the highest aim of moral life.[33] Does this not imply that in his research too, the individual should not strive for his own glory, as the Pythagoreans put it, that instead of insisting on his claim to truth, he should share it with his friends and, to use again the words of the Pythagoreans, make it common property? Thus Plato, if asked why he had made Socrates speak for him, could well have given an explanation similar to that proffered by the Pythagoreans, and could have justified the masking of his thought as they did theirs.

One must admit that Platonic anonymity is more striking than Pythagorean anonymity in so far as Plato is a more original philosopher than are the Pythagoreans. One cannot deny that his feeling of indebtedness to Socrates has a ring of sincerity and realism compared with which the gratitude of the Pythagoreans to their "teacher," who had lived long before their time, seems abstract and artificial.[34] Yet, in principle, Plato's procedure is the same as that followed by the so-called Pythagoreans. And an ethos of research like theirs provides an objective frame of reference for the explanation of Plato's self-effacement, and legitimates the undertones of personal gratitude as well as the artistic considerations influential in the choice of Socrates as his mouthpiece.[35]

[33] Cf. e.g. Plato's indictment of an "individualization" (*ἰδίωσις*) of feeling (*Republic,* V, 462 B [VIII, 547 B *ἰδιώσασθαι*], uttered in connection with his advocacy of "communism" (cf. 416 D), and the statement of the *Laws* (V, 731 D ff.) that "of all faults the gravest is one . . . conveyed in the maxim that 'every one is naturally his own friend' and that it is only right and proper that he should be so . . . whereas a man who means to be great must care neither for self nor for its belongings, but for justice, whether exhibited in his own conduct, or rather in that of another." Plato also quotes the *κοινὰ τὰ φίλων* (*Republic,* IV, 424 A; V, 449 C; *Laws,* 739 C *ἴδια . . . κοινὰ ἁμῇ γέ πῃ γεγονέναι*). Love of honor and distinction is to be rejected by the virtuous man (*Republic,* I, 347 B [*οὐ . . . φιλότιμον*]; cf. *Phaedrus,* 256 C). For *Symposium,* 208 C-D cf. below, p. 19.

[34] That the followers of Pythagoras wrote no dialogues, but treatises under the name of their master, or appended their views, as explanations, to his sayings (cf. e.g. Iamblichus, *De Vita Pythagorica,* 198 f.) is a difference that can safely be neglected in my context.

[35] According to Crossman, Plato does not distinguish between himself and Socrates also because any such distinction would have seemed

However, the hypothesis I have proposed concerning Platonic anonymity explains only half of the problem, and the lesser half I am afraid. For stranger still than Plato's use of the Socratic mask is the fact that it is not through Socrates alone that he conveys his thought. Not all the dialogues are Socratic dialogues, at least not to the same degree. In the *Timaeus*, the *Sophist*, and the *Politicus* Socrates merely listens to what others have to say. It is true that even when he is not speaking he may still be said to dominate the scene because, his silence notwithstanding, his very presence provides the standard by which everything is to be measured.[36] Nevertheless, one cannot deny that Socrates here plays a role very different from that which he has in the *Phaedo* or in the *Republic*, or in any of the dialogues where he investigates the case at hand. Moreover, in the *Laws*, he is given no part at all. Whatever Plato's motivation for depriving Socrates of his usual place in the setting of the dialogues, he can altogether dismiss him from the conversation.[37] And yet even when Socrates is not his protagonist, even when he is absent, Plato does not himself appear on the stage. Instead he invents imaginary figures—a Pythagorean philosopher, Timaeus,

unreal to him in view of the fact that "reason and truth are not the trappings of individual personalities; they are eternal and universal, and in them individual differences disappear" (*Plato Today*, pp. 72 f.). Though this characterization of the Platonic concept of truth and reason is quite correct (cf. below, note 45), it does not explain why Plato speaks above all through Socrates, as do the motives which the Pythagorean parallel suggests.

[36] Cf. Friedländer, I², pp. 141 f.

[37] Cicero, *De Legibus*, I, 5, 15 and the scholia on the *Laws* (A, *hypothesis*) identify the Athenian Stranger with Plato, the scholia for the reason that the Stranger admits to the authorship of two constitutions (cf. 739 A-E), the *Laws* and the *Republic*. Aristotle on the other hand speaks about "all the Socratic dialogues" (*Politics*, 1265 a 11) and then quotes a passage from the *Laws*. One has asked whether he talks carelessly or whether he deliberately identifies the Stranger with Socrates (W. D. Ross, *Aristotle's Metaphysics*, I [1924], p. XL). If the latter is the case, he might have interpreted the reference to another constitution as suggesting not the author of the *Republic* but the main speaker, Socrates. If Plato intended such an identification, one could only say that at the end of his life even Socrates became for him nameless. I side with those who believe that Socrates is not mentioned in the *Laws* because the subject and its treatment forbade his participation, cf. Friedländer, II (1930), p. 625 (see also I², p. 140, note 8).

a stranger from Elea, an Athenian citizen—and attributes his philosophy to them. Thus he always preserves his anonymity, but conceals himself in various ways, just as he retains the dialogue form in all his works, although he gives it many variations.

This use of many masks constitutes a unique feature of Platonic anonymity. The Pythagoreans always speak through the mouth of their master; they never speak through anyone else. And surely for an attitude such as the one taken by Plato the motive provided by the Pythagorean example fails to suffice. One can hardly assume that he credited imaginary characters with the truth in order to illustrate the conviction that all seekers after knowledge are engaged in a common enterprise. Still less would gratitude to Socrates have prevented him from speaking in his own name at the moment at which Socrates is not present or listens to the discourse of figures of Plato's invention. On these occasions he might well have "taken the word" himself as Aristotle was to do in his dialogues.[38] Nor are aesthetic demands inherent in the technique of the dialogue any longer relevant. For the argument has lost its unity; it is developed by different personalities. The interlocutors Plato creates certainly do not embody an identity of thought and action, of theoretical and practical life.[39] In short, there must be other reasons why Plato never lifts the veil of anonymity, reasons that may give a different coloring also to those which he shares with the Pythagoreans.

The nature of this peculiarly Platonic argument for renouncing one's claims to originality is, I think, suggested first by the manner in which Socrates' relationship to the truth is viewed in the dialogues. Plato's Socrates is unwilling to accept any statement on the authority of a great name; only if reason approves of it is it to be regarded as convincing (*Phaedrus*, 270 C). "We must not honor a man above truth, but . . . speak our minds" (*Republic*, X, 595 C), he maintains when opposing

[38] Friedländer says with regard to the *Laws* "Sich selbst einzuführen wäre für Platon gegen sein tiefstes Gesetz gewesen" (II, p. 625), but this "inner law" is certainly not adequately defined by any of the reasons usually given for Plato's silence.

[39] Cf. above, pp. 7 f.

others.[40] And he insists that those who converse with him take the same attitude with regard to his arguments: "But you, if you do as I ask, will give little thought (σμικρὸν φροντίσαντες) to Socrates and much more to the truth; and if you think what I say is true, agree to it, and if not, oppose me with every argument you can muster, that I may not in my eagerness deceive myself and you alike and go away, like a bee, leaving my sting sticking in you" (*Phaedo,* 91 C). To object to Socrates, he knows, is easy; to object to the truth, difficult (*Symposium,* 201 C). Thus the dialogues always divert attention from the person of Socrates and direct it to the truth; they always appeal not to his authority but rather to the strength of his argument. The name of Socrates obviously counts for little.[41] It is consistent with such a view—and another indication of Plato's concept of truth and of writing about truth—that when he gives the leading role in discussions of great importance to strangers from Elea and from Athens, he even allows them to remain nameless. Who they are, their identity, apparently is of no significance compared with the validity of their reasoning. Truth has nothing in common with names, one might say.

Why this is the case is explained, I think, by Plato's views on "the progress of the soul" toward knowledge. As he sees it, men are condemned to live with their eyes directed toward the shadows cast by the light rather than toward the light itself, and to mistake the shadows for reality. The first step in the process of their liberation is their "conversion," the turning of their necks, that makes them look in the direction where truth can be discovered. Were the world perfect—early training and

[40] On this passage which states the Platonic ethos most succinctly, cf. P. Shorey in his edition of the *Republic,* and *What Plato Said* (1957), *ad loc.* The Platonic spirit is preserved in the proverb *Amicus Plato, sed magis amica veritas* (cf. Aristotle, *Nicomachean Ethics,* 1096 a 16), not in the assertion that one would rather err with Plato than be right with Epicurus (Cicero, *Tusc. Disput.,* I, 17, 39).

[41] This verdict on Socrates and the truth obviously agrees with the Platonic concept of *eros* (cf. above, pp. 8 f.), and sharply contrasts with the attitude of the Pythagoreans. When they ascribe their newly won insight to their master, they make him the discoverer and possessor of all truth and represent him as the authority to be acknowledged. To them he is all-knowing, just as the allegorical interpretaton of Homer credits the poet with all knowledge (cf. the famous Pythagorean Αὐτὸς ἔφα, and also Iamblichus, *De Vita Pythagorica,* 158).

later education through the so-called sciences properly administered—dialectic would gently draw forth "the eye of the soul . . . sunk in the barbaric slough of the Orphic myth" (*Republic*, VII, 533 C), and lead it upward. As the world is, the first thing one has to learn through elenctic, and learns reluctantly, is that he is filled with error. It is an experience hard to bear, and one which, if accepted, humiliates him and shows him the worthlessness of what has been a source of pride for him—his opinions and judgments of things. But an unexamined life will never become a life worth living.[42]

When man has put away illusions and prejudices, he "finds" the truth. To speak in mythological terms: he remembers it; he knew the truth before he was born; it has always been with him, he has but forgotten it. To speak in more philosophical terms: he has failed to grasp the truth and to lay hold on it. Man merely acknowledges its being "there" and distinguishes it from falsehood, be it in the dialogue with others or in the dialogue within his own soul which constitutes thinking; he says yes or no, accepting what is true and rejecting what is false (*Theaetetus*, 189 E-190 A).[43] For truth is something outside of him. It is not made or invented; it is merely seen and recognized for what it is; it has independent existence. It masters man rather than being mastered by him.[44]

[42] This is asserted in the *Apology* (38 A) as well as in the *Sophist* (230 D). No matter how much the late dialogues may differ from the earlier ones, the principle of cross-examination prevails throughout.

[43] The phrase "dialogue within the soul" occurs only in *Theaetetus*, 189 E, and *Sophist*, 263 E. But it is only the later terminological formulation of a method which, from the first, determines the Socratic-Platonic dialogue with others. The "recourse to *logoi*," the "second voyage" (*Phaedo*, 99 D ff.), implies that in each case one regards as true what agrees with the assumed thesis and rejects what is not in accord with it.

[44] For speech or reason as personified, cf. Shorey, *What Plato Said*, p. 500 (*ad Protagoras* 361 A-B) and Friedländer, I², pp. 114 f. (*Theaetetus*, 173 C ["We are not the servants of the logos"], though expressing also the opinion of Socrates, merely states the fact that unlike the orator, the philosopher is not obliged to cut short his argument.) For Plato's concept of "seeing the truth" cf. Friedländer, I², pp. 86 f. I do not of course mean to say that Plato is the first to depersonalize the process of thinking. The "Word" of Heraclitus is identical with the law of the world (Friedländer, p. 114) and, as H. Cherniss reminds me, when Parmenides presents his philosophy as the teaching he received from the goddess, he also "objectifies" the truth.

Since truth comes to man in his humility and is not his truth, he who has discovered it has no claim on it, nor can he take pride in it. He can also no longer desire "to become known by name" (τοῦ ὀνομαστοὶ γενέσθαι) and to acquire everlasting fame (*Symposium*, 208 C). Such fame, and remembrance of oneself, is sought because man is longing for the immortal (τοῦ γὰρ ἀθανάτου ἐρῶσιν D-E). But having come to the end of the road, having reached knowledge, the aim of all love and desire (πρὸς τέλος ἤδη ἰὼν τῶν ἐρωτικῶν 210 E), he has gained that for which he has striven: he is in possession of the eternal, he lives in its contemplation (211 D); therefore, if anyone is immortal, it is he (212 A).[45] This is the reward for his trials and his labor, for his working "like a slave" to win knowledge (*Republic*, VI, 494 D).

How then could he be anxious to speak or write in his own name when telling others about his discoveries? To make much of himself might even persuade them to believe that they are being told personal opinions rather than truth itself; to make much of a name might induce them to ponder on the author rather than on what he has to say. In the *Phaedrus*, after Socrates has reported to his young friend the story he once heard about the King of Egypt, the god Thamus, who chided the god Theuth for inventing the art of writing and thus providing for man "the appearance of wisdom, not true wisdom," "an elixir not of memory, but of reminding" (275 A), Phaedrus exclaims: "Socrates, you easily make up stories of Egypt or any country you please" (275 B). Whereupon Socrates retorts: "They used to say, my friend, that the words of the oak in the holy place of Zeus at Dodona were the first prophetic utterances. The people of that time, not being so wise as you young folks, were content in their simplicity to hear an oak or

[45] However different the Platonic *eros* may be from Christian *Agape*, it too "seeketh not its own," it is not egocentric as is sometimes said (A. Nygren, *Agape and Eros*, I[2] [1941], pp. 137 f. where *Symposium*, 204 E and 208 D are quoted but 210 E and 212 A are not considered). What Plato means to express by his concept of philosophical *eros* undoubtedly is also that the truth of things is not their individual, but their universal character, that man's true existence lies not in the individuality that separates him from others, in his physical nature, but rather in reason which he shares with all men (cf. above, note 35). But this is not all he has to say, as is clear from the *Symposium*.

a rock, provided only it spoke the truth; but to you, perhaps, it makes a difference who the speaker is and where he comes from, for you do not consider only whether his words are true or not" (275 B-C).[46]

One may then well understand that Plato does not refrain from hiding behind a nameless speaker and that he distinguishes between Socrates and the truth for which he stands. Philosophy has nothing in common with names because it is not man but reason that speaks through philosophy. "Whithersoever the argument leads, one must go, just as the boat is carried by the wind" (*Republic*, III, 394 D).[47] To be sure, the individual must make an effort to descry the truth. He does not succeed all by himself. Many men have labored to fashion the knowledge which brings the boat to the end of its voyage. Remembering this, Plato is willing to ascribe the successful outcome to him from whom he learned, thereby expressing his gratitude for the help received from others. Still he never forgets that even the greatest philosopher and the most saintly man is merely the spokesman for a truth that is greater and nobler than he is himself. Such it would seem must be the conjecture which would explain Platonic anonymity in all its aspects.[48] And thus understood, Plato's silence not only betrays personal feelings and experiences, but has, I think, an important meaning for the adequate reading of his work.

For the dialogue form, more than any other form of philosophical communication, accentuates the fact that the truth is found through human beings and not through an impersonal process of reasoning. He who reads these conversations is asked to relive the argument within himself and make it his own. But bewitched as one is by the beauty of the world which Plato's

[46] H. N. Fowler, *Plato*, I (The Loeb Classical Library, 1919).

[47] P. Shorey takes this passage and similar ones to mean that Plato's "*dramatis personae* affect to follow whither the argument blows" (*The Unity of Plato's Thought* [1903], p. 5). To me it would seem that the metaphor of the *Republic* is indicative of Plato's earnest conviction that the investigator is at the mercy of the argument.

[48] Formulating the hypothesis in this manner, I am thinking of the Platonic work as a whole. It is quite possible, nay, probable, that starting with the Pythagorean example in mind, Plato in the course of time modified the principle of anonymity as he modified also the technique of the dialogue (cf. *Theaetetus*, 143 B-C).

genius has conjured up, by the brilliance with which he has endowed those whom he has speak, one loses oneself in the human world. There is danger that one forget about truth itself—about that "nature of wondrous beauty" which "in the first place is everlasting, not growing and decaying, or waxing and waning; secondly, not fair in one point of view and foul in another, or at one time or in one relation or at one place fair, at another time or in another relation or at another place foul, as if fair to some and foul to others, or in the likeness of a face or hands or any other part of the bodily frame, or in any form of speech or knowledge, or existing in any other being, as for example, in an animal, or in heaven, or on earth, or in any other place; but beauty absolute, separate, simple, and everlasting, which without diminution and without increase or any change, is imparted to the ever-growing and perishing beauties of all other things" (*Symposium*, 211 A-B).[49] Remaining silent about himself—the author, the human vessel of the truth—Plato eloquently directs the reader to the light of true being which here on earth is broken into the spectrum of individual existence—to that truth which is absolute, not relative. In this way Platonic anonymity symbolizes the objective element in his philosophy, the universality of reason, and is the ever-present correlative and corrective of its personal and subjective—or as one has come to call it, its existential—element, which is symbolized by the human dialogue, the "philosophizing together."[50]

Perhaps it will seem exaggerated to give so much significance to Platonic anonymity. Must it not be admitted, after all that has been said, that this anonymity is a pretense, a useless and meaningless fiction? Was it not known that the dialogues were the work of Plato? And was it not necessary that in the Academy, in the intellectual exchange between him and his associates, Plato took responsibility for what he said? Whether

[49] B. Jowett, *The Dialogues of Plato*, I[3] (1892).

[50] For the existentialist interpretation of Plato, cf. E. Frank, "The Fundamental Opposition of Plato and Aristotle," *A. J. P.*, LXI (1940), pp. 35 f. and 39 f.; Merlan (above, p. 3); and now Friedländer, I[2], pp. 243 ff. I am, of course, far from minimizing the importance of the existential element; my intention is merely to emphasize the corresponding importance of the objective factor. Both have to be taken into account if justice is to be done to the interrelationship of form and content in Plato's work.

he "lectured" on the Good or merely participated in the discussions that were going on, it was he who spoke, and he spoke in his own name.[51] In his daily existence, in the imperfection of this world, even the philosopher cannot live the insight which reason teaches. However, it is just for this reason, I venture to suggest, that Plato wanted to realize the truth "as far as possible" in the ideal philosophical life which the dialogues describe. His anonymity, myth or fiction that it is, is the "voluntary lie" that the good man has the courage to tell to himself as well as to others.[52] It reminds him and them of the fact, hard to grasp and even harder to understand, that what men consider their most personal and precious accomplishment is least theirs; that their life is not an isolated fragment, but part of a cosmos; that truth has been, is, and will ever be, regardless of whether or not men turn their eyes toward it and live according to its dictates.

LUDWIG EDELSTEIN.

[51] Friedländer (I², p. 134, note 3) doubts that there were any Platonic *Lehrschriften*; Cherniss suspects the reliability of the preserved reports concerning Plato's lecture on the Good (*The Riddle of the Early Academy*, pp. 13 ff.). Granted that the doubts and suspicions are justified, Plato can hardly have failed to discuss his philosophy with the members of the Academy and thus must "have given himself away." Such conversations would be "the very little" or "rarely," mentioned in the testimony on the Pythagoreans (cf. above, p. 12), the few occasions on which they too spoke in their own name.

[52] Cf. *Republic*, VII, 535 D-E; also II, 382 C ff., and Shorey's notes on these passages in his edition and translation of the *Republic*.

VII.—The Rôle of Eryximachus in Plato's *Symposium*

LUDWIG EDELSTEIN

THE JOHNS HOPKINS UNIVERSITY

The intention of this paper is to show that Plato's representation of Eryximachus is not a caricature of the physician; that Eryximachus plays an important rôle in the framework of the dialogue and that there is a relationship between the position given to him and the contents of the *Symposium*.

Among the speakers at the banquet that brought together Agathon, Socrates and Alcibiades (172A–B), Eryximachus is the representative of the medical art. There is almost general agreement among modern interpreters that Plato, in representing him, has drawn an ironical portrait of the pedantic expert and scientist. When once it was claimed that "nowhere in literature do we have such a charming picture illustrating the position of the cultivated physician in society as that given in Plato's Dialogues of Eryximachus," Gildersleeve retorted that Eryximachus was a pedant, a system-monger "who was only on sufferance in that brilliant company and whom Plato holds up to ridicule as incorporating the worst foibles of the professor of the healing art."[1] Most other criticisms have been in more or less the same vein.

This common verdict on Eryximachus is not restricted to details of Plato's portrayal. Wherever he appears on the stage, it is claimed, he is ridiculed as a pedant.[2] Even before he contributes his share to the contest of speeches on Eros, he is said to show his pedantry. Unable to forget his professional solemnity, he seizes every opportunity to display his medical knowledge: when he is first mentioned, he immediately delivers a lecture on μέθη (176C–D); later on he discourses on λύγξ (185D–E).[3] This censure is hardly justified. Eryximachus' first intervention is due to Pausanias' complaint that he is still weak from yesterday's bout and to his

[1] *AJPh* 30 (1909) 109. The statement is made in answer to W. Osler, *Counsels and Ideals* (Boston and New York, 1905) 24.

[2] Cf. U. v. Wilamowitz-Moellendorff, *Platon* I (3rd edition [Berlin, 1929]) 367: "Der Sprecher . . . soll unfreiwillig komisch wirken, wo immer er auftritt . . ."; cf. *ibid.* 361: "Der Arzt hat hier die Rolle des Pedanten."

[3] Cf. R. G. Bury, *The Symposium of Plato* (Cambridge, 1909) xxviii; A. Hug and H. Schöne, *Symposion* (*Platons Ausgewählte Schriften* 5 [3rd edition, Leipzig and Berlin, 1909]) xxxviii and 61, note 3.

request that the company consider how one could make today's drinking easy (176A). After Aristophanes has supported this wish for ease in drinking (176B) Eryximachus takes the platform. He inquires whether Agathon too finds himself not exactly in "good condition," and since this is admitted, and the other guests are not great drinkers anyhow (176B–C), he proceeds to state that excess in drinking is harmful and that he would advise against it, especially for those who are still somewhat heavy-headed (176D).[4] Advice has been sought, and who should be better prepared to give counsel than the physician who can rely on his medical experience? Does not the question asked clearly concern medicine?[5] Again, in proposing a cure for hiccoughs (185D–E), Eryximachus does not intrude on the company with his medical lore. It is not he who has brought up the subject. Aristophanes has turned to him because he thinks that the physician is the man to tell him how to stop his hiccoughs; Eryximachus only gives the advice for which he has been consulted. By making Eryximachus act as a physician whenever the occasion calls for medical opinion, Plato can hardly have intended to satirize him.

But even in his speech on Eros, Eryximachus talks as a physician. To this ancestor of Molière's Diafoirus, Robin claims,[6] everything in the world appears within the infinitely enlarged compass of his art. His oration is marred by pedantic mannerisms: "If Eryximachos is allowed to take up his parable," Gildersleeve contends,[7] "it is because Plato wished to let his humor play on the weak sides of the profession."

There is no gainsaying the assertion that Eryximachus loves to

[4] Eryximachus is not cut short by Phaedrus, as Hug-Schöne (see note 3) 21, note 2, maintain. He gives his counsel and has said all that he intended to say when he has finished.

[5] This is acknowledged in Phaedrus' words: *ἄττ' ἂν περὶ ἰατρικῆς λέγῃς* (176D). Physicians of the fourth century, not only philosophers like Antisthenes and Aristotle (cf. Hug-Schöne [see note 3] xxxviii, note 8), wrote on drunkenness and symposia; e.g. Mnesitheus (Athenaeus 11, p. 483f = Fr. 45 [H. Hohenstein, *Der Arzt Mnesitheus aus Athen*, Diss. Berlin, 1935]) and, in later times, Heraclides of Tarentum, Fr. 24 (K. Deichgräber, *Die griechische Empirikerschule* [Berlin, 1930]). Discussions of the influence of wine on men's health are also to be found in Hippocrates and Diocles; cf. Diocles, Fr. 141 (M. Wellmann, *Die Fragmente der sikelischen Ärzte* [Berlin, 1901]), and the parallels there given. Diocles recommends drinking *πρὸς ἡδονήν* (182, 1.2). The same expression is used in the *Symposium* (176E).

[6] L. Robin, *Le Banquet* (Platon, *Oeuvres Complètes*, 4.2 [Paris, 1929] Collection Budé) LII.

[7] *AJPh* 30 (1909) 109.

speak of medicine. Indeed, he begins his discourse with a dissertation on the medical art in order to pay homage to his profession, as he himself adds (186B). This, however, is not a sign of conceit on the part of the artisan; it simply shows a natural respect for his calling. Agathon too puts his art first, and in honoring poetry in this way, he expressly refers to the example of Eryximachus (196D).[8] Nor does Eryximachus give undue attention to his specialty. His analysis of medicine (186B–E) is shorter than his analysis of music (187A–E). To be sure, after having proved that Eros holds sway over medicine, he comes back to his art twice in order to elucidate certain points by comparison (187C; E), and once he speaks of health and disease when discussing the influence of Eros on the seasons of the year (188A–B). Such references, like the diction of his speech, clearly denote him as a medical man.[9] But after all, Eryximachus is a physician, and Plato apparently is interested in bringing out the typical characteristics of each speaker as well as the individual features of their personalities. Thus, in the speeches of Aristophanes and Agathon he uses motifs and stylistic devices that indicate the vocation of the two poets.[10] Aristophanes is pictured as "the very genius of the old comedy." He is "ready to laugh and make laugh before he opens his mouth, just as Socrates, true to his character, is ready to argue before he begins to speak."[11] The fact that Eryximachus talks like a physician, therefore, does

[8] Robin (see note 6) 24, note 2, concludes from the fact that Eryximachus discusses medicine first that for him it is *the* art. This judgment, in my opinion, is not justified because it does not take account of the motivation adduced by Plato. For another statement of Eryximachus that might be construed in Robin's sense, cf. below p. 89.

[9] A. E. Taylor, *Plato* (New York, 1936) 217, rightly says: "The style of the speech is appropriately sober, free from the artifices of rhetoric and marked by a plentiful use of professional terminology." Bury (see note 3) xxix notes the plainness of the oration and its lack of ornament but adds that its monotony (the recurrence of the same formulae) "marks it as the product of a pedantic, would-be scientific mind in which literary taste is but slightly developed and the ruling interest is the schematization of physical doctrines." Were such an evaluation made universal, many a great scientist, I am afraid, and even many a Greek scientist, would have to be classified as a pedant. P. Friedländer, *Platon* 2 (Berlin and Leipzig, 1930) 304, suggests that by emphasizing the pedantry of the arrangement Plato satirizes the style of certain Hippocratic writings. Could he not simply have imitated this style in order to give to Eryximachus' words their native color?

[10] For Aristophanes, cf. Bury (see note 3) xxx; Friedländer (see note 9) 306 ff.; for Agathon, cf. Bury xxxvi; B. Jowett, *The Dialogues of Plato* 1 (3rd edition [New York and London, 1892]) 531.

[11] Jowett (see note 10) 530.

not yet make him a pedant, and to those who interpret his medical air as a caricature of the expert, Eryximachus might well answer, as Aristophanes answered the physician when he blamed the comic poet for his buffoonery: I am not afraid to speak in this manner, for this is "the custom of my Muse" (189B).

On the other hand, if Eryximachus is reproached for "the dogmatism of his profession in trying to make good his pedantic correction of his predecessors,"[12] one should point out that the other speakers are dogmatic too. All of them give their opinions for what they are worth.[13] Besides, he is not the only one to detect the shortcomings of his rivals. Pausanias is dissatisfied with the speech of Phaedrus (180C); Aristophanes criticizes Eryximachus and Pausanias (189C); Agathon believes that his method of praising Eros is the correct one, while that of all the previous speakers was bad (194E); and Socrates charges that nobody so far has told the truth (198D). Moreover, if Eryximachus' argumentation seems a nuance too pedantic, this didacticism may have been intentional and meant to amuse himself and the rest of the company. The banquet is not a solemn affair. Those who are present are determined to have their fun; they indulge in jests and merrymaking, Aristophanes no more than Socrates and all the others.[14] At any rate, Eryximachus is quite capable of rising to the occasion. He defines medicine as the knowledge of separating fair love from foul (186C); he holds that Eros is the god who guides the work of the farmer and of the trainer (186E). Such ideas are fanciful and whimsical. He would certainly not have chosen the same language when conversing with his patients or with a peasant or a trainer. But for a party dedicated to the celebration of Eros his words are quite appropriate and give to his performance the mixture of the playful and the serious of which Agathon boasts in regard to his own oration (197E) and which is characteristic of all the speeches that are delivered.[15] Finally, that Eryximachus' professional atti-

[12] Gildersleeve (see note 1) 109; Friedländer (see note 9) 304, speaks of "Eitelkeit des Fachmanns" and "unliebenswürdige Krittelsucht."

[13] Cf. below p. 101.

[14] Taylor (see note 9) 217, was the first to suggest that Eryximachus' pedantry is "part of the fun of the evening and is presumably intentional." The gay tone of certain sections of the *Symposium*, the interplay of humor and seriousness, hardly need elaboration. Whether it is appropriate to contrast the *Symposium* as a comedy with the *Phaedo* as a tragedy (cf. Wilamowitz [see note 2] 356), is quite a different problem.

[15] Cf. Jowett (see note 10) 526.

tude and seriousness are tempered by a sense of humor is obvious also in his altercation with Aristophanes (189A–B). The poet is well aware of the physician's sarcasm when he answers him laughingly, and it is not for nothing that in his speech he guards himself repeatedly against any mocking remarks of Eryximachus (193B; D). Nor could Eryximachus have enjoyed the comic masterpiece of Aristophanes as much as he did (193E), had he himself lacked a sense of humor.[16]

Yet at this point one might object: even granted that the speech of Eryximachus is to some extent shaped by Plato's wish to characterize him as a doctor, that Eryximachus is not altogether portrayed as a pedantic fool, why is he made to claim that all he knows and all he is going to propound he has learned from medicine (186A–B)? How can medicine have taught him that Eros rules not only men and animals and plants, but all things, human and divine alike?[17] This assertion, it seems, indicates a rather ludicrous pride in the importance of the medical art and stamps Eryximachus as the prototype of the arrogant doctor. The speech as a whole, if not every detail of it, appears to be a travesty of the narrow-mindedness and conceit of the physician.[18]

It is true that Eryximachus' contention, at first blush, sounds preposterous. Yet before condemning him altogether it is perhaps pertinent to ask what exactly he has learned from medicine, what his art has led him to observe in regard to all the subjects which he mentions.[19] To put it briefly, it is this: the principle of a double

[16] Hug-Schöne (see note 3) xxxviii and 61, note 3, seem the only ones to allow Eryximachus "einen gewissen trockenen ärztlichen Humor."

[17] F. A. Wolf proposed to change the usual punctuation and to take the words *ὡς μέγας κτλ* as an independent sentence: nam ad *omnia* pertinere amorem, ad divinas etiam res ex arte medica discere non potuit (cf. G. F. Rettig, *Platons Symposion* 2 [Halle, 1876] 164). But such a change would be of no avail since the preceding *ὅτι* clause makes the same sweeping assumption. For the grammatical structure of the sentence, cf. Hug-Schöne (see note 3) 63, note 8.

[18] The statement made in 186A has been taken by K. F. Hermann (*Geschichte u. System der platonischen Philosophie* 1 [Heidelberg, 1839] 215) to show the pedantic self-complacency and glibness of the sophist; cf. also A. Schwegler, *Über die Composition des Platonischen Symposions* (Tübingen, 1843) 33. More recent interpreters are usually satisfied with pointing out that to Eryximachus medicine is the source of all knowledge (Hug-Schöne [see note 3] 63, note 7), and they parallel the assertion made here with that made in 176D. But the assumption that Eryximachus should have acquired from medicine a knowledge of all things human and divine is certainly a more far-reaching proposition than that medicine should have taught him a cure for hiccoughs.

[19] Thus, I think, one should best translate *καθεωρακέναι μοι δοκῶ ἐκ τῆς ἰατρικῆς*. The expression seems singular. Usually Plato says *καθορᾶν ἐν* (cf. F. Ast, *Lexicon*

Eros is valid in medicine, husbandry, gymnastics, music, astronomy and divination. Eryximachus' speech displays a familiarity with the basic presuppositions of the various arts, crafts and sciences.[20] Such knowledge, in my opinion, one should expect of a physician of the fifth century B.C., and Eryximachus may easily have acquired it in his pursuit of medicine.

In Eryximachus' time the value and nature of the arts were widely disputed. Many people asserted that the artisan did not accomplish anything through his art, that his success or failure depended entirely on chance. They went even so far as to deny that there was such a thing as an art; the word, they claimed, was an empty phrase behind which to hide one's ignorance and incompetence. To these attacks the artisans were forced to reply. By a careful analysis of the rules of the various arts they tried to establish the reality of their achievements which they contended were the results of insight and true understanding. Wherever men gathered to talk about problems important to them individually, or to the community as a whole, one professional after another would defend his art and define the nature of his technique. The physician naturally was among those who participated in these debates. The Hippocratic writing *On the Art* reflects the atmosphere in which such discussions took place.[21] Here a physician speaks in behalf of medicine. He quotes the objections of the adversaries and refutes them word by word. He points to the difficulties of the other arts, to the parallelism between the physician's procedure and that of other artisans. He is apparently well

Platonicum 2 [Leipzig, 1836]) *s.v.* Such phrases as *καθορῶντες ὑψόθεν* (*Sophistes* 216c) perhaps suggest that the words in question mean: looking out from medicine I have observed. . . .

[20] It has often been noticed that Eryximachus is preoccupied with the *τέχναι*. Cf. especially L. v. Sybel, *Platon's Symposion* (Marburg, 1888) 26 ff.; Bury (see note 3) xxix: "definitions of a precisely parallel kind for each of these departments [*sc.* of science] are evolved." Since these arts are concerned with all things human and divine, Eryximachus' talk assumes a cosmological aspect, but this tinge of natural philosophy is only incidental. In my opinion, he does not talk as a "Naturforscher," as has sometimes been held (e.g. Friedländer [see note 9] 305). The evaluation of Robin (see note 6) LII, note 1, seems more appropriate: "La *technicité* le préoccupe beaucoup plus que la *cosmologie*." The peculiarity of Eryximachus' approach is the more noteworthy since he was versed in natural philosophy, cf. below p. 93.

[21] *Hippocratis Opera*, ed. J. L. Heiberg, *Corpus Medicorum Graecorum* 1.1 (Leipzig and Berlin, 1927) 9 ff. This treatise gives the most vivid and most comprehensive picture of the problems debated, which are referred to also in the fragments of the Pre-Socratics and in the Platonic dialogues. In general, cf. also P. Shorey, *TAPhA* 40 (1909) 185 ff.; J. Wild, *Plato's Theory of Man* (Cambridge, 1946) 45 ff.

versed in their problems, and he also knows as much philosophy as is needed to provide a more general foundation for his statements.[22]

Eryximachus, then, must have been familiar with the methods and theories not only of medicine but also of the arts in general. The relationship of his profession to gymnastics and husbandry and music must have been a matter of interest to him. The subject which he chooses as his topic at the banquet, the way in which he approaches it, even his contention that medicine led him to observe the facts which he is about to recount, all these features characterize him as a physician of the classical period. The speech is not a caricature but rather an historically correct picture of a medical man of that time. It cannot have been Plato's intention to deride Eryximachus as a pedant, a system-monger, unduly fond of medicine.

Of course, this does not imply that Plato may not in some respects have made light of Eryximachus, just as he lets his humor play on Aristophanes and even on Socrates. Perhaps it is true that the physician "by his fine phrases works himself up to the belief in his own triumphant cleverness."[23] The words with which his encomium of Eros ends (188E) betray belief in his own wisdom and superiority, though it is fair to add that every one of the guests seems well content with his own contribution and that Eryximachus is at least aware of the possibility that involuntarily he may have omitted certain points or that Aristophanes might find a different manner of glorifying the god. This much, however, I venture to affirm: there is no reason to believe that Plato had only ridicule for Eryximachus' medical theories, or that he scoffed at his opinions in general and made him perform his assignment badly.[24]

[22] The essay *On the Art* is usually considered the work of a sophist; e.g. Robin (see note 6) 24, note 2. That it must have been composed by a physician I have tried to show in *Περὶ ἀέρων und die Sammlung der Hippokratischen Schriften*, *Problemata* IV (Berlin, 1931) 105 ff. (I should have known then that Wilamowitz, *Platon* 2 [Berlin, 1919] 253, has maintained the same view without, however, giving any further proof.) Even if the author were not a physician, no educated artisan of Eryximachus' time could be unaware of the issue; the exigencies of the situation in which he found himself demanded that he be concerned with it.

[23] Gildersleeve (see note 1) 109; cf. also Robin (see note 6) LVI.

[24] Cf. Wilamowitz (see note 2) 367: ". . . und für seine Medizin hatte Platon im Grunde nur Spott, denn sie war keine Wissenschaft"; also *ibid.* 362. Among the detractors of Eryximachus' entire performance, F. G. Rettig, *Platons Symposion* I (Halle, 1876) 13 ff., is one of the most outspoken representatives. But cf. also Hug-Schöne (see note 3) xxxix.

As far as it is possible to infer his doctrine from his brief résume of medicine, Eryximachus seems to have demanded that the physician do justice to the good desire of the body and restrain its bac desire, that he produce the one where it is missing, and alter the other where it is prevalent, distinguishing right and wrong in regard to repletion and evacuation (186B–D). Apparently the doctor can reach this goal only by prescribing an adequate regimen for the patient.[25] Now the "statesman" Plato rejects dietetic medicine: for the elaborate rules of diet, as he says in his criticism of the medical science proffered with so much severity in the *Republic*, are detrimental to the fulfilment of civic duties. Surgery and the application of drugs alone can therefore be considered legitimate means of treatment (405A–408B). Yet the "scientist" Plato judges dietetics as the only adequate control of sickness, while he condemns drugging as dangerous (*Timaeus* 89B–C).[26] Plato therefore must have felt some sympathy for Eryximachus' teaching. That he esteemed him and his father, that he respected their medical skill, is evident also from the *Phaedrus*. There the two are called upon as authorities (268A) together with other great artisans, Sophocles and Euripides (268C), and Hippocrates (270C), when the right procedure of any technique is examined.[27] Moreover

[25] Eryximachus expressly acknowledges that his art must take account of man's desires for the pleasure of eating (187E). The sources of his doctrine have been widely discussed. Taylor (see note 9) 218 holds that Pythagorean, Heraclitean and Empedoclean ideas are here amalgamated and that the theory as a whole is reminiscent of Sicilian medicine to which Plato was greatly indebted (*ibid.* 217). I hesitate to attach a label to Eryximachus' views; they are so vague that they seem compatible with the teaching of many schools. The closest parallel to Eryximachus' speech of which I am aware is to be found in the Hippocratic writing *On Ancient Medicine* where *πλήρωσις* and *κένωσις* are named as the tendencies to be considered in the healthy and in the sick (*CMG* 1.1 [see note 21] 42, lines 11–12; cf. 41, line 18, and *Symposium* 186C) and where the art of the physician is summarized as knowledge of the right kind of regimen. The passages adduced by Bury and Hug-Schöne (see note 3) *ad loc.* do not seem comparable; for in the Hippocratic books which they quote, *πλήρωσις* and *κένωσις* are not understood as tendencies of the body, as they are by Eryximachus, but rather as means of treatment on which the physician must rely.

[26] Note that Plato is aware of the seeming contradiction between his statements in the *Republic* and those in the *Timaeus*. For he recommends dietetics *καθ' ὅσον ἂν ᾖ τῳ σχολή* (*Timaeus* 89C). That most people have no leisure for the application of complicated dietetic rules was the decisive objection raised in the *Republic* (406C). Cf. also A. E. Taylor, *A Commentary on Plato's Timaeus* (Oxford, 1928) 628 [89c8].

[27] It is perhaps not amiss to point out that Eryximachus, "the noble son of a noble and sober father" (214B), attacks the bad habit of intoxication, and that Plato forbids the guardian of the *Republic* to indulge in *μέθη* (403E; cf. however *Laws* 637D ff.). Moreover, Acumenus, the father of Eryximachus, was fond of prescribing walks

in the *Protagoras*, Eryximachus' interest in questions of natural philosophy and astronomy is attested (315c). This too, in Plato's opinion, will have stood him in good stead.[28]

In his non-medical views Eryximachus is doubtless hinting at certain doctrines that are more fully developed in other Platonic writings. The sequence of arts which he advocates, the ascent from the bodily world through music and astronomy to the realm of the divine is the ascent which the *Republic* establishes in education and the *Timaeus* in the understanding of the cosmos. His definition of mantic foreshadows that given by Diotima.[29] The relative importance of his speech within the contest of orations is likewise obvious. It is his task to show the power of Eros in all departments of human activity. Phaedrus and Pausanias know only of Eros' significance for virtue, for morality. Aristophanes praises Eros as the aspiration of the soul that transcends itself and seeks its original unity. Agathon celebrates Eros as the possessor and dispenser of everything good. Eryximachus discusses one pertinent aspect of the subject that must be elaborated before Socrates can reveal the whole truth; and like all the other arguments, that of Eryximachus reappears in Socrates' encomium.[30]

(*Phaedrus* 227A). Simple kinds of gymnastics are advocated in the *Republic* (404B; E; 407B), and even in the *Timaeus* (89A), gymnastic exercises are defended as a method of purging and renewing the body. For Acumenus, cf. also Xenophon, *Memorabilia*, 3.13.2.

[28] Wilamowitz (see note 2) 361 infers even from the *Protagoras* that Plato dislikes Eryximachus, for he appears "im Gefolge des Allerweltsweisen Hippias, den Platon besonders gering schätzt." But Eryximachus does no more than ask Hippias "some questions"; this can hardly have been a crime in Plato's eyes. Eryximachus' philosophical knowledge is apparent also in his speech; he quotes Heraclitus (187A), and his theory of the double Eros of the body may reflect the teaching of Empedocles; cf. Hug-Schöne (see note 3) xxxix.

[29] I have followed almost literally formulations of Friedländer (see note 9) 305. Even Wilamowitz (see note 2) 367, grants that Eryximachus has some ideas. The agreement between his "Wissenschaftslehre" and that of Plato has been most thoroughly discussed by Sybel (see note 20) 26 ff. His admiration for Eryximachus' doctrine is perhaps exaggerated, though P. Cesareo (*I due Simposi in rapporto all'arte moderna* [Palermo, 1901] 114; cf. also Gildersleeve [see note 1] 110) is mistaken in claiming that Sybel identified Eryximachus with Plato; he clearly saw the limitations of the physician's thought (cf. 27 with 30). The physician indeed rests his case at the point from which Plato takes his flight, as Friedländer says (*ibid.*), who has also pointed to the unfortunate tendency of the critics either to admire or to condemn the speakers altogether ([see note 9] 299, note 2).

[30] Taylor (see note 9) 218, characterizes Eryximachus as the speaker who treats the cosmic aspect of Eros, but cf. above note 20. For the relation of Socrates' speech to the preceding ones, cf. Bury (see note 3) lvii ff. That the speech of Aristophanes

Some interpreters charge Eryximachus with sophistry, obscurity and arbitrariness in dealing with his theme. They criticize the dogmatic manner in which he treats the views of Heraclitus (187A).[31] Yet the arguments he advances are certainly not worse, they rather seem better than those of the others, Socrates excepted; at least, Eryximachus reasons and is conversant with philosophy. There may be ambiguities and inconsistencies in his oration. Still Socrates reserves for him the compliment that he "fought well" (193E–194A). This praise, even if touched with irony, cannot be discounted, for Socrates notes whether the others speak "sufficiently and well" (177E).[32] The statement must mean that to Plato, Eryximachus was not the least noteworthy of the speakers.

Contrary to the contention, then, that the physician is represented as a pedant, that he makes a fool of himself whenever he starts discussing a medical topic or when he elaborates the main subject of the evening, he is portrayed realistically and with sympathy. This result, I think, squares well with the fact that Eryximachus, in addition to giving the speeches that have been considered so far, plays an important rôle throughout the symposium. If one analyzes the framework of the dialogue carefully, he realizes that the physician is by no means just one of the guests among the others, but is a prominent figure at the banquet.

First of all, Eryximachus is responsible for the decision that the symposium be not devoted to excessive drinking which would make it impossible that speeches be given at all. On his advice the company resolves that everybody drink only according to his pleasure (176D–E).[33] Moreover, it is he who moves that the flute-girl be dismissed and that the entertainment be conversation rather than music (176E). And it is he again who suggests that each guest

is a satire on the theories of Eryximachus and of physicians in general is a contention of Bury (*ibid.*, xxxi ff.) which I do not find convincing; Wilamowitz (see note 2) 367 seems to agree with Bury.

[31] Cf. Bury (see note 3) *ad loc.*

[32] For the interpretation of the statement made in 177E, cf. Friedländer (see note 9) 299. Socrates' unqualified approval of Eryximachus can be fully appreciated only in comparison with his pretended praise of Agathon's speech which he immediately retracts (198A–B).

[33] Cf. above p. 86. Bury (see note 3) vii says that the potations are restricted on the proposal of Pausanias. But the latter asks only for deliberation (*σκοπεῖσθε* 176A) and is apparently not aware of a good way to reach the ease which he wishes to enjoy (*ibid.*). Taylor (see note 9) 211 is right in stating that "on the advice of the physician Eryximachus" it is resolved that there be no enforced deep "potting."

make a speech in honor of Eros (176E–177D).[24] To be sure, "the tale is not his," as he says himself (177A). Phaedrus has always wondered why none of the poets or sophists has ever given to Eros the praise due to him, and he has often expressed his astonishment to Eryximachus, his friend and lover (177A–C). But from Phaedrus' protestation no action would ensue here and now, were it not for Eryximachus. If Phaedrus is "the father of the subject" (177D) that will be discussed, Eryximachus, one might say, is "the father of the debate" that is about to take place. Intent on prescribing the proper diet for his friends, on checking their bad desire and on encouraging their good one, and being the good doctor that he is, he knows when the right moment has come for action. He has diagnosed that these people who are disinclined to drink would be willing to listen to his condemnation of drunkenness (176C). He also diagnoses that the present occasion provides the opportunity for doing a favor to Phaedrus by celebrating Eros (177C).[25] For he feels sure that the guests will be delighted to praise this god: they are all lovers and in love (177D–E). The physician is not mistaken in his judgment. His motion that the banquet be celebrated by speeches on Eros is unanimously accepted (177E–178A).

But it is not only the introductory scene which is dominated by Eryximachus; even later he continues to play an outstanding part. Together with Phaedrus, he is the president of the banquet. Whenever the speeches are formally introduced or concluded, either Phaedrus or Eryximachus is addressed; whenever difficulties arise or a diverting chat sets in, one of the two intervenes or is drawn into the conversation. Pausanias addresses Phaedrus (180C; 185C), and so do Agathon (197C; E) and Socrates (212B; C). Phaedrus also puts an end to the quarrel between Socrates and Agathon (194D–E), and he authorizes Socrates to talk as he pleases (199B–C). Eryximachus, on the other hand, is the "guardian" (189A) over the speech of Aristophanes who directs his oration to him (189C; 193D). Socrates turns to Eryximachus before and after Agathon's talk

[24] This fact, of course, is generally recognized. The statement of Wilamowitz (see note 2) 362 that Phaedrus "das Thema stellt" is obviously only a slip.

[25] In 176c, note the words: *ἐπειδὴ οὖν μοι δοκεῖ οὐδεὶς τῶν παρόντων προθύμως ἔχειν πρὸς τὸ πολὺν πίνειν οἶνον, ἴσως . . . ἧττον ἂν εἴην ἀηδής*, and again in 177c: *ἐν τῷ παρόντι πρέπον μοι δοκεῖ εἶναι ἡμῖν τοῖς παροῦσι.* To observe the *καιρός* is one of the main tasks of the physician, as is evident from the Hippocratic writings, cf. Edelstein (see note 22) 114.

(194A; 198A–B).[36] Last but not least, when Alcibiades threatens to make himself president of the banquet (213E) and urges the company to drink, Eryximachus saves the situation: he induces him to follow the procedure agreed upon at the beginning and to give a speech like the others (214A–C). Spurred on by Eryximachus, Alcibiades decides to praise Socrates (214D).[37]

In all the various acts of the symposium, then, Eryximachus appears as a person of distinction, a fact strangely neglected, it seems, by all modern interpreters in their evaluation of his rank among the guests. This physician is not simply on sufferance in the company with which he feasts.[38] He is their peer, nay, in some respects, their superior. For he exercises a certain authority over them. Within the framework of the dialogue, he is indeed more important than anybody else. Pausanias and Aristophanes and Socrates and even Agathon, the host, are but speakers; occasionally they participate in the interludes. Phaedrus assumes his place as president only through Eryximachus; it is mere politeness that he, to whom Eryximachus has given credit for his suggestion of the subject, is honored as the originator of the speeches. Eryximachus, however, lays the foundation for the whole contest. He holds the conversation together at the point where it is in danger of breaking up. As there would be no encomia of Eros without him, there would be no praise of Socrates without his insistence.

Now that the exceptional rôle of Eryximachus has become evident, one can hardly help asking whether it may be of some sig-

[36] Robin (see note 6) XIV seems astonished that Eryximachus fails to assume leadership in the conversation, while he characterizes Phaedrus as president of the banquet who is addressed by all the speakers. This has been shown to be erroneous. Incidentally, Socrates, though he addresses Phaedrus, also turns to the whole company (212B–C), and Alcibiades simply addresses the guests (215A), either because he considers himself president of the banquet (Robin, *ibid.*), or because the subject introduced by Eryximachus has been given up in favor of a new topic.

[37] That Socrates, too, is asked whether he agrees to Alcibiades' speaking (214E) seems natural and merely polite; it does not detract from the weight of Eryximachus' words. Bury (see note 3) xxiv has pointed out that in the "third act" account is taken only of Agathon, the host, Eryximachus and Socrates. Robin (see note 6) LII thinks that Eryximachus' rôle in the scene in question only serves to emphasize the contrast between Alcibiades' originality and adventurous fantasy, and the mediocrity of the physician of the "juste milieu." Such an interpretation, however, hardly does justice to the significance of Eryximachus' intervention.

[38] Contrary to Gildersleeve, cf. above p. 85. If among those who leave the symposium, Phaedrus and Eryximachus alone are mentioned by name (223B), this is again an indication of their importance within the framework of the dialogue as well as a feature that stresses their moderation (Bury [see note 3] xxviii).

nificance that it is a physician who is given such a prominent position. Of course, it could be merely by chance that Eryximachus stands in the foreground of the scene. It may be that Phaedrus really talked to him in the way described; it may be that Eryximachus did suggest a eulogy of Eros at a banquet of which Plato had heard, and that he acted as president of the gathering because he had introduced the motion that led to the contest of speeches. On the other hand, even supposing that there was some historical evidence on which Plato based his report, he has surely taken great pains in describing Eryximachus and in portraying the physician. Twice he shows Eryximachus acting in this capacity, at the very beginning when he advises against μέθη (176C–D), and in the middle of the piece when he cures Aristophanes' hiccoughs (185D–E). In the final part, again, Alcibiades solemnly refers to Eryximachus as a physician (214B). One is never allowed to forget that he is a doctor. Could this be without meaning, just a fortuitous circumstance?

Yet, as Jowett says: "If it be true that there are more things in the *Symposium* of Plato than any commentator has dreamed of, it is also true that many things have been imagined which are not really to be found there."[39] I should hesitate to suggest an answer to the question raised, were it not certain that for Plato, the physician was an exemplar, that in his ethical inquiries he used the medical art as a simile. That Plato's thought is tinged by medical concepts has often been maintained during the past few decades.[40] As a matter of fact, it has been contended that medicine influenced him as deeply as did mathematics: while the latter shaped his natural philosophy, the former is said to have molded his ethical doctrine. From medicine, it has been assumed, Plato took the distinction between art and chance, between conscious and purposeful actions and haphazard decisions; the dignity of a practical science to which he wished to raise ethics already had been realized in the science of medicine. Even the definition of the aim of moral endeavor, which is based on the concept of an innate good of the

[39] Jowett (see note 10) 524.

[40] One of the first to deal with the subject was H. Nohl, *Sokrates und die Ethik* (Tübingen, 1904) 34 ff. The discussion of the problem has been placed on a broader basis by E. Hoffmann, "Der gegenwärtige Stand der Platonforschung," Anhang zu E. Zeller, *Die Philosophie der Griechen* (2.1, 5th edition) 1070 ff. Cf. also W. Jaeger, *Paideia* 2 (Oxford, 1944) 131; 145; 321 f., and Taylor (see note 9) 217.

soul, seems indebted to definitions of medical treatment that are based on the concept of an innate good of the body. Whether such assumptions are correct or not, it is a fact that for Plato the relationship between the physician and his patient served as a model of human relationship, and it is with his use of this parallel alone that I am here concerned.[41]

Plato finds occasion to mention the physician in his discussion of rulership (*Politicus* 293A–C); for the physician, to him, is the ruler of his patients. Whichever method of healing he may employ, whether he follow books or not, whether he be poor or rich, he is called a doctor, if he has knowledge of medicine and acts for the benefit of the sick. All prescriptions which such a man gives, even those which mean temporary harm or pain, are considered justified because he is an expert in his art, and people submit to his ordinances. This common attitude toward the doctor indicates the criterion of right rulership. It is not the social standing of the ruler, nor the attestation of his prescripts, nor their specific content that matters; it is his knowledge alone that decides about his fitness. The example of the physician, to be sure, is not the only one through which Plato clarifies this view. He refers also to the trainer (294D), to the captain (297A), and finally to the weaver (308D). But the physician is the most representative type of the ruler and remains in the foreground of the discussion. He is mentioned together with the trainer (295C) and the captain (298A ff.), he alone is selected when the general definition of rulership is given (293C), and Plato says expressly that his art provides an especially good example of right rule (293B; cf. 296B–C).[42]

Moreover, there is apparently one characteristic of rulership that can be brought out solely by looking at the "image" of the

[41] In another paper I propose to deal in detail with the general bearing of medicine on Platonic ethics and at the same time to investigate the use of the simile of the physician in early and late Greek philosophy. Generally speaking, it seems to me that the distinction between τέχνη and τύχη is to be found not only in medicine but also in other arts, just as the innate good of the object is a concern not only of the physician but also of other artisans; e.g. *Gorgias* 503E, and P. Shorey, *The Idea of Good in Plato's Republic, University of Chicago Studies in Classical Philology* 1 (Chicago, 1895) 227. It is most of all the general analogy between body and soul that has influenced Plato's thought.

[42] Note the words: *τοὺς ἰατροὺς οὐχ ἥκιστα νενομίκαμεν*. L. Campbell, *The Sophistes and Politicus of Plato* (Oxford, 1867) *ad loc.*, translates "and physicians more especially." H. N. Fowler's translation (Plato 3 [Loeb] 1925), "And physicians offer a particularly good example," seems more adequate.

physician. He does not only command, he sees to it that his patients understand the rules given and follow them voluntarily. Certainly, the slave doctor behaves differently. Without asking the sick for an account of their diseases, he prescribes like an autocrat what he thinks necessary (*Laws* 720C). Not so, however, the freeborn doctor. He talks to his patients, he learns from them and in turn instructs them. He gives no prescription until he has persuaded the sick, and he leads them on by persuasion (*ibid.* 720D–E). For his leadership rests on persuasion, not on force (*ibid.* 722B). It is true that if the slave doctor were ever to meet the freeborn doctor and to witness his procedure, he would burst into laughter and say with contempt that the patient wishes to regain his health, that he does not wish to become a doctor himself (*ibid.* 857C–E). Yet it is exactly the aim of the good doctor to educate his patient as well as to heal him, and in this respect he is the model of the true ruler.[43]

The simile of the physician, then, has indeed great significance for Plato, though at the same time its limitations must not be overlooked. It is the statesman or the lawgiver rather than the philosopher whom he compares with the physician. Quite a different human relationship prevails between the philosopher and his pupil and the statesman or lawgiver and the citizen. For while the statesman is, or ought to be, an expert who rules over men through a knowledge which he has but they lack, or governs and educates them by means of laws, the philosopher does not exercise any rule, nor is he supposed to teach others the truth which he has in his possession. The philosopher, as Socrates says himself, practices the art of the midwife. He has no wisdom within himself, he can only help his fellows to bring forth their own knowledge (*Theaetetus* 149A ff.). Later philosophers glorify the philosopher as the physician of the soul. To Plato, however, philosophy is not a kind of medicine tending the patient on his sickbed and

[43] For *Laws* 720C ff. and 857C, cf. also W. Jaeger, *Paideia* 3 (New York, 1944) 215. I am not sure that Plato's account is historically correct in all respects. The distinction between slave doctors who treat slaves and freeborn doctors who treat freeborn patients is not warranted by the evidence available. On the other hand, the good doctor did hold converse with the sick, even though he did not educate them to be physicians, and medical men even wrote books on diseases for the use of laymen. Nor can there be any doubt that the physicians considered their relationship to their patients as that of a ruler to his subjects. Cf. in general Edelstein (see note 22) 102; 105, note 1.

putting him under the spell of sound and salutary tales through which he will be able to void his vast overload of sins and fill instead "his fearful emptiness of righteousness" (Philo, *Quis rer. div. heres*, 297). To Plato, the philosopher is not a physician, sitting in his clinic where people come with their sickness that he may lecture them and heal them through his words, imparting wisdom to them (Epictetus, 3.23.30). The Platonic philosopher is but a humble helper in the search for truth; unlike the statesman or lawgiver, he has no authority over men, nor does he strive for it.[44]

The comparisons of the philosopher with a midwife, of the statesman with a physician, occur only in the later works of Plato, the *Theaetetus*, the *Politicus*, the *Laws*. Yet they express in a pregnant form a belief that is inherent, I think, in all Platonic writings. The earlier dialogues, always ending with a negative result, are full of Socrates' protestation that "he does not know." The theory of recollection of the truth rests on the assumption that the knowledge resides in man's own thought. The method of the philosopher, as it is finally evolved, is that of dialectics, and it is his art of dialectics which Socrates likens to the art of midwifery (*Theaetetus* 161E). Even in the *Gorgias* where two arts are distinguished, the one dealing with the body, the other with the soul, it is legislation and justice, not philosophy, that are compared with gymnastics and medicine (464B). Nor is the fundamental distinction between philosopher and statesman impaired by Plato's assertion that one day the king must become a philosopher, or the philosopher a king, if the state of affairs in this world is ever to change for the better. In the exercise of their functions as philosopher and statesman there would still be the difference between authoritative rule and dialectical investigation. If the statesman rises above the sophist, the philosopher rises above the statesman in more than a geometrical proportion (*Politicus* 257B).

[44] As far as I know, it is only in *Phaedo* 89A that Socrates is said to act like a physician. But here, diagnosing his listeners' diseases — they are perturbed by the objections raised — he heals them through an exhortatory speech, not through philosophical teaching. In an analogous way, the simile is applied by Protagoras who states that in education the sophist changes the soul by the use of words, just as the physician changes the body by the use of drugs (*Theaetetus* 167A). The difference of the simile of the physician from that of the midwife has not sufficiently been stressed by Hoffmann (see note 40) 1075. Incidentally, Zeller ([see note 40] 637, note 2) claims that *Republic* 489B–C identifies the philosopher with the physician. Yet apart from the fact that only one detail is selected for comparison, in the passage in question the philosopher is viewed as the ruler of the many.

The bearing of the simile of the physician having been outlined, it should now be possible to conjecture with some assurance whether the rôle of Eryximachus in the *Symposium* has any meaning in regard to its content. That Plato, in depicting Eryximachus, was guided by his view of the physician's art as a model seems obvious. Eryximachus rules over his patients by virtue of his knowledge, he persuades them so that they obey him voluntarily. When he has learned from the guests what their complaints are, he gives his advice and they in turn are persuaded and obey him (176D). When Aristophanes turns to Eryximachus and informs him of his sickness, the physician enumerates in detail three possible means of treatment, and thus instructs Aristophanes how to take care of his ailment; he does not prescribe any one treatment in an autocratic manner.[45] Nor are Eryximachus' friends less aware of the fact than is Plato that the physician is a ruler, that he must be esteemed as such. When Alcibiades is asked by Eryximachus: "What are we going to do," he answers: "Whatever you command, for it is necessary to obey you; the leech is of the worth of many other men" (214B).[46] Of course, I do not mean to claim that all the features of Plato's interpretation of the doctor's relationship to his patients are woven into this dialogue. The representation of Eryximachus is not a paradigm of the medical art. But the essential characteristics of the good doctor are sharply accentuated in his portrait. He prescribes, the others follow his instructions. His wisdom is superior; the others, in their failings, acquire insight from him that they themselves do not possess. They are led to grasp the truth by persuasion.

And is this not exactly the experience of him who listens to the various speeches given at the banquet? Each of the speakers talks with authority, in a dogmatic fashion. Their teaching is non-dialectical and therefore unphilosophical. Even Socrates is not in his usual mood. Although he chides Agathon for believing that wisdom could flow from one person into another as water flows

[45] Much has been written on the meaning of this episode which causes Eryximachus to speak in place of Aristophanes. Within the context of the whole, the scene may have been introduced so as to make the intended order of the speeches appear incidental, cf. K. Reinhardt, *Platons Mythen* (Bonn, 1927) 63; Friedländer, *Platon* 1 (Berlin and Leipzig, 1928) 187 f., but it also serves to underline the position of the physician at the banquet.

[46] The verse from Homer (*Iliad* 11.517) is also quoted in the *Politicus* (297E), cf. above p. 98.

through wool from a fuller cup into one that is emptier (175D), later on he himself imparts the knowledge that he has obtained from Diotima with the assurance of the initiated. And could not all of the speakers say what Socrates says at the end of his oration (212B): of this I am persuaded and of this I try to persuade others? For they no less than Socrates have indulged in the recounting of mythical tales of the truth of which one cannot be sure, but can only be persuaded, and can only hope to persuade others.[47] Besides, their speeches are encomia (e.g. 177E), eulogies of a god or demon, just as Alcibiades' oration is an encomium (214D) of Socrates, who embodies the ideal of the good man. Such encomia the *Republic* leaves to poetry as its sole and justifiable province after Homer and the tragedians have been expelled from the city (607A). In the *Symposium* they are recited in competition with the works of poets and sophists who have neglected their duty of praising Eros (177A–B).[48] They are composed with that true rhetorical art which is allied with kingly statesmanship and uses myths for the persuasion of the many (*Politicus* 304C–D). Although they are so wondrous that one forgets oneself in hearing them and wishes them to be retold again and again, they do not convey the truth in philosophical terms; nor are they capable of doing so on account of their subject matter. For Eros leads man to the vision of the beautiful which he beholds but with "the eye of faith and desire,"[49] while it is thought that enables him to ascertain the good through dialectics, and thus to know.

That the physician, the exemplar of authority that persuades, is given such a significant rôle in the *Symposium*, is, I suggest, an intentional device of Plato. It is meant to emphasize the singularity of the content of this dialogue, the specific character of its method and instruction. Many other features of the framework of

[47] That the content of the *Symposium* is mythical has been acknowledged by Friedländer (see note 45) 207 and by Wilamowitz, who has especially stressed the non-dialectical character of its teaching ([see note 2] 360) and the fact that Socrates speaks only of persuasion ([see note 22] 170 f.). P. Frutiger, *Les Mythes de Platon* (Paris, 1930) 112 ff., judges differently, but he fails to account for the features just referred to. To be sure, the myth told by Socrates is a "true myth," based on the *logos*, while the others are not (cf. Friedländer, *ibid.* 207 f.). Fundamentally, however, all orations are unphilosophical, at least from the standpoint of the Platonic system.

[48] The relation of the passage in the *Republic* to the *Symposium* has been pointed out by Friedländer (see note 45) 142; the rhetorical character of the speeches has been stressed by Jaeger (see note 40) 180.

[49] Cf. Jowett (see note 10) 533.

the *Symposium* seem to serve the same purpose.[60] With the exception of Socrates, no philosopher is present at this banquet at which speeches are prescribed as a kind of diet for those who feel unable to drink as much as would fit the occasion. Even if these people are highly educated and cultured, they are not investigators of the truth in their own right. Nor do they belong to the inner circle of Socrates' friends; they are outsiders, living far apart from the man who is the wisest of his generation, or, like Alcibiades, unable to submit to his guidance. Even those who retell the conversation are among the least noble of Socrates' pupils; Aristodemus who apes him in externals (173B), and Apollodorus, a crazy fellow (173D), not a sober thinker but rather a passionate enthusiast who cannot control his emotions (*Phaedo* 117D). Finally, the people to whom the story is told are business men, men of the practical life (173C). It is as if Plato, by giving such a setting to his work, had attempted to treat with irony the teaching of that dialogue which to so many generations has seemed his greatest on account of the seducing splendor of its beauty. Perhaps he was aware of the fact that if it were taken as his final word, as his deepest insight, reason might find it difficult to assert the supremacy which he attributed to thinking, even above the claim of beauty.

[60] For the interpretation of the framework of the dialogue, cf. also Friedländer (see note 9) 295 ff.; Wilamowitz (see note 2) 359 f.

review are indeed applicable to him. But Randall is seldom willing merely to say that Aristotle is a functionalist or a behaviorist; he is usually "a thoroughgoing functionalist," "a thoroughgoing behaviorist," and the rest; and of this a sober reader will have his doubts, doubts that are nourished by what Randall himself says at other places in his book. Call it a remnant of Platonism or what you will, we find Aristotle eventually asserting that Being is more fundamental than Becoming, and grounding his naturalism in a higher order of "eternals" and "unchangeables." We must recognize that this aspect of Aristotle's thought also has its echoes among our contemporaries.

GLENN R. MORROW

UNIVERSITY OF PENNSYLVANIA

THIS "little book," as the author calls it in his Foreword, attempts to set forth what Professor Randall "has found to be the significance for the present day" of Aristotelian thinking; it is "a philosopher's delineation of Aristotle" (vii). Such evaluations of Greek philosophy have become rare, and yet they are badly needed if the thought of the past is to be made fruitful for the thought of today, if a consciousness of the continuity of the philosophical development is to be kept alive. Aristotle no doubt would heartily approve the approach here chosen in analyzing his work. It is the approach he himself is wont to use in the study of his predecessors. And every student of Aristotle, I think, must be grateful to the author of the book under review for having dared to write not another introduction to the *maestro di color che sanno,* but a book that proposes to philosophize with him and about him.

I should not, however, give the impression that Professor Randall's interpretation is unhistorical. To be sure, he does not present a complete picture of the Aristotelian system. In accordance with his aim, the emphasis laid upon the various philosophical issues is more often than not his rather than Aristotle's. And since he writes as a naturalist, he is interested in aspects quite different from those which a Thomist would accentuate (vii f.). But it is the author's opinion that the naturalism of Aristotle which he discusses is "the 'Aristotelianism' of Aristotle" (294; cf. 300); the ideas on which the investigation centers are "the more distinctly Aristotelian ideas" (295). In other words, the book is concerned with what Fichte in his interpretation of Kant calls "the spirit of the system."[1] And that the spirit of Aristotelianism is to be found in naturalism, Professor Randall, though not a philologist (vii), shows by employing the method of interpretation and by working with the results of philological criticism. Fond as he is of Santayana's *Secret of Aristotle* and willing, like Santayana, to tell Aristotle what he ought to have meant (103; 143), in order to point up mistakes, still he would not answer the question: "Is this truth to be found in Aristotle?" by saying, as Santayana does: "If it is the truth, it must have been his doctrine."[2]

The "Aristotelianism" of Aristotle is, of course, a term used in contrast with the "Platonism" of Aristotle, to denote the other component in his intellectual make-up, and consequently the problem of Aristotle's development, so important in recent literature, also looms large in the book. It is dealt with in a general manner in the second chapter (20 ff.) and taken up again incidentally in almost every one of the following chapters when the date of the writings on the several topics is discussed. Therefore it may not be inappropriate if, before speaking about the content of the interpretation itself, I say something about the view taken of Aristotle's development.

Professor Randall is a cautious and by no means orthodox adherent of the modern dogma. He preaches and practices a wise skepticism as to the possibility of distinguishing precisely the chronological layers of the various treatises (e.g., 22; 107; 259). For him, contradictions to be found in the texts are not necessarily indications of a Before and an After (29); he stresses the fact, so commonly forgotten by the "developmentists" and "separatists," that the writings give "the impression of forming an organic whole" (30). And though Professor Randall agrees that Aristotle—a full-fledged Platonist in his first published works, the dialogues—gradually formulated his own philosophy, he maintains that he never went so far as to cut himself off completely from Platonism. Aristotle's development was not so much "a movement 'away from' Platonic notions as an addition to them, a putting of them in a broader factual context" (21). There is no evidence that he slackened in his philosophical interests and turned scientist, even in his last years (cf. 29), as was the thesis originally advanced. This reinterpretation seems to me an especially important and needed improvement in the theory of development—

[1] *Grundlage der Gesamten Wissenschaftslehre*, II, 4 (*Werke* ed. F. Medicus, I, 1911), p. 381, note.

[2] *Dialogues in Limbo* (Ann Arbor Books, 1957), XIII, 244. For Professor Randall's "philological" attitude, see, e.g., 138.

as is, by the way, the admission that Aristotle had a genuine feeling for the appeal of Platonism (13).[3]

Even so, there remains room for debate, disregarding altogether the question whether the material preserved suffices for reconstructing the details of a development in Aristotle's thought. I am not sure that the fragments extant from the dialogues show that Aristotle ever wrote as a Platonist pure and simple (15 f.), or that the *Posterior Analytics* is an "early setting forth of the Platonic theory or ideal of science" (51). I doubt that prevalence of speculation suggests "youthful brashness and self-confidence" (161) in *On the Heavens,* and youthfulness of thought in the Lambda of the *Metaphysics* (107; 136), while the rejection of the Platonic Ideas is indicative of "maturity" (97).[4] Moreover, of all of Professor Randall's identifications of Platonism—it is said to be, among other things, a mystic faith (13), a religious attitude (18; 137), a love for a universal scientific method, for demonstration—the safest definition is perhaps (e.g., 32) that Platonism is "devotion to 'the Ideal,' the aspiration after what is deathless and eternal" (13). It is, if I am not mistaken, also the meaning most commonly given to the term by Professor Randall. Yet, though in this sense Aristotle does indeed remain a Platonist throughout his life, it will still be necessary to determine the specific form that such a Platonic ethos takes on in his philosophy.[5]

But Aristotle was by nature not only imaginative but also empirical; he exhibits "the temper of mind both of the Platonic dialectician and of the observant physician." His descent from a family of doctors, therefore, if not incontrovertibly attested, is at least "philosophically convincing" (12). It does apparently explain to a large extent his "Aristotelianism" and, in addition, why biology is the subject "where his heart lies" (219), "the central range from which his whole analysis springs" (220). Although such a connection between Aristotle's inheritance from

[3] The first decade of the debate on Jaeger's thesis has been surveyed by H. Cherniss in his review of R. Robinson's translation of Jaeger's *Aristoteles, American Journal of Philology,* 16 (1935): 261 ff. For later stages of the discussion see, e.g., D. S. Allan, *The Philosophy of Aristotle,* 1952, pp. 12 ff. Other literature I shall quote in the following wherever it has a special bearing on my review.

[4] Rejection of the Platonic Idea, I take it, is meant by the statement in question and not, as Professor Philip Merlan says in his review [*Philosophy and Phenomenological Research,* 22 (1961): 120], that the existence of God as pure form was ever denied by Aristotle. Concerning the *Posterior Analytics* cf. W. D. Ross, *Aristotle's Prior and Posterior Analytics,* 1949, Introduction, ch. II; concerning the *Protrepticus* and Gadamer's objections to the claim that it is a fundamentally Platonic dialogue, see Cherniss, *op. cit.,* pp. 266–268. Incidentally, the latter's warnings against any exaggerated trust in the possibility of retracing the development of Aristotle (270 ff.) seem to me to deserve more attention than they have received.

[5] See below, pp. 161 ff.

his father's side and his natural studies is almost universally assumed, the basis for this assumption is, I am afraid, most insecure.[6]

I shall not argue that, even admitting the correctness of the biographical tradition, a son cannot be expected necessarily to possess his father's interest and gifts. It is more to the point to insist that physicians of the classical period were not empiricists and experimentalists "by nature," as it were. Many, perhaps most of those who were not simple practitioners or craftsmen, were speculators. If "the physicians of the school of Hippocrates made the greatest achievements that empirical and experimental science was to attain before the Lyceum" (12 f.)—a claim that would be hard to justify—it is not known that Aristotle's father belonged to the circle of these Hippocratics. He who wishes to conjecture the antecedents of Aristotle's naturalism and of his concern with biology is on firmer ground believing that Aristotle happened to have eyes for the real no less than the ideal world. As for his emotions, they surely are aroused not by biology but rather by astronomy. Granted that he "grows lyrical" (148) about the fixed stars in his supposedly early and Platonic treatise *On the Heavens*, he is enthusiastic about astronomical knowledge also in the introduction to his late biological writings, for here it is said that the joy of a knowledge of heavenly phenomena surpasses the joy to be derived from any other knowledge "just as the joy of a fleeting and partial glimpse of those whom we love is greater than that of an accurate view of other things, no matter how numerous or how great they are" (*On Parts of Animals* 644b 33–35). Material for demonstration is no doubt more abundant in biological research than it is in the discipline of astronomy, not a negligible advantage (645a1 ff.). Yet inspiration comes from the contemplation of the heavens where the divine appears in perfection. There is, then, hardly any reason to interpret his philosophy, in so far as it may depend on scientific investigations, in the light of his work in natural history (224).[7]

I am, of course, far from minimizing the actual accomplishments of Aristotle's biological research or its historical significance.

[6] The generally held opinion is most succinctly expressed in E. Barker's saying that the interpreter of Aristotle has always to remember his "medical ancestry and interest" (*The Politics of Aristotle*, 1946, p. 242).

[7] For the origin of the view here rejected and the literature on it, see 223 f. That Aristotle, in the introduction to *On the Parts of Animals*, still shows a predilection for astronomy rather than biology has been stressed by Jaeger (*Aristoteles*, 1923, p. 361). Moreover, if his reconstruction of the *Protrepticus* is accepted (see above pp. 152, 153 and note 3), one must also admit with him that the concepts of *dynamis* and *energeia* are attested for that early dialogue and that their coinage has nothing whatever to do with Aristotle's biological studies (*Gnomon*, IV, 1928, pp. 632 ff.).

What had been done by earlier philosophers or philosophical scientists cannot compare in method and systematic breadth with his inquiries. The studies of "animal-life," fashionable in the Academy of his time, were attempts at classifications (Epicrates, Fr. 287 [Kock]) which may have aroused his interest in the subject, faulty as they seemed to him on account of their principle of division (*On Parts of Animals,* I, chs. 3–4).[8] The validity of the teleological principle, already vindicated for astronomy by Plato, still had to be established for biology against the "Darwinism" of the Pre-Socratics (642a24 ff.; cf. 640a19 ff.; b30 ff.). Throughout Aristotle's investigations the proof for the existence of God based on the movement of the heavenly bodies was complemented by the proof to be derived from the animal kingdom. Nevertheless, as a metaphysician he belongs rather to the philosophical movement which started with Anaxagoras and for which metaphysics is most intimately allied to astronomy. The latter is called "most akin to philosophy" even in the eighth chapter of Book Lambda of the *Metaphysics,* which, on account of the mention of Callippus, must have been written toward the end of Aristotle's career.[9]

To turn now to the interpretation itself, its main theme is Aristotle's functionalism (31; cf. 294) which is shown to pervade his epistemology (ch. V), his physics (chs. VIII–X) and biology (ch. XI), his "first philosophy" as pictured in Zeta, Eta, and Theta of the *Metaphysics* (ch. VI), and in his ethics and politics (ch. XII). In more distinct terms, Aristotle is viewed "as a behaviorist, an operationalist, and a contextualist, with a thoroughgoing philosophy of process" (31).

These "present-day labels . . . applied . . . to important aspects of Aristotle's thought" (31) generally speaking express Aristotle's theory on "Living and Desiring" (ch. IV) and are meant to translate a number of basic Aristotelian categories. Function and operation render *ergon* and *energeia,* respectively (64). Objective relativism or contextualism characterizes the fact that functions and activities are understood "in terms of that toward which they are directed, of that to which they are a response, 'their correlative objects' [*ta antikeimena*]" (66 f.). Behaviorism —a functional and contextual behaviorism, not a mechanistic one that explains the function by the structure of the mechanism or

[8] Jaeger (*Aristoteles,* p. 353; cf. pp. 16, 18), in my opinion, underestimates the importance of the biological studies of the Academy and without reason assumes that Aristotle's criticism of the Platonic method presupposes his own zoological investigations (p. 353, note 1).

[9] For Anaxagoras, cf. W. Dilthey, *Einleitung in die Geisteswissenschaften* (*Gesammelte Schriften* I, 1922), pp. 158 ff.; for Aristotle's place in the tradition of what Dilthey calls "monotheisthic metaphysics," *op. cit.,* pp. 211 ff.

instrument involved—is intended to cover Aristotle's explanation of the living organism through its *psyche*. Process is the equivalent of *kinēsis*.

To me translating the Greek technical vocabulary seems preferable to leaving it in the original as Professor Randall has decided to do in some cases. To say, for instance, "nousing" for *noein* (81), the elaborate commentary on the word notwithstanding (90, note 13), conjures up an esoteric mysticism of which the Greek is quite innocent. "*Nous* nousing *nous*" (144) is not too illuminating a formula for the activity of the best life. On the other hand, it is true that any modern word that one might choose has overtones inconsistent with the Aristotelian teaching. Even "actuality" and "potentiality" (127), in the usage of today, mean something different from what Aristotle meant by *energeia* and *dynamis*. But while the modern language is liable to certain misunderstandings, it allows one to make the relevance of Aristotle's thought for the present clearer and more precise, and this, one must not forget, is after all Professor Randall's aim.

At any rate one can hardly deny that what has come to be called naturalism and functionalism is one aspect of the Aristotelian system. That it is no more than one aspect, that it constitutes merely the range of "the more distinctly Aristotelian ideas," Professor Randall acknowledges himself, and he warns against the mistake of considering Aristotle a full-fledged naturalist and functionalist by stressing the fact that "the actual documents of the corpus are a combination of 'Platonism' and 'Aristotelianism' " and attest "a 'formalistic naturalism' or a 'structuralistic formalism' " (295) not to be neglected in a strictly historical presentation of Aristotle.[10] And as the author remains objective in admitting the difference of the Aristotelian view from a later unalloyed naturalism and functionalism in philosophy and science, so he is on the whole objective and fair also in his reading of the testimony. It is rarely that one feels he forces the meaning of words or sentences.[11] Only in the discussion of politics

[10] These quotations are from the last chapter. Only there, it is fair to say, are the limitations imposed upon the inquiry, though set forth in the Foreword and often referred to in the course of the argument, quite clearly formulated. This is unfortunate and could mislead the reader of the book. It is perhaps also one of the reasons why the author seems to Professor Merlan not to have given "an exegesis" of the text [*Philosophy and Phenomenological Research* 22 (1961): 121], and why Professor Haring compares his work unfavorably with the writings of Ross, Mure, and Allan [*The Review of Metaphysics*, 14 (1960): 293, note 3].

[11] It is for instance exaggerated, I think, to express Aristotle's concept of a basic temporal pattern of process through Leibniz's phrase "heavy with the past and big with the future" (170). And although Aristotle may be opposed to "what we call the method of reductive analysis" and may deal with what recent philosophers designate as " 'creative' or

and ethics, "the supreme achievement" (243) of Aristotle's objective relativism (252) and empirical and functional naturalism (257), has the evidence, in my opinion, been seriously slighted.

For it is not correct, I think, to claim that in Aristotle's moral theory, "what is good is always something plural, specific, and relative to a particular situation or context" (251) or that in "his practical science of ethics" no invariable structure can be found "that is true 'always or for the most part,' as is the case in the theoretical sciences, and is indeed the defining mark of those inquiries" (252). The adoption of the principle "a mean for us," or "a mean 'relatively' to us," the opposition to a Manichean naturalism, does not prevent Aristotle from holding that there are situations that allow of no mean and actions that are without exception bad and immoral (*Nicomachean Ethics* 1107a8 ff.). Nor is it justifiable to believe that the art of the statesman "might even divorce itself from moral considerations altogether," still less to say that "the more completely Aristotle approached the attitude of the *physikos*, the natural philosopher of politics, the nearer he came to the similar attitude of Machiavelli" (259). Investigating the advantages of all forms of state, Aristotle, despite his predilection for the rule of the middle classes, proffers advice also to the tyrant as to how he could preserve his rule. But the "advice," given after a description of the usual "arts of the tyrant" which "plumb the depth of wrong-doing," consists in the advocacy of a "second method, where the line of action followed is almost the very reverse" (1343a13–14; 30–32). If the tyrant, in consequence of such a different procedure, manages to hold on to power, it will come to pass that "his subjects will be men of a better stamp," that "he will himself attain a habit of character, if not wholly disposed to goodness, at any rate half-good half-good and yet half-bad, but at any rate not wholly bad" (1315a42–1315b11). This is hardly the voice of "the doctor . . . attracted to the diagnosis of symptoms and the suggestion of cures," as Barker puts it (266); it certainly is not the voice of Machiavelli.[12]

Whether or not Aristotle's philosophy can serve as the model for a modern reformed naturalism and functionalism, I do not feel called upon to decide. I should, however, at least mention that in the book under review it is not merely Aristotelian biology and

'emergent' evolution" (207), the coming-into-being of a new substance for him hardly is "creative of novelty" (210), the term being used without quotation marks.

[12] I do not wish to give the impression that the Aristotelian passages I have adduced are withheld from the reader of the book. They are quoted in full, 265 ff.

physics that are considered significant for present-day thought (e.g., 167), as they have been more and more often in recent years. The claim is extended to all the departments of inquiry so far considered.[13] Thus Aristotle is praised because for him the world of nature that man tries to understand is "an intelligible world," because experience is his opinion is not an "interaction between a 'merely' biological organism and a wholly illogical world" (106). He rightly assumes that "we see" rather than experience the truth; experience only "illustrates" laws; it does not "prove" their truth (45). He also is correct in holding that knowing is not a problem to be solved but rather a process to be described (105). If he errs in his teleology, he errs in not being enough of a teleologist for a post-Darwinian (129).[14]

With regard to logic and methodology, Professor Randall's approval is more reserved. To be sure, even in the field of language or formal logic Aristotle's teaching is "relevant and suggestive" for the modern philosopher (viii; cf. 298 f.). He saw that "knowing is a matter of language, of stating; it is not a 'having of sensations' or 'sense data' " (7). However, though he developed a formal logic (48) which has, as it ought to have, "ontological implications" (49), the needed functional analysis is missing in Aristotle, as it is missing even today (297; cf. 96).[15] And it can be said also of his actual practice of inquiry, which is entirely different from the practice proposed in the logic (52), that Aristotle discovered a fruitful procedure but failed in applying it. He opposed a universal scientific method and insisted on going to the facts. But he is deceived by his "confidence in

[13] One of the earliest appreciations of the modernity of Aristotle's biology is to be found in E. Frank's essay "Das Problem des Lebens bei Hegel und Aristoteles" (*Knowledge, Will, and Belief*, ed. L. Edelstein, 1955, pp. 218–220; the essay was originally published in 1927 in *Deutsche Vierteljahrsschrift für Literaturwissenschaft und Geistesgeschichte*). I may be permitted to point out in addition that the article in question deals in detail with one aspect of "The Heritage of Aristotle" briefly discussed by Professor Randall in ch. XII, the agreement and disagreement of Aristotle and Hegel, which is set forth with a view to the philosophical situation in the years after the First World War.

[14] Professor Randall's own philosophical point of view, which one must keep in mind in order to do justice to his *obiter dicta* on philosophical problems and individual philosophers, is expounded in his *Nature and Human Experience*, 1958. If in the *Aristotle* he acclaims the founder of the Peripatos for maintaining that sense perception is a "natural" event and not a "mental" one (87), he speaks of course as an unreconstructed naturalist. And the same holds true, I suppose, when he ascribes to Aristotle a "fitting humility," missing in Spinoza and Hegel, since for him "man is by no means the highest embodiment of the power of *nous*" (142).

[15] Yet it is to Aristotle's credit that the particular idea of science developed out of the discovery of the syllogism implies "a definite and determinate kind of world" (50 ff.). He is right also in stating that scientific assumptions are not arbitrarily chosen (55). On scientific argumentation and language see, moreover, 102, and on classifications 52.

observation"; he lacked even "the sense of the need of instruments"; because "he did not conceive the possibility of closer observation," he assumed "a finality in his explanations for everything." Not only was it impossible without instruments of observation to attain "any exact solutions to problems, . . . any precise verifications," but "he did not seek for such results" (54–58).

The verdict here rendered on Aristotle the "linguist" may be correct; the verdict on the logician and methodologist seems to me to require qualifications. The *Posterior Analytics* is not entirely concerned with "what a completed and perfected science is like" (33); it does after all deal with induction (42 f.). As Professor Randall points out himself, the method of the seventeenth-century pioneers of science was influenced by their study of the *Organon* (56). Again, Aristotle was hampered by the actual scarcity of instruments (e.g., 58); yet when he says that in the observation of the stars "we are far removed from the objects of our attempted inquiry, not in the obvious sense of distance of space, but rather because very few of their attributes are perceptible to our senses" (*On the Heavens* 286a4–7), he almost cries out for instruments of observation. He would, I believe, not only have been convinced by Galileo's telescope (162); he would have rejoiced in it as well. Nor can it be maintained, I think, that Aristotle's belief in the finality of his results had much to do with his thoughts about possible further research. He knew that certain facts "have not yet been sufficiently grasped" and that "whenever they will be, credit will have to be given to observation rather than to theories, and to theories only if what they affirm is in agreement with the observed facts" (*Generation of Animals* 760b30–33). Last but not least, he formulated physical laws in mathematical terms, although to be sure he did not often do so. Overconfident as he undoubtedly was with regard to the value of observation, he was more of a modern scientist than Professor Randall, with all his affection for the father of naturalism, concedes to him.[16]

More could, and should perhaps, be said about the interpretation Professor Randall provides of Aristotle's doctrine. But it is time to turn to a consideration of the final problem that the

[16] The mathematical implications of Aristotelian physics have been illustrated by J. E. Drabkin, "Notes on the Laws of Motion in Aristotle," *American Journal of Philology*, 59 (1938); 60 ff. I mention in passing that one would expect Professor Randall to do more justice, if not to the boldness of speculation, at least to the empiricism of the *On the Heavens*—the treatise to which ch. IV is devoted. But despite some occasional faint praise (e.g., 155), the verdict on the whole is quite unfavorable (e.g., 148); and the central interest of the discussion is said to be religious (148). See also below, p. 13 and note 19.

interpretation raises. If naturalism and functionalism are distinctly Aristotelian, it is no wonder that of Aristotle's *Metaphysics* the books Zeta, Eta, and Theta are reconcilable with "the dynamism of his analysis of the world of natural processes, the functionalism of his physics" (133), but that the concept of the Unmoved Mover enshrined in book Lambda must appear to be outside the "Aristotelianism" of Aristotle. And the same of course is true of the concept of the active intellect, as developed in the *On the Soul.* Could both be understood as immanent rather than transcendent, Aristotle's theology "would be sound, probably the only sound natural theology in the Western tradition" (144). But they can be understood in such a way, Professor Randall insists, only if one develops the meaning of Aristotle's words or if one states what ought to be their meaning if Aristotle is to be consistent (143; cf. 102). In other words, in feeling or language (cf. 141) the two theories imply transcendence. The belief in the Unmoved Mover is in fact "the expression of Aristotle's early Platonistic faith," a faith "gradually pushed into the background" (109). The active intellect is "the least important or significant part of the *De Anima* . . . it seems to be all that is left in the present text . . . of what had been in his early dialogues a much more important part of Aristotle's youthful Platonism" (102).[17]

For his thesis that the Unmoved Mover and the active intellect belong to the Aristotle who had not yet become himself, Professor Randall offers two reasons. First, book Lambda of the *Metaphysics* as well as the treatise *On the Soul* are "early" writings (102; 107). Second, when speaking of the active intellect Aristotle "resorts to a Platonic myth—he certainly employs in this paragraph the 'likely language' of myth" (100; cf. 104). Also "the Unmoved Mover may well be called a Platonic myth, like the 'Active Intellect' of the *De Anima*" (141), the language of Lambda being the likely language of which the *Timaeus* speaks (141). This assertion—be it noted—is not made in the spirit of disparagement. The naturalism Professor Randall professes allows him to admit that the concept of the active intellect "points to facts" (105), "paradoxical facts" (103). It is "a recognition of the cardinal difficulty in any naturalistic theory of knowing

[17] Some literature on the long debate about whether Aristotle's is a philosophy of transcendence or of immanence, is given 100 f. See also W. D. Ross, *Aristotle*, 1924, pp. 148 ff; 181 ff., and *Aristotle's Metaphysics* I, 1924, pp. cxxx ff. Professor Randall's statement of the case for immanence is very cautious indeed. Of the more recent publications, E. Frank's article on "The Fundamental Opposition of Plato and Aristotle," *American Journal of Philosophy*, 61 (1940): 34 ff.; 166 ff., now *Knowledge, Will and Belief* (pp. 86 ff.), probably makes the most outspoken claim for Aristotle's immanentism.

and intelligence," namely that in reaching truth "mind does seem to rise above the limitations and conditions of its bodily instrument" (103), that "'mind' is not a kind of cosmic accident" (105). And even when Professor Randall interprets the concepts of *nous* and of the Unmoved Mover as Aristotle should have interpreted them, the relation of God to the world is determined as "that which Whitehead has called 'internal-external'" (143; cf. 71, note 9). One must not forget that the naturalism advocated in the book hopes, under the guidance of Aristotle, "to arrive at last where he so often arrives himself in the end, at the Platonic *nous* which he shared to the full—the imaginative vision of truth" (300).

However, can one accept the arguments by which Professor Randall tries to prove the Platonism of those dogmas which the traditionalist would characterize as the most typically Aristotelian teaching, the quintessence of Aristotelianism? As for the early date of the treatise *On the Soul,* it is perhaps enough to state that, as Professor Randall indicates himself, there certainly is no unamimity in the matter (102). That the Lambda of the *Metaphysics* is "Platonic" is more than doubtful. Even the sentences in which Aristotle speaks of Platonic doctrines in the first person plural (107), it has recently been shown, do by no means prove his adherence to the Platonic dogma.[18] Of course, one cannot deny that Aristotle, in the treatise *On the Soul* as well as in the Lambda of the *Metaphysics*, uses Platonic expressions. In particular the comparison of the active intellect with light (430a15) is reminiscent of Plato's *Republic.* However, the introduction of such a metaphor does not yet justify the verdict that Aristotle is telling a "likely story," a myth (99 f.), not to mention the fact that the much later restatement of the theory which makes the active intellect come "from without" (*Generation of Animals* 736b28) is phrased in a direct and straightforward manner and belongs to a realm of discourse entirely different from Plato's language of probability. Nor does Aristotle's version of this language occur in the Lambda when he speaks about God (e.g., 141), but rather in the section on astronomy—and rightly from his point of view, since much in the explanation of astronomical phenomena can indeed be only a matter of "reasonable inference"

[18] See Frank, *op. cit.*, p. 119, note 1, and in general H. Cherniss, *Aristotle's Criticism of Plato and the Academy*, I, 1944, pp. 489 ff. (Appendix II). As for the *On the Soul*, J. Block has just argued that it was written after the (late) biological works had been completed ["The Order of Aristotle's Psychological Writings," *American Journal of Philology*, 82 (1961): 50 ff.]. He also has shown (74 ff.) that the active intellect is referred to not only in the supposedly early parts of book III, as Professor Randall seems to assume (102), but also in I, 408b18 and in II, 413b23-27.

(1074a24–25) or "plausible" as the *On the Heavens* puts it (288a1–2). Neither in time of origin nor in point of formulation can the concepts of the active intellect and of the Unmoved Mover be called Platonic.[19]

But the fact that the two concepts cannot be labeled as Professor Randall labels them naturally does not answer the question of how they are to be understood, still less the question of what Aristotle ought to have meant by them. And this issue in turn forces one to face the historical problem the author has raised. One cannot help asking whether he is right in his characterization of the "distinctly Aristotelian ideas" and in what sense it is justifiable to speak as he does of a dichotomy of the Platonic and the Aristotelian components in Aristotle's mental endowment, of a contrast of feeling and thinking which Aristotle's philosophy tries to harmonize (297).

Now to speak first of the active intellect and the Unmoved Mover, there can be no doubt that they have, in Aristotle's terminology, separate existence and, therefore, are transcendent rather than immanent. Yet what does separateness or transcendence mean to Aristotle? Certainly not the same it means to his master. Plato assumes a realm of ideas "there," completely distinct from the realm of things "here"; the Idea of the Good is beyond all being and knowing. Whether or not Aristotle ever was a faithful adherent of the Platonic doctrine of Ideas, in his preserved writings, the treatises, he denounces the Platonic concept of separation, of transcendence. Whereas for his teacher the Idea has an existence entirely different from that of the particular things that are merely "homonymous" with it, in Aristotle's opinion the universal character of things, though separated from them, exists in things; things are "synonymous" with universals. For as one has rightly said of his rejection of Plato, he attempts "somehow to determine the nature of *ousia* (of reality), by the conditions of sensible existence, whereas for Plato these are just the indications of a falling short of true reality of which consequently they cannot be the criteria."[20] The criticism of the Platonic principle

[19] What I have said about *Metaphysics* Lambda modifies of course also the verdict on the mention of the Unmoved Mover in the *Physics* (163), the other work in which Professor Randall finds a reference to this concept. There are no clear traces of it in the *On the Heavens*, he says (148). But see W. K. C. Guthrie in the introduction to his edition and translation of the latter book (Loeb Classical Series, 1953, pp. xxiii–xxv) for the *On the Heavens* in relation to Aristotle's philosophical development, xv ff., and for a discussion of Jaeger's claim that the Unmoved Mover appears "as early as the *De Philosophia*," Guthrie, especially xxv.

[20] Cherniss, *op. cit.*, p. 376. In the sentences preceding the quotation I have expressed the difference of Aristotelian from Platonic philosophy in the terminology in which it has been stated by Frank, pp. 86 f.

of *chorismos* is restated in the *Metaphysics* (1071b14 ff.) immediately before Aristotle expounds the concept of the Unmoved Mover. Clearly, his separateness is not thought to be a separateness such as attaches to the Idea of the Good or to any Platonic Idea.

One is therefore not astonished to find in other Aristotelian treatises a description of the existence of the Unmoved Mover couched in the language of immanence. Separate though God is from the world, he is said to touch the moved objects without being touched by them (*On Coming-to-be and Passing-away* 323 a30–34). He has his place in the circumference of the world (*Physics* 267b6–9; cf. *On the Heavens* 279a15–18). Both, God and *Nous,* are said to fall under the same category of substance which in the Aristotelian system applies to the existence of all things (*Nicomachean Ethics* 1096a24–25). And the active intellect, whether or not it is to be identified with the divine intellect, with God, does certainly, like the Unmoved Mover, also reside "here"; it is "in our souls" (*On the Soul* 430a13).[21] To be sure, such statements are few and must not be pressed too closely. Yet the passages attesting separateness are few also and cannot be taken in isolation. Taking into account the whole evidence, one must admit that while Aristotle tends to distinguish the existence of the Divine from the existence of things, he also tends, unlike Plato, to bring it, as it were, nearer home.[22]

I am not arguing that Aristotle succeds in his enterprise, that his solution to the problem of reality is consistent, or secure from the same objections he himself brings against Plato. I am claiming merely that his teaching cannot be understood so long as it is interpreted in a terminology that presupposes that transcendence and immanence are alternatives. His system is designed to maintain a position in between Platonic idealism and Presocratic materialism, integrating those features of both which to him seem true. As he says expressly, he wishes to be the arbiter of the contending philosophical factions. (*On the Heavens* 279a11; cf. *Physics* 206a13). It is neither transcendentalism nor immanentism that he professes, but rather a peculiar and unique combination of the two. *Idealrealismus* is perhaps the term that characterizes

[21] On the active intellect, see Ross, *Aristotle*, pp. 149; 153.

[22] Professor Randall, if I am not mistaken, refers only to *Metaphysics* 1075a12–17 (143) where the alternative of immanence and transcendence is raised and "both ways" of putting the case are said to be "probably" right. (The subject discussed here is strictly speaking the Good, but indirectly God, the Unmoved Mover; cf. Ross, *Aristotle's Metaphysic* I, p. cl). One of the passages I have quoted (*Nicomachean Ethics* 1096a24–25) seems to be considered inconsistent with Aristotle's own views by Cherniss (I, p. 363, note 27). But see Frank, *op. cit.*, p. 114, note 3, and H. H. Joachim, *Aristotle, The Nicomachean Ethics*, ed. D. A. Rees, 1951, pp. 31 ff. (*ad* 1096a11–1097a14).

best the main drift of his thought, just as it expresses most adequately the vision of the world elaborated by one of his greatest admirers and followers, the poet Goethe turned scientist and philosopher.[23]

If the description of Aristotelianism I have given is correct, if such is "the spirit of the system," to use Fichte's expression, would it have been consistent for Aristotle to propose the kind of "natural theology" that Professor Randall outlines; ought he to have meant what this theology implies? One can well imagine that Aristotle, had he been shown that change occurs in the heavenly regions, would have abandoned his theory of an inferior, sublunar world where alone things come into being and pass away. He was always willing to bow to facts. No argument, I venture to believe, would have induced him to accept a God who was merely an ideal (143). In this doctrine, even if it included the concept of the "internal-external" relation, he would have seen the victory of physics over metaphysics and, consequently, the downfall of metaphysics (1026a27 ff.). For Aristotle, separateness and eternity, though they are bound to the Here and to temporality, still remain different from them. Rejecting the analogical procedure of the *Republic*, he still establishes the concepts of Being, of the One, and of the Good, by the method of analogy.[24]

With this philosophy the philosophic critic naturally is free to take issue. He may point out to its author what he ought to have meant if he wished to be consistent, and it may well happen that the critic understands the author better than he understood himself. But if this criticism is made also in the name of "the spirit of the system," its pertinence depends on another factor: on the intentions of him who is criticized Very much like Aristotle, Kant, in his solution of the metaphysical riddle, tried to follow a middle path. As the Paralogisms of the first edition of the *Critique of Pure Reason* put it, one can and must be a "transcendental idealist" and an "empirical realist" as well; for although the categories of understanding through which the world is known are categories a priori, what is "given" to them in empirical experience is not subjective but real. Fichte saw

[23] For the term *Idealrealismus*, see P. Petersen, *Goethe und Aristoteles*, 1914, p. 58. The same ambivalence which characterizes Aristotle's understanding of the Being of God is found in his interpretation of divine thinking and cf Providence. No unqualifiedly transcendental or immanental interpretation such as Frank's (see above, note 17, and *op. cit.*, especially p. 117), therefore seems justifiable.

[24] Concerning Aristotle's *analogia entis*—a subject hardly touched upon in the book under review—and for its difference from Plato's concept of *analogia*, see Frank, *op. cit.*, p. 117, note 2.

"the spirit" of Kantianism in transcendental idealism. But his claim that the philosophy he formulated was the true consequence of Kant's insight was repudiated by the founder of critical philosophy—and not unjustly. Fichte's idealism, however true it may have seemed to Fichte and may seem to others, was not what Kant had aimed at. I cannot persuade myself that the case stands differently with regard to the naturalism Professor Randall upholds. Many of its features are, to be sure, Aristotelian. But the "more distinctive Aristotelian ideas" have, for better or worse, been omitted from it.[25]

From what has been said a final conclusion seems to follow. The distinction between the Platonist Aristotle and the Aristotelian Aristotle, which, like so many other interpreters, Professor Randall accepts, is perhaps not a fortunate one. Not only does it force the interpreter again and again to state that Aristotle is moving away from Plato and for no obvious reason returning to him in the end (e.g., 99); it is a distinction full of ambiguities and fraught with difficulties. Aristotle was a member of the Academy; he considered himself for a long time, maybe always, one of the Platonic circle. But in Plato's time the Academy had no official dogma. All the outstanding disciples of the master differed with him in important respects and had ideas of their own. One would be hard put to say what Platonism meant in detail for the men surrounding Plato. In a general sense their Platonism may be taken to stand for idealism, and in this sense Aristotle, too, was and remained a Platonist.[26] Yet even if after Plato

[25] It goes without saying that, as in the case of Aristotle (see above, p. 157), I am not presuming to decide whether Kant's philosophy is a successful solution to the riddle of the world. With regard to both I endeavor to set forth the premises of their thought from which their main theses follow. Recently "Some Assumptions of Aristotle" have been scrutinized by George Boas, *Transactions of the American Philosophical Society*, 49 (1959), part VI. In general one may say that much of the usual criticism of Aristotle (for which see Cherniss I, pp. 362, note 270; 475, note 426) is vitiated by the fact that the respective authors do not raise the historical problem as explicitly and straightforwardly as Professor Randall and that their strictures are a mixture of philosophical and historical remarks. Most often Aristotle is told that he does not say what Plato says and is therefore wrong, but not uncommonly he is told in addition that even from his own point of view he could not possibly take any other position than Plato's. Yet Aristotle did not believe that Plato was right, and he thought he had a better answer to the problem of separation posed by Plato. (This, in my opinion, is overlooked even by Boas, *op. cit.*, p. 79 b.) Unless due allowance is made for the specific premises advocated, one cannot appreciate the originality of either Aristotle or Kant.

[26] Professor Randall (see 13) is not unaware of the issue I have raised. He says, in fact, that Aristotle worked "at the problems he found in Plato's dialogues, but in his own spirit and manner" (15, cf. 18). Yet, in general he shares the common view of Aristotelian philosophy as a compromise (cf. Allan, *op. cit.*, p. 15). That his analysis of the characteristic features of Platonism seems to me debatable I have stated before (p. 153). This is too large an issue to be taken up here.

and Aristotle all men have been born either Platonists or Aristotelians, it is hard to imagine that Aristotle himself was born a Platonist and an Aristotelian. Should the truth not be rather that he was by nature an idealist as well as a naturalist, less of an idealist and more of a naturalist than the man who taught him and from whom he learned? And should not the fact that "the elements," to use Shakespeare's phrase, were "so mix'd in him" explain his difference from Plato and his agreement with him, the uniqueness and distinctiveness of his thought?

I started out by saying that Professor Randall modestly calls his book a little book; I hope that I have shown that it is also a weighty book. One cannot read it without seeing more clearly the "modernity" of the Aristotelian analysis of the world and the philosophical issues Aristotle tries to resolve, or without being drawn into renewed reflection upon the question "which was raised long ago, is still and always will be, and which always baffles us—'What is being?'" (*Metaphysics* 1028b2–4).

LUDWIG EDELSTEIN

THE ROCKEFELLER INSTITUTE

NOTES AND NEWS

The editors of the Journal regret to learn of the untimely death—at 53—of Paul Henle, professor of philosophy at the University of Michigan, in Paris, January 27, 1962. Professor Henle was on sabbatical leave in Paris when he died, studying and writing on logic and epistemology. He earned all his academic degrees at Harvard; taught there, at Smith, and at Northwestern during the course of his career; and served in the army during the war. He had been professor of philosophy at Michigan since 1950.

The Gifford Lectures on Natural Theology at the University of Glasgow were given this year by Dr. Charles W. Hendel, Emeritus Professor of Moral Philosophy and Metaphysics in Yale University. The subject of the series was "Politics: The Trial of a Pelagian Faith."

capable of improvement before the discovery, but, above all, he must be improved afterward. Anderson and Aristotle meet on the common ground of their interest in morality. If it is the "modern"thing to censure the ancient critic for drawing moral considerations into aesthetic criticism, what must we do about Anderson with his insistence upon moral realization? If it is sufficient justification for Anderson that he must meet the aspirations of his audience, perhaps it is sufficient for Aristotle too.

One other point remains before we are finished with the faulty hero—the nature of his fault. Aristotle rules out faults of vice and depravity and seems to prefer that the fault be a serious error of judgment (1453 a 8-17). As we can see in the quotation, Anderson generalizes on Aristotle and stipulates only the presence of a fault, perhaps a very slight one, which will allow the hero room for improvement.

On the third element, catharsis, Anderson does not have a great deal to say, but it is clearly a concomitant of the other two elements. At the beginning of his essay the dramatist refers to Aristotle's definition of tragedy "in his famous passage on catharsis" and poses the question "why the performance of a tragedy should have a cleansing effect on the audience" (3). Near the end of the essay he answers the question in a passage that ties together all three Aristotelian elements that we have discussed. The writer of tragedy

> must follow the ancient Aristotelian rule: he must build his plot around a scene wherein the hero discovers some mortal frailty or stupidity in himself and faces life armed with a new wisdom. He must so arrange his story that it will prove to the audience that *men pass through suffering purified*, that, animal though we are, despicable though we are in many ways, there is in us all some divine, incalculable fire that urges us to be better than we are (13, my italics).

In the light of Aristotle, several adaptations are at once apparent. First, whereas in Aristotle's view the purification is entirely an audience reaction (1452 b 30-1453 a 40, 1453 b 1-23), Anderson's audience sees it taking place in the soul of the hero and is then purified in its own collective soul by empathy. Second, Aristotle confines *suffering*, an element of the plot equal in importance to peripety and discovery, to destructive or painful actions on the stage—tortures, woundings, and the like (1452 b 10-3). Anderson makes the suffering introspective: it takes place within the soul of the hero. Third, Aristotle's tragedy effects the purgation of pity and fear (1449 b 27-8); Anderson says nothing of pity and fear, and it is evident that for him purification lifts men above all the dross of animalism and earth, so that they may "claim a kinship with a higher mortality than that which hems them in" (13). Last, of the two principal interpretations of the meaning of *κάθαρσις* Anderson chooses the moral one—that the emotions are left ennobled—rather than the medical one which has excess emotion purged away. The latter seems better established in Aristotle (Politics 1341 a 21-5, 1341 b 32-1342 a 16), but the former gives scope to the note of moral height on which a tragedy must end, according to Anderson, if it is to succeed in the theatre.

Anderson has combined into a working unit for dramatic writing three elements that Aristotle was inclined to think of separately, and in so doing he has broadened their scope to make the theatre "a religious affirmation, an age-old rite restating and reassuring man's belief in his own destiny and his ultimate hope" (14).

GEORGE YOST, JR.
UNIVERSITY OF PITTSBURGH

Aristotle and the Concept of Evolution

Nowhere in his writings does Aristotle state explicitly whether he believes or disbelieves in the eternity of the human race. Under these circumstances statements from which one could infer his opinion assume great importance. Platt, in his translation of De Generatione Animalium, comments on 762 b 28ff. in the following manner: "This is, I believe, the only passage from which we can gather anything about Aristotle's views on evolution. . . . It is clear that . . . he had no objection to the gradual development of man from some lowly organism, but also that he wisely maintained an attitude of absolute agnosticism on the question." And he adds that the passage "appears to have strangely escaped the notice of modern writers on the subject, at least I have found no reference to it in any whom I have consulted."[1]

It seems true that the words under discussion, important as they are, have not been heeded by those dealing with the history of biology, nor have they in general been given much attention by the commentators on Aristotle or by historians of philosophy. Yet more than eighty years ago J. Bernays took notice of the statement, and so did Susemihl and Zeller, following his example.[2] As Bernays pointed out, the theory of evolution is discussed by Aristotle as a mere hypothesis. He wishes to determine how man and four-footed animals could have developed if indeed they were "earth-born" as some say; and on this assumption he arrives at the conclusion that they must have originated from scolices.[3] Since Aristotle does not identify himself with this theory and since the concept of creation is irreconcilable with his philosophy, Bernays concludes

[1]Cf. The Works of Aristotle, ed. J. A. Smith and W. D. Ross, Oxford 1912, vol. V ad locum.

[2]Cf. J. Bernays, Theophrastus' Schrift über Frömmigkeit, 1866, 44ff.; E. Zeller, Die Philosophie der Griechen, II 2(3), 1879, 508, n. 1; F. Susemihl-R. D. Hicks, The Politics of Aristotle, 1894, ad 1269 a 5; cf. also below, note 5.

[3]The hypothetical form of the argument is stressed in the beginning (762 a 29) and at the end (763 b 3). The philoso-

hat Aristotle assumed the human race to be eternal. or such an interpretation he found confirmation in ristotle's insistence that all human knowledge, once ained, is lost and then again rediscovered. In this way, ernays said, Aristotle tried to defend the thesis of the ternity of mankind against the objection usually made at arts and sciences obviously were established at a latively late date in human history, a fact that seems rangely inconsistent with the claim that man existed ways.[4]

Bernays was certainly right in emphasizing the hypoetical form of Aristotle's statement. But his conusion, in my opinion, is open to two objections. First, ristotle's own views can hardly be deduced with cerinty from what he says in a passage where he is erely developing the theories of somebody else.[5] cond, not only those who admitted the eternity of ankind spoke of the repeated destruction and revery of arts and sciences. Plato did the same and t he left undecided whether man existed from the ry beginning of the world.[6] One must therefore rn to other passages in order to gain a more secure sis for deciding the issue at stake.

Now in the second book of De Generatione Animalm Aristotle proclaims that there is always a class of en and animals and plants (731 b 35 . . . *γένος ἀεὶ θρώπων καὶ ζῴων ἐστὶ καὶ φυτῶν*). At first thought might be doubtful whether the term "always" covers rnity *a parte posteriore* as well as *a parte anteriore*. t Aristotle holds that that which does not perish has ver been generated (De Caelo 282 a 31). Therefore cannot have assented to the theory of evolution ich he examines later on.[7] The assumption of a rld without men and plants and animals apparently foreign to Aristotle. So much is certain, even if his ief in the spontaneous generation of some animals d plants means that these several species were generd in course of time.[8] It is now safe to add that by theory concerning the history of arts and sciences istotle, like Thepohrastus and later Peripatetics, intended to support the supposition that the human race is eternal.[9]

The argument, as I have tried to put it, holds good also if confronted with the results of modern investigations into the chronology of the Aristotelian writings. According to these studies the biological works, of which De Generatione Animalium is part, are late; and De Caelo, where the concept of eternity is defined, though begun in Aristotle's middle period, embodies his views in their ultimate form.[10] The theory that all knowledge is lost and rediscovered is attested in the second book of the Politics (1269 b 1) that is early, but also in the late eighth chapter of Metaphysics Λ (1074 b 10.)[11] All the utterances adduced, then, are characteristic of what is held to be the final stage of Aristotelian philosophy.

I thought it worth while once more to call attention to the passage in De Generatione Animalium because of the intrinsic interest of the statement made. But there is also a more general consequence involved which should not be overlooked. The historians of science, generally speaking, characterize Aristotle as a philosopher who "saw a consistent evolution from lower to higher forms of being."[12] The historians of philosophy,

---

rs attacked are men like Anaximander (cf. also the interest- passage Diodorus I 7). Only two kinds of spontaneous eration are held conceivable by Aristotle: that from eggs that from scolices. But the former is rejected because it no analogy in reality (763 a 5ff.).

Cf. Bernays, 45ff.

Zeller seems also to have been dissatisfied with Bernays' cedure in this respect; for he quotes other Aristotelian pass- s from which the eternity of man follows, as he thinks (loc.). Susemihl, on the other hand, goes so far as to say that stotle, in De Generatione Animalium, refers to the evoluary views with "grave doubt" (loc. cit.).

Cf. Plato, Laws, 781 e-782 a and Bernays himself, op. cit. 171.

Cf. W. D. Ross, Aristotle's Metaphysics II, 1924, 357 (ad o a 21-6) who by the same argument refutes Brentano's m that "human reason, though imperishable, is not pre- stent from eternity."

Theophrastus thought that man was coexistent with the ld, but that trees and animals came into being only afterwards (cf. Porphyry, De Abstinentia II, 5; Bernays, op. cit. 39ff.). There is of course no reason to assume with Bernays (51) that Aristotle in later years might have admitted that animals developed after man. Bernays' claim is merely determined by his wish to make Theophrastus agree with Aristotle, but Theophrastus might well have been more independent than Bernays believes. For spontaneous generation of animals and plants according to Aristotle, cf. e.g. 761 b 23ff; 762 b 21ff.

9Cf. Bernays, 46ff., where the history of this debate is outlined.

10For the biological works cf. W. Jaeger, Aristoteles, 1923. 351ff. Jaeger does not mention De Generatione Animalium specifically, but this book presupposes the Historia Animalium written at the end of Aristotle's life (ibid. 352; 325, n. 1). P. Gohlke, Hermes LIX, 1924, 294ff. has not given any further clarification of the chronology of the biological writings. For De Caelo, cf. ibid., 316ff; especially 324, note 1.

11For Politics, cf. again Jaeger, 282; for Metaphysics cf. ibid., 230; for ch. 8, 368ff.

12E. Nordenskiöld, The History of Biology, 1932, 37; cf. also H. F. Osborn, From the Greeks to Darwin, 1929, 87. That at least in his later years Aristotle was favorably inclined towards the concept of evolution is assumed by C. Singer, A Short History of Biology, 1931, 39. One noteworthy exception is N. v. Hofsten, Isis, XXV, 1936, 81, who says: "Aristotle . . . has founded a general philosophic theory of evolution, but not the biological theory of evolution, viz., the theory of descent." Dr. I. E. Drabkin, in a personal communication, suggests that the identification of Aristotle with evolutionary theory is perhaps due in large measure to a curious error of Darwin. On the very first page of The Origin of Species, in the beginning of the "Historical Sketch," Darwin ascribes to Aristotle an evolutionary view, referring to Physics II 8, 198 b 18ff. But here Aristotle is citing this view only for the purpose of refuting it. For the interpretation of the Aristotelian passage itself, cf. also E. Zeller, Ueber die griechischen Vorgänger Darwin's, Vorträge und Adhandlungen, 3. Samml. 1884, 43ff., who is of the opinion that Aristotle outlines the theory as a mere experiment of thought, and that it cannot be attributed even to the pre-Socratics.

on the other hand, take the opposite stand. They deny that Aristotle's thought is suggestive of "evoluion in time, or from one species into another."[13] Both contestants in the main base their verdict on Aristotle's metaphysical and logical theories. In my opinion there can hardly be a doubt that the philosopher Aristotle was not an evolutionist. At any rate from De Generatione Animalium it follows that no protest can be entered against such a claim on the evidence of Aristotle's biological researches which in this connection certainly must be taken into account. The scientist Aristotle rejected that theory of evolution which t ancients knew. How much less can his system linked to evolutionary ideas of the nineteenth twentieth century! Where Aristotle speaks of man the highest and most perfect being, he envisages not process that leads to the evolution of man, but rath an eternal gradation inherent in the work of Natu whose ultimate aim, at least on this earth, is mankind

LUDWIG EDELSTEIN
THE JOHNS HOPKINS UNIVERSITY

COMMENT AND CONJECTURE ON MEDIAEVAL WORKS

Two Mediaeval Tours de Force

Poets from Homer to Catullus to Herrick have raved about the fascination of the human eye. The slender hand, the fair cheek, the glowing hair have all in turn furnished inspiration to sculptor and poet. But the beard —a mark of virility and dignity from Biblical times on to the modern Arab whose most sacred oath invokes the Prophet's beard—has lain unkempt and unsung.

Now the beard has not been altogether without its herald. The glorification of the beard is achieved in a religious allegory, an obscure dissertation dating from the twelfth century. The author is Burchardus de Bellevaux, a Cistertian abbot whose Apologia de Barbis was only recently discovered in Switzerland and edited, from a unique manuscript now in the British Museum, by E. P. Goldschmidt. The dissertation is addressed to the Brothers of the Monastery of Rosières in the Jura Mountains. As it stands, the manuscript consists of three sermons, divided into capita. From the general scheme and variety of the topics treated, the editor concludes that a considerable number of pages have been lost.

There had been a grim report that on account of certain disturbers of the peace—turbatoribus concordiae et dissidiosis quibusdam—the abbot had threatened to burn the beards of all the Brothers. The abbot, however, deprecates such an intention, except in the case of the guilty members. If that is not so, may his own beard not grow any more—desinat crescere barba mea.

Three things to be avoided in beards are lentipedes, spurcissima lendium caterva, pediculi. The ointment of Aaron's beard (unguentum barbae Aaron) destroys such vermin. This ointment has a triple virtue: puritas cordis, conscientiae bonitas, fidei veritas. The first type of worm clings to the flesh, the second to the hair, while the third runs over flesh and hair. There are three corresponding vitia: voluptas, associated with the first type of worm; inhonestas, with the second type; duplicitas, with the third. The unguentum barbae Aaron is to be used against lepra barbae. He who lapses into heres acquires lepra barbae.

Some condemn the saliva flowing from the bea but there is a moral significance attached to this co dition. David, pretending madness, let his saliva fl from his beard. He defiled his wisdom with humili just as he defiled his beard.

All references and discussions involving the be are closely and continuously linked with spirit values: types of beards and moustaches (grennone the size and trimming of moustaches; the spiritual i plications of the half-shaved messengers of David; w monks shave the beard; the tonsure; of a certain Ga who was barbata, and the medical advice that she jected; 'laughing in the beard'; why the goat is bea ed; the beard as a sign of courage and wisdom, w biblical illustrations; the fate of the beard in fut life. Throughout, there is a running closely reason exegesis, in St. Jerome's style, buttressed by numer allusions and citations, biblical, apocryphal, hag graphical, classical.

The syntax and vocabulary follow mediaeval—n ably ecclesiastical—usage, interspersed with rare pressions, colloquialisms, and neologisms—*rasbagi, b unitari, veraciter*, compounds of *barba*: *pleniberb barbilogia, tardiberbium, citiberbium*. There are oc sional proverbs borrowed from the literate mediae sermo, De cane quod canis est nec aqua nec pect tolles, In barba non iacet sapientia.

* * * * *

When the mediaeval scholars were academic th were not rarely dull; and when they attempted to whimsical and light, they were often still more so.

Poggio the Florentine, however, had the light tou as well as the weighty manner. One of his airier thin in this genre, is the little-known Dialogus an seni uxor ducenda. It was written about 1435 and first pu lished privately in Liverpool from a manuscript in Bibliothèque Nationale in 1805.

Ironically, this Ciceronian dialogue of Poggio Br

[13]L. Robin, Greek Thought and the Origins of the Scientific Spirit, 1928, 295; cf. also W. D Ross, Aristotle, 1924, 39.

[14]Cf. Zeller, 501ff, especially 505, note 1.

REVIEWS.

W. JAEGER. Diokles von Karystos. Die griechische Medizin und die Schule des Aristoteles. Berlin, 1938. Pp. 244.

Jaeger's book is the first modern monograph on Diocles, whose fame in antiquity almost equalled that of Hippocrates. That recent scholars have neglected him may partly be due to the fact that only fragments of his writings are preserved.[1]

Against the common belief Jaeger tries to demonstrate that Diocles did not live before Aristotle. Rose's opinion to the same effect did not carry any conviction, for it was made as an aperçue rather than elaborated as a doctrine. Maass' splendid observation that Diocles avoids hiatus elucidated a detail of his style, but did not prove that he lived in the last third of the 4th century B. C., as Maass suggested (cf. Jaeger, pp. 13 ff.). By placing the scattered references to Diocles into the framework of Greek philosophy Jaeger puts on a new basis the discussion of the problems involved, for he shows for the first time to what extent Diocles' language and thought coincide with Aristotelian formulations and ideas. Jaeger then concludes that Diocles must have been dependent on Aristotle and that he must have been at least his contemporary, for otherwise Aristotle would be dependent on Diocles, and that too in regard to important metaphysical and ethical concepts as well as characteristic scientific terms and stylistic devices.

Such a line of reasoning, no doubt, contains an *a priori* assumption which is not incontestable. Aristotle in many respects is dependent on his predecessors, and if it were certain that Diocles lived earlier, one would have to resign oneself to the fact that it is Diocles who taught Aristotle. Yet, whereas scholars so far had concluded from ancient testimony that Diocles died around 350 B. C., certainly before Aristotle formulated his own philosophical system, Jaeger infers from the fragments that he died after 300 B. C. and before 288/7 B. C. (p. 119). In an article, published shortly after his book had appeared, Jaeger goes even farther and tries to prove that Diocles lived from 340-260 B. C.[2] In both cases Jaeger's thesis is based on the interpretation of the same two statements which alone, it seems,

[1] M. Wellmann, *Die Fragmente der Sikelischen Ärzte Akron, Philistion und des Diokles von Karystos* (Berlin, 1901).

[2] *Vergessene Fragmente des Peripatetikers Diokles von Karystos, Abhandlungen der Preussischen Akademie der Wissenschaften*, 1938, Phil.-hist. Klasse, No. 3, p. 17. (This paper I shall quote as II, whereas the book will be quoted as I).

provide direct information about Diocles' lifetime, the one coming from Theophrastus (*Περὶ λίθων*, chap. 5 — frag. 166 Wellmann), the other from Athenaeus (II 59a — frag. 125 Wellmann).

Frag. 166, although of secondary importance for Jaeger, must be considered first, because of certain difficulties which it involves. It reads thus: *ἕλκει γὰρ* (*scil. τὸ λυγγούριον*) *ὥσπερ τὸ ἤλεκτρον, οἱ δέ φασιν οὐ μόνον κάρφη καὶ ξύλον, ἀλλὰ καὶ χαλκὸν καὶ σίδηρον, ἐὰν ᾖ λεπτός, ὥσπερ καὶ Διοκλῆς ἔλεγεν.* Originally Jaeger claimed that Diocles, who was still alive around 300 B. C., must have been dead at the time when these words were written (before 288/7 [I, p. 119]), since Theophrastus speaks of him in the imperfect. Later he maintains only, again on account of the use of the imperfect, that Diocles was not in Athens when Theophrastus wrote (II, p. 13), another possible explanation of the tense discussed by Jaeger in his book, but there rejected as unlikely (*loc. cit.*).

The possibility of such a flexible interpretation of the imperfect (cf. also I, p. 14), in my opinion, does not enhance confidence in the certainty of either the one or the other conclusion. Moreover, Pliny, in paraphrasing the passage, says (XXXVII, 53): *quod Diocli cuidam Theophrastus quoque credit.* Jaeger, referring to the somewhat deprecatory expression *Diocli cuidam*, says: "Dieser Unterschied in der Bewertung des Diokles bei Theophrast und Plinius würde allein schon fast genügen, um zu beweisen, dass es sich um den grossen peripatetischen Arzt handeln muss . . ." (I, p. 117); and he claims that Diocles "für ihn (*scil.* Pliny) keine greifbare Grösse mehr ist" (*loc. cit.*). Yet, since Theophrastus does not pass any judgment on Diocles' achievements, it is impossible to speak of differences in the evaluations pronounced by Theophrastus and by Pliny. Besides, it is hardly justifiable to cavil at Pliny's appreciation of Diocles' importance, for Pliny, who in other places mentions Diocles either simply by name or as the physician Diocles, calls him "the second in glory to Hippocrates" (XXVI, 10 — frag. 5 Wellmann). Since Pliny understood Theophrastus' statement to refer to a *certain* Diocles, this Diocles for Pliny could not be identical with the famous Diocles. Therefore it is dangerous, I believe, to use the fragment at all for determining the lifetime of Diocles of Carystus.[8]

[8] There is at least one other fragment the genuineness of which is doubtful (frag. 99 Wellmann), cf. J. Heeg, *Sitzungsberichte der Preussischen Akademie der Wissenschaften*, 1911, pp. 991 ff. Wellmann's revindication of the fragment (*Hermes*, XLVIII [1913], pp. 464 ff.) is not convincing. Another physician Diocles is known from Galen (XIII, p. 87 Kühn, and Wellmann, p. 65, n. 1), not to speak of all the others by that name referred to in ancient literature. Cf. also D'Arcy Wentworth Thompson, *The Philosophical Review*, XLVIII (1939), pp. 212-213.

The chronological evidence thus seems restricted to frag. 125: *Διοκλῆς δὲ κολοκύντας μὲν καλλίστας γίνεσθαι περὶ Μαγνησίαν, προσέτι τε γογγύλην ὑπερμεγέθη γλυκεῖαν καὶ εὐστόμαχον, ἐν Ἀντιοχείᾳ δὲ σικυόν, ἐν δὲ Σμύρνῃ καὶ Γαλατίᾳ θρίδακα, πήγανον δ' ἐν Μύροις.* The mention of Antioch, Jaeger says—taking up an argument of Rose entirely overlooked and forgotten later on—proves that Diocles was still alive when that city was founded or even for some time thereafter; Diocles must have lived, therefore, until 300 B. C. (I, pp. 67 ff.). Yet, as Theiler pointed out to Jaeger, Galatia is mentioned in the same fragment, and the name Galatia cannot have been used earlier than 270 B. C. (cf. II, p. 16). Jaeger, therefore, finally assumes as Diocles' term of life the years 340 to 260 B. C. (II, pp. 17; 36), and he claims that Diocles must have lived long enough to polemize against Herophilus whose *floruit* lies between 270 and 260 B. C. (cf. II, pp. 15; 36 ff.).

How does such a hypothesis fit in with the indirect evidence? When in his book Jaeger discusses Vindicianus' (4/5th century A. D.) doxographical survey of medical problems in which certain theories of Diocles are formulated as answers to the doctrines of Herophilus, he writes: "Wir müssen also entweder Wellmanns Voraussetzung preisgeben, dass in dem Exzerpt wörtliche Zitate aus Diokles vorliegen, oder folgern, dass Diokles im 3. Jahrh. lange genug gelebt habe, um eine Schrift gegen Herophilos verfassen zu können, der von Galen und anderen antiken Zeugen ausdrücklich als jünger als Diokles bezeichnet wird und nach herrschender Annahme erst vom zweiten und dritten Jahrzehnt an 'geblüht' hat. Dieser Synchronismus hat natürlich etwas Verlockendes, wenn man schon einmal dabei ist, die ganze Chronologie und Entwicklungsgeschichte der griechischen Medizin von Hippokrates bis zum Beginn des hellenistischen Zeitalters umzustossen. Aber hier stehen wir im Begriff, den Boden sicherer Tatsachen zu verlassen und statt der überwundenen Schwierigkeiten neue zu schaffen" (I, p. 200). Indeed, the assumption that Diocles could have opposed views held by Herophilus is inconsistent with the testimonies of Celsus and Galen (frags. 4; 16 Wellmann) who agree that Diocles wrote before Herophilus.

Why does Jaeger now (II, p. 15) consider as genuine the so-called answers of Diocles to Herophilus which he himself had shown to be arranged by Vindicianus, as is typical of this late compilatory literature (I, pp. 200 ff.)? His main reason for changing his mind is the reference to Galatia (II, p. 16); and yet, Kaibel, in his edition of Athenaeus, had already remarked: *γαλατείᾳ* C E, videtur corruptum; Kaibel's statement is probably due to stylistic considerations, as Jaeger explains (*loc. cit.*). Jacoby, too, regards *καὶ Γαλατίᾳ* as an obvious insertion which destroys the careful antithesis otherwise to be observed in these words (Jacoby *apud* Jaeger, *loc. cit.*, p. 16, n. 2). Moreover, since the statement apparently means to tell where the best kind of lettuce is grown, it would be hardly appropriate to name two places of production (Smyrna and Galatia); also in the words immediately preceding and following only one place is mentioned for the best kind of vegetables referred to there (cf. E. Kind, *Philologische Wochenschrift*, LIX [1939], p. 528). Finally, Diocles, in giving the places of origin, usually speaks of cities, not of countries (Jaeger, II, p. 16). One must conclude, I think, that καὶ Γαλατίᾳ is a later insertion; additions in statements of this kind are certainly nothing extraordinary.

At any rate, the contention that Diocles lived long enough to write against Herophilus—a claim which is refuted by all indirect testimony—cannot be established by the evidence adduced by Jaeger.[4] Besides, the content of Diocles' teaching is in no way linked to the work done by Herophilus and his associates; on the contrary, Diocles' doctrine and method are characteristic of the bent of the older generation. To give one striking example: Diocles' anatomy is animal anatomy, not human anatomy (cf. I, p. 165), which is a distinctive feature of Hellenistic medicine. It is safe to say that none of the new medical concepts, as conceived by the physicians of the first half of the third century B. C., is reechoed in the fragments preserved from Diocles' writings. Had he really lived and worked from 340-260 B. C. his system would be an outright anachronism. That it was is, of course, not impossible; yet this could be concluded only on the basis of irrefutable evidence.

If the chronological argument from the fragments allows of any conclusion at all, it proves that Diocles lived until 300 B. C., the time in which Antioch was founded, or shortly after, in other words perhaps from 375-295 B. C. Such a result is not incompatible with Pliny's and Galen's opinion that Diocles lived shortly after Hippocrates (frag. 5 Wellmann, *secundus aetate* (*scil.* Hippocratis); frag. 26 Wellmann, μικρὸν ὕστερον Ἱπποκράτους),[5] for Hippocrates probably died around 380 B. C. The new date for Diocles' lifetime can also be reconciled with Celsus'

[4] Consequently it seems impossible to accept either Jaeger's identification of Diocles of Carystus with the Diocles mentioned in the will of Strato (II, pp. 10 ff.), or his new dates for the physicians of the 4th century B. C., which he bases on his chronology of Diocles (II, pp. 36 ff.). Furthermore, if Jaeger's thesis as formulated in his article is adopted, it becomes even more doubtful that the so-called letter of Diocles to Antigonus is genuine (I, pp. 70 ff.), for Diocles could hardly write to the king on an equal footing around 305/4 (I, p. 79) if he was at that time 35 years old and at the beginning of his career.

[5] I fail to understand Jaeger's statement that a *floruit* of Diocles shortly before or around 300 B. C. is in agreement with Pliny's expression: *Diocles secundus aetate famaque Hippocratis* (II, p. 12), nor can I see that Galen's μικρὸν ὕστερον Ἱπποκράτους is already a misrepresentation of the tradition, because it puts Diocles immediately after Hippocrates (II, p. 37).

reckoning of generations (frag. 4, *post quem* (*scil.* Hippocratem) *Diocles Carystius, deinde Praxagoras et Chrysippus, tum Herophilus et Erasistratus*). Yet, I think one must admit that Diocles' lifetime then extends over a longer period or begins at a later date than one would have guessed from the indirect information.

Nevertheless, even if one is inclined to disregard the one direct testimony (frag. 125) entirely, since it certainly has been altered by addition, and since the foundation of Antioch seems a rather late *terminus post quem* for Diocles' death—even then it would be in accord with all the other ancient witnesses to assume that Diocles was a contemporary of Aristotle. Before Jaeger nobody ever seriously considered this possibility, for the close ideological and stylistic resemblance between the work of the two men had not been observed and the question of their mutual dependence consequently was no issue. Now that this observation has been made, one becomes aware that nothing prevents assuming Diocles to have been of the same age as Aristotle or somewhat younger.[6] On the contrary, the evidence points in this direction, for according to all sources Diocles was later than Hippocrates; there is no indication that the two were contemporaries, they are always distinguished as belonging to different generations. The chronological argument then, rightly considered, is in favor of Jaeger's first thesis of a close proximity of Diocles and Aristotle. This again makes it unnecessary to explain their agreement by presuming that Aristotle borrows from Diocles.

All these considerations do not, of course, indicate the extent of the reciprocal influence of the two men, or whose influence was the stronger and more important. It stands to reason that Diocles, in the methodological discussions in which he shares the views of Aristotle,[7] is dependent on him. Tradition does not suggest any philosophical originality of Diocles, and the fragments show a combination of different trends rather than a strongly personal point of view. Diocles may also have taken over the terminology, which in many respects closely resembles that of Aristotle (I, pp. 16 ff.).[8] Allowance must be made, however, for some exception to the contrary even in regard to this relation. Too little is known about Diocles to exclude the possibility of his having some philosophical ideas of his own or devising some stylistic novelty.[9] The statement of Diocles (II,

[6] Cf. Jaeger, I, p. 12: "Einen durchschlagenden Grund für . . . frühe Datierung des Diokles gibt es in der Tat nicht."

[7] *ποιότης* (?), *ὅμοιον, ἀρχαὶ ἀναπόδεικτοι, ἁρμόττον* (I, pp. 25 ff.; 37 ff.); the concept of teleology (pp. 51 ff.).

[8] *ἐνδέχεσθαι* (I, p. 23); *ποσαχῶς λέγεται* (p. 24); *συμβαίνειν εἴωθε* (p. 31).

[9] Especially if he had been a *ῥήτωρ* (frag. 99 Wellmann, and Jaeger I, p. 2). But Wellmann's emendation was rejected and the genuineness of the fragment disputed by Heeg (cf. *supra* n. 3).

pp. 5 ff.) in which he disagrees with Aristotle in the explanation of winds shows that, in spite of all his dependence on Aristotelian philosophy, Diocles was able to judge for himself even in questions of natural philosophy. Nor is there any reason why it should have been necessary for him to learn what he learned by a careful study of the published *Ethics* as well as from the oral lectures which he had heard.[10]

Yet, if it is reasonable to assume Diocles' dependence on Aristotle in these matters, a similar subordination of Diocles the zoologist and physician is not probable. It is hardly a "Skandalon der historischen Vernunft" (I, p. 177) that Diocles' work is represented as one of the sources of Aristotle's zoological writings. In the first place, Diocles discussed questions of zoology not only in his meager dietetical books, as Jaeger at one place says (I, p. 176), but also in his treatise on anatomy, the first ever written (Galen, II, p. 282 Kühn = frag. 23 Wellmann). This book, then, could have been a source of information for Aristotle, as Jaeger elsewhere admits (I, pp. 183-4), and a source of special importance if Aristotle himself did not write on anatomy (I, p. 165, n. 1). Such a work presupposes systematic knowledge and most probably contained a description of animal parts (contrary to Jaeger, *loc. cit.*); there is certainly no proof that it was unsystematic or lacking in description. Moreover, even disregarding the problem of the Coan zoological system (I, pp. 167 ff.), Aristotle himself testifies to his knowledge of forerunners in the field; he cannot have been the first to establish a system of zoology.[11] This fact in no way detracts from the remarkable qualities of his work or from the incomparable greatness of his achievement. Even where he takes over his knowledge, he maintains his independent attitude. Jaeger was doubtless correct when in his book he interpreted *De Generatione Animalium* II 7, 745 b 33-746 a 28 as a polemic against Diocles' divergent opinions (I, p. 166) and suggested that there may be many other such polemics in the Aristotelian writings (I, p. 167).[12] Still, even controversy does not exclude dependence, in the case of Aristotle any more than in the case of Diocles, the natural scientist.

[10] I, p. 59: "Nun scheint mir aber aus unserer Untersuchung zugleich unwiderleglich hervorzugehen, dass Diokles die ethische Lehre des späten Aristoteles nicht *nur* aus mündlichem Vortrag, sondern in ihrer genauen schriftlichen Formulierung gekannt hat, wie sie in der Nikomachischen Ethik uns vorliegt."

[11] Cf. I. V. Carus, *Geschichte der Zoologie* (1872), pp. 57 ff.; 77. If Buffon, Cuvier, and Alexander v. Humboldt are inclined to see in Aristotle the first whom tradition mentions, the originator of zoology and its system (I, pp. 167-8), Aristotle himself answers (*Poetics*, 1448 b 27-30): *τῶν μὲν οὖν πρὸ Ὁμήρου οὐδενὸς ἔχομεν εἰπεῖν τοιοῦτον ποίημα, εἰκὸς δὲ εἶναι πολλούς.*

[12] Attention must be called, however, to the fact that this interpretation of these passages cannot be reconciled with the chronology set up in Jaeger's later article.

As for Diocles the physician—no general considerations make it probable or acceptable that he, the son of a physician, wherever his opinions coincide with those of Aristotle, even in medicine, must be borrowing from him, or that in these instances both go back to the same source (I, pp. 218-19). To be sure, it would be hopeless to collect all the cases of their agreement and to divine which one is following the other (Jaeger, *loc. cit.*). Yet there are also cases in which Diocles deviates from Aristotle (e. g. I, p. 166); and certainly, if Diocles even as a physician had nothing to offer Aristotle he could not have been "the second in glory to Hippocrates" and one of the doctors whom Aristotle praises by saying: "those physicians who have subtle and inquiring minds have something to say about natural science and claim to derive their principles therefrom."[13] Finally, Aristotle asserts that philosophers should discuss the causes of death and disease only up to a certain point (μέχρι του); he does not say that they have to become physicians themselves (*ibid.*). Why, then, should he not have learned from Diocles?

To sum up: Jaeger has shown, I believe, that Diocles was a contemporary of Aristotle and deeply influenced by Aristotelian philosophy, the first physician of the "synthetic type" (I, pp. 5; 220), integrating, as a true Aristotelian, the achievements of the whole past (I, p. 224). These results of Jaeger's interpretation, results of the greatest importance, must be protected and upheld against certain exaggerations to which he himself is liable in determining the rôle of Aristotle as compared with that of Diocles; they must be kept safe against the new position which Jaeger has later taken in regard to the chronological questions. Only then will a more appropriate appreciation of Diocles' achievements be reached.[14]

LUDWIG EDELSTEIN.

THE JOHNS HOPKINS UNIVERSITY.

ETTORE BIGNONE. Studi sul Pensiero Antico. Naples, Luigi Loffredo, 1938. Pp. viii + 355. L. 15.

This interesting volume represents a collection of articles dealing with Antiphon the sophist, Plato, Aristotle, Epicurus, and Ennius. All of these articles had already appeared in Italian periodicals. In fact, one of them, "Il pensiero platonico ed il Timeo," was published as far back as 1910; and I feel some doubt as to whether it was really wise to include it, almost

[13] *De Respiratione* 480 b 22 ff., Hett's translation (Loeb Classical Library [1935], p. 479).

[14] When this was already in page-proof there appeared (*Philos. Rev.*, XLIX [July, 1940], pp. 393 ff.) an article of Jaeger's summarizing the views expressed in his book and paper here reviewed.

AMERICAN JOURNAL OF PHILOLOGY

Founded by B. L. GILDERSLEEVE

Edited by

HENRY T. ROWELL

VOLUME LXXVI

BALTIMORE: THE JOHNS HOPKINS PRESS
LONDON: ARTHUR F. BIRD
PARIS: ALBERT FONTEMOING LEIPZIG: F. A. BROCKHAUS

1955

REVIEWS.

FRITZ WEHRLI. Die Schule des Aristoteles, Texte und Kommentar. Heft IV: Demetrios von Phaleron. Pp. 89; Heft V: Straton von Lampsakos. Pp. 83; Heft VI: Lykon und Ariston von Keos. Pp. 67; Heft VII: Herakleides Pontikos. Pp. 124. Basel, Benno Schwabe, 1949-1953.

Wehrli's new edition of the remains of the Peripatetic writings down to the first century B. C. has been proceeding with admirable speed. Three fascicles appeared between 1944 and 1948.[1] By 1953, four more had come out. To be sure, in regard to the authors covered by the latter series, excellent preparatory work had been done during recent years. Yet it is no mean achievement that within less than a decade Wehrli was able to finish seven out of the ten volumes projected to make up the great work he has undertaken single-handed.

Starting with fascicle IV, the principles followed in editing the texts have been slightly changed. Fragments doubtfully attributed are now indented; the critical apparatus lists the manuscripts from which the various readings are cited (*Nachwort*, H. IV).[2] These are welcome improvements. It remains regrettable that Wehrli has not seen fit to add an *index locorum* to each fascicle. (All indices are to appear in the final volume which will contain an analysis of the development of the Peripatetic doctrine.) Moreover, in the case of authors like Demetrius and Heraclides, where the editions of Jacoby and Voss respectively are commonly referred to in the pertinent literature, a concordance of the old and the new numeration of the fragments would have been most desirable.

That Wehrli's collection integrates all the evidence hitherto known, one will take for granted. Does it also bring new material? For an answer to this question no criterion is provided by the mere number of fragments as compared with that in earlier editions, e. g. 181 fragments of Heraclides in Wehrli as against 107 in Voss. Unlike the latter, Wehrli does not distinguish *testimonia* and fragments; passages are broken up into small pieces and are sometimes repeated; if no other statement can be traced to titles mentioned in book lists, they reappear as separate fragments, a fact which accounts for 27 "fragments" of Heraclides (and incidentally for 34 out of the 150 fragments of Straton). On the other hand, certain testimonies overlooked by Voss are now included (e. g. Heraclides, 145; 162); parallels not indicated by him have been added (e. g. 51b; c); more recent editions of papyri have yielded additional information (e. g. 9; 13c; 14b). On the whole however one gains the impression that the additions concern only minutiae and that it

---

[1] Cf. the reviews of H. Cherniss, *A. J. P.*, LXIX (1948), pp. 455-7; LXX (1949), pp. 414-18.

[2] P. von der Mühll put his collations of the manuscripts of Diogenes Laertius at Wehrli's disposal, cf. VII, p. 9, line 9.

has proved impossible to discover important new testimony. And a comparison of Wehrli's material on Lycon, Ariston, Demetrius, and Straton with that to be found in Mueller, Jacoby, and the studies by Gercke, Capelle, and others, leads to the same conclusion.[3]

Wherever the attribution of individual fragments is debatable, Wehrli takes a commendably conservative and cautious attitude (e. g. Demetrius, Fr. 114; Heraclides, Fr. 164). Yet one cannot help feeling that his reasons for accepting or rejecting a certain piece of evidence in many instances are stated rather briefly or dogmatically (e. g. Demetrius, Frs. 25; 38 f.; 134; Straton, Fr. 113). Straton, Fr. 128, where the name Straton is a conjecture by Diels, is taken as genuine without an adequate refutation of Capelle's contention that the ascription is "absolutely uncertain" (*R.-E.*, IV A, *s. v.*, col. 305). If Heraclides of Ainos rather than Heraclides of Pontos is referred to in Fr. 11, as Wehrli seems to admit in his commentary (cf. also Zeller, *Philosophie der Griechen*, II, 1[4], p. 989, n. 3), the story contained in Fr. 16, which in Diogenes Laertius follows immediately and is told on the same authority, must be suspected too; it is in fact excluded from Voss' collection (cf. also Daebritz, *R.-E.*, VIII, *s. v.*, cols. 473 f.). In the case of Straton, Wehrli refuses, rightly I think, to follow Diels in considering the introduction to Hero's *Pneumatics* merely a "shortened summary" of Straton's views, and consequently restricts himself to printing only a very few excerpts. To determine how much Hero derived from Straton, he says (p. 57), would demand a special investigation. It is too bad that Wehrli himself did not provide such an analysis for which he was better prepared than anyone else. Without this, the selection made by him must remain unconvincing, and it might have been better to exclude the indirect evidence altogether—as Wehrli usually does—despite the fact that parallels are adduced to establish at least the authenticity of the passages included.

The testimony on Ariston raises a particularly difficult problem. Even the ancients themselves found it hard to separate the work of the Peripatetic Ariston from that of his Stoic namesake (Fr. 9). That the Philodemus quotations (Frs. 13-15) must go back to Ariston, the Aristotelian, Wehrli reaffirms with new arguments. I am less sure that I can follow him when he claims for Ariston of Keos four of the fragments ascribed to Ariston of Chios by v. Arnim (Frs. 16; 21; 25; 26; cf. I, 401; 390; 402; 400 Arnim), with whose position Wehrli otherwise agrees (cf. *ad* Fr. 9), thus indirectly rejecting the attempt of Gercke to foster upon the Peripatetic philosopher even the fragments quoted from a book entitled Ὁμοιώματα (cf. *Arch. f. Gesch. d. Philos.*, V [1892], p. 205; also *R.-E.*, *s. v.* "Ariston," no. 52). Now, Fr. 26 Wehrli derives from Stobaeus, who in Arnim's opinion is borrowing consistently from the Stoic work just mentioned. Nor is an interest in the Spartan laws on marriage, though in line with Platonic and Aristotelian teaching (Commentary, *ad loc.*), necessarily alien to a Stoic. Zeno's *Politeia* was modelled after that of Lycurgus (I, 261 Arnim). The other three references

---

[3] Since the lack of indices makes it difficult to render a precise estimate, I should mention that at least in regard to Demetrius my judgment is confirmed by P. De Lacy, *C. P.*, XLVI (1951), p. 132.

are taken from Plutarch who knows both the Stoic and the Peripatetic Ariston. Physiognomic observations like those contained in Fr. 21, even if Platonic in flavor, square well with remarks attributed to Zeno (I, 204; cf. also 248 Arnim), and to Cleanthes (I, 618 Arnim), and with other statements traceable to the Stoic Ariston (I, 388 Arnim). And I should think that it is quite compatible with the "cynic coarseness" of Ariston's style to compare the beauty of the body which betrays the beauty of the soul with a well-fitting shoe pointing up the shapeliness of the foot. Again, the fact that Fr. 25 reflects a "realistic" point of view can hardly be considered sufficient reason for proving Peripatetic authorship. Ariston, the Stoic, was not a rigorous adherent of the dogma, as Wehrli dubs him (p. 64). His heterodoxies were many and were vehemently censured by the school (cf. e.g. Pohlenz, *Die Stoa,* I [1948], pp. 27 f.). In moral actions he ascribed a positive value to the prevailing circumstances, a point upon which Wehrli himself comments in connection with Demetrius, Fr. 84, where he also points out Ariston's influence on the unorthodox Panaetius. Would such an heretical view not imply a realistic outlook on human affairs? Finally, that Fr. 16 fits in with the other remains of the book entitled Ὁμοιώματα even Wehrli does not deny (p. 62). There seems no firm ground then for the redistribution of the fragments which he proposes.[4]

As for the commentary on the various authors, it provides a good starting point for the study of the fragments. The literary and rhetorical evidence, which forms the greater bulk of the material in the fascicles under review, is treated very fully. The remarks on Ariston's description of the various types of character (Frs. 13-16) and on Demetrius' theory of rhetoric are models of annotation that greatly helps to clarify the subject. On the other hand, issues of detail raised in the earlier debate often do not find an answer. Thus nothing is said about Jacoby's suggestion (*F. Gr. Hist.*, II D, *Kommentar*, p. 649, 35 ff.) that the last sentence of Demetrius, Fr. 166, may not belong to the quotation from Demetrius, or that, on the contrary, it may be necessary to print even more, namely the passage which links Fr. 166 to Fr. 161. Again, in commenting on Demetrius, Fr. 154, Wehrli maintains that Demetrius in his report on Isocrates must have connected the latter's voluntary death with the battle of Chaeroneia; his only reference is to Wilamowitz, *Hermes*, XXXIII (1898), p. 495. But Jacoby takes a different view (*Kommentar*, p. 651, 41 ff.), in confirmation of which he quotes *Philol. Unters.*, XVI (1902), p. 342, notes 1-2. Furthermore, it seems to me that the strictly philosophical testimony has received not quite the same consideration as the rest of the evidence. To be sure, Straton's doctrine of perception (Frs. 107 ff.) is fully discussed, and so is Heraclides' astronomical theory (Frs. 104-17). But Wehrli's commentary on Straton hardly absolves the reader from constantly checking back to Capelle's penetrating criticism of the fragments.

In the four commentaries there are of course a great number of individual problems that would deserve notice. Instead of scrutinizing these, however, I shall endeavor to discuss at least some aspects of the general evaluation of the different personalities as it emerges from Wehrli's statements.

---

[4] For the material on Ariston, cf. also below, pp. 418-19.

While earlier interpreters were inclined to deny to Demetrius any interest in metaphysical or logical investigations (e. g. E. Bayer, *Tüb. Beitr. z. Altertumswissenschaft*, XXXVI [1942], p. 150; cf. p. 154), Wehrli is willing to allow for the possibility that Demetrius may have written on epistemological and dialectical problems (Frs. 187; 155). To me, this suggestion is very plausible. A writer whose aim it was to mediate between philosophy and rhetoric by making both serve the truth (Fr. 157; pp. 79 f.) can easily be credited with studies on the question of knowledge, and the title *Περὶ τοῦ δόκου* (Fr. 187) is best explained as pointing to a work of this kind. To doubt with Jacoby (*Kommentar*, p. 644, 14 ff.) the genuineness of the ascription of such a book to Demetrius is warranted only if one sees in him a mere *littérateur*. I wonder whether the treatise *Περὶ πίστεως* (Fr. 87) was not another essay in epistemology, a possibility which Wehrli considers, but finally rejects in favor of the assumption that the subject dealt with was ethical. Philodemus (Fr. 157) criticizing Demetrius for his attempt "to deprive the philosopher of the search for truth and giving it to the rhetorician instead," charges that Demetrius tried to transfer the authority he once held in political affairs to the realm of inquiries that require proof (*καὶ ἐπὶ τὰς σκέψεις μετάγει τὰς πίστεως δεομένας*). Had Demetrius really written on proof, the rebuttal would be especially poignant and deadly. It is true, the essay in question is mentioned among the ethical writings of Demetrius, but the order followed in the book list shows other inconsistencies (cf. *ad* Frs. 74-6).

The fact that Straton selected Lycon as his successor (Frs. 4-6), Wehrli characterizes as "*Notlösung*" (p. 2), but he admits that Lycon's general orientation may have seemed a desirable change from the tendencies represented by Straton. This interpretation, I think, is the most convincing yet proposed of Straton's will. Wehrli rightly disagrees with Wilamowitz' total condemnation of Lycon and rather sides with Brinck's more positive characterization of his policy (*R.-E.*, Suppl. VII, *s. v.* "Peripatos," cols. 932 f.). Wehrli himself has put Lycon's achievement in proper perspective by pointing out that his definition of the end of life came to be included in the doxographical tradition (*ad* Fr. 15, p. 24). He probably is also right in claiming (*ad* Fr. 20) that Lycon by the true joy of the soul meant the joy derived from a good education rather than that resulting from contemplation. This no doubt would involve a certain deviation from the teaching of Aristotle. That nevertheless the definition retains at least the Aristotelian spirit may perhaps become clearer through a comparison with the one proposed by Ariston's fellow-student, Hieronymus, who under the influence of the Cyrenaic and Epicurean schools taught that the aim of life consists in freedom from pain (Cicero, *Acad. prior.*, II, 42, 131). In the issue that split the Peripatos—Hieronymus founded a school of his own—Lycon remained in opposition to the then ascending moral ideal of imperturbability and freedom from emotions. If his approval of natural goods made him liable to the charge of "luxurious living," one will do well to remember that the same charge was brought by followers of Crates against Theophrastus and Xenocrates (Metrocles, *apud* Teletem, p. 40, 4 ff. Hense), even before it was raised against Demetrius or Lycon (*ad* Fr. 7).

Lycon and his pupil Ariston both were assiduous students of the Aristotelian works (Lycon, Fr. 9). Both were engaged primarily in ethical or rhetorical investigations, but in addition were probably also concerned with inquiries into nature (Lycon, Frs. 28-30; Ariston, Frs. 34-35). On the basis of Stobaeus' report (*Eclog.*, I, p. 347, 21 W.) about the various faculties of the soul according to "Ariston," Zeller (*op. cit.*, II, 2[3], p. 926, n. 3) assumed that Ariston was interested also in epistemology and psychology. Arnim has attributed the fragment from Stobaeus to the Stoic Ariston (I, 377), and Wehrli seems to agree with him; at any rate, he does not include the Stobaeus passage in his collection. But within the context of Stoic philosophy, and of the philosophy of the Stoic Ariston in particular, the statement is extremely hard to understand. Two parts of the soul are distinguished, the one capable of sensory perception, the other "by itself and separate from [any] organs"; the latter is either non-existent in animals, or inadequately developed, and has therefore no name; in men, however, in whom alone it appears, it is called reason (νοῦς). Now, the Stoics of Ariston's time were sensualists; none of them taught that reason could function independently of the senses or any bodily organs; they made a sharp distinction between animals and men and attributed reason to man alone.[5] Ariston himself rejected all physical and logical inquiries and restricted philosophy to ethical questions. The theory outlined then is hardly reconcilable with his point of view, and would surely be unique within the context of the other fragments. But it fits in well with the Peripatetic investigations on the psychology of animals known to have extended to Lycon's time (cf. Regenbogen, *R.-E.*, Suppl. VII, *s. v.* "Theophrastos von Eresos," col. 1432). Straton had gone so far as to attribute reason (νοῦς) even to animals (Fr. 48). The author quoted by Stobaeus seems to have been a Peripatetic who made an attempt to return to the Aristotelian notion according to which reason is not bound up with the body or any organ (cf. *De Anima*, 429 a 26; b5), and also to oppose Straton's revolutionary doctrine without completely rejecting all its implications. And is it not most likely, as Zeller maintains, that the Ariston mentioned by Stobaeus is Ariston of Keos? The other Peripatetic by this name who lived in the first century B. C. is a rather unimportant figure and is known only for his natural and logical studies (cf. Zeller, *op. cit.*, III, 1[3], p. 614, n. 1; pp. 627 f.). Ariston, the friend or pupil of Critolaus (Sextus Empiricus, *Adv. Math.*, II, 61; Quintilian, II, 15, 19), as I believe with Zeller (*op. cit.*, II, 2[3], p. 925, n. 2), is identical with Ariston of Keos; for since the name Ariston is absent from some of the lists of the Peripatetic scholarchs (cf. Wehrli, *ad* Fr. 7), he may easily have been described as a friend

[5] Sextus Empiricus, *Adv. Math.*, VII, 359, ascribes to some dogmatists a theory in certain respects similar to that of Ariston, namely that the soul is said to be endowed with δύναμις ἀντιληπτική, and Arnim, II, 849, takes him to refer to the Stoics. Even if this were correct, it would still be true that Ariston assumes two different parts of the soul, the perceptive and the rational, while the "Stoics" try to show that the faculties of the soul are not separable, but rather coexistent with each other. Nor is there any implication that mind is here conceived of as independent of organs.

of Critolaus in that branch of the tradition which made Critolaus the successor of Lycon. Finally, a psychological dogma as it is intimated in the account of Stobaeus squares well with Plutarch's assertion that in the essay called after his teacher Lycon, Ariston dealt with doctrines concerning the soul (Fr. 33, where I consider Wehrli's restoration of the text preferable to that of the other editors). If this interpretation is correct, the picture of Ariston is much enriched. In his psychological teaching he Aristotelianizes. In his rhetorical views (according to Sextus and Quintilian, he considered persuasion the aim of rhetoric), he also follows Aristotle. Thus his work in its manysidedness forms a transition to the activity of Critolaus, who took up even the metaphysical speculations of Aristotle. It becomes increasingly clear, I think, that even under the leadership of Lycon and Ariston Peripatetic teaching was not as exclusively ethical and historical as one used to assume.

To turn to Heraclides, Wehrli counts him among the Peripatetics, at least in the wider sense of the term (p. 61); following the tradition to be traced to Sotion, he rightly points out that it cannot be by mistake that Heraclides' *vita* appears in Diogenes Laertius' account of the Peripatetic school. But of course, Wehrli does not discount altogether the Platonic influence on Heraclides which was important enough to have instigated many ancient and modern historians to consider Heraclides a Platonist. Neither one of these labels seems quite appropriate, for Heraclides though stimulated by diverse philosophical movements followed his own bent of mind. His originality and the philosophical and scientific character of his work, in my opinion, are underrated in Wehrli's commentary. Little is made of Heraclides' peculiar atomic theory (Frs. 118-20). His dialectical and geometrical writings mentioned by Diogenes Laertius (Fr. 22 *finis*) are not set off as separate fragments. He is denied even the epithet "*wissenschaftlicher Astronom*" (p. 95). Granted that Heraclides was not the original astronomer he was once held to be, and that in his writings he popularized the views of others, he surely had a perfect grasp of the subject matter, and the dialogue form of most of his works did not necessarily preclude strictly scientific exposés. Nor do his studies on music show only that an "amalgamation of mythological fable and scientific data is characteristic of Heraclides" (p. 115). I shall not argue that a history of music which traces the origin of the great musical heroes to the Muses (Frs. 159 f.) is not necessarily mythology, although Apollodorus' use of Heraclides (*F. Gr. Hist.*, 244 F 146) would strongly suggest this. Nor shall I contend that the derivation of all musical genera from Apollo's trimetre (Fr. 158), or the statement that Amphion was the son of Zeus (Fr. 157) are by themselves no sufficient evidence for stamping Heraclides as a mythologist. Any mythologizing tendency on his part is amply counterbalanced by his scientific musical theories concerning the relation of sound and air movement. Wehrli's reasons (p. 113) for athetizing the passage in which they are mentioned (Porphyry, *Comment. in Ptolemaei Harmonica*, p. 30 Düring) and for excluding it from his collection seem quite unconvincing to me.[6] And I find it equally unjustifiable to

[6] The genuineness of the fragment has been advocated again by B. L. van der Waerden, *Hermes*, LXXVIII (1943); cf. *idem*, *Verh. d. Konin-*

maintain that Heraclides was the first to have had a yearning for the miraculous (p. 75, *ad* Fr. 49), that he fought against the proponents of enlightenment (p. 74, *ad* Fr. 46), or that he belonged among the faithful (p. 74, *ad* Fr. 47; cf. also p. 104). It is true, he sometimes gives a religious interpretation of historical events (Fr. 49). On the other hand, he also traces the misfortunes of men to moral and political causes; miraculous happenings he recounts only in accordance with current reports (Fr. 50: φασί); sometimes it remains unclear which side he himself endorses (Frs. 46 f.). After all, the testimonies are taken from dialogues where different opinions were represented. How would one judge Heraclides' view on pleasure if by chance only its praise (Fr. 55) had been preserved? Heraclides doubtless shared the Platonic belief in the immortality of the soul, and the Academic belief in prophecies (cf. *ad* Frs. 76-89; also p. 104). But while it must be admitted that nineteenth-century scholars, like Brandis and Zeller, tended to minimize the "antiscientific" evidence, it seems that now the interpretation tends toward the opposite extreme and comes dangerously close to the biased verdict of Timaeus who was himself so much given to superstition and belief in miracles: διὰ παντός ἐστιν Ἡρακλείδης τοιοῦτος παραδοξολόγος (Fr. 84).

Finally, the comments on Straton. The ancients considered him preëminently a natural philosopher—Polybius was perhaps the first to have held this view (Fr. 16; cf. Capelle, *R.-E., s. v.*, col. 284). Wehrli rightly stresses the fact that such an opinion is onesided and that Straton dealt also with moral theories and with philosophy in general (Fr. 15), even though the extant fragments, due to the interest of the ancients in the naturalist Straton, happen to concern mostly his "physics." In evaluating his physical doctrine Wehrli, in agreement with the more recent investigations, speaks of Straton's "positivistic science" (p. 46, *ad* Fr. 8) or "positivistic attitude" (p. 81, Fr. 143). The dialectical method, he says almost apologetically, was not absent from Straton's work, in spite of his reliance on experiments (*ad* Fr. 19). Such statements, I am afraid, must give rise to misunderstandings. Straton's experiments are "perceptual demonstrations" of logically proved theories. The role of the experiment in ancient physics is not to be equated with that which it plays in modern research. Moreover physics itself in antiquity was part of philosophy; it was never cut loose from metaphysical principles.[7] One can therefore hardly argue against Straton's having written a book *On the kingship of philosophy* because such an emphatic profession in favor of the predominance of philosophy would be unlikely for a "physicist" (p. 78, *ad* Fr. 133).

As regards the details of Straton's physical doctrine, Wehrli, like all modern interpreters since Rodier, holds that according to Simplicius, Straton abandoned Aristotle's concept of the changelessness of forms (p. 61, *ad* Fr. 72). However, if this were so, could Sim-

klijke Nederl. Akad. van Wetenschappen, Afd. Natuurkunde, Ser. 1, XX, 1 (1951), p. 63. Zeller, *Philos. d. Gr.*, II, 1^4, p. 1036, n. 1 already noted the connection of Heraclides' musical theory with his atomic speculations.

[7] Cf. H. Leisegang, *s. v.* "Physik," *R.-E.*, XX, 1, col. 1041; in general L. Edelstein, *Journ. of the Hist. of Ideas*, XIII (1952), pp. 577 f.

plicius cite Straton's views with approval (καὶ καλῶς γε οἶμαι ὁ Στράτων)? In the words immediately preceding the quotation he identifies himself with Aristotle's position according to which it is the subject, not the form that changes in the process of alteration (*In Phys.*, p. 806, 28 ff. Diels); as he puts it briefly here (p. 807, 2-3; 6-10) and explains at length later (p. 809, 3 ff.), the subject changes essentially, while the forms change but incidentally. Now Straton, as Simplicius relates, assumed that movement takes place not only in the subject that is moved (τὸ κινούμενον), but also in the "whence" (ἐξ οὗ) and in the "whither" (εἰς ὅ), though in each of these it takes place in a different manner. In the subject, movement is change (μεταβάλλει); in the "whence" and "whither," it is passing away and coming into being. If Simplicius calls this an adequate statement of the matter, he must have recognized in Straton's distinction of two kinds of movement the Aristotelian distinction of essential and accidental change just mentioned. His endorsement of Straton is the more noteworthy since he is not remiss elsewhere in pointing out Straton's deviations from Aristotle (e. g. Fr. 75), and he takes issue with Theophrastus for the very reason that the latter fails to differentiate between essential and accidental movement (p. 861, 24 ff.).[8] How Straton worked out the details of his theory of movement, the fragments do not tell. That he was more of an Aristotelian than is generally granted on the basis of Simplicius' testimony, to me seems certain.

The supposition that Straton rejected Aristotle's concept of form is usually coupled with the contention that he discarded teleological considerations altogether (p. 61; cf. *ad* Frs. 36-9). I see little reason for this assumption. To be sure, Straton considered natural weight and motion sufficient to explain everything (Fr. 32); in his opinion, qualities and forces were the last principles (Frs. 42-9). But he also held that nature, though not possessed of feeling or body, contained within itself divine power, the causes of growth and decay (Frs. 33; 37). One could refer to him as one of those who involuntarily testify to the existence of the divine, even though he put nature in its place (Fr. 36). It is more probable therefore that Straton in his concept of necessity (Fr. 35, and commentary) included the teleological aspect, just as his pupil, the physician Erasistratus, combined mechanistic and teleological principles. After all, even Epicurus, with whom Straton had so much in common, redefined necessity in such a way that it became a substitute for the rational and purposive element in Platonic and Aristotelian philosophy.[9]

In my discussion of the problems arising in connection with the general evaluation of the various personalities I could do no more than ask some questions and make certain suggestions. The final clarification of these matters will have to wait for Wehrli's fully

---

[8] H. Cherniss, whom I consulted about the meaning of the Simplicius passage, drew my attention to the fact that G. Rodier, *La physique de Straton de Lampsaque* (1890), p. 62, n. 2, who has been followed by later interpreters, omits the phrase ἄλλον δὲ τρόπον ἐν ἑκάστῳ. These words, however, are essential in the argument, at least for Simplicius' identification of Straton's views with those of Aristotle.

[9] Cf. H. Armstrong, "The Gods in Plato, Plotinus and Epicurus," *C. Q.*, XXXII (1938), p. 192.

documented history of the Peripatetic doctrine which he promises to give in his last volume. That he may reach his goal before long must be the wish and hope of everybody interested in Hellenistic thought.

LUDWIG EDELSTEIN.

THE JOHNS HOPKINS UNIVERSITY.

ERWIN R. GOODENOUGH. Jewish Symbols in the Greco-Roman Period. Vol. I: The Archaeological Evidence from Palestine. Pp. xvii + 300; Vol. II: The Archaeological Evidence from the Diaspora. Pp. xi + 323; Vol. III: Illustrations. Pp. xxxv + 10 (indexes); 1209 figs.; Vol. IV: The Problem of Method. Symbols from Jewish Cult. Pp. xiii + 235; 117 figs. New York, Pantheon Books, 1953-54. (*Bollingen Series*, XXXVII.)

It was a Christian theologian, Karl Watzinger who, together with the architect Heinrich Kohl, published, in the year 1916, the first description and reconstruction of the synagogs in Palestine. And again it is a Christian theologian who presents us with a work scheduled to have seven quarto volumes, four of which have already appeared, dealing with the complete range of Jewish art objects: Erwin R. Goodenough, Professor of History of Religion at Yale University.

Both men were guided in their research by similar trains of thought. Watzinger found in the synagogs of Galilee the forerunners of Christian churches, at least as far as the eastern part of the Roman Empire was concerned. And Goodenough, already as a young man, while regarding the mosaics of Sta. Maria Maggiore in Rome, had discovered motifs: the white garment of Jesus and his rod, similar to that of Moses, or the prominence of groups of three figures, indicating Jewish prototypes, or the writings of Philo.

At that time, the number of well-known Jewish monuments was not yet as great as it is today. One need only remember that the mosaic floors in Palestine and the Biblical mural paintings of the synagog in Dura Europos were found during the last decades. Goodenough began to collect burial places and their contents, synagogs and their plastic and painted decorations, lamps, vessels of earthenware and glass, amulets, coins and even inscriptions; he collected them, described and interpreted them, and had their pictures made. And he was not satisfied to select, for instance, a few characteristic pieces from an abundant number of small lamps, often similar to one another; but he described and reproduced each piece he could lay hands on, with the patience and punctiliousness that mark the true scholar.

His collector's activities range in time from the first to the seventh century of the Christian era, in space over the vast territory that had Jewish settlements. The Jews had penetrated beyond Palestine already before the Roman domination, but now, after the destruction of Herod's temple in 70 A. D., we find them all over the Mediter-

ner im Hinblick auf die von Prof. Jeffery von der amerikan. Univ. in Kairo für Zwecke der Mission geplante kritische Koranausgabe. In engster Zusammenarbeit mit Jeffery und nach genauer Abgrenzung der beiden verschiedenen Arbeitsziele wird B. sich damit begnügen, für diejenigen Gelehrten, die sich selbständig mit dem Korantext beschäftigen und daher auf die Quellen zurückgehen, das notwendige kritische Material mit allen Hinweisen in Umschrift bereitzustellen. Alle Koranlesarten, die in der älteren Literatur, d. h. in den Kiraat-Werken, den Kommentaren, den Traditionssammlungen und den grammatischen Werken erreichbar sind, sowie diejenigen, die sich bei Prüfung der bisher etwas unterschätzten kufischen Koranhandschriften ergeben werden, werden von ihm verarbeitet und jeweils getrennt geboten werden nach konsonantischen Abweichungen innerhalb des osmanischen Textes, nach Vokalisierungsmöglichkeiten dieses Textes und endlich nach den Abweichungen vom osmanischen Text. Der Übersichtlichkeit und schnelleren Auswertung wegen wird B. der Materialsammlung sogleich eine kritische Wertung der Varianten beigeben und diejenigen Abweichungen vom textus receptus, denen besondere Bedeutung zukommt, durch den Druck hervorheben. Wortregister und grammatische Übersichten werden den reichlichen Stoff nach anderer Richtung erschließen.

Der 6. deutsche Orientalistentag, der im vorigen Jahre in Wien stattfand, hat diesen ebendort von B. vorgetragenen Plan aufs lebhafteste begrüßt und seine Ausführung als ein dringendes Bedürfnis der Wissenschaft bezeichnet. Über diese Beifallskundgebung hinaus sollten alle Arabisten B. bei seiner mit so viel Opfermut und selbstlosem Sinn durchgeführten Arbeit wenigstens so weit helfend zur Seite stehen, daß sie ihm von dem Vorhandensein kufischer Koranmanuskripte und von solchem Variantenmaterial Kenntnis geben, das sich an abseits liegenden Stellen der arabischen Literatur verbirgt.

Berlin. Gotthold Weil.

Griechisch-Lateinische Literatur

Karl Deichgräber [Privatdoz. f. Klass. Phil. an d. Univ. Berlin], Die griechische Empirikerschule. Sammlung der Fragmente und Darstellung der Lehre. Berlin, Weidmannsche Buchh., 1930. VIII u. 398 S. 8⁰. M. 25,—.

Die Empirikerschule ist eine Gegenbewegung gegen die beiden dogmatischen Ärzteschulen des Hellenismus: die Schulen des Herophilos und des Erasistratos. Bis auf einen Kommentar des Apollonios von Kition zu Hippokrates περὶ ἄρθρων und die wenigstens empirisch beeinflußte Enzyklopädie des Celsus ist das literarische Werk der Schule wie das ihrer Gegner nur in Fragmenten erhalten. Diese hat Deichgräber auf Anregung Hermann Schöne's zum ersten Mal zu einer Einheit zusammengefaßt.

Die Sammlung, die er gibt, zerfällt in drei Teile: die Zeugnisse über die Empirikerlehre im allgemeinen, die Fragmente einzelner Empiriker, die Kommentare zu Hippokrates. Das Material stammt in der Hauptsache aus Galen, Celsus, Aurelian, Plinius und Athenäus und besteht fast ausschließlich in indirekten Referaten. Ich finde unter den Fragmenten der einzelnen Ärzte nur zwei direkte Zitate (53, 12 ff.; 175, 29 ff.), abgesehen von pharmazeutischen Rezepten, die unter einem bestimmten Namen erhalten sind (e. g. fr. 237). D. hat dieses Material dort, wo ausreichende Texte noch nicht vorliegen, neu ediert (30 ff.). Vor allem ist der Text der aus Galen genommenen Zitate durch Heranziehung der Handschriften gesichert. Die Fortschritte, die allein dadurch erreicht werden konnten, sind zahlreich (e. g. 91, 28; 153, 4, 23). Daneben finden sich auch viele Emendationen des Textes. Manche Korrekturen durch leichte Veränderung der überlieferten Buchstaben sind evident (90, 25; 91, 1; 106, 1; 126, 23). Manche Zusammenhänge werden durch Veränderung oder Hinzufügung eines Wortes, gestützt auf sprachliche Parallelen, klargestellt (103, 1 δυνατοί st. δυνατόν; 104, 18 συστῆναι δυνατὸν <τὸ> ὑπάρχειν nach Galen IX 18/19). Mancher weitgehende textkritische Eingriff dagegen ist gewagt und kaum richtig. So ist die Emendation des großen Heraklideszitates (176, 17), wie mir scheint, unmöglich. Der Sinn der Worte ist: man darf den medizinischen Vorgang, um den es geht, nicht rein verstandesmäßig beurteilen (176, 13). Weil in ihm bestimmte Erscheinungen tatsächlich gegeben sind, muß man sie eben als tatsächlich annehmen, da dieses (das Tatsächliche) zu suchen, nützlich ist, wenn es auch nicht immer das Gewöhnliche ist (κοινόν). Setzt man nun statt κοινόν, wie D. will, ἀναγκαῖον, so sagt der Empiriker, es sei zwar nützlich, auf die Erfahrung zu achten, wenn es auch nicht immer notwendig ist, was doch nicht stimmen kann. Ebenso ist die Ersetzung von εὑρών durch εἰπών (240, 13), wie mir scheint, nicht angängig. Es handelt sich in diesen Ausführungen um die Möglichkeit, aus dem Vorkommen gleicher oder ähnlicher Worte auf die Identität des Schriftstellers zu schließen. Wenn man bei einem alten Autor das Stammwort findet, kann man nicht sagen, daß ihm die Ableitung bekannt sein muß. Wenn man die Ableitung findet (εὑρών), darf man kühnlich (θαρραλέως) das Stammwort verwenden; wieder handelt es sich um einen Schluß von dem, was man bei einem Schriftsteller findet, auf das, was man sonst als seinen Sprachgebrauch voraussetzen darf.

Über die Textkonstituierung der Einzelheiten, von der eben die Rede war, geht der Versuch D.s hinaus, den ursprünglichen Text eines für die Geschichte der empirischen Schule wichtigen Dokumentes überhaupt erst herzustellen: er hat die nur lateinisch erhaltene subfiguratio empirica des Galen ins Griechische zurückübersetzt. Die aus anderen Werken des gleichen Übersetzers bekannte Technik seiner Übertragungen (8 ff.) erlaubt diese Rekonstruktion des Originals. Die Textgestaltung im einzelnen ist durch fortwährende Hinweise auf den sonstigen Sprachgebrauch Galens gesichert. Die Übersetzung ist eine philologische Leistung, deren Zweck und Wert in ihr selbst liegt. Man darf bei der Verwendung der Übersetzung aber nicht vergessen, daß sie immer Interpretation und Hypothese ist. Auch der lateinische Text bietet ja schon Schwierigkeiten. Gut sind die von D. gegebenen leichten Besserungen und Umstellungen (43, 16; 51, 9; 53, 26). Die Veränderung von appar*ente* in appar*eat* (45, 19) ist vielleicht richtig, wenn auch für die Beibehaltung der Überlieferung die dann gegebene Gleichordnung mit den vorhergehenden Worten spricht; es würden in diesem Falle wie öfter zwei Begriffe den gleichen Vorgang charakterisieren. Dagegen ist, wie mir scheint, die Ersetzung von melior eo minodotus durch melior quam minodotus (87, 24) falsch. Der Sinn des Satzes ist: Heraklides, der die Realität eines logischen Vermögens im Menschen anerkannte, diese Fähigkeit aber nicht ausbildete, ist als Arzt soviel geringer als Hippokrates, wie Menodot mehr ist als er, da Menodot das logische Vermögen für die Medizin neben der Erfahrung fruchtbar machte (vgl. die von D. gegebene Charakteristik des Menodot in der Einleitung zu seinen Fragmenten 212, 30 und zum Logischen überhaupt die Ausführungen 306). Ändert man mit D., so bezieht sich der Gebrauch logischer Prinzipien in der Medizin auf Heraklides, obwohl doch gerade gesagt wurde, daß er sie zwar anerkannte und gelegentlich anwendete, aber sich nicht in ihnen ausbildete, während ihre bewußte Anwendung und Ausbildung für Menodot charakteristisch ist. Der griechische Text muß dementsprechend wohl heißen: ὅσῳ βελτίων ἐστὶν αὐτοῦ Μηνόδοτος. Was die Schrift als Ganzes angeht, so kann ich D. nicht folgen, wenn er sie mit Ilberg für uneinheitlich hält (16). Galen soll als Absicht einmal die reine Darstellung der empirischen Lehre hinstellen (43, 17), ein ander Mal den Nachweis der Unmöglichkeit einer empirischen Lehre (88, 18). Doch auch an der zweiten Stelle (88, 18) bezeichnet es Galen als seine Absicht, in diesem Buch darzulegen, wie es möglich sei (quo modo possibile sit), nicht, wie es unmöglich sei, die Medizin rein empirisch, ohne jede rationale Erkenntnis aufzubauen. Er setzt hinzu: für jemanden, der darauf verzichtet, die ganze Materie zu untersuchen und zu klären (ei qui permittet substantiam totam invenire). Was damit gemeint ist, zeigen die vorhergehenden Erörterungen des 12. Kap.s. Alle logischen Untersuchungen gehören nach rein empirischer Ansicht, die Galen ja vortragen will (43, 17), nicht zur empirischen Medizin. Bestimmte Empiriker haben den Fehler gemacht, sie doch hereinzuziehen (Herakleides, Menodot). Darüber hat Galen in anderen Büchern gehandelt. In diesem Buch will er zeigen, wie der, der darauf verzichtet, die ganze Materie (logischer Probleme) zu untersuchen und zu behandeln, die Medizin rein empirisch aufbauen kann.

In Untersuchungen, die D. dem Text beigibt, begründet er seine Stellung zu einzelnen Problemen der Sammlung. Er spricht über Schulzugehörigkeiten der einzelnen Empiriker; diese Ausführungen ermöglichen jetzt die einfachste Orientierung über alle die empirische Schule angehenden Fragen und die Literatur zu ihnen. Viele Einzelheiten sind neu gesehen oder richtiggestellt. Die Benutzung empirischer Kommentare im Galenschen Kommentar zum 3. und 6. Epidemienbuch ist, wie mir scheint, schlagend nachgewiesen (25). Ausführliche Indices, die D. angelegt hat, ermöglichen die Verwendung des ganzen Materials als Einheit, und so führt die mit eindringender Kenntnis gegebene Zusammenfassung des verstreuten, wenn auch bekannten Materials zu etwas Neuem und macht den Weg für eine gründliche Bearbeitung der Einzelheiten frei.

Aber D. gibt in seiner Arbeit nicht nur das philologisch hergerichtete Quellenmaterial, alles sicher Empirische, sondern auch einen philosophiegeschichtlichen Beitrag: die Darstellung der Lehre, und zwar fast ausschließlich der empirischen Wissenschaftstheorie. Die

Praxis wird nur gestreift, die Darstellung der Chirurgie und Pharmazie unterbleibt (vgl. Vorwort). Diese Darstellung des hellenistischen Systems einer induktiven Logik trägt wieder alles Material aufs sorgfältigste zusammen und zergliedert den Erfahrungsbegriff bis in alle Einzelheiten (288 ff.). Es wird gezeigt, wie die empirische Schule versucht, die Medizin ganz auf Erfahrung, ohne jedes logische Dogma, aufzubauen. Was D. sagt — und seine Ausführungen erschöpfen das schwierige Thema —, führt die Arbeiten von Schöne und Wellmann weiter und schließt sie ab.

In der empirischen Schule selbst sieht D. ein typisches Phänomen des Hellenismus (269). Sie entstand als Reaktion auf die dogmatischen Schulen; der Wissenschaftsbegriff, auf den sie ihre Lehre gründet, ist mit dem der skeptischen Schule identisch und wurde durch die Lehren des Demokrit, Nausiphanes und Epikur vorbereitet. In der hippokratischen Medizin finden sich nach D.s Meinung nur Andeutungen empirischer Lehren (271), wenn man auch aus der platonischen Erwähnung des Hippokrates schließen muß, daß es zu jener Zeit auch Ärzte gab, die bewußt den empirischen Standpunkt vertraten (273 Anm. 1).

Nun liegt der eigentliche Unterschied der dogmatischen Medizin des Hellenismus von der empirischen, bei weitgehender Übereinstimmung in der Behandlung der Kranken, in einem Unterschied der Fragestellung. Die Empiriker lehnen die Frage nach der Natur des Menschen, nach den Ursachen der Krankheiten und der innerorganischen Vorgänge ab. Über all das gibt es, meinen sie, keine Erfahrung und darum keine Erkenntnis. Schon in der hippokratischen Medizin aber finden sich verschiedene Einstellungen zu diesem Problem, wenn auch immer eine positive Lösung versucht wird. Denn der Autor der Schrift περὶ φύσιος ἀνθρώπου legt Wert darauf, daß seine Erklärung der Natur des Menschen und der Krankheiten empirisch nachweisbar ist, nicht etwa nur rational begründet sei. Die verschiedenen Stoffe, die er annimmt, lassen sich im Menschen empirisch nachweisen; ihre Verschiedenheit ist zu sehen und zu fühlen (cp. 5 VI 40/42 L.). Darum ist seine Erklärung richtig. Ebenso sind die Stoffe, aus denen der Autor der Schrift περὶ ἀρχαίης ἰητρικῆς die Natur des Menschen und der Krankheiten im Gegensatz zu Erklärungen aus abstrakten Qualitäten (warm, kalt usw.) herleitet, sichtbar und darum wahr (Hippokrates CMG I 1 45,25). Die Lösung dieser Fragen wird also bewußt durch eine empirische Methode gewonnen, die sich selbst als Gegensatz zur rationalen, dogmatischen Methode empfindet und dadurch eine Vorstufe der Methode der späteren Empirikerschule ist. Die hellenistischen Empiriker lehnen diese Fragen ganz ab, weil die skeptische Überlegung den Erfahrungsbegriff vollkommen zersetzt hat, so daß der Mut zur Erfahrung in der gleichen Weise eingeengt ist wie der Mut zum Analogieschluß durch die systematischen und logischen Untersuchungen der aristotelischen Schule (vgl. O. Regenbogen, Quellen und Studien zur Geschichte der Mathematik, Abt. B., Bd. I, 156 ff.). Die einfachen Beobachtungen, die dem hippokratischen Arzt als Erklärung der Natur des Menschen ausreichten, genügen nicht mehr. Aber die Unterschiede heben die Übereinstimmung im wichtigsten, in der Methode, nicht auf; die Empirikerschule steht in einer reichen medizinischen Tradition. Schon in der Schrift περὶ φύσιος ἀνθρώπου wird, wie später in der empirisch skeptischen Lehre, der dogmatische Gegner durch die ἰσοσθένεια der verschiedenen sich gegenseitig aufhebenden Meinungen widerlegt (cp. 1). Schon in der Schrift περὶ ἀρχαίης ἰητρικῆς findet sich die für den späteren Empiriker so bezeichnende Wertschätzung der Individualität (cp. 20 cf. D. 311).

Wenn aber D. mit Usener den Wissenschaftsbegriff der Empiriker von Demokrit herleitet, so muß man einwenden, daß Demokrit wie Epikur eine rationale Naturerkenntnis lehren und mit voller Sicherheit über das Unsichtbare und Unerfahrbare urteilen. Das skeptische Moment der empirischen Lehre ist historisch nur aus dem Agnostizismus des Protagoras und der Skepsis des Gorgias herzuleiten. Die Tendenz aber, die Erfahrung als einzigen Grund der Erkenntnis anzusehen, scheint durch eine andere Philosophie bedingt oder wenigstens an ihr orientiert. Die Schrift περὶ φύσιος ἀνθρώπου, die ja bewußt empirisch vorgeht, erklärt das Leben als Mischung der Elemente, den Tod als Auflösung, in der jeder Bestandteil des Körpers dorthin zurückkehrt, woher er kam (cp. 3 Ende). Das ist empedokleisch (Diels B. 6—15). Die Ärzte, die die Krankheiten des Menschen oder seine Natur aus e i n e m Prinzip verstehen, vertrauen einer einzelnen ihrer Erfahrungen, während doch das Richtige ist, wie man nach dem Vorgehen des Autors schließen muß, nicht einer einzelnen Erfahrung, sondern der Gesamtheit der Erfahrungen zu vertrauen (cp. 6). Dieser Lehrsatz klingt wie eine Umschreibung der empedokleischen Lehre, man müsse keinem einzelnen Sinn, sondern nur allen zusammen — dazu gehört auch das Denken — trauen, um die Wahrheit zu finden (B. 4). Die Menschen sind von dem überzeugt, was sie gerade erleben, und meinen, es sei das Ganze (B. 2). Die Polemik gegen das Eine als Prinzip des Entstehens (cp. 3), kann von Empedokles zur Begründung seiner Vierelementetheorie in ähnlicher Weise geführt worden sein. Schließlich bestimmt der φύσις-Begriff der Schrift die Natur des Menschen als Mischungsverhältnis der im Körper befindlichen Stoffe (VI 40, 1 L.), nicht etwa als ein statisches Sein. Das entspricht einer charakteristischen Definition des Empedokles (B. 8). Ich untersuche nicht, ob die Viersäftetheorie der Schrift auch empedokleisch ist (vgl. Wellmann, Fragmente der sizilischen Ärzte, Berlin 1901, S. 74/75). Jedenfalls finden sich diese empedokleischen Gedanken im Zusammenhang mit einer empirischen Theorie. Wenn die empirische Schrift περὶ ἀρχαίης ἰητρικῆς gegen Empedokles polemisiert, weil seine Fragestellung noch zu philosophisch sei (CMG I i 51, 10), ein Vorwurf, der ja nicht nur ihn, sondern viele trifft, so liegt gerade in dieser namentlichen Erwähnung ein Hinweis auf die Bedeutung, die Empedokles für die empirischen Ärzte hat. Mir scheint also die empirische Medizin des Hellenismus außer durch bestimmte medizinische Lehren des 5. Jh.s mit durch die Philosophie des Empedokles bedingt zu sein. So haben ja auch die Empiriker selbst ihre Schule aus der sizilischen Ärzteschule hergeleitet (42, 21), also aus der von Empedokles beeinflußten ärztlichen Richtung des 5. Jh.s, wenn sie auch im allgemeinen nur Schüler der Natur, nicht eines Menschen sein wollten. Die empedokleische Philosophie, die den Menschen auf seine Erfahrung als einzigen Quell der Erkenntnis hinwies, und die ihn nur menschliche Erkenntnisse lehren wollte (B. 2), mußte die empirische Forschung beeinflussen und fördern.

Alle diese Bewegungen sind natürlich nur Vorstufen der empirischen Schule des Hellenismus. Der Empiriker dieser späten Zeit ist ganz Skeptiker. Sein Wissenschaftsbegriff ist ebenso wie seine praktische Haltung skeptisch. Er will nach den Dingen, die man nicht sehen kann, nicht mehr fragen; er erklärt weder die Natur des Menschen, noch die der Krankheiten. Seine Abgeklärtheit äußert sich praktisch als Menschenfreundlichkeit, wie er ja auch die Sektion nicht nur als wissenschaftlich unbrauchbar sondern auch als grausam ablehnt. Die Empiriker waren als Ärzte wohl kaum gewinnsüchtiger als die anderen (D. 322/323); immer haben nur wenige Ärzte, wie Galen selbst an der Stelle sagt, auf die sich D. bezieht, aus Menschenfreundlichkeit behandelt. Auch würde ich Skeptizismus nicht so sehr mit Untätigkeit und Apathie gleichsetzen, wie D. es immer wieder tut (e. g. 294; 298), obwohl er selbst auf die aktiven Momente des empirischen Erfahrungsbegriffes hinweist; man muß wohl mehr an den Begriff der tätigen Skepsis denken. Die Vergleiche der alten Anschauungen mit modernen, die D. als Charakteristik liebt (e. g. 280), scheinen mir nicht nötig und nicht fördernd.

Aber das sind Einzelheiten der Deutung. Sie fortzuführen und zu vertiefen, ist jetzt endlich möglich, nachdem D. in mühevoller Arbeit das Material einheitlich zusammengestellt hat. Darüber hinaus wird jede Weiterarbeit an der Medizin des Hellenismus überhaupt von der Grundlage ausgehen, die er durch seine Sammlung geschaffen hat.

Berlin. Ludwig Edelstein.

Germanische Literaturen

Alfred Hübner [Dr. phil., Göttingen], Die »mhd. Ironie« oder die Litotes im Altdeutschen. [Palaestra 170. Untersuchgn. u. Texte aus d. dtsch. u. engl. Philol. Begr. v. A. Brandl u. Er. Schmidt† hrsg. v. A. Brandl u. Jul. Petersen. Leipzig, Mayer & Müller, 1930. VIII u. 210 S. 8⁰. M. 15,—.

Die Stilfigur der Litotes hatte bisher für die altdeutsche Zeit keine umfassende Darstellung gefunden. Was die antike Litotes betrifft, sei auf Carl Weyman: »Studien über die Figur der Litotes« in den Jbb. f. klass. Phil., 15. Suppl. Bd., verwiesen. Was ihre Art im Altdeutschen anbelangt, hat Lörcher über dieses Stilmittel bei Otfrid und im Heliand, Beitr. 25, 544, kurz berichtet, und von Arthur Krause liegt eine Würzb. Diss. (1913) vor: »Die Litotes und ähnliche Figuren im Nibelungenlied«. Auch im allgemeinen Stiluntersuchungen ist vielfach über diese Redefigur gehandelt. So ist es sehr dankenswert, daß Hübner die Frage für die gesamte mhd. Literatur untersucht. Er hat zu diesem Zwecke fast $1^1/_2$ Millionen Verse durchgelesen und über 10 000 Beispiele gesammelt (von denen er natürlich nur einen ausgewählten Teil vorlegt), sich also eine verläßliche Grundlage geschaffen.

Die antike Litotes drückt (in der Regel) einen Behauptung durch Verneinung ihres Gegenteiles aus. Sie ist zweigliedrig, besteht aus einem Verneinungsworte und einem negativen Ausdruck. Das 2. Glied ist zumeist ein Adj. (*no*

AMERICAN JOURNAL OF PHILOLOGY

Founded by B. L. GILDERSLEEVE

Edited by
HENRY T. ROWELL

KEMP MALONE, BENJAMIN D. MERITT, JAMES H. OLIVER
EVELYN H. CLIFT: Secretary

Honorary Editor
DAVID M. ROBINSON

VOLUME LXXII

BALTIMORE: THE JOHNS HOPKINS PRESS
LONDON: ARTHUR F. BIRD
PARIS: ALBERT FONTEMOING LEIPZIG: F. A. BROCKHAUS
1951

MAX POHLENZ. Die Stoa, Geschichte einer geistigen Bewegung. Göttingen, Vandenhoeck und Ruprecht, I (1948), pp. 490; II (1949), pp. 230.

Pohlenz' book climaxes a lifelong study of Stoic philosophy. Concerned with particular aspects of Stoicism ever since he published his dissertation in 1898 (II, pp. 7 f.), he now traces the entire development of the school and its influence on other movements. He does not restrict himself to an analysis of the philosophical problems, but also sets the Stoa against the background of ancient civilization. The same familiarity with Greek and Roman literature and life which distinguishes all of Pohlenz' writings and which is to be found now only in few others is characteristic of this new work and is not in need of my further praise.

Of the two volumes, the first gives the history of the Stoa uninterrupted by the discussion of controversial matters, and generally even without reference to the passages on which the interpretation rests. The second contains the "footnotes" and the criticism of modern literature. Such an arrangement, no doubt, has the advantage of making the text eminently readable. The disadvantage, to my mind, is that if one wishes to find out about the arguments underlying any of the views stated, he must constantly switch from the first tome to the second, where the material is arranged according to paragraphs and lines of the former.

As for the general approach to his subject, Pohlenz tries to strike a balance between the older attitude of overemphasizing the unity of Stoic thought and the more recent attempts at restoring the individual tenets of the various members of the school. The doctrine of the Old Stoa is represented as one, yet the specific contributions of Zeno, Cleanthes, Chrysippus and their pupils are clearly marked. With the Middle Stoa, the school dogma begins to be contrasted with individual systems, namely those of Panaetius and Posidonius. In regard to the final period, from which alone complete works have survived, short outlines of the common Stoic teaching are followed by characterizations of the various philosophers, such as Musonius, Seneca, Epictetus, and Marcus Aurelius.

Pohlenz' concept of Stoic philosophy is determined first of all by his belief that Zeno's doctrine was formulated in answer to that of Epicurus and in opposition to the latter's ideas (e. g. I, pp. 23; 113). Now, it is true that Epicurus was older than Zeno, and he seems to have started his school before the Stoa was founded. Zeno's dependence on Epicurus may therefore appear plausible, although, as far as I can judge, it cannot be proved. The Zenonian fragments never mention Epicurus directly, nor is it possible to demonstrate an implied polemic of Zeno against his contemporary. Diogenes Laertius, VII, 85, a passage which Pohlenz singles out as evidence of such a polemic (II, p. 65), is not necessarily directed against Epicurus alone, to disregard the fact that Zeno's name does not occur here.[1] However, Pohlenz makes one aware of the insufficient

[1] Epicurus' concern with the Stoics, on the other hand, is attested (cf. Diogenes Laertius, VII, 9), and a coloring of certain of his state-

reasons for the usual treatment of the two schools which in the histories of philosophy almost without exception are dealt with independently of each other, the Stoic teaching being placed in advance of that of the Epicureans.

Another basic consideration emphasized by Pohlenz throughout his book is the influence which the Semitic origin of most of the Stoic philosophers presumably had on their thought. To discriminate between the Semitic and the Greek components in the Stoic doctrine indeed constitutes one of his "main problems" (I, p. 31; cf. *Neue Jahrbücher für Wissenschaft und Jugendbildung*, II [1926], pp. 257 ff.). Of course, Pohlenz is not unaware of the difficulties of this attempt; as he says himself, little is known about the culture of the countries from which Zeno or Chrysippus sprang (e.g. pp. 31; 164). Nevertheless, he hazards judgments and compiles a whole catalogue of Semitic traits. Hairsplitting (p. 51), fanaticism, fatalism, the postulate of the "you ought," an uncompromising dualism of body and soul, a lack of half tones, of anything between love and hatred (pp. 164 f.)[2]—all these, to Pohlenz, are Semitic characteristics, and they are those that he finds "foreign and disagreeable" in Stoic philosophy (p. 165). With the advent of the Middle Stoa, or as Pohlenz prefers to say, with the Hellenization of the Stoa (p. 191), they "disappear by themselves" in the system of the Dorian, Panaetius (p. 207; cf. p. 192). Even the Syrian, Posidonius, because of his intellectual attitude, is now considered to have had "predominantly Hellenic and Macedonian blood in his veins" (p. 208).

Reading these statements one wonders about the hairsplitting of early and late Greek sophists; about the one Greek among the older Stoics, Cleanthes, who unlike Panaetius failed to Hellenize the Stoa and in his fanaticism went so far as to demand that Aristarchus be punished for impiety; about the fatalistic astrological theories of Hipparchus; about Plato's moral imperatives and, most of all, about his dualism (cf. Pohlenz, p. 377). Moreover, if Zeno as a foreigner was inclined to stick to the "true meaning" of words, to be interested in their etymology (p. 116), what about the etymologies recounted even in Attic tragedies (or to use a modern example, those adduced by Hegel)? Needless to add that Pohlenz' theory does not hold its ground even within his own interpretation. He admits that Zeno and Chrysippus separated themselves from the land of their birth and found a new physical and spiritual home in Greece (p. 367); Zeno, whose thought was deeply Hellenized (p. 113; cf. p. 164), was able to convince people because he spoke to them in their own spirit (p. 165); Diogenes, the Babylonian, recognizing the significance of music in education thereby made himself the interpreter of old Hellenic views (p. 184). The reader cognizant of these inconsistencies and perhaps less certain than Pohlenz of a scientific

ments by Stoic terms has been shown to be probable by C. Bailey, *The Greek Atomists and Epicurus* (1928), pp. 531 f. Cf. also Pohlenz, I, p. 363.

[2] The two last categories Pohlenz borrows from S. A. Cook's analysis of the Semitic spirit (*The Cambridge Ancient History*, I [1923], p. 196).

basis for the assumption that racial factors determine the human intellect, can easily remove the racial tag attached to almost every one mentioned, be it Ariston (p. 163) or Marcion (p. 410), Musonius (p. 303) or Tertullian (p. 437). But one truly lamentable weakness resulting from these speculations, I think, remains: the individual character and personality is not given its desert (e. g. p. 69); sentiments and impulses (pp. 68; 107 f.) are the main categories in explaining ideas, while the history of problems is depreciated (p. 68), and with it, the search for truth in which the philosopher is engaged. What constitutes the Greek character—the political, the ethical combined with the aesthetic, the sensuous in addition to the rational (p. 207)—is inferred from its manifestation at one arbitrarily chosen point, rather than from its display during the entire process of Greek history, and thus the attempted and badly needed rehabilitation of the Hellenistic period (pp. 166 f.) is fundamentally vitiated.

To turn now to Pohlenz' evaluation of the various phases of Stoicism, the Old Stoa (pp. 22-190) is seen in the following way. Zeno devised the scheme of the whole doctrine (p. 161); Cleanthes contributed hardly more than his pantheistic religious pathos, without changing the essence of the system (p. 163); Chrysippus, the second founder of the Stoa, seemingly expounding Zeno's views, but actually responsible for its extreme monism, built up an intellectualistic psychology, clarified the issues of fate and of the freedom of the will, and, great systematizer that he was, also created a systematic dialectics (pp. 163 f.). This appraisal restores Chrysippus to his rightful place, of which he has been deprived by those who believe Stoic philosophy to be the achievement principally of Zeno (e. g. F. Ueberweg—K. Praechter, *Die Philosophie des Altertums*[12] [1926], pp. 410 ff.), or of Zeno and Cleanthes (e. g. A. C. Pearson, *The Fragments of Zeno and Cleanthes* [1891], p. 48), thus reducing the share of Chrysippus to a mere systematization of earlier ideas. Sometimes Pohlenz may be too ready with a "probably Chrysippus" (e. g. p. 74), but in general he seems to make good his claim as to Chrysippus' importance. Zeno, on the other hand, occasionally is credited with more than is his due. That he was the one who formulated the doctrine of self-preservation and self-love (pp. 113 ff.) is at least doubtful, for the evidence marshalled (II, p. 65) is but indirect. And no full justice is done to the role of Cleanthes. The decisive theory of "tension," if not altogether his addition, certainly was greatly elaborated by him, as was the whole topic of natural inquiry.[3] In connection with this, Cleanthes reshaped ethics; the introduction of the term "nature" into the Zenonian

[3] Pohlenz, on the evidence of Frs. 99 and 106 Arnim, traces the doctrine to Zeno (II, pp. 42 f. *ad* I, pp. 74 f.). But in Fr. 99 τείνεσθαι is a conjecture of Diels, and in Fr. 106 (p. 30, line 35), as Pohlenz says himself, the words πνευματικὸς τόνος may be a later addition. Cf. also Pearson, *op. cit.*, pp. 41 f. and *ad* Fr. 56, line 54; in general P. Barth-A. Goedeckemeyer, *Die Stoa*[6] (1946), p. 49, a book that makes the philosophical implications of Stoicism admirably clear and that I should be inclined to judge more favorably than Pohlenz seems to do (II, p. 12).

definition of the aim of life (I, pp. 116 f.) is only one of his significant contributions. Cleanthes' discussion of poetry and its place in philosophical teaching also is of wider significance than one would gather from Pohlenz' mention of it (pp. 53 f.).

The interpretation of the Middle Stoa (pp. 191-276) summarizes Pohlenz' well-known investigations of Panaetius and Posidonius and integrates them into an impressive picture of their teaching and of their impact on their contemporaries. The method followed in the reconstruction of these systems is quite different from that applied in the chapter on the Old Stoa. There, Pohlenz generally clings to the attested material and tries rigorously to separate the known from the unknown (to name one outstanding example, he shows that the famous terms *λόγος ἐνδιάθετος* and *λόγος προφορικός* are not to be found in the fragments of the older Stoics and probably are not even of Stoic coinage [II, p. 21]). Here, he concerns himself with passages which he assumes echo the views of Panaetius and Posidonius. Nowhere, so far as I can see, does Pohlenz argue about the objections which during the past few decades have been raised by many scholars against such a procedure, and I shall not attempt to restate them now. As regards Panaetius, the matter has been settled, I think, by van Straaten's recent collection of the fragments. As for Posidonius, a final decision will have to wait for the reediting of the testimony.[4]

In the next chapter, on the Stoa of the imperial age (I, pp. 277-366), Pohlenz maintains the common thesis that the Roman Stoa marks the return to Chrysippus' doctrine (pp. 291 f.), yet he also makes it evident—and perhaps more evident than any previous writer—how many new and different trends appear in the philosophy of the Roman Stoics. There is Musonius' insistence on habituation and practice in ethics (p. 301); Seneca's concept of anticipation (pp. 307 f.) and premeditation (p. 309), his gentlemanly *ars vivendi* (p. 313), his stress on man's conscience (p. 317) and on man's will (pp. 319 f.); Epictetus' division of philosophical topics (p. 329), his theory of choice (p. 332), his evaluation of *αἰδώς* and *πίστις* (p. 335); and Marcus Aurelius' anthropology (p. 343). One might add that the *principium individuationis* obtained a metaphysical, ethical, aesthetic, and pedagogical significance which it hardly had in earlier times (Seneca, *Ep.*, 113, 13-16; 114; 115). Moreover, this generation lives in the here and now. Teaching by example replaces teaching by theorem, and models are found in contemporary men and events, rather than in the ancient poets.[5] Not only do the

[4] Cf. *A. J. P.*, LVII (1936), pp. 286-325; LXXI (1950), pp. 78-83. The collection of the Posidonian fragments on which I am working is scheduled to appear in the near future. I should add that Pohlenz in a book that has just come out (*Stoa und Stoiker* [1950], 386 pp.) has translated not only fragments hailing from the Old Stoa, but also fragments of Panaetius and Posidonius, as well as passages which he thinks can be traced to these authors.

[5] This is especially true of Epictetus. Cf. also his general criticism of poetry, I, 4, 26; 28, 12, 32. Chrysippus was famous for his predilection for poetical quotations (I, p. 29), and the same is true of Posidonius,

Roman Stoics emphasize the inner, subjective moment in man's decisions, but also the realization of philosophical truth in action—one is almost tempted to say, in the philosopher's own existence—becomes one of their principal concerns (Epictetus, I, 29, 55-57). In some of these traits one might discern the influence of Panaetius and Posidonius on the Roman Stoa, and I should be inclined to rate this influence higher than does Pohlenz, at least where he speaks in general terms (p. 291; but e. g. pp. 321; 338; 348). Cleanthes' admiration of Zeus permeates the monotheism of Epictetus and Marcus Aurelius. Many of the new doctrines take their departure from Chrysippus. Nevertheless, the thesis of the preponderance of Chrysippus' authority seems much in need of a revision, and it might be well to take the words of Epictetus more literally when he says that Chrysippus "shows us the way" (I, 4, 30). Chrysippus may have provided the intellectual tools for the younger Stoics. Fundamentally, their views are new, and these representatives of Stoicism, no less than their predecessors, in their factiousness and independence of judgment are like "oligarchs," to use Numenius' happy phrase (II, 20 Arnim).

Another view that Pohlenz shares with many interpreters of Stoicism also, in my opinion, calls for reconsideration, namely the assumption of a special affinity between the Roman spirit and that of Stoic philosophy. This thesis, propounded by Pohlenz first in his chapter on the Middle Stoa (pp. 257-76), naturally gains momentum in his analysis of the later Stoa. Is it really true that in the first centuries of our era Stoicism among all the philosophical schools "remained the only one which suited the Romans and acquired significance for their way of life" (p. 279)? Certainly, during the first 150 years in which philosophy made an impress on Rome, the Epicureans were in the ascendency. Cicero's assertion *Italiam totam occupaverunt* (*Tusc.*, IV, 3, 7) may be exaggerated. Yet, the poets of the late Republic testify to the strong hold which Epicureanism alongside Stoicism had over the Roman mind. And was it not the typically Roman attitude that shaped also Epicureanism? Is Lucretius' Epicurean ethics not expressive of the Roman *Willenshaltung* (cf. W. Y. Sellar, *The Roman Poets of the Republic*[3] [1899], pp. 358 f.)? Just as Seneca infuses into the Stoic language the Roman simile of war and of the warrior, so does Lucretius revel in pictures of war and fighting.[6] Varro dared to contend that the dissension between the Stoa and the Garden was but a *Logomachia* (*Menippeae*, 243; cf. Pohlenz, p. 275), and he was quite right for his own time, in which Epicureanism changed greatly and acknowledged even political responsibility. In the first century of our era Epicurus'

who in addition used examples from past history (Galen, *De Placitis Hippocratis et Platonis*, p. 372 M.).

[6] For the Roman simile of fighting and military service, cf. Pohlenz, I, p. 314, and O. Regenbogen, *Die Antike*, XII (1936), pp. 115 f. However, one should not overlook the fact that the simile is also related to the language of the mysteries, cf. R. Reitzenstein, *Die Hellenistischen Mysterienreligionen*[3] (1927), p. 192; the comparison of philosophy with the mysteries is significant for Lucretius, as well as for Seneca and Epictetus.

doctrine did not cease to have faithful adherents among the Romans, not to mention that the Stoic, Seneca, showed an outspoken friendliness toward its teachings (pp. 306; 322); in the second century its authority rose steadily.[7] Even granting that under Augustus it may have looked for a moment as if Stoicism would emerge as the national philosophy of Rome (p. 276), this dream did not come true. The initial opposition to the monarchy, so prominent among the Stoics, though not absent among the Epicureans, gave the Stoa the prestige of upholding the old Roman creed. But the Stoa, too, eventually made its peace with the empire (pp. 286; 314), and the ethics which a man like Hierocles taught his pupils, despite its lip service to patriotism, is concerned mostly with the petty problems of daily life (p. 288). Under these circumstances I think it would be safer to speak of an affinity between individual Romans and Stoicism, rather than of one between Rome and the Stoa.

Pohlenz' last chapter (pp. 367-465) deals with the influence of the Stoic doctrine on other philosophies. He makes much of the Stoicism of Philo (pp. 367 ff.), whom Wolfson, admitting the frequency of Stoic terminology and phraseology, has just characterized as more of a critic than a follower of the Stoa (*Philo*, I [1947], pp. 111 f.). In opposition to Reitzenstein, Pohlenz sees a Stoic tinge in the Gnostic doctrine (p. 381), he underlines the Stoic views in the Hermetic writings (p. 383) and sifts out the Stoic elements in Neopythagoreanism and Neoplatonism (pp. 386 ff.). Special attention is paid finally to the sway of Stoic ideas over Christianity (pp. 400 ff.). While in its very beginning Christianity was impervious to philosophy—even the thought of St. Paul and St. John was not tinted with Stoicism (pp. 403; 405)—from the time of the Apologists (pp. 406 ff.) the development of the new religion cannot be understood without taking its contact with the Stoa into account (p. 463).

To be sure, in this survey on late ancient beliefs Pohlenz does not neglect to underline the Platonic trend noticeable in the various philosophical schools, as well as in Christianity. He points to the fact that Stoic materialism was abandoned in favor of Platonic idealism, that monism receded before dualism. Yet he is inclined to put the decisive emphasis on the Stoic share, especially in the formulation of Christian ethical concepts (e. g. p. 415). That he should speak of the Stoic explanation of evil as the necessary antithesis of the good (pp. 430; 445), an explanation which Chrysippus himself used with express reference to Plato (II, 1169 Arnim; cf. *Phaedo*, 60 C; also *Theaetetus*, 176 A), can be but a slip of the pen.

[7] For the history of Epicureanism in general, cf. H. Usener, *Epicurea* (1887), pp. LXXIII ff.; for the second century, cf. F. Ueberweg-K. Praechter, *Die Philosophie des Altertums*[12] (1926), pp. 578 ff. For the names of Roman Epicureans, cf. E. Zeller, *Die Philosophie der Griechen*, III, 1[3] (1880), p. 375. The claim that the philosophers expelled by Vespasian practically were all Stoics and Cynics (Pohlenz, I, p. 286) seems not justified to me.

To what an extent Stoic ethics itself is tinged by Platonism is a vexed problem.[8] This much, however, is certain: the "Socratic medicine" of which Chrysippus talked (III, 424 Arnim) became more and more potent in Musonius, in Seneca, and in Epictetus, the very men who transmitted Stoic ethics to the Christians. Even in regard to their moral doctrines, then, Clement and the other Christian philosophers took over almost as much Platonism as Stoicism. Nor should one forget that the Stoa had learned a good deal from its interchange with the Academy and the Peripatos (pp. 248 ff.; 354 ff.).

Saying this, I do not wish to identify myself with Shorey's opinion that Stoicism is only an episode in the history of Platonism, much as I agree with his strictures on the usual representations of the influence exercised by Stoic philosophy on later generations (*Platonism—Ancient and Modern* [1938], pp. 19 ff.). The peculiarity of the Stoic dogma has clearly been demonstrated by Pohlenz and he has set in sharp relief the originality of the Hellenistic systems against those of the Pre-Socratics, of Plato, and of Aristotle. The Stoic sage is more than "the stony similitude of a Platonist," and Stoic philosophy as a whole is more than decayed Platonism. In their metaphysics, and above all in their interpretation of natural phenomena, their teleology, the Stoics held their own. Their contribution to all natural sciences, no less than to the humanities, was great indeed. It is on the basis of such an evaluation alone that one can understand the survival of Stoic ideas in the Middle Ages, and the impetus that Stoicism gave to the philosophers of the Renaissance, as well as to the rationalists of the succeeding centuries.[9]

In this review I have outlined only the principal components of Pohlenz' picture of Stoicism. I have not attempted to give an impression of the innumerable details which he discusses and clarifies, or of the wealth of material incorporated into his book. In this regard, it may suffice to say that the reader will find a most complete account of all aspects of Stoicism, of the lives of the philosophers as well as of their theories. I need hardly add that the modern literature too is thoroughly covered. There is now no more comprehensive and no more up-to-date introduction to Stoic philosophy than the one which Pohlenz provides, and therefore the book will be widely read. However, using it the reader, in my opinion, should be aware that the main theses of Pohlenz' interpretation are still controversial, and it is for this reason that I have drawn attention to them here.

LUDWIG EDELSTEIN.

UNIVERSITY OF CALIFORNIA, BERKELEY.

[8] Cf. the remarks of O. Rieth, "Grundbegriffe der stoischen Ethik," *Problemata*, IX (1933), pp. 169 f.

[9] Cf. Pohlenz' short survey of the Stoa in the Middle Ages and in modern times (pp. 466-73), and for the latter period also Barth-Goedeckemeyer, *op. cit.*, pp. 308-49.

AMERICAN JOURNAL OF PHILOLOGY

Founded by B. L. GILDERSLEEVE

Edited by
HENRY T. ROWELL

KEMP MALONE, BENJAMIN D. MERITT, JAMES H. OLIVER
EVELYN H. CLIFT: Secretary

Honorary Editor
DAVID M. ROBINSON

VOLUME LXXI

BALTIMORE: THE JOHNS HOPKINS PRESS
LONDON: ARTHUR F. BIRD
PARIS: ALBERT FONTEMOING LEIPZIG: F. A. BROOKHAUS

1950

carefully than hitherto for such indications as there may be of eastern or western origin. In the absence of evidence one must either presume a western origin or be content with a *non liquet*." But it is hoped that the author's skepticism will not rob scholars of an open mind for the possibility of an eastern origin of early post-classical editions of classical works.

HANS JULIUS WOLFF.

OKLAHOMA CITY UNIVERSITY.

M. VAN STRAATEN. Panétius, sa vie, ses écrits et sa doctrine avec une édition des fragments. Amsterdam, H. J. Paris, 1946. Pp. xv + 399.

In recent discussions of the philosophy of the Middle Stoa attention has centered on Panaetius, the founder of the school. Van Straaten bases his interpretation of Panaetius' theories upon a new collection of the evidence. This fact alone makes his book noteworthy. The editions of van Lynden (1802) and Fowler (1885) are antiquated and hard of access. Progress could be achieved only by making the material available and studying it afresh.

To speak first of the collection of the fragments (Part II, pp. 227-393), van Straaten rightly follows the example of van Lynden and also prints the data concerning Panaetius' life and activities, which Fowler omitted (p. 229). Again in contrast to Fowler, the author does not attempt to group the fragments together according to the books from which they may be derived (*ibid.*), but arranges the material according to subjects (pp. 234 f.). This procedure, too, I find convincing, since with one exception (frags. 34-44) hardly more than the titles are known of these books (frags. 33; 45-51).

As for the content of the collection, van Straaten includes not only the statements which ancient authors ascribe to Panaetius, but also some which modern scholars have attributed to him. He does so, although he is by no means an ardent believer in *Quellenforschung*. As a matter of fact, in very detailed and circumspect analyses he refutes the belief that Panaetian good can be recovered from Cicero's *Tusculanae Disputationes*, II (pp. 266 f.; 285-92), *De Finibus* (pp. 292-94), *Laelius* (pp. 294-96), *De Republica* (pp. 302-15), *De Legibus* (pp. 315-19), or from Philo's *De Aeternitate Mundi* (pp. 255-57), or from Plutarch's *Περὶ εὐθυμίας* (pp. 296-300), or from Seneca's *De Tranquillitate Animi* (pp. 300-02). Nemesius' *Περὶ φύσεως ἀνθρώπου* he considers a doubtful source (pp. 267 f.). Even Augustine's famous distinction of the various types of theology (*De Civitate Dei*, IV, 27) he does not trace to Panaetius (pp. 259-62). Passages in Cicero's *De Officiis* and in Sextus Empiricus are the only indirect testimony that remains; indeed the reasoned exclusion of the other sources is one of the most important results of van Straaten's studies.

Now, since in the *De Officiis* Cicero, according to his own admission, adapts Panaetius' *Περὶ τοῦ καθήκοντος*, it is possible that the "main passages," selected by the editor because it seemed unfeasible to reprint books I and II in their entirety (pp. 230 f.), echo the thoughts of Panaetius. But it is equally possible that Cicero added ideas of his own, as he certainly did in some instances (p. 277). In my opinion, it would have been better to leave out all statements that are not attested by ancient tradition. At any rate, it is gratuitous to assume that Sextus speaking of the younger Stoics and their logical doctrines must necessarily have had Panaetius in mind (pp. 269 ff.). His reference is so vague that it cannot be made the cornerstone of a reconstruction of the lost logical theories of Panaetius (frag. 91; pp. 130 ff.).

The incorporation of uncertain material accounts in part for the larger number of fragments which van Straaten's collection contains, as compared to that of Fowler (165, as against 57). Furthermore, one must remember that a good many fragments had to be repeated under various headings, and that the author numbers consecutively the fragments and the testimonies concerning Panaetius and his pupils.[1] On the other hand, some of his scientific theories (e. g. frags. 51, 136) are listed which are missing in Fowler, not to mention the rich documentation of Panaetius' life that has been brought together. Thus van Straaten's collection constitutes a definite improvement over the work of his predecessors. The material is reproduced with utmost care and from the best modern editions.[2] To my knowledge, it is complete, with the exception of two statements in Porphyry's commentary on the *Harmonics* of Ptolemy. One of these is especially interesting, because it comes from an otherwise unknown book of Panaetius and is a literal quotation, while all the other fragments are merely paraphrases (pp. 26; 234). Since the passages, so far as I can see, have not yet been taken into account in the literature on Panaetius, I shall cite them here:[3]

Porphyry, pp. 65, 21–66, 15: *Εἴρηται δὲ καὶ Παναιτίῳ τῷ νεωτέρῳ ἐν τῷ Περὶ τῶν κατὰ γεωμετρίαν καὶ μουσικὴν λόγων καὶ διαστημάτων συντόμως περὶ τούτων μετ' εὐλόγου ἀπολογίας τῆς ὑπὲρ τῶν πρεσβυτέρων καὶ διδασκαλίας τῆς κατὰ τοὺς ἀριθμοὺς χρήσεως. γράφει γὰρ ὧδε.*

'Καὶ κατὰ μουσικὴν δὲ τὸ λεγόμενον ἡμιτόνιον κατάχρησίς ἐστιν ὀνόματος. ὁ γὰρ οἰόμενος τὸ μεταξὺ διάστημα ὀξέος καὶ βαρέος διχοτομεῖσθαι μέσῳ τινὶ φθόγγῳ ὅμοιός ἐστι τῷ τὸ μεταξὺ λευκοῦ καὶ μέλανος

[1] Frags. 1-63 give the testimonies, titles of books, and general characteristics of Panaetius' philosophy, frags. 137-63 concern the pupils of Panaetius; *ca.* 22 fragments are of doubtful authenticity. I should mention that van Straaten also includes passages which he thinks are more or less likely quotations from Panaetius. These are inserted after fragments of a similar content and are distinguished by the addition of a, b, c, etc. to the numeral (p. 232).

[2] For the editions used, cf. pp. 232 ff., for the sigla of the MSS, cf. pp. 379-89. That the apparatus criticus is too conservative—van Straaten retains even the *ego* of the various editors and their cross references to earlier or later passages—has been pointed out by J. H. Turner, *C. J.*, XLIV (1948), p. 64.

[3] Cf. *Porphyrios Kommentar zur Harmonielehre des Ptolemaios*, ed. I. Düring, *Göteborgs Högskolas Årsskrift*, XXXVIII (1932), 2. For the interpretation of the passages, cf. again Düring, *op. cit.*, XL (1934), 1, pp. 168 f.; 177. As Düring has seen, the first fragment confirms Suidas' mention of a younger Panaetius (frag. 1 van Straaten, and pp. 235 f.).

ἢ θερμοῦ καὶ ψυχροῦ διχοτομεῖσθαι λέγοντι. οὐ γὰρ παρὰ τὰ μεγέθη τῶν φθόγγων ἡ περὶ τὰ σύμφωνα πραγματεία, ἀλλὰ περὶ τὰς ποιότητας. οἱ δ' ἀπὸ τῶν μαθημάτων ἐπειδὰν λέγωσι τὸ διὰ πασῶν ἐν διπλασίονι λόγῳ, οὐ τοῦτο λέγουσιν, ὅτι τὸ μέγεθος τοῦ φθόγγου τῆς νήτης διπλοῦν ἐστι τοῦ μεγέθους τῆς ὑπάτης ἢ ἀνάπαλιν. τεκμήριον δέ, ἐάν τε γὰρ σφόδρα πλήττωσι τὰς χορδάς, ἐάν τε τὴν μὲν μᾶλλον, τὴν δ' ἧττον—τὸ μὲν διάστημα ταὐτόν—ἡ δὲ μᾶλλον πληττομένη χορδὴ μείζονα ἀποτελεῖ ἦχον, ὥστ' ἔοικεν οὐκ ἐν μεγέθει τὸ διάστημα λέγεσθαι. πῶς οὖν εἴπερ ἐν ποιότησίν ἐστι, τὸ μὲν διὰ πασῶν ἐν διπλασίονι λόγῳ λέγεται, τὸ δὲ διὰ τεσσάρων ἐν ἐπιτρίτῳ καὶ τὸ διὰ πέντε ἐν ἡμιολίῳ καὶ τὸ διὰ πασῶν καὶ διὰ πέντε ἐν τριπλασίῳ, τὸ δὲ δὶς διὰ πασῶν ἐν τετραπλασίονι; ὅτι οὔτε τῆς ὄψεως ἰσχυούσης κρίνειν τὰ σύμμετρα τῶν μεγεθῶν ἀλλ' εὑρημένου μέτρου, ᾧ καταμετρούμενα τὰ σύμμετρα κρίνεσθαι πέφυκεν, οὔτε τῆς ἁφῆς ἰσχυούσης κρίνειν τὴν κατὰ τὰ βάρη σύγκρισιν, ἀλλ' εὑρημένου ζυγοῦ, ᾧ κρίνεται τὰ βάρη. ἄτοπον δὲ δοκεῖ τὴν ἀκοὴν πολὺ ἀσθενεστέραν ὑπάρχουσαν τῆς ὄψεως χωρὶς μέτρου τινὸς καὶ κανόνος κρίνειν τὰ σύμφωνα τῶν διαστημάτων. οἱ γὰρ αὖ τῇ αἰσθήσει προσέχοντες ὡς ἐκ γειτόνων φωνὴν ἀκούοντες, ὅμοιοι φαίνονται τοῖς χωρὶς μέτρου διὰ τῆς ὄψεως περὶ τῆς κατὰ τὰ μεγέθη συμμετρίας ἀποφαινομένοις, οἳ πολὺ ἀφαμαρτάνουσι τῆς ἀληθείας.'

Porphyry, p. 88, 1-7: δεῖ δὲ γινώσκειν, ὅτι κἂν ποιότητες ὦσιν αἱ διαφοραὶ τῶν ψόφων αἱ κατ' ὀξύτητα καὶ βαρύτητα, οὐδὲν κωλύει ὡς περὶ ποσὸν ποιεῖσθαι τὸν λόγον τῶν φθόγγων ὡς τῇ ποσότητι τοῦ ὑποκειμένου ἐπιγίνεσθαι ταύτας τὰς διαφοράς, ἢ ὥσπερ ὁ Παναίτιος ἔφασκε, 'μέτρα τινὰ τοὺς παλαιοὺς κατ' ἀναλογίαν τοῖς φθόγγοις παραβάλλειν ἀπὸ τῶν ἀριθμῶν, οἷς χρωμένους ἡμᾶς τὸ παχὺ καὶ ἀβέβαιον τῆς ἀκοῆς ἐκκλίνειν.'

To turn now to van Straaten's analysis of Panaetius' views (Part I, pp. 3-226), the ethical doctrine, the core of the philosophy of Panaetius, is convincingly expounded and with admirable clarity set against the background of older theories. Like all Stoics, Panaetius defines the moral aim as "life in accordance with nature" (frag. 109; p. 140); like all of them, he distinguishes between the general, cosmic law and the particular, human one. Yet he puts more emphasis on the latter, on the individual values, and he stresses the content of man's action rather than his mental attitude. Not only should man learn to accept his fate, he should above all else strive to attain that which is good and fitting (pp. 139-58). Acquiescence of the mind is less important than active achievement. Thus, it becomes clear for the first time why Panaetius went even so far as to consider virtue not self-sufficient, but rather dependent upon health, money, and strength (frag. 110; p. 154). A positive evaluation of reality is basic for the new *ars vivendi* (p. 163). It is connected with, or derived from, the recognition of the dualism in man's nature (pp. 95-129).

Van Straaten's analysis of Panaetius' physics (pp. 63-94) I find less acceptable. Panaetius, he holds, believed in the eternity of the cosmos (p. 68). This, to be sure, is what Diogenes Laertius says (frag. 66), and what Philo also attests (frag. 65), if the name Panaetius is here correctly restored. Yet frag. 69, which is taken from Stobaeus, or rather from Arius Didymus (cf. H. Diels, *Doxographi Graeci*, p. 469, b7-10), asserts only that in Panaetius' opinion the assumption of the eternity of the world was more probable and more satisfactory. Cicero too mentions only that Panaetius doubted the Stoic dogma of an eventual disintegration of the world (frag. 64).[4] Similarly, according to Diogenes Laertius, Panaetius denied the real existence of mantic (frag. 73), while, according to Cicero, he was only doubtful about it, yet refrained from committing himself definitely, did not dare to make a decision, and was satisfied with a *non liquet* (frags. 70, 71; cf. also 82). The better and older authorities, then, attest no more than a questioning and undecided attitude on the part of Panaetius. The later sources, it seems, tend to state Panaetius' opinions more dogmatically than he did himself.[5] It was not only in regard to the problem of mantic that Panaetius took the position of the academic Sceptics with whom he had so much in common; he apparently did the same in regard to metaphysical issues. With this in mind, one can also appreciate the assertion of Epiphanius: . . . *καὶ τὰ περὶ θεῶν λεγόμενα ἀνῄρει. ἔλεγε γὰρ φλήναφον εἶναι τὸν περὶ θεοῦ λόγον* (frag. 68). Epiphanius by no means accuses Panaetius of atheism, and there is no reason to reject his testimony, as has generally been done (p. 87); all he intends to say is that Panaetius did away with investigations into the divine, because to him theology was "idle chatter." In the same way, the Sceptics refuted all positive statements about the gods, without, however, denying their existence.[6]

So far, I have spoken only of Panaetius the philosopher. But Panaetius, one of the most learned men of his time (frags. 8, 48), was also a scientist and a scholar. His interest in research, greater than that of the early Stoics, foreshadows the attitude of his pupil, Posidonius. Van Straaten pays scant attention to this side of Panaetius' work. I shall try at least to characterize the main aspects which can now be established on the basis of the evidence available.

Sceptical as Panaetius was in metaphysical questions, he had a rather dogmatic confidence in the results of natural studies, and especially of astronomy. Here, he talked as if he could see nature at work and touch her with his hands (frag. 77). Distrusting the sight of the eyes, the most deceiving of the senses (frag. 90 = 74),

[4] Zeller, *Die Philosophie der Griechen*, III, 1 (1880), p. 561, no. 2, claims that *addubitare dicebant* in frag. 64 is an addition of Cicero. This, I think, is beyond proof, and it is highly improbable in view of the fact that Cicero, as will be shown immediately, is consistent in his representation of Panaetius' sceptical attitude.

[5] Perhaps Panaetius, like Balbus (*De Natura Deorum*, II, 85), considered alternate possibilities of the fate of the cosmos, and the doxographers chose whichever formulations suited them best. This would explain the discrepancies in the content of frags. 64-69.

[6] For the identity of arguments proffered by Panaetius and Carneades, cf. frags. 72, 74 *finis*, and pp. 50 ff. For the sceptic polemic against the proofs of the existence of gods, cf. Zeller, *op. cit.*, pp. 505 ff. The statement in Libanius, *Ep.* 803, 4: *ὃς καὶ τοὺς θεοὺς ἡγεῖτο εἶναι φλήναφον*, which may be a misquotation from Panaetius, by contrast helps to clarify the meaning of frag. 68. The possibility that some of the heterodoxies of Panaetius were stated only in the form of doubts of the general Stoic dogma, has been stressed by F. Ueberweg-K. Praechter, *Die Philosophie des Altertums* (1926), p. 477.

he relied heavily upon reason (cf. Porphyry, p. 65, 21 ff.). Moreover, all physical problems seem to have attracted him in like manner.[7] He occupied himself with anthropology (frag. 76). He wrote on geography (frags. 76, 135, 136), and I see no reason to reject with van Straaten (p. 37) Pliny's admission (frag. 51) that he made use of a geographical treatise of Panaetius.

Literary studies apparently fascinated Panaetius even more. Remarkably enough, he was concerned not only with Greek, but with Roman literature as well. It was he who pointed out to the Romans the greatness of their early poetry (frag. 47). He dealt with problems of genuineness and attribution of writings (frag. 123), with the identification of homonymous authors (frag. 124), and he was also concerned with language, with the pure Attic form that prevailed in Plato's time (frag. 92). Nor did he neglect higher criticism. He judged poems in relation to the temper of the time in which they were written (frag. 125). He praised Demosthenes' moral courage and ranked him with Cimon, Thucydides, and Pericles (frag. 94), an evaluation that cannot have been without influence on Cicero's enthusiasm for Demosthenes (*Ad Att.*, XV, 1b, 2; Plutarch, *Cicero*, 24), and the later fame of this writer. In his remarks on the history of philosophy Panaetius shows disgust for the petty anecdotes and the gossip to be found in peripatetic biographies (frags. 132, 133). The Platonic and Socratic dialogues more than anything else (frags. 126-30) naturally held the attention of the devotee of Plato (frag. 56). He even challenged the picture of Socrates which Aristophanes gives in his *Clouds* (frag. 134). Throughout his literary investigations Panaetius appears as a follower of Crates of Mallos whose pupil he was, according to his own words (frag. 5, cf. p. 7).

Political history, too, was of interest to Panaetius, and he did not disdain inquiry into minute details. He studied inscriptions and dated them according to the type of their lettering (frag. 131). His interpretation of history in general is particularly remarkable. In contrast to the majority of ancient historians, he was willing to acknowledge the share of common men in military and political achievements. Themistocles, Pericles, Cyrus, Agesilaus, Alexander, he says, could not have done what they did without the help of the people. Cicero is hardly right in considering this a trite observation, not worthy of the lengthy discussion that Panaetius devoted to it (frag. 117). Panaetius' concern with the problem is quite in keeping with the realism of his political treatises (pp. 203-11), which he wrote *ad usum popularem et civilem* (frag. 61; cf. p. 58).

Behind such an attitude one senses the humanism of Panaetius, the strong and independent personality of the man who showed moderation in word and deed (frag. 27, cf. 32; also 114), who was able to realize that in human relations sometimes kindness rather than truth is the higher value (frag. 95). What this celebrated humanism meant in detail (pp. 201; 218 ff.) it is too early to ask, nor can one as yet define the influence of Panaetius' doctrine on later generations (pp. 223 ff.). For the development of the school

[7] For Panaetius' musical theories, known only from Porphyry, cf. Düring, *op. cit.*, 1934. Here, I should note only that they show him once more in agreement with Plato (*Republic*, VII, 531a). For Panaetius and Plato, cf. van Straaten, pp. 48 ff.

which he founded is still unknown. The first phase of the history of the Middle Stoa, however, has been greatly clarified by van Straaten's book.

LUDWIG EDELSTEIN.

UNIVERSITY OF CALIFORNIA, BERKELEY.

Phyllobolia für Peter von der Mühll zum 60. Geburtstag am 1. August 1945. By OLOF GIGON, KARL MEULI, WILLY THEILER, FRITZ WEHRLI, and BERNHARD WYSS. Basel, Benno Schwabe & Co., 1946. Pp. 288.

This handsome volume contains five essays written by five of Professor von der Mühll's former pupils, all of whom are scholars of international reputation teaching in Swiss institutions of higher learning. In the first and briefest of these essays, "Der erhabene und der schlichte Stil in der poetisch-rhetorischen Theorie der Antike" (pp. 9-34), Fritz Wehrli connects the conception of the "elevated" style with Democritus' theory of inspiration, to which he would also assign the notion of the "magnetic" transfer of enthusiasm from poet to performer to audience which is proposed in Plato's *Ion*;[1] and he contends that the influence of Democritus is to be reckoned with wherever in ancient theory the "elevated" style is held to be the expression of πάθος or higher sentiment as it is in the Περὶ Ὕψους. He argues that the inspirational theory of poetry in the *Ion*, the *Apology*, and the *Phaedrus* is Democritean though mixed with Gorgianic elements, Gorgias having elaborated the aperçus of Democritus into a system of rhetoric and poetics which swiftly became common property, so that neither Plato nor Aristophanes before him needed to get his knowledge of it from any particular writing of Democritus or Gorgias. This last point is apparently a concession to Kranz's criticism[2] of Pohlenz's thesis[3] that Aristophanes used as his source for the *Frogs* a specific book of Gorgias. Pohlenz, moreover, had maintained that this book contained a comparison of the styles of Aeschylus and Euripides;[4] but Wehrli, though he believes Gorgias to have been the source of the Aeschylean defence of the "lofty" style, sees behind the Aristophanic criticism of Aeschylus which is put into the mouth of

[1] Wehrli does not attempt to prove that the theory of "magnetic transference" belonged to Democritus himself, and he does not mention Delatte's attempt to demonstrate it (*Les Conceptions de l'Enthousiasme chez les Philosophes Présocratiques*, pp. 59 ff.). Neither Wehrli nor Delatte observes that in introducing the theory (*Ion* 533 D) Socrates refers to Euripides for the name λίθος Μαγνῆτις, and that in the fragmentary passage of the *Oeneus* which is presumably meant (frag. 567 [= 571]) Euripides compares to a magnet the influence of someone or something upon the human mind. One might suppose that by this Plato meant to indicate that Euripides was the immediate inspiration of his figure in the *Ion*.

[2] W. Kranz, *Stasimon*, p. 268.

[3] *Gött. Nachr.*, 1920, pp. 142-178.

[4] *Op. cit.*, pp. 158, 162.

cially controversies which involve the authenticity of primary source material. As it is, the reader who is not a specialist will not always understand the relation to the text of the studies listed in the bibliographies. The propriety of dismissing the political forensic speeches as a mere detail in Demosthenes' career as logographer (28) is at least debatable; the Leptinean oration is not even mentioned, I believe, in the text, though passages are cited once or twice on minor points. The attempt (282) to reconstruct the defense of Demosthenes in "l'affaire d'Harpale" from passages in the speeches of Hyperides and Dinarchus which are simply stock rhetorical commonplaces is, in my opinion, futile. Cloché accepts the time-honored belief that Demosthenes recovered little or nothing from the guardians, but grew rich so fast from his earnings as a logographer that within four years he was in the trierarchic census (27 f.); both assumptions might profitably be tested by the actual evidence. I note a few minor inadvertences. The statement (25) that the elder Demosthenes entrusted his cutlery business to "l'affranchi Milyas" is inaccurate, since we learn from Dem., xxix, 26 (which on p. 27 is treated as authentic) that Milyas was manumitted only when his master lay dying. Two or three years preceding the trial of Demosthenes *vs.* Aphobus could not have been consumed in discussions "devant l'arbitre public" (27), since those officials functioned only after filing of the complaint; possibly the author is thinking of the conferences mentioned in Dem., xxx, 6. There seems to be a confusion (76) of the reserve force of fifty triremes (Dem., iv, 16) with the field army of 2000 infantry and 200 cavalry, to be supported by ten fast triremes (*ib.*, 20-22). The translations, which usually are from the *Collection Budé*, occasionally suffer from being stripped of context; "pour le moment" (88) will scarcely do for εἰς τὸ παρόν (iii, 10), and "pour l'ombre d'un avantage à Delphes" (120) emasculates the fine close of the speech *On the Peace*.

The printer has allowed an attractive format and clear typography to be marred by many misprints and misspellings.

GEORGE M. CALHOUN.

UNIVERSITY OF CALIFORNIA.

LOTTE LABOWSKY. Die Ethik des Panaitios (Untersuchungen zur Geschichte des Decorum bei Cicero und Horaz). Leipzig, F. Meiner, 1934. Pp. 124.

In her attempt to present the ethical system of Panaetius, Miss Labowsky chooses as her main theme the conception of decorum because of its decisive importance for Panaetius' philosophy and because of its great influence on later centuries (p. 4). The purpose of her interpretation is not to sum up the various testimonies in a doxographical form but rather to elucidate the basic principles of Panaetius' thinking in their inner relation and balance (p. 3).

Miss Labowsky starts her attempt at reconstruction with a passage from the only treatise which can with certainty be traced back to Panaetius (p. 2), Cicero's discussion of decorum in *De officiis* (I, 93-151). She is aware of the fact that even here it is necessary to separate the thought of Panaetius from the transformation or addition made by Cicero, and it is especially this that she wants to achieve in her analysis (p. 3). Her conclusion is that the passage, in the main, gives the original sentences of Panaetius, only abbreviated by Cicero, who also inserted the Roman examples (pp. 67 ff.). This conclusion is primarily based on internal evidence, on the interpretation of the text and its coherence. It may very well be that the difficulties which the reader notes in perusing the argumentation can be explained by Cicero's hasty and careless method of working. Miss Labowsky, in general, does not think too highly of Cicero as a philosophical writer; she expressly adopts Usener's unfavourable judgment about him (p. 3). Yet, granted that consistency has been proved, this would not permit any conclusion about the source of Cicero's text. He himself admits that in writing this book he is often (multum, II, 17, 60) or mostly (potissimum, III, 2, 7; cf. Labowsky, p. 2, n. 3) following Panaetius. But it is precisely in the introduction to the *De officiis* that he defines his method of following the Greek examples thus: sequemur igitur hoc quidem tempore et hac in quaestione potissimum Stoicos, non ut interpretes, sed, ut solemus, e fontibus eorum iudicio arbitrioque nostro quantum quoque modo videbitur hauriemus (I, 2, 6). Cicero was not such a bad writer as not to be able to compose out of divergent material a correct sequence of ideas. Starting from the internal evidence that the text is intact, one can prove that it is the text of Panaetius only by presupposing his authorship. If one does so, one can agree with Miss Labowsky and take the whole Ciceronian passage, without any limitations, as a reproduction of Panaetius' philosophy.

Next, the *Ars poetica* is discussed from the point of view of the conception of decorum and from that alone (pp. 74 ff., p. 76). Referring to Kroll's more general assertion (p. 75, n. 8) Miss Labowsky proves in detail that this conception is a constituent factor of the disposition; furthermore, she explains how it was possible for Horace in adhering to such a philosophical idea still to achieve a work of art (pp. 77, 98). The line of reasoning in the *Ars poetica* thus becomes much clearer. Horace, so far as he is concerned with ethical decorum, is considered by Miss Labowsky to be determined by Panaetius' shaping of the subject (p. 98). Nothing new can be concluded from his poem in this respect, but the aesthetical decorum which he stresses gives her the opportunity to bring out more sharply an aspect of the decorum conception which she deems to be significant for Panaetius' thinking.

For in the last part of her book Miss Labowsky, after having outlined the history of decorum,—her study was published shortly after Pohlenz' essay on decorum had appeared (p. 4, n. 14)—characterizes the ethics of Panaetius as an *ars vitae* in the proper sense of the word (p. 113). Unity of action and influence on the spectator are characteristic of the work of art as well as of the moral attitude of human beings; the dynamic power can be realized in the individual form alone, yet it coincides with, and is subordinated to, the general rule (p. 112). The aesthetical and moral values are fused into one, into the old conception of *καλοκαγαθία* (p. 121). In this sense Panaetius is viewed as the last Greek philosopher (p. 1). His doctrine historically must be understood as a Platonizing of Stoic theories (p. 116). But it is no mere external combination of opposite ideas; it is the expression of the "ursprüngliche, aller dialektischen Zerspaltung vorausgehende Lebens- und Wertgefühl" of the later centuries, and in this sense it is more than an individual conception (pp. 1-2).

The interpretation which Miss Labowsky gives is subtle, sometimes, I am afraid, even exaggerated and sophisticated. Thus, for example, she expresses in seven lines the meaning which an *enim* in the text of Cicero is supposed to have (pp. 18-19). But generally her remarks are very illuminating. She always traces the late ideas to their origin, and she connects the single facts with the general trend in the development of philosophical thought. Her interpretation reads like a commentary on the discussion with which it deals and as such is indispensable for everyone interested in these texts.

I must restrict myself here, however, to that problem which is the main object of the book and of which the analysis of Cicero and Horace is meant to be only the first step: the representation of the ethical system of Panaetius. And for this point I do not feel that Miss Labowsky has proved her thesis. I accept those testimonies which she uses as the only basis for a reconstruction and do not inquire into how far it would be possible to come to conclusions taking into account the other fragments of Panaetius as well as his whole philosophical system of which the ethics, after all, is only a part. Even then there arise great difficulties.

Miss Labowsky credits Panaetius, first of all, with separating the ethical reflection from the contemplation of the wise man, with speaking only of the average individual who is perfecting himself in virtue. The proof for this statement is found in the ironical and contemptuous answer given by Panaetius to a young fellow who asked him whether the wise man should love or not: "De sapiente, inquit, videbimus: mihi et tibi, qui adhuc a sapiente longe absumus, non est committendum, ut incidamus in rem commotam . . ." (Seneca, *Epistle*, 116, 5; fr. 56 [Fowler]; Labowsky, pp. 115-16). Even if one is inclined to find in this anecdote an indication that Panaetius' belief in the wise man was not that of the other Stoics—a conclusion which is by no means necessary and convincing—, what exactly is meant by the words "de sapiente videbimus" nobody can tell; it would be hard to assert that Panaetius did more than doubt the existence of the wise. For his scepticism never leads him to anything more than doubt in all the important problems in which he disagrees with the old Stoa. It is, therefore, not at all certain that Panaetius denied the reality of the existence of the wise man, that he rejected, from the beginning, every argument concerning his attitude as being wrong (p. 115). And what evidence is there that he ascribed to the wise man and to the idea of honesty transcendental existence alone (p. 116)? Miss Labowsky emphasizes the importance of the reference made by Cicero-Panaetius to the Platonic *Phaedrus:* formam quidem ipsam . . . et tamquam faciem honesti vides, "quae si oculis cerneretur, mirabiles amores" ut ait Plato, "excitaret sapientiae"; and she declares these words to be the motto of the ethics of Panaetius (p. 116). The idea of honesty cannot be seen, but it becomes apparent in the individual human actions (pp. 116; 9). Yet, this is not a Platonic solution of the problem of how the world of the phenomena and that of thinking are related to each other; it is not the transformation of the πρῶτον φίλον and its dynamics into Stoic philosophy—at least as long as the idea is understood to be the Stoic ἔννοια and the nature of man is interpreted as rational only. And that this is the case, Miss Labowsky herself states (pp. 116-17). It is the old Stoic doctrine, I think, expressed perhaps in a terminology similar to the Platonic one: Panaetius was a great admirer of Plato; Cicero was an Academic philosopher. But if there were any real relationship between the προκόπτων of Panaetius and the φιλόσοφος of Plato (p. 116), Panaetius would have had to change the psychological dogmas of the Stoics and their definitions of virtues and vices as Posidonius did later on.

I do not believe, therefore, that the ethical system of Panaetius, as a whole, has been adequately reconstructed by Miss Labowsky. It is the historical interpretation of detail which makes her book valuable.

LUDWIG EDELSTEIN.

INSTITUTE OF THE HISTORY OF MEDICINE,
THE JOHNS HOPKINS UNIVERSITY.

AMERICAN JOURNAL OF PHILOLOGY

Founded by B. L. GILDERSLEEVE

Edited by

TENNEY FRANK

With the coöperation of

HAROLD CHERNISS (assistant editor), KEMP MALONE
BENJAMIN DEAN MERITT, DAVID MOORE ROBINSON

VOLUME LVII

BALTIMORE: THE JOHNS HOPKINS PRESS

LONDON: ARTHUR F. BIRD

PARIS: ALBERT FONTEMOING   LEIPZIG: F. A. BROCKHAUS

1936

THE PHILOSOPHICAL SYSTEM OF POSIDONIUS.

Since only a few fragments of the works of Posidonius have survived, it is necessary to reconstruct his philosophical system. Such a reconstruction was first attempted in the beginning of the 19th century after the fragments had been collected.[1] It was naturally restricted to the understanding of those testimonies. But then, from the end of the 19th century on, the fragments were supposed not to be sufficient material. Scholars therefore tried to replace the missing direct data by tracing down the influences of Posidonius on later philosophers. Many theories were granted as being indirectly Posidonian, because they seemed to fit either to one of the fragments itself or to the consequences to be drawn from it.[2] This method was applied even down to the most recent times. For in regard to the basic principle, it is no essential alteration that the "inner form" of Posidonian thinking, felt intuitively rather than demonstrated, decided what theories could be attributed to Posidonius.[3]

The interpretation of the Posidonian philosophy changed a good deal with the modification of the method of reconstruction. First, the system was visualized as a Stoic theory influenced more or less by Plato and Aristotle. Posidonius was believed to be an eclectic thinker of not too great importance and in-

[1] *Posidonii Rhodii reliquiae* collegit I. Bake, Lugd. Bat., 1810. The collection, motivated only by the intention to bring together the statements of the pupil of Panaetius (p. 262), is far from being satisfactory. Some fragments are missing, some quotations have been discovered since that time. The text is to a great extent incorrect since the editions used by Bake are antiquated.

[2] This begins with the dissertation of P. Corssen, *De Posidonio auctore*, 1878. Cf. O. Gruppe, *Berichte über die Literatur zur antiken Mythologie und Religionsgeschichte*, 1898-1905, p. 168, and R. Jones, *Classical Philology*, XVIII (1923), p. 202. Later, many books were written following the same procedure, the most important of which are W. W. Jaeger, *Nemesios v. Emesa*, Berlin, 1914, p. 2, and I. Heinemann, *Poseidonios' metaphysische Schriften I*, Breslau, 1921; *II*, Breslau, 1928. Cf. also R. Hirzel, *Untersuchungen zu Ciceros philosophischen Schriften*, Leipzig, 1882, *II*, pp. 1 ff.

[3] K. Reinhardt, *Poseidonios*, München, 1921, p. 2 (in the following quoted as Reinhardt, I).

dividuality.[4] But when the new method of tracing down the influences was introduced, the Posidonian philosophy was regarded as the starting point of Neoplatonism. Posidonius passed for a religious thinker, for the first to connect Oriental and Greek thought. Almost all Greek philosophy of later centuries was based on his work.[5] Finally, Posidonius was characterized as a philosopher whose system is founded on sciences. To him spirit and nature were only two different aspects of the same power; he was a monistic thinker, the first vitalist of antiquity. Posidonius was now considered to be the last Greek philosopher before the beginning of that epoch during which Greek and Oriental thought were united.[6]

These three conceptions of Posidonian philosophy stand in opposition to one another. Which of them really represents his system? At the moment, this question cannot be answered. But the dilemma must be solved. The study of the influence of Posidonius on later authors led at best to probabilities which are worthless, since the different theories refute one another.[7] Certainty can only be reached by determining the work of Posidonius, proceeding from those fragments alone which are

[4] Cf. H. Ritter, *Geschichte der Philosophie*, 1836-38, III, p. 701. Ch. A. Brandis, *Handbuch der Geschichte der griechischen Philosophie*, Berlin, 1866, II, 2, p. 236 (Die Eklektik und Synkretistik (!) 4. Abschnitt). E. Zeller, *Geschichte der Philosophie der Griechen*, Leipzig, 1880, III, 1, pp. 570 ff., although he accepts some results of Corssen and later authors, is more inclined to the previous manner of interpreting the philosophy of Posidonius; cf. especially pp. 577, 578, 579. He is therefore criticized by Jaeger, *l. c.*, p. 25, 1.

[5] Cf. A. Schmekel, *Die Philosophie der mittleren Stoa*, Berlin, 1892, p. 400; Jaeger, *l. c.*, p. 120, p. 2 and *passim*. It is above all Jaeger's interpretation which is adopted by Überweg-Praechter, *Grundriss der Geschichte der Philosophie*, Berlin, 1926, I, p. 478, 2; cf. R. Reitzenstein, *Die Hellenistischen Mysterienreligionen*, Leipzig, 1927, p. 5.

[6] K. Reinhardt, *l. c.*, pp. 3-18 and *Kosmos und Sympathie*, München, 1926 (in the following quoted as Reinhardt, II). A change of Reinhardt's opinion pointed out by M. Pohlenz, *Göttinger gelehrte Anzeigen*, 1926, p. 306, is denied by Reinhardt himself, "Poseidonios, Über Ursprung und Entartung," *Orient und Antike*, VI (1928), p. 54.

[7] The first to contradict this method as such was Gruppe, *l. c.* Through philosophical argumentation, it was rejected by Jones, *l. c.* and *The Platonism of Plutarch*, Chicago, 1916, since Neoplatonism ought to be traced to Platonic sources not to Stoic dogmas. Cf. also the objections of Crönert, *Gnomon*, VI (1930), pp. 152 ff.

preserved as direct quotations under his name. And yet, such an interpretation was always made in a fortuitous rather than in a deliberate and comprehensive manner.[8] Whether the interpretation cannot succeed in reproducing the system or it is possible to understand the philosophy from the fragments—in either case, the basis of judgment should have been established in this way.[9]

It is my aim, therefore, to attempt the reconstruction of the philosophical system by interpreting the fragments alone. I shall presume only that Posidonius was a Stoic philosopher, deeply influenced like his teacher Panaetius by Platonic and Aristotelian theories. So much is certain.[10] In order to understand the scattered and abbreviated testimonies, it is necessary, therefore, and advantageous to correlate them to the general Stoic theory as well as sometimes to the philosophy of Plato and Aristotle.

I.

Division and Aim of Philosophy.

Posidonius divides philosophy into three parts: physics, ethics, and logic, and believes that it is necessary to begin the

[8] Bake collects the material without interpreting it. In the works of Ritter and Brandis the general outlines of the philosophy of Posidonius are very briefly sketched. His scientific research is not taken into account at all. Zeller uses many of the Posidonian fragments for the reconstruction of the Stoic philosophy, but in speaking about Posidonius he does not consider them again, *l. c.*, p. 584, 3. No special inquiry into Posidonian philosophy restricted to the fragments has ever been made.

[9] Reinhardt, I, pp. 39 ff. declares the understanding of the doxographical material to be impossible. Through this study of the fragments the further question may also be decided, as to whether the new collection of the available material, demanded by Reinhardt (I, *praef.*) and Pohlenz, *Göttinger gelehrte Anzeigen*, 1922, p. 164, would be useful or not. Moreover the form such a collection should take has to be determined in this way: it is necessary to decide whether direct quotations alone should be printed or influenced passages too and, if so, which ones. Cf. n. 131.

[10] Galen, *de placitis Hippocratis et Platonis*, ed. I. Müller, Leipzig, 1874, e.g. p. 405, 9. Strabo, II, 3, 8, p. 104. As regards Panaetius cf. Zeller, *l. c.*, p. 560, 4.

philosophical inquiry with physics.[11] It is important, however, to emphasize that these three spheres cannot be separated from one another. The parts of philosophy cannot be compared with the parts of a garden, with plants and fruits and walls. They belong together, like the parts of the human organism. Physics has to be compared with blood and flesh, logic with bones and nerves, ethics with the soul.[12] As certain as the inseparable connection of those provinces may be, still it is not clear whether they are merely co-ordinated or to a certain extent subordinated.[13] In any case, the goal of philosophy is to lay down the principles which are the presuppositions of knowledge, to find general statements, not special statements, to understand the whole, not the individual.[14] And one should not stand aloof from philosophy because of the disagreement of opinion, for by such an argument life as a whole would be destroyed.[15]

[11] Diogenes Laertius, VII, 39: Τριμερῆ φασὶν εἶναι τὸν κατὰ φιλοσοφίαν λόγον. εἶναι γὰρ αὐτοῦ τὸ μέν τι φυσικόν, τὸ δὲ ἠθικόν, τὸ δὲ λογικόν. οὕτω δὲ . . . καὶ Ποσειδώνιος. VII, 41: Παναίτιος δὲ καὶ Ποσειδώνιος ἀπὸ τῶν φυσικῶν ἄρχονται, καθά φησι Φανίας ὁ Ποσειδωνίου γνώριμος ἐν τῷ πρώτῳ τῶν Ποσειδωνείων σχολῶν. The subdivision of physics made by Posidonius (cf. *ibid.*, VII, 84) is not preserved.

[12] Sextus Empiricus, *adversus logicos*, I, 19: ὁ δὲ Ποσειδώνιος, ἐπεὶ τὰ μὲν μέρη τῆς φιλοσοφίας ἀχώριστά ἐστιν ἀλλήλων, τὰ δὲ φυτὰ τῶν καρπῶν ἕτερα θεωρεῖται καὶ τὰ τείχη τῶν φυτῶν κεχώρισται, ζῴῳ μᾶλλον εἰκάζειν ἠξίου τὴν φιλοσοφίαν, αἵματι μὲν καὶ σαρκὶ τὸ φυσικόν, ὀστέοις δὲ καὶ νεύροις τὸ λογικόν, ψυχῇ δὲ τὸ ἠθικόν.

[13] According to Zeller, *l. c.*, pp. 60-62, it is possible to determine the sequence of the parts of philosophy by some general considerations. About this problem cf. n. 126. As regards the rôle of the organism in the Posidonian system, cf. p. 299.

[14] Cf. Plutarch, *Pompeius*, chap. 42, 5: Ποσειδώνιος δὲ καὶ τὴν ἀκρόασιν ἀνέγραψεν ἣν ἔσχεν ἐπ' αὐτοῦ (sc. τοῦ Πομπηΐου) πρὸς Ἑρμαγόραν τὸν ῥήτορα περὶ τῆς καθόλου ζητήσεως ἀντιταξάμενος. and the interpretation of H. v. Arnim, *Leben und Werke des Dion von Prusa*, Berlin, 1898, p. 93. Simplicius, *in Aristotelis Physic.*, ed. H. Diels, Berlin, 1882; *Commentaria in Aristotelem Graeca*, X, pp. 291, 34-292, 31. The characterization of the Posidonian system by Reitzenstein (*Hermes* 65 [1930], p. 81, and *Mysterienreligionen*, *l. c.*, p. 135) is based entirely on indirect conclusions. The same is true of Reinhardt's interpretation, *I*, pp. 43 ff. Concerning the relation between philosophy and the individual sciences cf. pp. 319 ff.

[15] Diogenes Laertius, VII, 129: δοκεῖ δ' αὐτοῖς μηδὲ διὰ τὴν διαφωνίαν ἀφίστασθαι φιλοσοφίας, ἐπεὶ τῷ λόγῳ τούτῳ προλείψειν ὅλον τὸν βίον, ὡς καὶ Ποσειδώ-

II.

Physics.

Posidonius like all the other Stoics holds two principles to be existent in the universe, the active and the passive. The passive is the unqualified substance, the matter; the active is the reason contained in it, the God. For He is everlasting and throughout the whole of matter He creates each individual thing.[16] It is matter and God, then, which constitute the universe.

The first of these two principles Posidonius defines more accurately as follows: "The matter and substance of all things is without quality and form as far as it has no distinct form of its own or quality in itself. But always it is in a certain form and quality. And as far as reality is concerned the existing substance is different from the matter only in our thought."[17] What does that mean? The Stoics, in general, distinguish between matter and elements. To them matter, the passive principle, is unqualified substance, incorporeal and destitute of form. The existing substance, the elements, are endowed with form and quality. They are created by God from the principle of matter, and, therefore, they are really differentiated from the latter in regard to their existence.[18] Posidonius, too, assumes

νιὸς φησιν ἐν τοῖς προτρεπτικοῖς. Although Posidonius is here in agreement with other Stoics, the theory is of special significance for him. Cf. Diogenes Laertius, VII, 91 and p. 318. Cf. also H. G. Gadamer, Hermes 63 (1928), pp. 145-6.

[16] Diogenes Laertius, VII, 134: *Δοκεῖ δ' αὐτοῖς ἀρχὰς εἶναι τῶν ὅλων δύο, τὸ ποιοῦν καὶ τὸ πάσχον. τὸ μὲν οὖν πάσχον εἶναι τὴν ἄποιον οὐσίαν τὴν ὕλην, τὸ δὲ ποιοῦν τὸν ἐν αὐτῇ λόγον τὸν θεόν. τοῦτον γὰρ ἀΐδιον ὄντα διὰ πάσης αὐτῆς δημιουργεῖν ἕκαστα. τίθησι δὲ τὸ δόγμα τοῦτο . . . καὶ Ποσειδώνιος ἐν τῷ δευτέρῳ τοῦ φυσικοῦ λόγου.* The subdivision of physics, made by Posidonius (cf. VII, 84 and 132), is not preserved.

[17] Doxographi Graeci, p. 458, 8-11: *Ἔφησε δὲ ὁ Ποσειδώνιος τὴν τῶν ὅλων οὐσίαν καὶ ὕλην ἄποιον καὶ ἄμορφον εἶναι, καθ' ὅσον οὐδὲν ἀποτεταγμένον ἴδιον ἔχει σχῆμα οὐδὲ ποιότητα καθ' αὑτήν. ἀεὶ δ' ἔν τινι σχήματι καὶ ποιότητι εἶναι. διαφέρειν δὲ τὴν οὐσίαν τῆς ὕλης τὴν οὖσαν κατὰ τὴν ὑπόστασιν ἐπινοίᾳ μόνον.*

[18] Diogenes Laertius, VII, 134, 136, 137. Sextus Empiricus, *adversus mathematicos* X, 312. *Stoicorum Veterum Fragmenta*, ed. H. v. Arnim, II, frags. 303, 321. Seneca, *de providentia* V, 9. Zeller, *l. c.*, p. 130, 2.

a matter which is unqualified and destitute of form. But this matter can be distinguished only by thought. It is a kind of logical presupposition. All that is real is existing substance, the elements. Posidonius then renounces the real existence of matter as such, and, in consequence of that, the creation of elements from matter. The elements exist always as the material principle. Compared with the general Stoic dogma this conception of matter is heretical. Posidonius also refutes the Platonic dogma according to which matter is unqualified.[19] He agrees with Aristotle in the denial of the existence of matter destitute of all attributes. But, whereas the difference between matter and elements is considered by Aristotle to be the difference between potentiality and actuality of the same substance, it is established by Posidonius as a difference between existence in thought and in reality.[20] The Posidonian definition of the first principle of the universe is original with him.

As regards the second principle, Posidonius declares: "God is intellectual spirit extending throughout the whole substance."[21] God is omnipresent intellect. And "God is intellectual spirit like fire. He has no form, but He can be altered into what He wants and can become equal to what He wants."[22] The existence of God is destitute of form. The quality of His essence, although it is definite, may be changed into everything. The whole world, therefore, is declared again to be the substance of God.[23] The action of God consists in His ruling of the world: "God governs the whole."[24] The Stoics, in general, also define God as material reason extending throughout matter

[19] Plato, *Timaeus* 51a.

[20] Zeller, *l. c.*, II, 2, pp. 315-17; Bernays, *Abhandlungen der Berliner Akademie*, 1876, p. 12. Concerning the difference between thought and reality cf. p. 317.

[21] *Commenta Lucani*, ed. H. Usener, *ad* v. 578, p. 305: ait enim Posidonius: *θεός ἐστι πνεῦμα νοερὸν διῆκον δι' ἁπάσης οὐσίας.* deus est spiritus rationalis per omnem diffusus materiam. Cf. Reinhardt, II, p. 202.

[22] *Doxographi Graeci*, 302b 22: *Ποσειδώνιος πνεῦμα νοερὸν καὶ πυρῶδες, οὐκ ἔχον μὲν μορφὴν μεταβάλλον δὲ εἰς ὃ βούλεται καὶ συνεξομοιούμενον πᾶσιν.* Cf. Reitzenstein, *Die hellenistischen Mysterienreligionen*, *l. c.*, p. 135.

[23] Diogenes Laertius, VII, 148: *Οὐσίαν δὲ θεοῦ . . . τὸν ὅλον κόσμον . . . καὶ Ποσειδώνιος ἐν πρώτῳ Περὶ θεῶν.*

[24] Laurentius Lydus, *de mensibus* IV, 48: Ποσειδώνιος τὸν Δία τὸν πάντα διοικοῦντα.

and to be found everywhere. But this reason creates the qualities of the elements as well as of all things, it is seminal reason.[25] Posidonius does not mention such a creative power of God. The action of God apparently is restricted to the ruling of the world. He can only become accommodated to that which exists. This doctrine is entirely different from the Platonic one, according to which God is the maker of the world. The God of Aristotle is form without substance, the God of Posidonius is substance without form. The Aristotelian God is separated from the world of which he is the unmoved mover. The Posidonian God is within the world. Thus, the definitions of the second principle of the universe are also original.

But it might be by chance that in these definitions of God His power of creation is never mentioned. Furthermore, if God is not seminal reason, how is it possible for him to become the artificer of all things in the world, as Posidonius nevertheless assumes?[26] However, according to Posidonius, qualified matter is not created at all. From the beginning, the elements have always existed as one of the principles of the world. Finally, all the Stoics declare: God is the same as nature and fate.[27] God, the seminal reason, is, therefore, identical with nature, a skilful fire, proceeding methodically with its work of creation, and it is identical with fate, the continuous cause of the existent things or reason by which the world is administered.[28] Posidonius alone contends: "Fate is in the third place from Zeus. The first is Zeus, the second, nature, the third, fate."[29] Thus Posidonius gives a sequence of three powers differing in the matter of which they are composed. Accordingly, he derives divination from God, fate, and nature, taking

[25] Diogenes Laertius, VII, 136.

[26] Cf. Diogenes Laertius, VII, 134.

[27] Diogenes Laertius, VII, 135. *Doxographi Graeci*, 322b 9; 323a 9. Cleanthes subordinates fate at least, *Stoicorum Veterum Fragmenta* II, frags. 933. Cf. Zeller, *l. c.*, III, 1, p. 143, 3.

[28] Diogenes Laertius, VII, 156 (cf. 148) and 149.

[29] *Doxographi Graeci*, 324a 4: *Ποσειδώνιος τρίτην ἀπὸ Διός. πρῶτον μὲν γὰρ εἶναι τὸν Δία, δεύτερον δὲ τὴν φύσιν, τρίτην δὲ τὴν εἱμαρμένην*; *ibid.* 324b 11; 620, 20. Cf. Plato, *Republic* X, 597e: *τοῦτ' ἄρα ἔσται καὶ ὁ τραγῳδοποιός, εἴπερ μιμητής ἐστι, τρίτος τις ἀπὸ βασιλέως καὶ τῆς ἀληθείας πεφυκώς, καὶ πάντες οἱ ἄλλοι μιμηταί.* Cf. *The Republic of Plato*, ed. by James Adam, II, Cambridge, 1902, p. 464, who already quotes the Posidonian parallel.

them as three separate instances.[30] To Posidonius, therefore, God is not identical with nature and fate. He does not at all identify reason either with the creative power of the world or with the continuous cause of existence. In this distinction, he agrees with Aristotle and Plato.[31] So it seems to be certain that, according to Posidonius, God is not seminal reason. But how then is God able to create all things? What are the nature and fate from which he is to be distinguished? Since their definition is not preserved, it is possible only to infer their mode of existence, and in order to do this it is necessary to determine the essence of the world and the manner of processes going on in it.

There exists only one world, directed by reason and providence. Since providence governs the world, divination is a real science, as is also proved by some other facts.[32] The heaven, the ruling power of the world, is one and finite, having a spherical form, the most suitable for motion.[33] The world itself is an animal and rational and endowed with a soul and with intellect.[34]

The processes of this world have neither beginning nor end. Posidonius denies every real generation and destruction. He says: There exist four generations and destructions from the being into the being. For he denies that such a process from

[30] Cicero, *de divinatione* I, 125: Quocirca primum mihi videtur, ut Posidonius facit, a deo de quo satis dictum est, deinde a fato, deinde a natura, vis omnis divinandi ratioque repetenda.

[31] Zeller, *l. c.*, II, 2, p. 387; *Doxographi Graeci*, p. 324, 29.

[32] Diogenes Laertius, VII, 143: *ὅτι δ' εἷς ἐστι (sc. ὁ κόσμος) . . . καὶ Ποσειδώνιος ἐν πρώτῳ τοῦ φυσικοῦ λόγου. ibid.* 138: *Τὸν δὴ κόσμον διοικεῖσθαι κατὰ νοῦν καὶ πρόνοιαν . . . καὶ Ποσειδώνιος ἐν τῷ τρίτῳ Περὶ θεῶν. ibid.* 149: *καὶ μὴν καὶ μαντικὴν ὑφεστάναι πᾶσάν φασιν, εἰ καὶ πρόνοιαν εἶναι. καὶ αὐτὴν καὶ τέχνην ἀποφαίνουσι διά τινας ἐκβάσεις, ὥς . . . καὶ Ποσειδώνιος ἐν τῷ δευτέρῳ τοῦ φυσικοῦ λόγου καὶ ἐν τῷ πέμπτῳ Περὶ μαντικῆς.* cf. Cicero, *De divinatione* I, 6; II, 35.

[33] *Ibid.* 139: *Ποσειδώνιος ἐν τῷ Περὶ θεῶν τὸν οὐρανὸν . . . τὸ ἡγεμονικὸν τοῦ κόσμου.* 140: *Ἕνα τὸν κόσμον εἶναι καὶ τοῦτον πεπερασμένον, σχῆμ' ἔχοντα σφαιροειδές. πρὸς γὰρ τὴν κίνησιν ἁρμοδιώτατον τὸ τοιοῦτον, καθά φησι Ποσειδώνιος ἐν τῷ πέμπτῳ τοῦ φυσικοῦ λόγου.* Cf. R. Jones, *Classical Philology* 27 (1932), p. 126, who rightly rejects the assertion that Posidonius can be named the inventor of the solar-theology, since he, in contrast to Cleanthes, made the heaven the ruling power of the world. Concerning the origin of this theory in general cf. Jones, *l. c.*

[34] Diogenes Laertius, VII, 142: *Ὅτι δὲ καὶ ζῷον ὁ κόσμος καὶ λογικὸν καὶ ἔμψυχον καὶ νοερὸν . . . καὶ Ποσειδώνιος.*

non-being into non-being is existent. As regards the changes concerning being, he assumes one by separation, another by alteration, another by mixing together, another by dissolution from the whole. The change by alteration concerns the substance, whereas the three others concern the individual phenomena which derive from substance.[35] This conception of Posidonius' is heretical. It follows that the world cannot be destroyed by the annihilation of substance as most of the Stoics believe.[36] Moreover, it seems improbable that the world can be destroyed at all. And it has even been claimed that Posidonius denies the destruction of the world.[37] But on the other hand, Posidonius

[35] Areios Didymos, fr. 27 (*Doxographi Graeci*, p. 462,13 ff.): *Ποσειδώνιος δὲ φθορὰς καὶ γενέσεις τέτταρας εἶναί φησιν ἐκ τῶν ὄντων εἰς τὰ ὄντα γιγνομένας. τὴν μὲν γὰρ ἐκ τῶν οὐκ ὄντων καὶ τὴν εἰς <τὰ> οὐκ ὄντα, καθάπερ εἴπομεν πρόσθεν, ἀπέγνω ὡσὰν ἀνύπαρκτον οὖσαν. τῶν δ' εἰς <τὰ> ὄντα γινομένων μεταβολῶν τὴν μὲν εἶναι κατὰ διαίρεσιν, τὴν δὲ κατ' ἀλλοίωσιν, τὴν δὲ κατὰ σύγχυσιν, τὴν δὲ ἐξ ὅλων, λεγομένην δὲ κατ' ἀνάλυσιν. τούτων δὲ τὴν κατ' ἀλλοίωσιν περὶ τὴν οὐσίαν γίγνεσθαι, τὰς δὲ ἄλλας τρεῖς περὶ τοὺς ποιοὺς λεγομένους τοὺς ἐπὶ τῆς οὐσίας γιγνομένους.* I follow Usener in reading *ἀπέγνω ὡσὰν* against Diels who writes *ἀπέγνωσαν*. It is impossible to assume that all the Stoics denied any destruction into non-being. The conjecture of Heeren seems to be unnecessary, the emendation of Usener is the best and the easiest one. In the following words Posidonius describes how, in consequence of his theories, the generations of the individual things take place: *ἀκολούθως δὲ τούτοις καὶ τὰς γενέσεις συμβαίνειν. τὴν γὰρ οὐσίαν οὔτ' αὔξεσθαι οὔτε μειοῦσθαι κατὰ πρόσθεσιν ἢ ἀφαίρεσιν, ἀλλὰ μόνον ἀλλοιοῦσθαι, καθάπερ ἐπ' ἀριθμῶν καὶ μέτρων [καὶ] συμβαίνειν ἐπὶ <δὲ> τῶν ἰδίως ποιῶν οἷον Δίωνος καὶ Θέωνος καὶ αὐξήσεις καὶ μειώσεις γίνεσθαι. διὸ καὶ παραμένειν τὴν ἑκάστου ποιότητα [τὰ] ἀπὸ τῆς γενέσεως μέχρι τῆς ἀναιρέσεως, <ὡς> ἐπὶ τῶν ἀναίρεσιν ἐπιδεχομένων ζῴων καὶ φυτῶν καὶ τῶν τούτοις παραπλησίων.* Then, the fragment of Areios speaks about the general Stoic dogma: *ἐπὶ δὲ τῶν ἰδίως ποιῶν φασι δύο εἶναι τὰ δεκτικὰ μόρια.*

[36] Cf. e. g., Cicero, *de natura deorum* II, 118-19.

[37] Philo, *de aeternitate mundi* II, 497 M: *Βόηθος, καὶ Ποσειδώνιος, καὶ Παναίτιος, ἄνδρες ἐν τοῖς Στωικοῖς δόγμασιν ἰσχυκότες, ἅτε θεόληπτοι, τὰς ἐκπυρώσεις καὶ παλιγγενεσίας καταλιπόντες πρὸς θειότερον δόγμα τῆς ἀφθαρσίας τοῦ κόσμου παντὸς ηὐτομόλησαν.* Bernays, *Abhandlungen der Berliner Akademie*, 1876, p. 72; 1882, p. 248, 11, reads instead of *Ποσειδώνιος* according to the manuscript *Βόηθος ὁ Σιδώνιος*. Already Gaisford noticed that Posidonius is very often misspelled *Σιδώνιος* (in his edition of Suidas *s. v.* Poseidonios). Pasquali (*Storia della tradizione*, 1934, pp. 43 ff.) again emphasizes that the old editions sometimes give the correct tradition. And Bernays' manuscript itself, in the same place, wrongly gives *Πανετος* instead of *Παναίτιος*. Still, this testimony cannot be regarded as absolutely cer-

discusses the space into which the world is to be resolved after its ruin and determines it to be finite.[38] It is, therefore, hard to believe that he did not consider the destruction of the world. If he did, his reasons for such a catastrophe must have differed from the reasons other Stoic philosophers had in mind. And this contradiction of the data may derive from the fact that Posidonius himself did not solve this problem definitely, but admitted it to be an alternative.[38a]

The definition of time by Posidonius fits this theory of generation and destruction. For he ascribes an infinite extension to time as a whole. Past and future, not absolutely but relatively infinite, are terminated by the present, the smallest thinkable unit of time, acknowledged by Posidonius as a discrete entity in opposition to Chrysippus. Time is the measure of the velocity of things. Movement, therefore, should always have been existent and should last forever.[39]

tain. Also Posidonius' belief in the golden age which was much better than the others seems to presume some kind of change or destruction of the world. Cf. Seneca, *Epistle* 90, 5.

[38] *Doxographi Graeci*, p. 338a 18, b 19: Ποσειδώνιος ἔφησε τὸ ἐκτὸς τοῦ κόσμου οὐκ ἄπειρον, ἀλλ' ὅσον αὐταρκες εἰς διάλυσιν. Diogenes Laertius, VII, 142: περὶ δὴ οὖν τῆς γενέσεως καὶ τῆς φθορᾶς τοῦ κόσμου φησὶ . . . καὶ Ποσειδώνιος ἐν πρώτῳ περὶ κόσμου. But Posidonius wrote no book about the subject, cf. Diels, *Doxographi Graeci*, p. 9.

[38a] Concerning the possibility of such an unsolved alternative cf. the statement of the Stoic in Cicero, *De natura deorum* II, 85: "Quae (coniunctio mundi partium) aut sempiterna sit necesse est hoc eodem ornatu quem videmus, aut certe perdiuturna, permanens ad longinquum et immensum paene tempus. Quorum utrumvis ut sit. . . . Cf. *ibid.* 118.

[39] Areios Didymos, fr. 26 (*Doxographi Graeci*, p. 461, 13 ff.): Ποσειδώνιος. τὰ μὲν ἐστι κατὰ πᾶν ἄπειρα, ὡς ὁ σύμπας χρόνος. τὰ δὲ κατά τι, ὡς ὁ παρεληλυθὼς χρόνος καὶ ὁ μέλλων. κατὰ γὰρ τὸν παρόντα μόνον ἑκάτερος πεπέρανται. τὸν δὲ χρόνον οὕτως ὁρίζεται, διάστημα κινήσεως ἢ μέτρον τάχους τε καὶ βραδύτητος. ὅπως ἔχει τὸ ἐπινοούμενον· [καὶ] κατὰ τὸ πότε τοῦ χρόνου τὸν μὲν εἶναι παρεληλυθότα, τὸν δὲ μέλλοντα, τὸν δὲ παρόντα, ὃς ἐκ τινος μέρους τοῦ παρεληλυθότος καὶ τοῦ μέλλοντος περὶ τὸν διορισμὸν αὐτὸν συνέστηκε. τὸν δὲ διορισμὸν σημειώδη εἶναι. τὸ δὲ νῦν καὶ τὰ ὅμοια ἐν πλάτει χρόνου καὶ οὐχὶ κατ' ἀπαρτισμὸν νοεῖσθαι. λέγεσθαι δὲ τὸ νῦν καὶ κατὰ τὸν ἐλάχιστον πρὸς αἴσθησιν χρόνον περὶ τὸν διορισμὸν τοῦ μέλλοντος καὶ παρεληλυθότος συνιστάμενον. In assuming that matter and time are eternal Posidonius follows Aristotle (cf. *Physics* IV, 10-11; Zeller, *l. c.*, II, 2, p. 398), and he agrees with him also in the belief that space cannot be infinite (cf. *Doxographi Graeci*, p. 338a 18, b 19). About the Chrysippean definition of time cf. Areios Didymos, fr. 26 (*Doxographi Graeci*, p. 461, 23 ff.).

This world, not created in time and, perhaps, indestructible, is a system made up of heaven and earth and the natures in them, or a system constituted by God and by men and all things created for their sake.[40] What are these natures meant to be, by what principles are they guided? Within this world there are plants, animals, human beings, gods. According to the general Stoic dogma, nature is the creative power of plants, and certain processes of a vegetative kind are carried out in animals too.[41] Posidonius "embraces the Platonic dogma about the faculties of the soul." Supposing emotions to be movements of illogical faculties, namely of those which Plato names appetitive and passionate, he must have understood these faculties in the Platonic sense.[42] He must therefore have ascribed to plants at least the appetitive soul, desire and sensation.[43] Again in accordance with Plato, Posidonius takes for granted that animals are endowed with the passionate part of the soul. He refutes the Stoic theory by which emotions are restricted to men.[44] Human

[40] Diogenes Laertius, VII, 138: *καὶ ἔστι κόσμος . . . , ὥς φησι Ποσειδώνιος ἐν τῇ μετεωρολογικῇ στοιχειώσει, σύστημα ἐξ οὐρανοῦ καὶ γῆς καὶ τῶν ἐν τούτοις φύσεων ἢ σύστημα ἐκ θεῶν καὶ ἀνθρώπων καὶ τῶν ἕνεκα τούτων γεγονότων*, if the second definition also belongs to Posidonius. This is not absolutely sure.

[41] Diogenes Laertius, VII, 86; *Stoicorum Veterum Fragmenta* II, 708-10.

[42] Galen, *De placitis*, 397, 1: (Ποσειδώνιος) . . . *πρεσβεύων αὐτοῦ* (sc. Πλάτωνος) *τά τε περὶ τῶν παθῶν δόγματα καὶ τὰ περὶ τῶν τῆς ψυχῆς δυνάμεων*. *ibid.* 405, 12 ff.: *τὰ πάθη δεικνύων . . . κινήσεις τινὰς ἑτέρων δυνάμεων ἀλόγων, ἃς ὁ Πλάτων ὠνόμασεν ἐπιθυμητικήν τε καὶ θυμοειδῆ.*

[43] Praechter (*l. c.*, p. 480) says: "Die Pflanze, nach der Stoa nur von der *φύσις*, nicht von *ψυχή* geleitet, besitzt <nach Posidonius> mit dem *ἐπιθυμητικόν* (Plato *Timaeus* 77b) die *θρεπτική* u. *αὐξητικὴ δύναμις*, das Tier, nach der Stoa niederster Besitzer der *ψυχή*, fügt dazu nebst dem *θυμοειδές* die *αἴσθησις* sowie das *ὀρεκτικόν* und *κινητικὸν κατὰ τόπον*." This is not correct. Plato expressly states that the plants have sensation together with desire, cf. *Timaeus* 77b: *αἴσθησις ἡδεία καὶ ἀλγεινὴ μετὰ ἐπιθυμιῶν.*

[44] Galen, *De placitis*, 457, 2: (Χρύσιππος) *τῶν ἀλόγων ζῴων ἀφαιρεῖται τὰ πάθη φανερῶς ἐπιθυμίᾳ τε καὶ θυμῷ διοικουμένων, ὡς καὶ ὁ Ποσειδώνιος ὑπὲρ αὐτῶν ἐπὶ πλέον διεξέρχεται.* He adds: *ὅσα μὲν οὖν τῶν ζῴων δυσκίνητά τέ ἐστι καὶ προσπεφυκότα δίκην φυτῶν πέτραις ἤ τισιν ἑτέροις τοιούτοις, ἐπιθυμίᾳ μόνῃ διοικεῖσθαι λέγει αὐτά, τὰ δὲ ἄλλα ἄλογα σύμπαντα ταῖς δυνάμεσιν ἀμφοτέραις χρῆσθαι, τῇ τε ἐπιθυμητικῇ καὶ τῇ θυμοειδεῖ.* This apparently is a restriction of the previous statement. Animals are endowed with the two powers of the soul,

beings participate in the three powers of the soul: the appetitive, the passionate, and the rational.[45] Finally there are still other animate beings in the world: the stars which are gods, as the heaven itself is a god.[46]

These stars are bodies composed of ether, lucid and like fire, never at rest, but always moving in cycles. Especially the sun and the moon are *ἄστρα*. But it is necessary to differentiate between *ἀστήρ* and *ἄστρον*. Every *ἀστήρ* is an *ἄστρον*, but the converse is not true.[47] The *ἀστήρ* has identical qualities with the *ἄστρον*, but it also shares in the same quality of the place in which it is.[48] The *ἄστρα* include, besides sun and moon, all the planets. The *ἀστέρες* are the so-called fixed stars which are also in eternal motion. Since they are ethereal heavenly bodies, the only other place in which they can circulate, the only other

yet those (*ὅσα μὲν οὖν*) which like plants lack motion share only in one of these powers. The passionate faculty is inseparably connected with the faculty of changing place. Cf. Zeller, *l. c.*, III, 1, p. 581, 3.

[45] Galen, *De placitis*, 457, 8: *τὸν ἄνθρωπον δὲ μόνον ταῖς τρισί, προσειληφέναι γὰρ καὶ τὴν λογιστικὴν ἀρχήν.* Posidonius, like Aristotle does not distinguish species or parts of the soul but faculties of one essence derived from the heart, Galen, *ibid.* 501, 10: *ὁ δὲ Ἀριστοτέλης τε καὶ ὁ Ποσειδώνιος εἴδη μὲν ἢ μέρη ψυχῆς οὐκ ὀνομάζουσιν, δυνάμεις δὲ εἶναί φασι μιᾶς οὐσίας ἐκ τῆς καρδίας ὁρμωμένης.* The partition of the soul, ascribed to Posidonius by Tertullian (*De anima*, chap. 14), is not quite perspicuous: (anima dividitur in partes) duodecem apud quosdam Stoicorum, et in duas amplius apud Posidonium, qui a duobus exorsus titulis principali, quod aiunt *ἡγεμονικόν*, et a rationali, quod aiunt *λογικόν*, in decem et septem exinde prosecuit. *Tertulliani Opera*, ed. Reifferscheid-Wissowa, I (1890) against Diels, *Doxographi Graeci*, pp. 205-6. Concerning the general Stoic distinction of the parts of the soul, cf. Diogenes Laertius, VII, 157.

[46] Diogenes Laertius, VII, 148: *οὐσίαν δὲ θεοῦ . . . φησί . . . τὸν οὐρανόν . . . καὶ Ποσειδώνιος ἐν πρώτῳ Περὶ θεῶν.* *Doxographi Graeci*, p. 466, 18: *ἄστρον δὲ εἶναί φησιν ὁ Ποσειδώνιος σῶμα θεῖον.*

[47] Areios Didymos fr. 32 (*Doxographi Graeci*, p. 466, 18): *ἄστρον . . . σῶμα θεῖον ἐξ αἰθέρος συνεστηκός, λαμπρὸν καὶ πυρῶδες, οὐδέποτε στάσιν ἔχον, ἀλλ' αἰεὶ φερόμενον ἐγκυκλίως. ἰδίως δὲ τὸν ἥλιον καὶ τὴν σελήνην ἄστρα λέγεσθαι. διαφέρειν δὲ ἀστέρα ἄστρου. εἰ μὲν γάρ τίς ἐστιν ἀστήρ, καὶ ἄστρον ὀνομασθήσεται δὲ ὄντως, οὐ μὴν ἀνάπαλιν.*

[48] Achilles Tatius, *Isagoge in Arati Phaenomena*, chap. 10: *ἀστήρ ἐστι κατὰ Διόδωρον σῶμα θεῖον οὐράνιον τῆς αὐτῆς μετειληφὸς οὐσίας τῷ ἐν ᾧ ἐστι τόπῳ, σῶμά τι λαμπρὸν καὶ οὐδέποτε στάσιν ἔχον ἀλλ' ἀεὶ φερόμενον κυκλικῶς. ὡσαύτως δὲ ὡρίσατο καὶ Ποσειδώνιος πρὸ αὐτοῦ ὁ Στωϊκός.*

substance in which they can share seems to be the air.[49] The fixed stars are signs, whereas sun and moon and, maybe, all the planets have real influence.[50] The stars are generally called demons. For demons are named in this manner because their quality is taken and separated from the ethereal substance.[51] And

[49] That follows from a statement about Diodorus who agrees with Posidonius in the definition of the stars as well as in the distinction of *ἀστήρ* and *ἄστρον*: *Διόδωρος δὲ καὶ οἱ ἄλλοι μαθηματικοὶ ἰδίως καὶ κοινῶς τὰ ζῴδια ἄστρα καλοῦσι καὶ ἀστέρας παρατιθέμενοι Πλάτωνα μάρτυρα ἄστρα τοὺς ἑπτὰ πλανήτας ἐν τῷ Τιμαίῳ εἰρηκότα, τὸν κύνα μέντοι ἀστέρα ὄντα ἐν τῷ βίῳ ἄστρον λέγομεν. ἀλλ' ὁ μὲν ἀστὴρ καὶ ἄστρον, οὐκέτι δὲ τὸ ἀνάπαλιν.* (cf. Diels, *Doxographi Graeci*, p. 20). It is in this sense that "Posidonius censet in natura signa quaedam rerum futurarum. Etenim Ceos accepimus ortum Caniculae diligenter quotannis solere servare coniecturamque capere, ut scribit Ponticus Heraclides, salubrisne an pestilens annus futurus sit. Nam si obscurior et quasi caliginosa stella exstiterit, pingue et concretum esse caelum, ut eius aspiratio gravis et pestilens futura sit; sin illustris et perlucida stella apparuerit, significari caelum esse tenue purumque et propterea salubre." (Cicero, *De divinatione* I, 130); another quotation taken from Heraclides by Posidonius is preserved, cf. n. 128.

[50] For Signa rerum concerning the dog-star cf. Cicero, *De divinatione* I, 130. Cf. *Doxographi Graeci*, p. 383b 7: *Ποσειδώνιος ὑπὸ μὲν τῆς σελήνης κινεῖσθαι τοὺς ἀνέμους, ὑπὸ δὲ τούτων τὰ πελάγη.* Concerning the sun cf. Pliny, *Naturalis historia*, II, 23 [21]. Cf. the Stoic theory in Cicero, *De natura deorum* II, 54: stellae inerrantes . . . nec habent aetherios cursus neque caelo inhaerentes . . . non est enim aetheris ea natura ut vi sua stellas complexa contorqueat . . . habent igitur suam sphaeram stellae inerrantes ab aetheria coniunctione secretam et liberam. As regards the difference between stars as signs and as influences cf. E. Pfeiffer, *Studien zum antiken Sternglauben*, *Stoicheia* II (1916), p. V; 84 ff. Did Posidonius also place the fixed stars very near to the earth behind the planets, like the moon which is so close to the earth and therefore mixed with air (Diogenes Laertius, VII, 145)? That would explain why they partake of the changes of the air, probably of the atmosphere, not of the always pure and liquid air; this distinction is to be found in Pliny, *Naturalis historia* II, 23 [21]). Cf. F. Boll, *RE* VI, p. 2413, s. v. Fixsterne.

[51] Cornificius *apud* Macrobius, *Saturnalia* I, 23, 7: (*δαίμων*) ut Posidonius scribit in libris quibus titulus est *περὶ ἡρώων καὶ δαιμόνων* quia ex aetheria substantia parta atque divisa qualitas illis est." Since Posidonius gave this explanation in the book *περὶ ἡρώων καὶ δαιμόνων* did he understand the *ἀστέρες* to be heroes, beings wrapped with air? cf. *Etymologicum Magnum*, *s. v. ἥρωες*: . . . *ἢ ἀπὸ τοῦ ἀέρος, ὥς φησιν Ἡσίοδος, Ἠέρα ἑσσάμενοι, πάντῃ φοιτῶντες ἐπ' αἶαν.* Concerning explanations of words by etymology cf. p. 317.

Posidonius defines the stars also as living animals, created by the ether.

Plants, animals, human beings and stars, all these natures found in the world, like the world itself, are guided by the soul. This soul is a warm breath, by which we become animate and are moved.[52] Its function is to hold the body together. For it is not the body which holds together the soul, it is the soul which holds together both itself and the body.[53] Unity of the body, therefore, can only be found where the soul is dominant. Even the bones of the human frame contain a part of the soul.[54] Posidonius apparently subscribes to the definition according to which only living beings, only plants and animals, can be recognized as unified bodies. Stones and wood are not unified bodies. In organic nature alone is there to be found a coherence in which no part can be harmed without harm being done to the other parts too, without mutual sympathy.[55] And

[52] Diogenes Laertius, VII, 157: *Ποσειδώνιος πνεῦμα ἔνθερμον εἶναι τὴν ψυχήν. τούτῳ γὰρ ἡμᾶς εἶναι ἐμπνόους καὶ ὑπὸ τούτου κινεῖσθαι.* Movement, therefore, is essential for the soul, cf. *Timaeus* 77b, where Plato assumes movement even as regards plants.

[53] Achilles Tatius, *Isagoge in Arati Phaenomena*, chap. 13: *οἱ δὲ Ἐπικούρειοί φασι μὴ εἶναι ζῴδια (sc. τὰ ἄστρα), ἐπειδὴ ὑπὸ σωμάτων συνέχεται. οἱ δὲ Στωικοὶ τὸ ἀνάπαλιν. Ποσειδώνιος δὲ ἀγνοεῖν τοὺς Ἐπικουρείους ἔφη, ὡς οὐ τὰ σώματα τὰς ψυχὰς συνέχει, ἀλλ' αἱ ψυχαὶ τὰ σώματα ὥσπερ καὶ ἡ κόλλα καὶ ἑαυτὴν καὶ τὰ ἐκτὸς κρατεῖ.* Concerning the dependence of this statement on Aristotle, *De anima* 411b 6; cf. Jones, *Classical Philology*, XXVII (1932), p. 115 and Heinemann, *l. c.*, II, p. 33.

[54] *Scholion T in Homerum M*, 386: *δοκεῖ αὐτῷ (sc. τῷ Ὁμήρῳ) καὶ τοῖς ὀστοῖς τὸ ψυχικὸν παρεσπάρθαι ὡς καὶ Ποσειδώνιος ἐν γ' περὶ ψυχῆς. ὁ μὲν γὰρ Πλάτων* (cf. Plato, *Timaeus* 73b) *καὶ τοὺς δεσμοὺς αὐτῆς ἐν ταῖς τοῦ ὀστοῦ ῥίζαις φησὶν εἶναι.*

[55] Sextus Empiricus, *adversus mathematicos* IX, 78-81: *τῶν τε σωμάτων τὰ μέν ἐστιν ἡνωμένα, τὰ δὲ ἐξ συναπτομένων, τὰ δὲ ἐκ διεστώτων. ἡνωμένα μὲν οὖν ἐστι τὰ ὑπὸ μιᾶς ἕξεως κρατούμενα καθάπερ φυτὰ καὶ ζῷα . . . ἐπὶ δὲ τῶν ἡνωμένων συμπάθειά τις ἔστιν, εἴ γε δακτύλου τεμνομένου τὸ ὅλον συνδιατίθεται σῶμα.* In the same place the general Stoic theory is pictured (IX, 81) according to which even stones and wood belong to the class of unified bodies and participate at least in habit, whereas plants are ruled by nature. The heretical Stoic definition again in Cicero, *De natura deorum* II, 75: omnes res subiectas esse naturae sentienti, a statement which is explained later (82) in the following way: sed nos cum dicimus natura constare administrarique mundum, non ita dicimus ut glaebam aut fragmentum lapidis aut aliquid eius modi nulla cohaerendi

this whole organic world, even in the most primitive form of organism, is dominated by the soul. Where the others recognise the effects of nature, Posidonius recognises the effects of soul. In him the power of nature is always elevated to the plane of a sensitive being. Nature is identical with soul which again, as the Stoics believe, is simply nature, endowed with sensation.[56]

Is the soul mortal or immortal? No fragment directly refers to this problem.[57] But Posidonius attributes to Plato the opinion that only the soul of the world is immortal. It is certainly right to conclude that Posidonius could not believe in the immortality of the individual soul when he restricts the Platonic theory to the immortality of the world-soul alone.[58] Furthermore, this doctrine was ready to Posidonius' hand. Aristotle and Panaetius were of the same opinion, and the Stoics in general did not believe in personal immortality either.[59] In any case, no fragment proves the immortality of the soul, not even its immortality for the period till the destruction of the world.

But sensitive nature, soul, is restricted to the organic realm. What about the inorganic world, what about stones and wood and all the other material bodies? Posidonius thinks that matter

natura, sed ut arborem ut animal, in quibus nulla temeritas sed ordo apparet et artis quaedam similitudo.

[56] Diogenes Laertius, VII, 156: *ψυχὴ αἰσθητικὴ φύσις.*

[57] Cicero, *De divinatione* I, 64 relates that Posidonius explains divination by the fact that "plenus aer sit immortalium animorum, in quibus tamquam insignitae notae veritatis appareant." Already the fact that signs of truth are said to appear in these immortal spirits would hint at a statement concerning stars. The fixed stars are godly bodies, living in the air, cf. n. 49. *De divinatione* I, 130, in the same connection, these stars are expressly mentioned. As it seems to me, it is impossible to conclude from this statement that Posidonius believed the *human* soul to be immortal, especially since all his other statements do not correspond to such a thesis.

[58] Cf. Hermias' *Commentarius in Platonis Phaedrum*, ed. P. Couvreu (1901), p. 102: *οἱ μὲν γὰρ περὶ τῆς τοῦ κόσμου μόνης* (sc. *ψυχῆς*) *ᾠήθησαν εἶναι τὸν λόγον . . . ὧν ἐστι καὶ Ποσειδώνιος ὁ Στωικός. οἱ δὲ περὶ πάσης ἁπλῶς.* Already Reinhardt, II, p. 91, 1 interprets these words in a similar manner.

[59] Cf. Aristotle, *De anima* 415b 26, *De generatione animalium* 731b 31. Panaetius *apud* Cicero, *Tusculanae disputationes* I, 32, 79 and Zeller, *l. c.*, III, 1, p. 563, 1. Only Cleanthes holds that all souls last till the conflagration, Diogenes Laertius, VII, 157; cf. also 151.

always existed in some quality and form.[60] Material qualities and forms, therefore, have existed independently from the beginning. Posidonius expresaly states that some of these everlasting qualities have a special faculty of forming the matter. In this conception he follows Aristotle and Theophrastus. Like them Posidonius declares the warm and light element to be the formative and moving element throughout matter.[61] Inseparably connected with it, this power exists eternally like the other elements. Since all things are composed of matter, the material principle really dominates everything. It may, therefore, be called fate according to which all things happen.[62] Reason governs the universe, sensitive nature holds together the bodies, fate creates the movement within the world.

The world is really ordered by three materially distinct powers, each of which is a cause. It seems consistent with this division that Posidonius should define cause quite differently from all the other Stoics. By them matter, reason, and form are taken into account, whereas the teleological cause is entirely neglected. But matter, from which all things are created, cannot, since it has no power of its own, be separated from the reason, which creates all things. Matter, therefore, is not recognized as cause. Form, according to the Stoics, is a part of reason and, therefore, does not constitute a separate cause. Reason as material cause, accordingly, is the only cause to be assumed by the Stoics in general.[63] The identity of reason and matter, of God, nature,

[60] Cf. the interpretation pp. 290-1.

[61] *Scholia in Aristotelem* 517a 28 (Cf. Simplicius, *in De caelo* 309b 2 K): *ἄλλος δὲ ὁ τρόπος οὗτός ἐστι τῆς εἰς τὰ εἰδικὰ καὶ ὑλικὰ τῶν τεσσάρων στοιχείων διαιρέσεως καὶ ἄλλος ἐκεῖνος καθ' ὃν τὰ μὲν βαρέα καὶ ψυχρὰ ὕλης λόγον ἔχει τὰ δὲ κοῦφα καὶ θερμὰ εἴδους. αὐτὸς δὲ ὁ Ἀριστοτέλης ἐν ἄλλοις λέγει καὶ Θεόφραστος ἐν τῷ περὶ τῆς τῶν στοιχείων γενέσεως καὶ Ποσειδώνιος ὁ Στωϊκὸς παρὰ τούτων λαβὼν πανταχοῦ χρῆται.* In regard to this theory Reinhardt (II, p. 347; I, p. 149) refers to Seneca, *Naturales Quaestiones* II, 10, 4. But there the name of Posidonius is not mentioned. He also emphasizes that Posidonius is the founder of the dogma of the "Wärmelehre." As it seems to me, this assumption is rejected already by the words of the *Scholion* which derives the doctrine of Posidonius from Aristotle and Theophrastus. Besides, Posidonius defines the different qualities of the elements like the other Stoics, taking for granted that the air is a cold element (cf. Plutarch, *De primo frigido*, chap. 16).

[62] Diogenes Laertius, VII, 149: *καθ' εἱμαρμένην δέ φασι τὰ πάντα γίνεσθαι . . . καὶ Ποσειδώνιος ἐν δευτέρῳ Περὶ εἱμαρμένης.*

[63] Seneca, *Epistle* 65, 2-11.

and fate is presupposed by this theory. Consequently Zeno and Chrysippus define cause as that through which things are.[64] It is Posidonius alone who distinguishes three causes: "The cause of something is that through which it exists or the prime active power or the principle of activity. And cause is real and bodily; that of which it is the cause is neither real nor bodily, but accidental and predicate."[65] Now, that through which the thing exists is apparently matter, acknowledged as a separate cause and not identified with reason, since matter is considered by Posidonius to be an independent power. The principle of activity must correspond to the reason which governs the universe. The prime active power, then, can only be understood as the soul which is itself a source of motion besides that caused by material forces.[65a]

These are the three powers which govern the world. But how is it at all possible to assume two principles, as Posidonius does, and yet to distinguish three materially different powers within the world? Why is God the first, nature the second, fate the third? The manner in which matter exists is as solid body, extended in three dimensions, length, breadth, depth. God exists as matter without form or, so to say, without dimension; since He has to be contemplated as material existence, it is necessary to ascribe to him at least punctual existence.[66] But besides these two forms of reality Posidonius recognizes yet another: "Under surface are understood the limits of the solid body, or

[64] Areios Didymos, fr. 18, *Doxographi Graeci*, p. 457, 4 ff.

[65] *Ibid.* 457, 14 ff.: Ποσειδώνιος δὲ οὕτως· αἴτιον δ' ἐστί τινος, δι' ὃ ἐκεῖνο ἢ τὸ πρῶτον ποιοῦν ἢ τὸ ἀρχηγὸν ποιήσεως. καὶ τὸ μὲν αἴτιον ὂν καὶ σῶμα, οὗ δὲ αἴτιον οὔτε ὂν οὔτε σῶμα, ἀλλὰ συμβεβηκὸς καὶ κατηγόρημα. It is possible that because of this differentiation of causes, Strabo blames Posidonius for being too much inclined to the Aristotelian method. Not that it is, however, characteristic of Stoic philosophy to renounce causation as such: "πολὺ γάρ ἐστι τὸ αἰτιολογικὸν παρ' αὐτῷ καὶ τὸ ἀριστοτελίζον, ὅπερ ἐκκλίνουσιν οἱ ἡμέτεροι διὰ τὴν ἐπίκρυψιν τῶν αἰτιῶν" (Strabo, II, 3, p. 104).

[65a] Posidonius expressly mentions the teleological moment: Diogenes Laertius, VII, 140 (cf. note 33) and Simplicius, *in Aristotelis Physica*, *l. c.*, p. 292, 6 (cf. note 128). Is this meant to be the equivalent to the godly reason (cf. Aristotle, *De Gen. Animal.* 731b 24)? Yet it is not clear how Posidonius divides the various factors, although he apparently follows Plato and Aristotle, at least to a certain extent.

[66] In regard to such a punctual existence cf. the definition of time.

that which only has length and breadth, but no depth. Posidonius admits this surface to exist in thought as well as in reality."[67] The Stoic school took it for granted that mathematical figures are existent only in thought.[68] To Posidonius the limits of the solid body have a real existence. The forms are entities. The limits are the reason of the mathematical figures. The form, not the contents, is constitutive.[69] The soul which holds together the bodily existence, like the limits which constitute the body, is declared by Posidonius to be idea, or form.[70] The mode of existence of this soul, therefore, seems to be a mathematical figure. The soul is an entity which is extended in two dimensions, whereas the body is extended in three dimensions and the divine matter is extended in one dimension.

Can this identification of soul and geometrical figure be proved? It may be ascertained by the definition of the soul, ascribed to Plato by the pupils of Posidonius. In the interpretation of the *Timaeus* they suppose that the divisible substance of the limited is meant in respect to the bodies, and they combine it with the intelligible and declare the soul to be the idea, the form of the space in which is inherent a harmony of numbers. For the mathematical figures are between the first intelligible substances and that which can be seized by the senses, and, therefore, they are placed apart from both. In the same way the soul shares in the eternal qualities of the intelligible and the passive qualities of the perceptible; and, there-

[67] Diogenes Laertius, VII, 135: *ἐπιφάνεια δέ ἐστι σώματος πέρας ἢ τὸ μῆκος καὶ πλάτος μόνον ἔχον, βάθος δὲ οὔ. ταύτην δὲ Ποσειδώνιος ἐν τρίτῳ Περὶ μετεώρων καὶ κατ' ἐπίνοιαν καὶ καθ' ὑπόστασιν ἀπολείπει.* cf. Aristotle, *Metaphysics*, III, 5; VII, 2.

[68] Proclus, *in Euclidem*, p. 89, 16; cf. Bréhier, *Revue des études Greques*, XXVII (1914), p. 44.

[69] Cf. Proclus, *l. c.*, p. 143, 8. This definition goes back to Plato's *Meno*, cf. Bréhier, *l. c.*, p. 56, 2.

[70] Macrobius, *in Somnium Scipionis* I, 14, 19: Posidonius animam ideam (cf. Diels, *Doxographi Graeci*, p. 213). It is impossible to understand idea in the Platonic sense of the word. The existence of an immaterial substance is not recognized by Posidonius. But he apparently used to call the soul an idea. Plutarch, *De procreatione animae* 1023d, attacks Posidonius because he applied the word idea to the moving soul. Cf. concerning this passage and that quoted R. M. Jones, *The Platonism of Plutarch*, p. 74.

fore, the appropriate place of its substance is between the substance of the divisible and that of the intelligible.[71] This definition comes from the interpretation of the *Timaeus*, but it exactly corresponds to the conclusion which seems to follow from the Posidonian fragments.[72]

At the same time it becomes understandable why Posidonius was able to assume only two principles of the universe, although he distinguishes three different powers within the world. The soul is different from God and matter, but it is composed of them. Obviously God is superior to matter. He therefore, occupies the highest place, and since the soul is in the middle be-

[71] Plutarch, *De procreatione animae* chap. 22, 1023 (cf. Taylor, *A Commentary on Plato's Timaeus*, 1928, pp. 118-9 and R. M. Jones, *The Platonism of Plutarch*, pp. 73 ff.): ὅμοια δὲ τούτοις ἐστὶν ἀντειπεῖν καὶ τοῖς περὶ Ποσειδώνιον. οὐ γὰρ μακρὰν τῆς ὕλης ἀπέστησαν ἀλλὰ δεξάμενοι τὴν τῶν περάτων οὐσίαν περὶ τὰ σώματα λέγεσθαι μεριστὴν καὶ ταῦτα τῷ νοητῷ μίξαντες ἀπεφήναντο τὴν ψυχὴν ἰδέαν εἶναι τοῦ πάντῃ διαστατοῦ κατ' ἀριθμὸν συνεστῶσαν ἁρμονίαν περιέχοντα. τά τε γὰρ μαθηματικὰ τῶν πρώτων νοητῶν μεταξὺ καὶ τῶν αἰσθητῶν τετάχθαι, τῆς τε ψυχῆς τῶν νοητῶν τὸ ἀΐδιον καὶ τῶν αἰσθητῶν τὸ παθητικὸν ἐχούσης προσῆκον ἐν μέσῳ τὴν οὐσίαν ὑπάρχειν.

[72] In this connection the discussion may be mentioned as to whether Posidonius wrote a commentary to Plato's *Timaeus* or not. Taylor, *l. c.*, p. 35 upholds the existence of the Posidonian commentary against Reinhardt's denial. The latter certainly is right in maintaining that the existence of such a commentary cannot be concluded from the words: ὁ Ποσειδώνιος τὸν Πλάτωνος Τίμαιον ἐξηγούμενος. (Sextus, *adversus dogmaticos* I, 93). The introduction to Plutarch, *De procreatione animae* shows that ἐξηγεῖσθαι may be used for occasional references to Platonic passages in various writings. On the other hand the explanation of Plato's *Timaeus* by Posidonius and his pupils is so important that already Plutarch places it beside the explanation of Crantor. (The whole question is now summarized by H. O. Schroeder, *Galeni in Platonis Timaeum Commentarii fragmenta, Corpus Medicorum Graecorum*, Supplementum I [1934], pp. ix ff.). Whether Posidonius wrote commentaries to Platonic dialogues or not, he interpreted them, and his interpretation soon became famous. Cf. concerning other explanations of Platonic passages n. 58 and Taylor, *l. c.*, 35 n. The interpretation of the *Timaeus* as well as the definition of the soul by Posidonius explain why throughout antiquity he was so famous for his geometrical skill. Galen believes that the whole originality of his philosophy and particularly its difference from the Stoic dogma is based on his geometrical studies (*De placitis*, 362, 5; 653, 14). One remembers the Platonic ἀγεωμέτρητος μηδεὶς εἰσίτω. Posidonius is scarcely an "Augendenker" (Reinhardt, I, p. 5).

tween God and matter, matter must have the last rank. The first is Zeus, the second nature, the third fate. Ruled by these three materially distinct powers the process of the world goes on.[73]

These are the outlines of the physical system of Posidonius. Compared with the general Stoic system it is heretical. Although it is influenced by Platonic and Aristotelian thought, it is neither Platonism nor Aristotelianism; it is original. The physical fragments are only a few, and they do not give a complete picture. But the fundamental principles, I think, are clear.

III.

Ethics.

Posidonius, whose ethical precepts are very famous,[74] in agreement with the Stoic school subdivides the ethical branch of philosophy as follows: the subject of appetition and that of things good and evil and that of the emotions and of virtue and the aim and the first value and the actions and the appropriate encouragement and dissuasion.[75] Such a subdivision is not to be found in the books of Zeno and Cleanthes. It is customary only since the time of Chrysippus. What each of these branches is like cannot be found out exactly. Nor does it become clear how many parts of ethics Posidonius distinguished in detail.

But so much is certain: Posidonius believes that the understanding of the nature of emotions is the basis of all ethical philosophy. He says: with the theory of the emotions is bound together the teaching concerning the virtues and that concerning the end, and as a whole all the dogmas of ethics are

[73] It is important to notice that almost all the heretical theories are preserved by Areios Didymos. Thus they go back to the first generation after Posidonius, to a man who certainly knew Posidonian philosophy (cf. Diels, *Doxographi Graeci*, pp. 69, 77). The tradition which Aetius and Diogenes Laertius follow is apparently more assimilated to the general Stoic dogma. Accordingly Diogenes does not consider Posidonius a heretic.

[74] Seneca, *Epistles* 104, 22; 108, 38; 33, 4.

[75] Diogenes Laertius, VII, 84: *τὸ δὲ ἠθικὸν μέρος τῆς φιλοσοφίας διαιροῦσιν εἴς τε τὸν περὶ ὁρμῆς καὶ εἰς τὸν περὶ ἀγαθῶν καὶ κακῶν τόπον καὶ εἰς τὸν περὶ παθῶν καὶ περὶ ἀρετῆς καὶ περὶ τέλους περί τε τῆς πρώτης ἀξίας καὶ τῶν πράξεων καὶ περὶ τῶν καθηκόντων προτροπῶν τε καὶ ἀποτροπῶν. οὕτω δὲ ὑποδιαιροῦσιν οἱ περὶ Χρύσιππον . . . καὶ Ποσειδώνιον.*

dependent on the knowledge of the faculties of the soul as on a string.[76]

"There is no need to explain in many words or with very exact conclusions what the emotions of the soul are like. It is only necessary to remember what human beings always experience." [77] Emotions are not judgments nor do they ensue upon judgment; they are caused by the appetitive and passionate faculty of the soul.[78] They are the movements of these faculties which Posidonius calls "movements destined to suffer." [79] In assuming such a theory, Posidonius is entirely at variance with the Stoic dogma. He embraces, as he believes, the theory of the older philosophers. He follows Pythagoras and Plato and Aristotle and he presumes that Zeno and Cleanthes were inclined to these theories too. To Chrysippus he is bitterly opposed.[80]

The division of the emotions according to Posidonius is as follows: "Some emotions are psychic, some are bodily. And those not caused by the soul but concerning the soul are bodily; those not caused by the body but concerning the body are psychic. And psychic, in the simple sense, are those in judgments and representations, for instance, desire, fear, wrath. Bodily, in the simple sense, are fever, coldness, thickness, looseness. Concerning the soul but bodily are lethargy, melancholy, sting,

[76] Galen, *De placitis*, 397, 5-8: *συνῆφθαι δὲ καὶ τὴν περὶ τῶν ἀρετῶν διδασκαλίαν τούτοις (sc. τοῖς πάθεσιν) φησὶ καὶ τὴν περὶ τοῦ τέλους καὶ ὅλως πάντα τὰ δόγματα τῆς ἠθικῆς φιλοσοφίας ὥσπερ ἐκ μιᾶς μηρίνθου δεδέσθαι τῆς γνώσεως τῶν κατὰ τὴν ψυχὴν δυνάμεων.*

[77] Galen, *ibid.* 487, 7-10: *οἷάπερ ἐστὶ τὰ πάθη τῆς ψυχῆς, οὐ μακρῶν λόγων οὐδὲ ἀποδείξεων ἀκριβεστέρων δεόμενα, μόνης δὲ ἀναμνήσεως ὧν ἑκάστοτε πάσχομεν, ὡς καὶ Ποσειδώνιος εἶπεν.* Cf. Zeller, *l. c.*, III, 1, p. 580, 3.

[78] Galen, *ibid.* 348, 12-16: *Ποσειδώνιος μέν γε τελέως ἀπεχώρησεν ἀμφοτέρων τῶν δοξῶν. οὔτε γὰρ κρίσεις οὔτε ἐπιγινόμενα κρίσεσιν εἶναι ἀλλὰ ὑπὸ τῆς θυμοειδοῦς τε καὶ ἐπιθυμητικῆς δυνάμεως ἡγεῖται γίνεσθαι τὰ πάθη κατὰ πᾶν ἀκολουθήσας τῷ παλαιῷ λόγῳ.* Cf. 397, 8-12.

[79] Galen, *ibid.* 443, 9-11: *τὰ πάθη . . . παθητικαὶ κινήσεις. οὕτω γὰρ ὁ Ποσειδώνιος ὀνομάζειν εἴωθεν.* Cf. 405, 9-14; 442, 3: *ἡ παθητικὴ ὁλκή.*

[80] The opposition of Posidonius to the Stoic dogma cf. Galen, *De placitis*, 407, 1-3. His agreement with the dogma of the older thinkers *ibid.* 396, 1-3; of Pythagoras: 401, 13-15, 459, 2-5; of Plato: 405, 9-14, 461, 4-6, 463, 1-3; of Aristotle: 432, 9-11, 461, 4-6, 463, 1-3; of Zeno: 362, 5-11, 458, 12-13, 456, 4; of Cleanthes: 456, 4, 654, 2-3. His opposition to the theories of Chrysippus *Stoicorum Veterum Fragmenta* III, pp. 54, 41; 62, 14; 112, 10; 120, 1; 131, 2; 116, 37; 118, 14.

fantasies, relaxation. On the other hand, concerning the body but psychic are tremblings and pallor and change of the behavior to fear and distress."[81] No definition of the single emotions is preserved.[82]

All these conditions are dependent on the form of the bodily existence. They are changed together with the changes of the body.[83] Posidonius, therefore, follows Plato in the method by which the emotions are to be treated.[84] He also believes in the possibility of education.[85] He believes in physiognomy; he thinks that the character of a man is influenced by the country in which he lives.[86] Taking this theory as a basis of explanation,

[81] Plutarch, *Utrum animae an corporis sit libido et aegritudo* (*Plutarch*, ed. Wyttenbach, V pars II, p. 700 A): *ὅ γέ τοι Ποσειδώνιος τὰ μὲν εἶναι ψυχικὰ* (sc. *τῶν παθῶν*), *τὰ δὲ σωματικά. καὶ τὰ μὲν οὐ ψυχῆς, περὶ ψυχὴν δὲ σωματικά. τὰ δὲ οὐ σώματος, περὶ σῶμα δὲ ψυχικά. καὶ ψυχικὰ μὲν ἁπλῶς τὰ ἐν κρίσεσι καὶ ὑπολήψεσι, οἷον ἐπιθυμίας λέγων φόβους ὀργάς. σωματικὰ δὲ ἁπλῶς πυρετοὺς περιψύξεις πυκνώσεις ἀραιώσεις. περὶ ψυχὴν δὲ σωματικὰ ληθάργους μελαγχολίας δηγμοὺς φαντασίας διαχύσεις. ἀνάπαλιν δὲ περὶ σῶμα ψυχικὰ τρόμους καὶ ὠχριάσεις καὶ μεταβολὰς τοῦ ἤθους κατὰ φόβον ἢ λύπην.* Cf. Zeller, *l. c.*, III, 1, p. 583, 2 who is not right in stating that this fragment shows a dualistic attitude. It includes the same distinction of three powers which is to be found in the physics, the third being a combination of the two others.

[82] Bake, *l. c.*, p. 222 believes that at least the definition of wrath is preserved, but Lactantius, *De ira*, chap. 17 does not give the definition of Posidonius himself but his testimony about the definition of some other philosophers.

[83] Galen, *De placitis*, 442, 14-15: *τῶν παθητικῶν κινήσεων τῆς ψυχῆς ἑπομένων ἀεὶ τῇ διαθέσει τοῦ σώματος.*

[84] Galen, *ibid.* 436, 7-10: *μὴ τοίνυν θαυμάζωμεν ἔτι μηδὲ ὅτι τὰς θεραπείας τῶν παθῶν ὀρθῶς μὲν ὁ Πλάτων ἔγραψεν, ὡς καὶ ὁ Ποσειδώνιος αὐτῷ μαρτυρεῖ, μοχθηρῶς δὲ ὁ Χρύσιππος.* cf. 396, 14 ff.

[85] Galen, *ibid.* 445, 4-12: *ταῦτά τοι καὶ ὁ Ποσειδώνιος αὐτῷ* (sc. *τῷ Χρυσίππῳ*) *μέμφεται μετὰ τοῦ καὶ θαυμάζειν, ὅσα Πλάτων εἶπεν ὑπὲρ τῆς τῶν παίδων ἔτι τε κυουμένων ἐν τῇ μήτρᾳ διαπλάσεως ἀποκυηθέντων τε τροφῆς καὶ παιδείας, καὶ γέγραφεν οἷον ἐπιτομήν τινα κατὰ τὸ πρῶτον αὐτοῦ περὶ παθῶν σύγγραμμα τῶν ὑπὸ Πλάτωνος εἰρημένων, ὡς χρὴ τρέφεσθαι καὶ παιδεύεσθαι τοὺς παῖδας ὑπὲρ τοῦ τὸ παθητικόν τε καὶ ἄλογον τῆς ψυχῆς σύμμετρον ἀποφαίνεσθαι ταῖς κινήσεσι καὶ τοῖς τοῦ λόγου προστάγμασιν εὐπειθές.* cf. n. 107.

[86] Galen, *ibid.* 442, 7-443, 3: *συνάπτει δὲ εἰκότως τοῖς λόγοις τούτοις ὁ Ποσειδώνιος τὰ κατὰ τὴν φυσιογνωμίαν φαινόμενα. καὶ γὰρ τῶν ζῴων καὶ τῶν ἀνθρώπων, ὅσα μὲν εὐρύστερνά τε καὶ θερμότερα, θυμικώτερα πάνθ' ὑπάρχειν φύσει, ὅσα δὲ πλατυΐσχιά τε καὶ ψυχρότερα, δειλότερα. καὶ κατὰ τὰς χώρας*

Posidonius considers it possible to explain all the difficulties which the previous philosophers, especially Chrysippus, could not solve.[87]

Such an heretical dogma of the emotions should establish the foundation of ethics. As Posidonius always stresses: "From the right understanding of the emotions, there may be derived the right understanding of things good and evil, of the virtues and of the aim of life."[88] How does Posidonius define these three constitutive parts of ethics in detail?

As regards things good and evil, he is of the opinion that wealth and health are to be counted among the good things.[89] This statement at first glance seems to be refuted by another one: "Things which do not provide the soul either with magnanimity or trust or security are not good. Riches and health and things similar to them, however, do not accomplish anything of this kind; therefore, they are not good."[90] But the two statements are not contradictory. First of all, in the same connection in which health and wealth are declared not to be good, Posidonius states, "that riches are a cause of evil, not since they themselves do any evil, but since they instigate men to do it. For the efficient cause which must hurt immediately, is one thing; the antecedent cause is another thing. Riches are imbued with the antecedent cause."[91] Riches, then, and apparently

δὲ οὐ σμικρῷ τινι διενηνοχέναι τοῖς ἤθεσι τοὺς ἀνθρώπους εἰς δειλίαν καὶ τόλμαν ἤτοι φιλήδονόν τε καὶ φιλόπονον. . . .

[87] Galen, *ibid.* 348, 16-351, 2; concerning fear 453, 11 ff.; 454, 7 ff.; concerning the acquiescence of emotions 397, 10. Posidonius does not compare the disease of the soul with the disease of the body like the other Stoics, cf. *ibid.* 409, 5-410, 2; 371, 1-13. As far as I know, this theory of the emotions never was controversial.

[88] Galen, *De placitis* 448, 9-11: νομίζω γὰρ καὶ τὴν περὶ ἀγαθῶν καὶ κακῶν καὶ τὴν περὶ τελῶν καὶ τὴν περὶ ἀρετῶν ἐκ τῆς περὶ παθῶν ὀρθῶς διασκέψεως ἠρτῆσθαι.

[89] Diogenes Laertius, VII, 103: Ποσειδώνιος μέντοι καὶ ταῦτά φησι (sc. πλοῦτον καὶ ὑγίειαν) τῶν ἀγαθῶν εἶναι. Cf. *Doxographi Graeci*, p. 593, 9: Ποσειδώνιος Ἀπαμεὺς ἔλεγε τὸ μέγιστον ἐν ἀνθρώποις ἀγαθὸν εἶναι πλοῦτον καὶ ὑγείαν.

[90] Seneca, *Epistle* 87, 35: Posidonius sic interrogandum ait: "quae neque magnitudinem animo dant nec fiduciam nec securitatem, non sunt bona. Divitiae autem et bona valetudo et similia his nihil horum faciunt; ergo non sunt bona."

[91] Seneca, *Epistle* 87, 31: Posidonius, ut ego existimo, melius, qui ait

health, too, are not bad in themselves. They themselves do no evil. In the same sense, Posidonius does not acknowledge the truth of the statement that riches are not a good and refutes the negation, like Antipater. He, therefore, must have assumed the positive character of riches themselves.[92] And that exactly is the meaning of the dogma that wealth and health too are counted among the good things. They are in a positive sense good and in a positive sense bad. It is impossible to call them neutral or indifferent things, as do the Stoics, things which may only be used in a bad or good sense.[93]

It is consistent that, in Posidonius, the illogical faculties of the soul should suffer good or bad from illogical powers. The reason alone is influenced by the logical faculties. The illogical faculties of the soul are by nature desirous of joy and victory and they are satisfied only by illogical things.[94] It is, therefore, impossible that Posidonius should deny the positive value of things like health and wealth. But although they are good in one respect, they may be called evils in another. It is because "they incite the mind and beget arrogance; they cause envy and alienate the mind so far that the fame of wealth pleases us who shall still be harmed by it. All good things, however, should be free from fault; they are spotless, they do not corrupt the spirit; they do not seduce. Yet they elevate and dilate, but without puffing up. Things that are good give trust; riches, however, audacity. Things that are good give magnanimity; riches,

divitias esse causam malorum, non quia ipsae faciunt aliquid, sed quia facturos inritant. Alia est enim causa efficiens, quae protinus necesse est noceat, alia praecedens. Hanc praecedentem causam divitiae habent; . . .

[92] Seneca, *Epistle* 87, 38.

[93] Diogenes Laertius, VII, 102-103. It is in contradiction to this Stoic theory that Diogenes speaks about the statement of Posidonius. It is not justifiable to blame the testimony of Diogenes as exaggerated, as does Überweg-Prächter, *l. c.*, p. 480, and the usual explanation of these passages.

[94] Galen, *De placitis*, 400, 5-9: *οὐδὲν γὰρ οὕτως ἐναργές ἐστιν, ὡς τὸ δυνάμεις τινὰς ἐν ταῖς ἡμετέραις εἶναι ψυχαῖς ἐφιεμένας φύσει, τὴν μὲν ἡδονῆς, τὴν δὲ κράτους καὶ νίκης, ἃς ἐναργῶς ὁρᾶσθαί φησι κἀν τοῖς ἄλλοις ζῴοις ὁ Ποσειδώνιος.* *Ibid.* 453, 10-11: *τῷ μὲν γὰρ ἀλόγῳ (sc. τῆς ψυχῆς) διὰ τῶν ἀλόγων ἥ τε ὠφέλεια καὶ ἡ βλάβη, τῷ λογικῷ δὲ διὰ ἐπιστήμης τε καὶ ἀμαθίας.*

insolence. Insolence is nothing but a false semblance of magnanimity." [95]

It is on this theory about things good and evil that the doctrine of duties is based. Panaetius divided this subject into three branches: the first in which we reflect on what is right and what is wrong; the second on whether it is useful or not; the third on how a decision should be reached when there seems to be a conflict between the answers to the first two questions. Posidonius has dealt with this third case.[96] For Panaetius wrote that he would expound the subject later on; but he did not keep his promise, although he lived thirty years after his book was finished. The subject is, however, touched upon by Posidonius in certain papers, although with astonishing brevity, since he actually points out that no other single topic in all philosophy is so necessary.[97] One of the problems discussed by him in this connection is whether the duty towards society, the most natural duty, should always be preferred to temperance or modesty. Posidonius answers in the negative. For some things are either so vile or so flagitious that a wise man would not practise them even to save his country. Posidonius collects many of these facts, some so horrid, some so obscene that it seems scandalous even to speak about them. The wise man, however, will not

[95] Seneca, *Epistle* 87, 31: . . . inflant animos, superbiam pariunt, invidiam contrahunt et usque eo mentem alienant, ut fama pecuniae nos etiam nocitura delectet. Bona autem omnia carere culpa decet; pura sunt, non corrumpunt animos, non sollicitant. Extollunt quidem et dilatant, sed sine tumore. Quae bona sunt fiduciam faciunt, divitiae audaciam. Quae bona sunt magnitudinem animi dant, divitiae insolentiam. Nihil autem aliud est insolentia quam species magnitudinis falsa.

[96] Cicero, *Ad Atticum* XVI, 11, 4: Illius tres sunt; sed, cum initio divisisset ita, tria genera exquirendi officii esse, unum, cum deliberemus, honestum an turpe sit, alterum, utile an inutile, tertium, cum haec inter se pugnare videantur, quo modo iudicandum sit, . . . Eum locum Posidonius persecutus est.

[97] Cicero, *De Officiis* III, 2, 7-8: Panaetius . . . de tertio autem genere deinceps se scripsit dicturum nec exsolvit id, quod promiserat. Quod eo magis miror, quia scriptum a discipulo eius Posidonio est triginta annis vixisse Panaetium, posteaquam illos libros edidisset. Quem locum miror a Posidonio breviter esse tactum in quibusdam commentariis, praesertim cum scribat nullum esse locum in tota philosophia tam necessarium.

do such things for his country, and his country will not even require him to do them.[98]

Finally, Posidonius in opposition to the general Stoic dogma assumes that there are not only immoral men and wise men but also men who make moral progress.[99] In this theory he follows the Aristotelian philosophers. Consequently, he distinguishes between different moral attitudes. The immoral, of course, are inclined to things good and evil according to their pleasure. The men who make moral progress feel no emotions in misfortune or, at least, they feel no more than is appropriate. Although they admit suffering under evils, they will not follow the emotions, but the logical power of the soul.[100] The wise man is he who acknowledges everything honest to be good, and these honest things are the goods for which he will offer prayers to God. He is entirely free from all emotions. He does not experience them even in fortunate circumstances.[101]

[98] Cicero, *De officiis* I, 45, 159: Illud forsitan quaerendum sit, num haec communitas, quae maxime est apta naturae, sit etiam moderationi modestiaeque semper anteponenda. Non placet; sunt enim quaedam partim ita foeda, partim ita flagitiosa, ut ea ne conservandae quidem patriae causa sapiens facturus sit. Ea Posidonius collegit permulta, sed ita taetra quaedam, ita obscena, ut dictu quoque videantur turpia. . . .

[99] Diogenes Laertius, VII, 91; cf. *ibid.* 127.

[100] Galen, *De placitis*, 392, 9: *οἱ δὲ (προκόπτοντες) ἐν μεγίστοις κακοῖς ἑαυτοὺς ὑπολαμβάνοντες εἶναι ὅμως οὐ γίνονται διὰ τοῦτο ἐν πάθει. Ibid.* 370, 12: *ὁμοίως δὲ καὶ τοὺς προκόπτοντας μεγάλας βλάβας ὑπὸ τῆς κακίας ὑπολαμβάνοντας πεπεῖναι ἔδει καὶ ὑποφέρεσθαι φόβοις καὶ λύπαις περιπίπτειν μὴ μετρίαις, ὅπερ οὐδὲ αὐτὸ συμβαίνει.* Cicero tells (*Tusculanae Disputationes* II, 61) that Posidonius in the presence of Pompey discussed the thesis that the honorable alone is good and, suffering an attack of pain, often said: "You will not succeed, pain; as grievous as you are, I shall never concede that you are an evil." Itaque narrabat (Pompeius) eum graviter et copiose de hoc ipso, nihil esse bonum nisi quod esset honestum, cubantem disputavisse, cumque quasi faces ei doloris admoverentur, saepe dixisse: "Nihil agis, dolor! quamvis sis molestus, numquam te esse confitebor malum." This story only proves that Posidonius has to be considered as a man who made moral progress (against Zeller, *l. c.*, III, 1, p. 214, 2; 582, 4).

[101] Galen, *De placitis*, 370, 3-7: *οἱ σοφοὶ μέγιστα καὶ ἀνυπέρβλητα νομίζοντες εἶναι ἀγαθὰ τὰ καλὰ πάντα οὐκ ἐμπαθῶς κινοῦνται ὑπὸ αὐτῶν ἐπιθυμοῦντές τε ὧν ὀρέγονται καὶ περιχαρεῖς γινόμενοι ἐπὶ τοῖς αὐτοῖς, ὅταν τύχωσιν αὐτῶν.* 392, 8: *οἱ μὲν (σοφοὶ) γὰρ ἐν μεγίστοις ἀγαθοῖς . . . ἑαυτοὺς ὑπολαμβάνοντες εἶναι ὅμως οὐ γίνονται διὰ τοῦτο ἐν πάθει.* Diogenes

Like the teaching about things good or evil, virtues as well are based on the right understanding of the emotions. This Posidonius stresses over and over again.[102] Man's primary art is virtue itself. There is joined to this the useless and fleeting flesh, fitted only for the reception of food, as Posidonius remarks.[103] He then distinguishes between logical and illogical virtues; the illogical virtues are faculties of the soul, the logical virtue is knowledge. Besides, he divides virtue into four types.[104] The proof that virtue really exists is the fact that the followers of Socrates, Diogenes, and Antisthenes made moral progress. And the proof of the existence of vice as a fundamental fact is that it is the opposite of virtue.[105] Posidonius, however, does not believe that virtue is self-sufficient, but he contends that health is needed, and wealth and strength.[106]

Virtue can be taught.[107] Posidonius held that not only precept-

Laertius, VII, 124: *εὔξεταί τε, φασίν, ὁ σοφός, αἰτούμενος τὰ ἀγαθὰ τῶν θεῶν, καθά φησι Ποσειδώνιος ἐν τῷ πρώτῳ περὶ καθηκόντων.* Wisdom may be lost in consequence of drunkness or melancholy, cf. Diogenes Laertius, VII, 127. As regards this problem, Posidonius defended the statement of Zeno, cf. Seneca, *Epistle* 83, 10.

[102] Galen, *De placitis*, 654, 3-6: *καὶ μέντοι καὶ τὸν περὶ τῶν ἀρετῶν λόγον ἐπὶ ταύταις ταῖς ἀρχαῖς ὀρθῶς φησι περαίνεσθαι καὶ δείκνυσιν αὐτὸ τοῦτο διὰ μεγάλης πραγματείας ἰδίᾳ γεγραμμένης αὐτῷ.*

[103] Seneca, *Epistle* 92, 10 (ed. with an English translation by R. M. Gummere, Loeb Classical Library): prima ars hominis est ipsa virtus; huic committitur inutilis caro et fluida, receptandis tantum cibis habilis, ut ait Posidonius.

[104] Galen, *De placitis*, 446, 13: *ἕπεται δὲ εὐθὺς τοῖσδε καὶ ὁ περὶ τῶν ἀρετῶν λόγος αὐτοῦ ἐλέγχων τὸ σφάλμα διττόν, εἴτε ἐπιστήμας τις ἁπάσας αὐτὰς εἴτε δυνάμεις ὑπολάβοι. τῶν μὲν γὰρ ἀλόγων τῆς ψυχῆς μερῶν ἀλόγους ἀνάγκη καὶ τὰς ἀρετὰς εἶναι, τοῦ λογιστικοῦ δὲ μόνου λογικήν. ὥστε εὐλόγως ἐκείνων μὲν αἱ ἀρεταὶ δυνάμεις εἰσίν, ἐπιστήμη δὲ μόνου τοῦ λογιστικοῦ.* Diogenes Laertius, VII, 92: *τέτταρας δὲ (ἀρετὰς) οἱ περὶ Ποσειδώνιον.* For this doctrine in the Academy cf. Διαιρέσεις Ἀριστοτέλους § 2 (V. Rose, *Aristoteles Pseudepigraphus*, p. 679).

[105] Diogenes Laertius, VII, 91: *τεκμήριον δὲ τοῦ ὑπαρκτὴν εἶναι τὴν ἀρετήν φησιν ὁ Ποσειδώνιος ἐν τῷ πρώτῳ τοῦ ἠθικοῦ λόγου τὸ γενέσθαι ἐν προκοπῇ τοὺς περὶ Σωκράτην καὶ Διογένην καὶ Ἀντισθένην. εἶναι δὲ καὶ τὴν κακίαν ὑπαρκτὴν διὰ τὸ ἀντικεῖσθαι τῇ ἀρετῇ.*

[106] *Ibid.* VII, 128: *ὁ μέντοι Παναίτιος καὶ Ποσειδώνιος οὐκ αὐτάρκη λέγουσι τὴν ἀρετήν, ἀλλὰ χρείαν εἶναί φασι καὶ ὑγιείας καὶ χορηγίας καὶ ἰσχύος.*

[107] *Ibid.* VII, 91: *διδακτήν τε εἶναι αὐτήν, λέγω δὲ τὴν ἀρετήν, καὶ Ποσειδώνιος ἐν τοῖς προτρεπτικοῖς.*

giving, but even persuasion, consolation, and encouragement are necessary in this teaching. To these he adds the investigation of causes. He remarks that it will also be useful to illustrate each particular virtue; this science he calls ethology, while others call it characterization. It gives the signs and marks which belong to each virtue and vice, so that by them distinction may be drawn between like things.[108] For the teaching of ethics and especially of virtues cannot be done in a few words, since the emotions are only to be treated by persuasion. Posidonius says: "I do not think that Plato's laws should have the preambles added to them. For a law should be brief, in order that the uninitiated may grasp it all the more easily. It should be a voice, as it were, sent down from heaven. It should command, not discuss. Nothing seems to me more dull or more foolish than a law with a preamble. Warn me, tell me what you wish me to do, I am not learning but obeying." [109] Ethical philosophy, the theory about virtues, has not to command but to discuss.

The last of the constitutive parts of ethics is the theory of the aim of life. The end is life in accordance with nature, which is to live in accordance with virtue, for it is virtue toward which nature leads us.[110] But it is necessary to define correctly what is meant by living in agreement with nature. Posidonius says: "Some disregard this necessity, and they contract the meaning of living in accordance with nature into doing everything pos-

[108] Seneca, *Epistle* 95, 65: Posidonius non tantum praeceptionem, nihil enim nos hoc verbo uti prohibet, sed etiam suasionem et consolationem et exhortationem necessariam iudicat. His adicit causarum inquisitionem, aetiologian quam quare nos dicere non audeamus, cum grammatici, custodes Latini sermonis, suo iure ita appellent, non video. Ait utilem futuram et descriptionem cuiusque virtutis; hanc Posidonius ethologian vocat, quidam characterismon appellant, signa cuiusque virtutis ac vitii et notas reddentem, quibus inter se similia discriminentur.

[109] Seneca, *Epistle* 94, 38: (Posidonius) qui "inprobo," inquit, "quod Platonis legibus adiecta principia sunt. Legem enim brevem esse oportet, quo facilius ab imperitis teneatur. Velut emissa divinitus vox sit; iubeat, non disputet. Nihil videtur mihi frigidius, nihil ineptius quam lex cum prologo. Mone, dic, quid me velis fecisse; non disco, sed pareo."

[110] Diogenes Laertius, VII, 87: *Ζήνων . . . τέλος εἶπε τὸ ὁμολογουμένως τῇ φύσει ζῆν, ὅπερ ἐστὶ κατ' ἀρετὴν ζῆν. ἄγει γὰρ πρὸς ταύτην ἡμᾶς ἡ φύσις. ὁμοίως δὲ καὶ . . . Ποσειδώνιος.*

sible in order to attain the things by nature primarily good. They come near to determining the aim as joy or freedom from disturbance or something similar. But this is obviously in contradiction to the word itself and nothing good or conducive to happiness. It necessarily follows the end but is not itself the end. If the aim is rightly defined, however, it is possible to use the definition to solve the dilemma brought forward by the Sophists, a solution rendered impossible by the definition of life as experience of the happenings in the whole of nature. This is of the same value as the definition of life in accordance with nature if there is no desire to gain the indifferent things in a mean way."[111] Thus it is extremely important to know exactly the aim of life and Posidonius again attacks Chrysippus very severely.[112]

In more detail he states in regard to the aim: "The reason for the emotions, that is for their inconsistency and for life possessed by an evil genius, is that they do not follow in every respect the demon in themselves, born with us and having the same nature as the demon governing the whole world, but that they are led by the brutish and worse demon. Men who do not realize this neither acknowledge the right cause of the emotions, nor do they judge rightly about true happiness in conformity with nature. For they do not see that the first thing is not to be led at all by the illogical and godless part of the soul which is possessed by an evil demon."[113] And he declares, "The sum-

[111] Galen, *De placitis*, 450, 5: "*ἃ δὴ παρέντες ἔνιοι τὸ ὁμολογουμένως ζῆν συστέλλουσιν εἰς τὸ πᾶν τὸ ἐνδεχόμενον ποιεῖν ἕνεκα τῶν πρώτων κατὰ φύσιν ὅμοιον αὐτὸ ποιοῦντες τῷ σκοπὸν ἐκτίθεσθαι τὴν ἡδονὴν ἢ τὴν ἀοχλησίαν ἢ ἄλλο τι τοιοῦτον. ἔστι δὲ μάχην ἐμφαίνων κατὰ αὐτὴν τὴν ἐκφοράν, καλὸν δὲ καὶ εὐδαιμονικὸν οὐδέν. παρέπεται γὰρ κατὰ τὸ ἀναγκαῖον τῷ τέλει, τέλος δὲ οὐκ ἔστιν. ἀλλὰ καὶ τούτου διαληφθέντος ὀρθῶς ἔξεστι μὲν αὐτῷ χρῆσθαι πρὸς τὸ διακόπτειν τὰς ἀπορίας, ἃς οἱ σοφισταὶ προτείνουσιν, μὴ μέντοι γε τῷ κατὰ ἐμπειρίαν τῶν κατὰ τὴν ὅλην φύσιν συμβαινόντων ζῆν, ὅπερ ἰσοδυναμεῖ τῷ ὁμολογουμένως εἰπεῖν ζῆν ἡνίκα μὴ τοῦτο μικροπρεπῶς συντείνει εἰς τὸ τῶν ἀδιαφόρων τυγχάνειν.*"

[112] *Stoicorum Veterum Fragmenta* III, p. 5, 4; p. 112, 10 cf. n. 80.

[113] Galen, *De placitis*, 448, 15: *τὸ δὴ τῶν παθῶν αἴτιον τοῦτ' ἔστι τῆς τε ἀνομολογίας καὶ τοῦ κακοδαίμονος βίου, τὸ μὴ κατὰ πᾶν ἕπεσθαι τῷ ἐν αὐτοῖς δαίμονι συγγενεῖ τε ὄντι καὶ τὴν ὁμοίαν φύσιν ἔχοντι τῷ τὸν ὅλον κόσμον διοικοῦντι, τῷ δὲ χείρονι καὶ ζῳώδει ποτὲ συνεκκλίνοντας φέρεσθαι. οἱ δὲ τοῦτο παριδόντες οὔτε ἐν τούτοις βελτιοῦσι τὴν αἰτίαν τῶν παθῶν οὔτε ἐν τοῖς*

mum bonum is living in contemplation of the truth and order of all things and fashioning oneself as far as possible in accordance therewith, being led aside as little as possible by the irrational part of the soul."[114] The end of life, according to Posidonius, is a merely theoretical one. It is knowledge alone for which the wise man is striving, knowledge which is the task of reason. Thus, the whole character of the Stoic philosophy changes. Theoretical knowledge had always been refuted as the aim of life. It had been considered by Chrysippus to be equivalent to joy, which was rejected.[115]

This definition of the aim of life is independent of any form of eschatology. There is no eschatological fragment and no proof whatever that Posidonius assumed the human soul to be immortal.[115a] On the other hand, the aim of life is understood in a more active sense. The resignation to fate, thus, is over-

περὶ τῆς εὐδαιμονίας καὶ ὁμολογίας ὀρθοδοξοῦσιν. οὐ γὰρ βλέπουσιν, ὅτι πρῶτόν ἐστιν ἐν αὐτῇ τὸ κατὰ μηδὲν ἄγεσθαι ὑπὸ τοῦ ἀλόγου τε καὶ κακοδαίμονος καὶ ἀθέου τῆς ψυχῆς. In order to understand the meaning of demon, it seems necessary but also sufficient to compare Parmenides, fr. 12 (Diels) and Plato's *Timaeus* 90a, quoted by Galen, *De placitis*, 502-3. It is also important to note, that Posidonius, like Hipparchus, believes in astrology, cf. Augustine, *De civitate Dei* V, 2, cf. also 9. Concerning Plato's adherence to the astrological belief cf. Pfeiffer, *l. c.*, p. 46, 8. Concerning the *συγγένεια* of the stars cf. *ibid.*, pp. 116-17. Besides, Posidonius calls the stars demons. Cf. n. 51.

[114] Clement, *Stromateis* II, 129: *τὸ ζῆν θεωροῦντα τὴν τῶν ὅλων ἀλήθειαν καὶ τάξιν καὶ συγκατασκευάζοντα αὐτὸν κατὰ τὸ δυνατόν, κατὰ μηδὲν ἀγόμενον ὑπὸ τοῦ ἀλόγου μέρους τῆς ψυχῆς.* By this definition of the aim of human life the *πολυμάθεια* ascribed to Posidonius is to be understood, Strabo, XVI, 753. Cf. Seneca, *Epistle* 78, 28: "Unus dies hominum eruditorum plus patet quam imperitis longissima aetas, ut ait Posidonius."

[115] Cf. Zeller, *l. c.*, III, 1, p. 52 and O. Rieth, *Hermes* 69 (1934), pp. 13 ff. Cf. again Cicero, *De natura deorum* II, 153: quae contuens animus accedit ad cognitionem deorum, e qua oritur pietas, cui coniuncta iustitia est reliquaeque virtutes, e quibus vita beata existit par et similis deorum, nulla alia re nisi inmortalitate, quae nihil ad bene vivendum pertinet, cedens caelestibus.

[115a] Diels, *Doxographi Graeci*, p. 587, 19 only assumes Posidonius to be the author of a passage which deals with immortality. Reinhardt, I, p. 471 does not consider eschatology at all, but in his second book he tries to ascertain it, starting from the conception of demons, cf. however Jones, *Classical Philology*, XXVII (1932), p. 113.

come to a certain extent. The Stoics contend that fate leads men who are willing to be led, and forces those who resist. Posidonius says: "There are never any occasions when you need think yourself safe because you wield the weapons of Fortune; fight with your own! Fortune does not furnish arms against herself; hence men equipped against their foes are unarmed against Fortune herself."[116]

Thus, Posidonius, starting from a heretical definition of emotions builds up an entirely heretical system of ethics. The individual theories are closely connected and cannot be separated from one another. The teaching on ethics, as he himself always contends, is based on the right understanding of the emotions. And the ethics correspond to the heretical physics.[116a]

IV.

Logic.

As regards the logic of which again the subdivision is unknown,[117] the material preserved is very meager. Mention is made of the distinction of three causes by Posidonius.[118] The efficient cause and the antecedent cause are differentiated.[119] The names of some forms of conclusions are given.[120]

[116] Seneca, *Epistle* 113, 28: "Non est quod umquam fortunae armis putes esse te tutum; tuis pugna. Contra ipsam fortuna non armat; itaque contra hostes instructi, contra ipsam inermes sunt."

[116a] It is certainly incorrect to state: "Diese Abweichungen von der Stoischen Überlieferung (in der Anthropologie) hatten nun zwar auf die übrigen Lehren des Poseidonios nicht den Einfluss, den man nach seinen eigenen Äusserungen erwarten könnte; so entschieden er vielmehr die Abhängigkeit der Ethik von der Ansicht über die Affekte anerkannte, so wird uns doch aus seiner Sittenlehre nichts berichtet, was mit der Stoischen Moral in Widerspruch stände; denn (!) die Angaben des Diogenes . . . haben wir bereits als unglaubwürdig erkannt." (Zeller, *l. c.*, III, 1, p. 582). The most adequate interpretation of the Posidonian ethics I know of, is given by A. Modrze, *Philologus*, 87 (1932), pp. 300 ff., although it is primarily based on indirect testimonies.

[117] Diogenes Laertius, VII, 84.

[118] Areios Didymos fr. 18, cf. n. 65.

[119] Seneca, *Epistle* 87, 31: praecedens causa, efficiens causa.

[120] Galen, Εἰσαγωγὴ διαλεκτικὴ ed. Kalbfleisch (1896), p. 47, 16 ff.: *τοὺς δὴ τοιούτους ἅπαντας συλλογισμοὺς τῷ γένει μὲν ἐκ τῶν πρός τι ῥητέον, ἐν εἴδει*

More important is the Posidonian definition of categories. It is said that he, like other philosophers, "separates two classes, word and things. As regards the word, he considers it necessary to ask if the word means anything; what it means; how many meanings it has; in what way it means anything. As regards the things, use must be made of conjecture which he names both *κατ' αἴσθησιν* and quality; and of definition which he names both *κατ' ἔννοιαν* and concerning something."[121] These, then, are the two fundamental aspects of judgment. The word, as one of them, has to be studied in every respect. So it also becomes understandable why Posidonius attributed significance even to etymologies.[122] The distinction between conjecture according to apprehension and definition according to thinking reflects the distinction between existence in reality and existence in thought often to be found in the fragments. It is in this sense that Posidonius defends, against Epicurus, the possibility of statements concerning existence proceeding from logical presuppositions.[123]

Connected with the distinction of categories is the definition of the standard of truth by Posidonius. He says in his exposition of Plato's *Timaeus*, "Just as light is apprehended by the luciform sense of sight, and sound by the aeriform sense of hearing, so also the nature of all things ought to be apprehended by its kindred reason."[124] What does this mean? To Posi-

δὲ κατ' ἀξιώματος δύναμιν συνισταμένους, ὥσπερ καὶ ὁ Ποσειδώνιός φησιν ὀνομάζειν αὐτοὺς συνακτικοὺς κατὰ δύναμιν ἀξιώματος. Cf. Seneca, *Epistle* 87, 38.

[121] Quintilian, III, 6, 37: In duo et Posidonius dividit, vocem et res. In voce quaeri putat an significet, quid, quam multa, quo modo? In rebus coniecturam quod *κατ' αἴσθησιν* vocat, et qualitatem, et finitionem, cui nomen dat *κατ' ἔννοιαν* et ad aliquid.

[122] Cf. the etymologies of demon (n. 51) and of sight: *ὄψις ὡς μὲν Ποσειδώνιος παρὰ τὸ ἅπτω* (*Etymologicum Magnum*).

[123] Proclus, *in Euclidem*, pp. 216, 20-217, 3; 217, 24-218, 11; cf. Bréhier, *l. c.*, p. 53.

[124] Sextus Empiricus, *Adversus Logicos* I, 93 (ed. with an English translation by R. G. Bury, Loeb Classical Library): *καὶ ὡς τὸ μὲν φῶς, φησὶν ὁ Ποσειδώνιος τὸν Πλάτωνος Τίμαιον ἐξηγούμενος, ὑπὸ τῆς φωτοειδοῦς ὄψεως καταλαμβάνεται, ἡ δὲ φωνὴ ὑπὸ τῆς ἀεροειδοῦς ἀκοῆς, οὕτω καὶ ἡ τῶν ὅλων φύσις ὑπὸ συγγενοῦς ὀφείλει καταλαμβάνεσθαι τοῦ λόγου.* Is it really by chance that in the following words, according to the Pythagorean theory, reason is identified with number? Posidonius was well ac-

donius every act of recognition is a kind of growing together. This is valid for hearing, seeing, feeling and thinking.[125] Something in the apprehending subject always has to correspond to the object outside which is to be apprehended, and it has to be similar to this object. The nature of all things, therefore, can only be seized by the cognate faculty of the human being: reason. If it is necessary to judge about the essence of things, the basis of judgment is no apprehending presentation, coming from a real object, no sensation, no preconception. The Stoic school in general believes in such criteria. Only a few older philosophers acknowledge the right reason to be the standard of truth, as Posidonius contends.[126]

This theory symbolizes the whole system. Materialism is still recognized by Posidonius. But mere empiricism is overcome by his philosophy. Thinking, too, is able and destined to judge reality. Matter and God exist. Emotions are as real as reason. Sensation and reason are forms of cognition. The proof of vice is found in the fact that it is the opposite of virtue, which really exists.[127] The rules of logic are the rules of the world. Opposition is a fundamental fact of reason and, therefore, of existence. That is the reason that no quality can be without its opposite. On the other hand, although there are opposites,

quainted with the dogma of this school. And one should conclude the same identification from his interpretation of the soul in the *Timaeus*, since the first intelligible things are apparently meant to be numbers (against Zeller, *l. c.*, III, 1, 578, 4).

[125] No details are known about Posidonius' theory of vision. Cf. concerning this problem and the interpretation of Reinhardt, H. Cherniss, *American Journal of Philology*, LIV (1933), pp. 154 ff.

[126] Diogenes Laertius, VII, 54; concerning the general Stoic dogma cf. *ibid.* and 42. It is for this reason, too, that I deal with logic as the last branch of philosophy, and give ethics, the theory on the soul and its faculties, the middle place between physics and logic. If it is necessary to begin philosophical inquiry with physics, as Posidonius thinks, logic must be the end, since it corresponds to reason, the highest principle. I cannot prove that this sequence is correct, but it seems to me to follow from the interpretation of the fragments (against Zeller, cf. n. 13).

[127] Cf. n. 105 and the definition of dialectic. Diogenes Laertius, VII, 62: *διαλεκτικὴ δέ ἐστιν, ὥς φησι Ποσειδώνιος, ἐπιστήμη ἀληθῶν καὶ ψευδῶν καὶ οὐδετέρων.* Cf. Zeller, *l. c.*, III, 1, p. 64.

one of them is considered to be the more important factor or the true reality. God is the first. Reason is superior to emotions. For thought does not only distinguish, it orders and subordinates things.

But since reason governs the whole and is the fundamental law of order, since the world, in its last principle, can only be understood by reason, not by experience, the difference between the philosophical task and the scientific research is conceived by Posidonius in a distinctively new manner. Discussing the study of the philosopher and of the mathematician in regard to astronomy he says: "It is the subject matter of the physical theory to inquire into the substance of the heavens and of the stars and into the power and quality and into generation and destruction; and by Jove! it is able to point out the magnitude of things and their figure and order. Astrology does not try to tell anything of this kind, but it points out the order of the heavenly bodies, showing the heaven to be a real cosmos; it speaks about the figure and the magnitude and the distance of the earth as well as of the sun and the moon, and about eclipses and encounterings of the stars, about their quality and quantity, and their orbits. It, therefore, naturally needs arithmetic and geometry, since as far as figures are concerned it touches upon the question of how great and how much and in what manner. And in regard to these problems, the explanation of which it alone promises to give, it is valid to bring about this explanation by arithmetic and geometry. The astrologer and the physicist indeed very often aim at proving the same points: for instance, that the sun is great, that the earth is spherical; yet, they do not take the same road. One of them proves everything starting from the substance or the power or from the criteria of what is better or from the generation and change, and he thus proves everything; the other starts from the consequences of the figures or the magnitude or from the greatness of the movement and the harmony of time therewith. The physicist often touches upon the causes, with the active power in mind, the astrologer, concluding from the external consequences, does not sufficiently recognize the cause; for instance, when he determines the earth or the stars to be spherical in shape. He sometimes does not even want to ascertain the cause, for instance if he discusses the eclipses, but sometimes he finds out the facts by granting an hypothesis, some forms by which the phenomena are preserved, for instance an inquiry into the reasons by which sun and moon and the planets seem to move irregularly. In regard to these problems, if we presuppose their circuits to be eccentric or the stars to move in epicycles, their apparent irregularity is preserved. And it is necessary to find out, too, which of these orbits the phenomena may possibly traverse, so that the subject of the planets seems to belong to the aetiology, given according to the possibility of orbits. Thus, a certain Heracleides of Pontus came and said that the apparent anomaly concerning the sun might be preserved also, if the earth were moving and the sun were stationary. For it is not at all the province of the astrologer to ascertain whether something is at rest by nature and what is moving, but, introducing hypotheses according to which some bodies stand still, some move, he has to inquire which hypothesis the phenomena of the heavens will obey. He has to take from the physicist the principles that the movements of the stars are simple and kindred and orderly, and from them he will point out that the choral dance of all the stars is cyclical whether they move in parallels or in crosswise circles."[128]

[128] Simplicius on Aristotle's Physics, *Commentaria Graeca* ed. H. Diels, IX (1882), pp. 291, 21-292, 31: ὁ δὲ Ἀλέξανδρος φιλοπόνως λέξιν τινὰ τοῦ Γεμίνου παρατίθησιν ἐκ τῆς ἐπιτομῆς τῶν Ποσειδωνίου Μετεωρολογικῶν ἐξηγήσεως τὰς ἀφορμὰς ἀπὸ Ἀριστοτέλους λαβοῦσαν. ἔχει δὲ ὧδε. τῆς μὲν φυσικῆς θεωρίας ἐστὶ τὸ σκοπεῖν περί τε οὐσίας οὐρανοῦ καὶ ἄστρων καὶ δυνάμεως καὶ ποιότητος γενέσεώς τε καὶ φθορᾶς καὶ νὴ Δία τούτων περὶ μεγέθους καὶ σχήματος καὶ τάξεως ἀποδεικνύναι δύναται. ἡ δὲ ἀστρολογία περὶ τοιούτου μὲν οὐδενὸς ἐπιχειρεῖ λέγειν, ἀποδείκνυσι δὲ τὴν τάξιν τῶν οὐρανίων κόσμον ὄντως ἀποφήνασα τὸν οὐρανόν. περί τε σχημάτων λέγει καὶ μεγεθῶν καὶ ἀποστημάτων γῆς τε καὶ ἡλίου καὶ σελήνης καὶ περὶ ἐκλείψεων καὶ συνάψεων τῶν ἄστρων καὶ περὶ τῆς ἐν ταῖς φοραῖς αὐτῶν ποιότητος καὶ ποσότητος. ὅθεν ἐπειδὴ τῆς περὶ ποσὸν καὶ πηλίκον καὶ ποιὸν κατὰ σχῆμα θεωρίας ἐφάπτεται, εἰκότως ἀριθμητικῆς τε καὶ γεωμετρίας ἐδεήθη ταύτῃ. καὶ περὶ τούτων, ὧν ὑπισχνεῖτο μόνων λόγον ἀποδώσειν, δι' ἀριθμητικῆς τε καὶ γεωμετρίας συμβιβάζειν ἰσχύει. πολλαχοῦ τοίνυν ταὐτὸν κεφάλαιον ἀποδεῖξαι προθήσεται ὅ τε ἀστρολόγος καὶ ὁ φυσικός, οἷον ὅτι μέγας ὁ ἥλιος, ὅτι σφαιροειδὴς ἡ γῆ οὐ μὴν κατὰ τὰς αὐτὰς ὁδοὺς βαδιοῦνται. ὁ μὲν γὰρ ἀπὸ τῆς οὐσίας ἢ τῆς δυνάμεως ἢ τοῦ ἄμεινον οὕτως ἔχειν, ἢ ἀπὸ τῆς γενέσεως καὶ μεταβολῆς ἕκαστα ἀποδείξει, ὁ δὲ ἀπὸ τῶν συμβεβηκότων τοῖς σχήμασι ἢ μεγέθεσι ἢ ἀπὸ τῆς ποσότητος τῆς κινήσεως καὶ τοῦ ἐφαρμόττοντος αὐτῇ χρόνου. καὶ ὁ μὲν φυσικὸς τῆς αἰτίας πολλαχοῦ ἅψεται εἰς τὴν ποιητικὴν δύναμιν ἀποβλέπων,

The investigation of general principles, then, is the task of the philosopher. The scientist has to solve only the individual problems. To a certain extent, Posidonius again follows Aristotle.[129] But his statement goes further than does Aristotle's.

To Posidonius, the philosopher alone is able to establish the fundamental principles of science. The scientists have to respect the limits which philosophy traces out. All the sciences are based on philosophical presuppositions which cannot ultimately be proved by science.[130] It is the last task of philosophy to lay down these general principles. If in the Golden Age everything was under the jurisdiction of the wise man or the philosopher, now science at least is under his government.

What consequences are to be drawn from this attempt to reconstruct the Posidonian philosophy proceeding from those fragments alone which are preserved under the name of Posi-

ὁ δὲ ἀστρολόγος ὅταν ἀπὸ τῶν ἔξωθεν συμβεβηκότων ἀποδεικνύῃ οὐχ ἱκανὸς θεατὴς γίνεται τῆς αἰτίας, οἷον ὅτε σφαιροειδῆ τὴν γῆν ἢ τὰ ἄστρα ἀποδίδωσιν, ἐνιαχοῦ δὲ οὐδὲ τὴν αἰτίαν λαβεῖν ἐφίεται ὡς ὅταν περὶ ἐκλείψεως διαλέγηται: ἄλλοτε δὲ καθ' ὑπόθεσιν εὑρίσκει τρόπους τινὰς ἀποδιδούς, ὧν ὑπαρχόντων σωθήσεται τὰ φαινόμενα. οἷον διὰ τί ἀνωμάλως ἥλιος καὶ σελήνη καὶ οἱ πλάνητες φαίνονται κινούμενοι; ὅτι εἰ ὑποθώμεθα ἐκκέντρους αὐτῶν τοὺς κύκλους ἢ κατ' ἐπίκυκλον πολούμενα τὰ ἄστρα, σωθήσεται ἡ φαινομένη ἀνωμαλία αὐτῶν, δεήσει τε ἐπεξελθεῖν καθ' ὅσους δυνατὸν τρόπους ταῦτα ἀποτελεῖσθαι τὰ φαινόμενα, ὥστε ἐοικέναι τῇ κατὰ τὸν ἐνδεχόμενον τρόπον αἰτιολογίᾳ τὴν περὶ τῶν πλανωμένων ἄστρων πραγματείαν. διὸ καὶ παρελθών τίς φησιν Ἡρακλείδης ὁ Ποντικός, ὅτι καὶ κινουμένης πως τῆς γῆς τοῦ δὲ ἡλίου μένοντός πως δύναται ἡ περὶ τὸν ἥλιον φαινομένη ἀνωμαλία σώζεσθαι. ὅλως γὰρ οὐκ ἔστιν ἀστρολόγου τὸ γνῶναι τί ἠρεμαῖόν ἐστι τῇ φύσει καὶ ποῖα τὰ κινητά, ἀλλὰ ὑποθέσεις εἰσηγούμενος τῶν μὲν μενόντων, τῶν δὲ κινουμένων σκοπεῖ τίσιν ὑποθέσεσιν ἀκολουθήσει τὰ κατὰ τὸν οὐρανὸν φαινόμενα. ληπτέον δὲ αὐτῷ ἀρχὰς παρὰ τοῦ φυσικοῦ, ἁπλᾶς εἶναι καὶ ὁμαλὰς καὶ τεταγμένας κινήσεις τῶν ἄστρων, δι' ὧν ἀποδείξει ἔγκυκλον οὖσαν τὴν χορείαν ἁπάντων τῶν μὲν κατὰ παραλλήλους, τῶν δὲ κατὰ λοξοὺς κύκλους εἰλουμένων. οὕτως μὲν οὖν ὁ Γέμινος ἤτοι ὁ παρὰ τῷ Γεμίνῳ Ποσειδώνιος τὴν διαφορὰν τῆς τε φυσιολογίας καὶ τῆς ἀστρολογίας παραδίδωσιν ἀπὸ τοῦ Ἀριστοτέλους τὰς ἀφορμὰς λαβών. Cf. concerning the distinction between *θέσις* and *ὑπόθεσις* Plato, *Republic* 511b; *Epistle* VII 342a ff. and K. v. Fritz, *Philologus* 87 (1932), pp. 40 ff.; 136 ff.

[129] Cf. Aristotle, *De respiratione* 480b21 ff.

[130] Reinhardt states (I, p. 53) that to Posidonius sciences are the basis of philosophy. The consequences Reinhardt draws chiefly from indirect evidence are contradictory to the fragment taken from Simplicius.

donius? It follows first of all that the fragments are sufficient material to give a picture which, if not complete in every respect, is still clear and exact enough to permit an understanding of the system. It is not necessary to base the interpretation of the philosophy of Posidonius on indirect testimonies.[131] At the same time it is now possible to establish the influences which Posidonius' system had on philosophers as well as scientists. If the fragments did not show enough, these influences could not be determined conclusively. While this is very important from the historical point of view, it is so in no other respect. If the influences are supposed to disclose new material, not contained in the fragments, such an interpretation necessarily remains a mere guess. For it can never be decided whether the new thought really has to be traced back to Posidonius or is a later transformation of his ideas.

The reconstructed Posidonian system, moreover, is distinct in its originality. To be sure, it is a Stoic system. But Posidonius is strongly influenced by Aristotle and Plato as well as by other great philosophers. These various influences, different to the modern mind, seem homogeneous to him and, above all, they do not destroy his individuality. On the contrary, they seem to unfetter his own thought. They are material molded by him according to the Stoic mentality. Posidonius is a comprehensive personality. He is inclined to face facts; he does not want to evade reality. But he is also a very good mathematician and logician, a man trained in literature as well as in history, a scientist and at the same time active in politics, a thinker and an explorer. His fundamental experience seems to be the variety of interests and opinions integrated, however, as the unity of life, an experience which he translates into his own existence.

Posidonius, such as he really is, cannot influence his own or later generations to any considerable extent. He is, of course, well known to his contemporaries. Cicero estimates his work

[131] A collection of the fragments, however, would be useful, and it could be made without regard to ail the passages which are believed to be influenced by Posidonius' thought. It is my intention to undertake this in regard to the philosophical as well as the scientific material.

highly, but Panaetius, Chrysippus, and Zeno have at least the same rank as Posidonius. Besides there are still other Stoics who are very famous. As a whole, the influence of the Epicurean and Academic philosophy is much greater during the lifetime of Posidonius than the influence of the Stoic school. When in the 1st Century A. D. the Stoic philosophy finally becomes the dominant system, it is the old Stoa, not the philosophy of Posidonius, which is recognized. Seneca admires Posidonius as a great philosopher, but it is Chrysippus whom he follows in regard to the essential theories—Chrysippus whom Posidonius so bitterly attacks. And the same is valid for the whole Stoicism of this epoch and of later centuries.[182] Posidonius does not agree with the thinking of this period or of the following ones. He is, therefore, soon forgotten. Scientists may use his books because they appreciate the material available in them. Galen may quote him in renouncing the general Stoic dogma, because he thinks it convenient to refute the Stoics by a Stoic. But no philosopher thinks it worthwhile to discuss the Posidonian system as such. In the 4th Century A. D. nobody ever reads Posidonius.[183] Nowhere is he characterized as an outstanding figure. The name of Posidonius is very seldom, almost never, mentioned even in the doxographical material.

Not even the Neo-Platonists consider the philosophy of Posidonius. How could they? To Posidonius God and matter are fundamental principles, independent of each other, as are virtue and vice, experience and reason. The contrast of God and matter, the contrast of good and evil is an eternal fact, not the

[182] *Stoicorum Veterum Fragmenta*, collegit Ioannes ab Arnim, Vol. I, Praefatio III: Ita enim res se habet: eam Stoicae doctrinae formam, quae imperatorum Romanorum aetate fuit, uberrimis testimoniis illustrare possumus eademque ex Chrysippi auctoritate tota pendet. Galen (ed. G. Kühn), IV, 819: *ὁ πάντων ἐπιστημονικώτατος ὁ Ποσειδώνιος, ἐν οἷς ἐπαίνων ἐστὶ μεγίστων ἄξιος, ἐν τούτοις αὐτοῖς μὲν ὑπὸ τῶν ἄλλων οὐχ ἕπεται τῶν Στωϊκῶν.*

[183] Cf. Jaeger, *Nemesios v. Emesa*, p. 68: "Den Poseidonios hat weder Nemesios noch sonst ein Mensch des ausgehenden 4. Jahrhunderts mehr gelesen, und wie wenige werden seinen Namen noch gewusst haben!" And yet, Simplicius is the first to say that the Stoic books are becoming rare, cf. Simplicius *in categorias*, *Scholia in Aristotelem*, 49a, 16: *παρὰ τοῖς Στωϊκοῖς, ὧν ἐφ' ἡμῶν καὶ ἡ διδασκαλία καὶ τὰ πλεῖστα τῶν συγγραμμάτων ἐπιλέλοιπεν.*

consequence of guilt or punishment. No fragment therefore, shows religious feeling; no fragment deals with eschatology. The soul which guides all the natures does not strive for redemption. It is striving for knowledge, knowledge of this world. The nature of man is neither ecstatic nor faithful. Acquiescence in the harmony of the world is an attitude unfamiliar to Posidonius.[184] The order of the world has to be grasped by reason. His system is rational, yet it acknowledges experience. The triumph over the emotions is not won by seclusion from the world; it is gained in the study of the phenomena. If the fragments are taken into account, Posidonian philosophy is the opposite to Neo-Platonism. What is the use then of calling Posidonian philosophy the turning point to religious and mythical feeling? His system is not more responsible for Neo-Platonic philosophy than any other philosophical system is the presupposition of the subsequent one.

The new era does not begin with Posidonius. With him the Hellenic period comes to an end. Posidonius is the last great philosopher of this epoch. His philosophy is essentially Greek, not Oriental. It is because of just this fact that his influence on later centuries is so small. To him spirit and nature are contraries; they are not two different aspects of the same thing. It is, therefore, impossible to prove that he was a monistic thinker. Furthermore, no fragment speaks of vitalism, of life as force and effect. Life, according to Posidonius, is formed by the soul, the sensitive nature. The power of sympathy is not recognized by Posidonius more than by many other philosophers. If the interpretation is restricted to the material which is certain and which alone should be used, all these theories cannot be taken for granted.[185]

To be sure, the reconstruction now given according to the

[184] In the characterization of Neo-Platonism I mostly follow Jaeger, *l. c.*, p. 2 and *passim*. The conception of *δεσμός*, characteristic for this school, is mentioned in the fragments only in a negative sense: *ἐκ πάντων δὴ τούτων φησὶ δείκνυσθαι διότι ἡ οἰκουμένη κύκλῳ περιῤῥεῖται τῷ ὠκεανῷ: "οὐ γάρ μιν δεσμὸς περιβάλλεται ἠπείροιο, ἀλλ' ἐς ἀπειρεσίην κέχυται. τό μιν οὔτι μιαίνει."* (Strabo, II, 100).

[185] But it is Reinhardt who recognized the essentially Greek character of the Posidonian philosophy. Concerning the *ζωτικὴ δύναμις* cf. Crönert, *Gnomon* VI (1930), p. 152, 1.

fragments does not solve all the problems involved. There are certain questions to which the preserved material gives no answer. The arrangement of the single theories is unclear. It may be that the tenor of some fragments is influenced by the conceptions of later writers; only a few passages are literally preserved, most of them are indirect reports. Many problems remain, simply and solely because the works of Posidonius are lost.[136]

LUDWIG EDELSTEIN.*

THE JOHNS HOPKINS UNIVERSITY.

[136] Zeller, *l. c.*, III, 1, p. 49, is right in saying: "Aber doch bleibt immer noch (bei dieser Rekonstruktion) ein doppelter Übelstand übrig. Fürs erste nämlich werden uns in der Regel nur die einzelnen Lehrsätze der Stoiker und höchstens noch einzelne Beweise dafür mitgeteilt, die innere Verknüpfung dieser Sätze dagegen und ihre ursprünglichen Motive müssen wir grossenteils durch eigene Schlüsse ergänzen. Hätten wir die Werke eines Zeno und Chrysippus in ihrem vollständigen Zusammenhang, so würden wir in dieser Beziehung von einer viel gesicherteren Grundlage ausgehen, und weit weniger auf blosse Vermutung beschränkt sein."

* I wish to express my gratitude to Mrs. C. L. Temkin for revising my English.

VIII.—Primum Graius Homo
(Lucretius I.66)

LUDWIG EDELSTEIN

THE JOHNS HOPKINS UNIVERSITY

In the opening passage of his poem Lucretius praises the courage of him who first among mortals dared to oppose religion and first desired to understand nature. This eulogy on a "man of Greece" (*Graius homo*) and his achievements (I.66ff.) is generally understood to refer to Epicurus.[1]

That such an interpretation of the verses involves great difficulties nobody will deny. As a matter of fact, Epicurus was not the first fighter against religion, nor was he the first investigator into nature; how, then, can Lucretius represent him as such? To make Lucretius' deviation from the truth acceptable, it will hardly do to take refuge in such explanations as "enthusiasm" or "poetical license"; the historical inaccuracy of the statement is too flagrant.[2] It is not convincing either to claim that Lucretius, by eulogizing Epicurus as he does, wishes to indicate that the master was self-taught. Epicurus' refusal to learn from others what he could have learned did not in fact make him the first instigator of philosophical research.[3] And even if it were true that nobody before Epicurus had repudiated religion in the form of organized state-cults, as has been said in justification of Lucretius' words, it would not follow that he was also the first explorer of the universe.[4] The fact, then,

[1] Cf. e.g. H. A. J. Munro, *T. Lucreti Cari, De Rerum Natura Libri Sex* (London, G. Bell, 1928), II, *ad* 62–79.

[2] Cf. C. Giussani, *T. Lucreti Cari, De Rerum Natura Libri Sex* (Torino, E. Loescher, 1896), II, *ad* 66: "Entusiasmo o poetica libertà non bastano a spiegare questa ingiustizia storica." Strangely enough, Munro does not discuss the question at all in his commentary (*ad locum*). Cf. however the argumentation of W. A. Merrill, *T. Lucreti Cari, De Rerum Natura Libri Sex* (New York, American Book Company, 1907), 277–78.

[3] Therefore I cannot agree with Giussani, *op. cit.* (see note 2): "Nell' affermazione di Lucrecio c'è un' eco del noto vanto di Epicuro d'essere autodidatto;" as to the notion of Epicurus' independence of his predecessors, see note 20.

[4] Cf. B. Farrington, *Science and Politics in the Ancient World* (New York, Oxford University Press, 1940), 176: "Here it is surely clear that the religion which lowered upon mortals with dreadful mien, and of which the most typical representative is Zeus with his thunderbolt, is that useful political variety we met with in Theognis,

remains that Lucretius' praise, taken as a tribute to Epicurus, is in contradiction to the historical data. I may note in passing still another difficulty: the unemphatic expression, *Graius homo*, as referring to Epicurus, is unparalleled in Lucretius. Though the poet usually speaks of his master without mentioning his name, he always calls him divine or at least emphasizes his superhuman rank.[5]

Since the accepted interpretation is admittedly unsatisfactory, is it not possible to assume that Lucretius, in composing the encomium, was thinking of someone else rather than of Epicurus? That this is really the case seems to be indicated by the fact that the language of the passage in question is reminiscent of that found in arguments concerning the origin of philosophy and science; the topics discussed by Lucretius and by those who celebrate the accomplishments of the Pre-Socratics are identical.[6] Needless to say, a praise of the Pre-Socratics, not of Epicurus, as the first to interpret nature and to fight religion, would be historically correct, but I contend that eulogizing these men would also be in agreement with Lucretius' views of the development of natural philosophy and of the historical dependence of the Epicurean system in particular. Finally, I suggest that such a praise of others beside Epicurus would be compatible with Lucretius' general attitude toward his master, with his appreciation of Epicurus' original contribution to philosophy, and with his evaluation of the essence of Epicureanism.

As to the phraseology and the topics of the *laus inventoris*, as the whole encomium (I.62–79) is called in the oldest manuscript,[7]

Pindar, Critias, and Plato. And this identification may help us to understand, what is otherwise obscure, why Lucretius should claim priority for Epicurus in his daring venture. Of critics of popular religion there had been plenty before Epicurus; but, as we have seen, no one before him had organized a movement to emancipate men from the terrors of the organized State cults." I am, of course, not concerned here with Farrington's general thesis; for his interpretation of this particular passage, see note 14.

[5] Cf. V.8: deus ille fuit, deus; III.15: divina mente; VI.5–7: virum . . . divina reperta; III.3: o Graiae gentis decus; cf. also III.1042ff. O. Regenbogen, *Lukrez, Neue Wege zur Antike*, II.Reihe, Interpretationen, Heft 1 (Leipzig, Teubner, 1932), 39, note 2, points out that Epicurus' name is omitted for stylistic reasons ("gehobener Stil"); the only exception (III.1042) is due to the fact that in this passage the names of others are also given.

[6] W. A. Heidel, "On Certain Fragments of the Pre-Socratics, Critical Notes and Elucidations," *Proceedings of the American Academy of Arts and Sciences* XLVIII (1913), 682, was the first to draw attention to this similarity by explaining Pliny *Nat. Hist.* II.8. 31 (= 12A 5, H. Diels, *Die Fragmente der Vorsokratiker*,[5] ed. W. Kranz [Berlin, Weidmann, 1934]) through Lucretius I.66ff.; see note 11.

[7] Cf. H. Diels, *T. Lucreti Cari, De Rerum Natura Libri Sex* (Berlin, Weidmann,

Lucretius ascribes to a Greek the first attempt to oppose religion and understand nature—that is, he finds the elements of philosophy in Greece, not in the Orient. To deal with the racial origins of philosophy and science as a whole is quite a common proposition; the problem is brought up at the beginning of almost every ancient history of philosophy. That Greek philosophy was derived from Oriental knowledge was a widespread opinion in Lucretius' time; Posidonius had just claimed that the atomic system was a Phoenician invention. It is, then, appropriate for Lucretius to stress the essentially Greek character of philosophical inquiry, especially here, where he addresses Memmius, the Graecophile, whose favor he is courting. When he speaks of a Greek or the Greek, whereas others are wont to speak of Thales as the first philosopher, his words are reminiscent of Theophrastus' judgment that the name of the man who was really the first philosopher is unknown.[8] Again, Lucretius emphasizes his belief that it was a mortal man who dared to raise his eyes against the heavens. Obviously he is referring to the con-

1923), I.61a. The verses themselves read thus:

> Humana ante oculos foede cum vita iaceret
> in terris oppressa gravi sub religione
> quae caput a caeli regionibus ostendebat
> horribili super aspectu mortalibus instans,
> primum Graius homo mortalis tollere contra
> est oculos ausus primusque obsistere contra,
> quem neque fama deum nec fulmina nec minitanti
> murmure compressit caelum, sed eo magis acrem
> inritat animi virtutem, effringere ut arta
> naturae primus portarum claustra cupiret.
> ergo vivida vis animi pervicit, et extra
> processit longe flammantia moenia mundi
> atque omne immensum peragravit mente animoque,
> unde refert nobis victor quid possit oriri,
> quid nequeat, finita potestas denique cuique
> quanam sit ratione atque alte terminus haerens.
> quare religio pedibus subiecta vicissim
> opteritur, nos exaequat victoria caelo.

[8] For the general problem involved cf. e.g. Diodorus I.96; Diogenes Laertius I.prooemium; cf. also A. Kleingünther, "Πρῶτος εὑρετής," *Philologus Supplement*, XXVI.1 (1934), 145ff.; 52ff. For Posidonius' opinion cf. Strabo XVI.757; Sextus Empiricus *Adv. Mathematicos* IX.363. For Memmius' attitude toward Greek literature cf. Cicero *Brutus* 247. For Theophrastus, who is known to Lucretius, either directly or indirectly, cf. E. Reitzenstein, *Theophrast bei Epikur und Lukrez* (*Orient und Antike* II [Heidelberg, C. Winter, 1924]); cf. *Doxographi Graeci*,[2] ed. H. Diels (Berlin, De Gruyter, 1929), 475, 10ff. For the indefinite expression *Graius homo*, cf. e.g. Critias 88 B25, 12; *ibid.* 41 Diels; Vergil *Georgics* I.141ff., and such expressions as Pliny VI.33. 211: scientia Graecae inventionis; Ovid *Fasti* II.38: Graecia principium moris fuit.

troversy as to whether philosophy, and more specifically the understanding of the heavenly phenomena which is the first step in the direction of a rational interpretation of nature, was discovered by men or whether it was originally revealed by a god. Like all philosophers and in contrast to the Oriental prophets, like Ovid and in contrast to Manilius, he decides in favor of the more enlightened view.[9] Moreover, Lucretius calls the deed of the Greek a daring venture. In the same way earlier and later writers are in the habit of commemorating the venture of those who, in the remote past, were the first to undertake scientific or philosophical research.[10] Finally, Lucretius glorifies the man who first broke the barriers at the gates of nature, just as Pliny says of Anaximander, whom many considered the inaugurator of philosophy, that by his discoveries he opened the doors of the cosmos.[11]

In consequence of the first daring venture of a Greek, so Lucretius continues, the human mind succeeded in traversing the universe and in gaining the knowledge of the laws of nature (I.72ff.). This simile of the flight of the mind through the universe is often used to celebrate philosophical thinking by which men grasp the truth about those objects which they are unable to apprehend with their senses.[12] Lucretius, then, in the rational explanation of the

[9] I.66–67: homo mortalis tollere contra/ . . . oculos, cf. A. Ernout, L. Robin, *Lucrèce, De rerum natura Commentaire exégétique et critique* (Paris, Collection Budé, 1925), *ad locum:* "le rapprochement *homo mortalis* est intentionnel; l'auteur de la révolte est le fils d'un homme, non d'un dieu." Cf. Ovid *Fasti* I.297ff.; Pliny II.12. 53–54; the opposite opinion is expressed by Manilius I.25ff.; cf. also the parallels in A. E. Housman, *M. Manilii Astronomicon, Liber Primus* (London, G. Richards, 1903), *ad* 30; Manilius II.105ff. deals only with the divine inspiration of later astronomers.

[10] I.67: est . . . ausus; cf. ἐτόλμησε Agathemerides (Eratosthenes) 12 A 6 Diels; cf. also 12 A 7; in general Strabo I.1; Eustathius (*Geographi Graeci Minores*, ed. C. Müller [Paris, Didot, 1861]), II.208: τολμηρὸν ἡ φιλοσοφία; cf. W. A. Heidel, "Anaximander's Book, the Earliest Known Geographical Treatise," *Proceedings of the American Academy of Arts and Sciences* LVI (1921), 247; Chalcidius, 24 A 10 Diels; Ps. Apuleius *De Mundo*, ch. 1.

[11] Cf. Heidel, *loc. cit.* (see note 6), 682. Pliny says: obliquitatem eius (*sc.* zodiaci) intellexisse, hoc est rerum fores aperuisse, Anaximander Milesius traditur primus. Cf. also Pliny XXXV.9. 61: ab hoc (*sc.* Apollodoro) artis fores apertas Zeuxis Heracleotes intravit (the passage is apparently characteristic of the literature Περὶ εὑρημάτων). For I.71: cupiret, cf. Cicero *De Natura Deorum* I.11. 26 (59 A 48 Diels): Anaxagoras . . . primus omnium rerum discriptionem . . . confici voluit.

[12] Cf. e.g. Cicero *De Natura Deorum* I.20. 54; *De Finibus* II.31. 102 (Epicurean source); *Acad. Priora* II.39. 122 (Sceptical source); Ps. Aristotle Περὶ κόσμου 391 A 8ff. (Ps. Apuleius *De Mundo* Intr., Stoic-Dogmatic source), and in general R. M. Jones, "Posidonius and the Flight of the Mind through the Universe," *Class. Phil.* XXI (1926), 97ff. The simile is often taken as a symbol of mystical or religious revelation: Heidel, *loc. cit.* (see note 6); R. Reitzenstein, *Die hellenistischen Mysterienreligionen* [3] (Leipzig,

principles of this world acknowledges a victory which raises man to heaven; he contends that the destruction of religious fear goes together with the rise of philosophy, and he glories in the triumph thus achieved. Even Pliny realizes that through philosophical speculation men have gained access to the heavens; even he insists that Pre-Socratic philosophy has resulted in liberating the human mind from the bondage in which it had been held by superstition; even he hails the genius of those who through their arguments have vanquished men and gods.[13] Last, but not least, Lucretius indignantly refers to the Greeks who sacrificed Iphigenia, since, ignorant of the natural reasons for the calm which they had encountered, they believed it necessary to propitiate the divine wrath in order to obtain favorable winds (I.84ff.). In the same way Pliny, praising the deeds of the Pre-Socratics and early astronomers, contemptuously tells of Nicias, the leader of the Athenians, who destroyed Athens' might because he did not dare to leave the harbor on account of a lunar eclipse, the true cause of which he did not comprehend and which he therefore took as a bad omen.[14] To be sure, Lucretius wishes to illustrate the sinister aspect of religion, the

Teubner, 1927), 133ff.; Regenbogen, *op. cit.* (see note 5), 42–43; J. Kroll, *Gott und Hölle, Studien der Bibliothek Warburg* (Leipzig, Teubner, 1932), XX.506ff.; Jones (*loc. cit.*, 113, note 1) at least doubts that Lucretius is conscious of any allusion to mysteries. The poet, however, who finds more certainty in philosophy than in oracles (I.736–39) has just stressed the human character of the daring deed (see note 9); the simile rather expresses the self-sufficiency of the human mind, as it does in the parallels previously given, and is used as impersonally as is the expression *Graius homo*. That the simile is original with Lucretius and was not used by Epicurus has been suggested by N. W. DeWitt, "Epicurus, Περὶ φαντασίας," *T.A.P.A.* LXX (1939), 424ff.

[13] Cf. Pliny II.11. 49: Haec ratio mortales animos subducit in caelum, ac velut inde contemplantibus trium maximarum rerum naturae partium magnitudinem detegit (cf. also Ovid *Fasti* I.297–98: Felices animae, quibus haec cognoscere primis/ Inque domus superas scandere cura fuit!; *ibid.*, 307: Sic petitur caelum . . .); cf. again Pliny II.12. 54: et misera hominum mente jam soluta, in defectibus scelera aut mortem aliquam siderum pavente; and finally Pliny II.12. 55: argumenti repertores quo deos hominesque vicistis! While Lucretius mentions that in consequence of the victory the limits and qualities of all things have become known, Cicero speaks of Anaxagoras as the one who tried first to give: omnium rerum discriptionem et modum mentis infinitae vi ac ratione (*De Nat. Deorum* I.11. 26); see note 11.

[14] Cf. Pliny II.12. 54. For the example given in Pliny and Lucretius cf. Lucian Περὶ θυσιῶν, and J. Geffken, "Menippos Περὶ θυσιῶν," Hermes LXVI (1931), 347ff., who traces the Iphigenia story to Varro (Menippos); cf. also Regenbogen, *op. cit.* (see note 5), 63, note 2. I wish at least to mention that this story does not fit in with Farrington's claim that in writing the eulogy Lucretius was thinking of Epicurus who opposed "the organized religion of the great" (*op. cit.* [see note 4], 177). Surely here it is the political leaders, the supposed inventors of religion, not the deceived masses who pay the penalty for the belief in gods.

impiety which religion itself might bring about, whereas Pliny is content with pointing out the political mischief which might result from superstition; as to their fundamental attitude, they do not differ.

To sum up all that has been said so far: the phraseology used throughout the eulogy on a Greek and his achievements, and the topics discussed, are those which one would expect to find in an encomium dedicated to the Pre-Socratics, not to Epicurus. The verses in question, it seems, give the typical representation of the beginnings of scientific and philosophical research, of the victory of the human mind over the difficulties encountered in that undertaking.[15]

Yet, here the question arises as to whether Lucretius really viewed the Pre-Socratics as the interpreters of nature and the antagonists of religion before Epicurus, whether he really considered the understanding of nature as a victory of philosophy itself. Certainly, the poet ascribes a special significance to the philosophical systems of the early period before Socrates. That he discusses the Pre-Socratic theories at all in expounding the principles of the philosophy of nature would not be astonishing; to do that is quite customary for an Epicurean.[16] Lucretius, however, goes much further than the average Epicurean: he accepts certain concepts of the Pre-Socratics, especially certain ideas of Empedocles and Anaxagoras; he praises these men much more highly than is usual for his school.[17] Most important, he directly acknowledges that

[15] The *laus inventoris*, as I have tried to interpret it, would fall under the "encomia on πράγματα" which are mentioned by Hermogenes (*Progymnasmata*, ch. 7; L. Spengel, *Rhetores Graeci* [Leipzig, Teubner, 1854], II.13, 14ff.). The detailed rules for such encomia are not preserved, yet it is said that they start out with the praise of the inventors, their bodily and intellectual qualities; cf. in general R. Volkmann, *Die Rhetorik der Griechen und Römer* (Leipzig, Teubner, 1885), 336. That Lucretius follows rhetorical patterns has been shown by Regenbogen, *op. cit.* (see note 5), 27ff. The discussion of the specific inventions of the Pre-Socratics is already found in Callimachus (11 A 3a Diels; cf. 58 B 3) and Eudemus (12 A 19 Diels).

[16] H. Usener, *Epicurea* (Leipzig, Teubner, 1887), Fr. 231ff., and especially Philodemus *De Pietate* and Cicero *De Nat. Deorum* I (*Doxographi Graeci* [see note 8], 531ff.). All authors are, of course, considered in these doxographies; though Lucretius does not write as a doxographer or a historian of philosophy, it may even be significant that he confines himself to the Pre-Socratic theories.

[17] In general cf. I.635ff.; 716ff.; 830ff. (I.705ff.; 565ff.) and G. P. Eckman, *Controversial Elements in Lucretius* (New York, Ch. B. Jackson, 1899), 19ff. Concerning Empedocles cf. Regenbogen, *op. cit.* (see note 5), 44ff. and F. Ueberweg-K. Praechter, *Die Philosophie des Altertums*[12] (Berlin, E. S. Mittler, 1926), 451 (in reference to Lucretius I.1021ff.); concerning the general attitude toward Empedocles cf. e.g. *Diogenes Oenoandensis*, ed. I. William (Leipzig, Teubner, 1907), Fr. 35; Ueberweg-Praechter, *op. cit.*, 580.

all Pre-Socratics, those whom he praises and those whom he belittles, have contributed to the discovery of truth. Though they fail in the right understanding of the principles, they are "the authors of many excellent and godlike discoveries, they have given responses from so to say their hearts' holy of holies with more sanctity and on much more unerring grounds than the Pythia who speaks out from the tripod and laurel of Phoebus" (I.734–39).[18] Lucretius, to be sure, is no less emphatic in heaping reproaches on their mistakes. He is in possession of the truth, and whoever lives in the truth, be he poet or philosopher, has little patience with those who live in error.[19] But his abruptness and harshness cannot obscure the fact that he also finds truth in the Pre-Socratic teaching. Small wonder! Epicureanism, being the exact counterpart of the Platonic and Aristotelian explanations of natural phenomena, is indeed the continuation of tendencies dominant in the earlier phases of Greek thinking. Not only is the Epicurean system as such dependent on Democritus, as everybody knew and even Epicurus admitted; there are in addition many ideas which the Epicureans had in common with Anaximander and some of his contemporaries. It suffices to refer to the assumption of innumerable worlds and to the belief in the impossibility of recognizing the adequate explanation of the phenomena even if it had been found. Ancient and modern historians of philosophy have stressed these trends which Epicurus' doctrine has in common with that of the Pre-Socratics.[20]

[18] Munro's translation, *T. Lucreti Cari, De Rerum Natura Libri Sex* translated by H. A. J. Munro (London, G. Bell, 1920). Even Heraclitus is included in this praise. Note, moreover, that the epithet divinitus (I.736) is identical with the epithets given to Epicurus (see note 5; cf. also III.371: Democriti . . . sancta sententia).

[19] Contrary to C. Bailey, "The Mind of Lucretius," *American Journal of Philology* LXI (1940), 289, who says: "Nor has Lucretius the true calm of the philosophical temperament; he does not weigh and balance different possibilities, but dogmatically asserts —and often passionately—his own point of view. This may be seen conspicuously in his treatment of previous Greek thinkers in Book I. He does not take the theories of Heraclitus, Empedocles, and Anaxagoras for what they are worth and estimate their merits. He brushes them aside and points out where they fall short of the true doctrine of atomism."

[20] Epicurus as a pupil of Nausiphanes, cf. Fr. 233, 235 Usener; his dependence on Anaxagoras (and Archelaus) Fr. 240 Usener (Anaxagoras' concept of the νοῦς and his explanation of the natural phenomena as independent of it [Plato *Phaedo* 97 C ff.] is like a foreshadowing of Epicurus' assumption of the existence of gods and that of a world which is neither created nor influenced by them). Epicurus and Anaximander, cf. Simplicius *Physics* 1121, 5; cf. also J. Burnet, *Early Greek Philosophy* [4] (London, A. & C. Black, 1930), 59; *Greek Philosophy* (London, Macmillan, 1928), I.23. Epicurus and Xenophanes, Burnet, *Greek Philosophy*, 36. Epicurus and Democritus, Burnet, *Greek Philosophy*, 194; *Early Greek Philosophy*, 341ff.

Lucretius, too, realizes the interdependence of their thought, and he is quite willing to admit it.

Even more: Lucretius says that in the books dealing with natural philosophy he is going to translate "the findings of the Greeks" into his native tongue (I.136–37); so strong is his feeling that he does not recount the findings of his master alone.[21] The poet is keenly aware of the gradual development of organic life, of culture in general, and of all the arts in particular, "for things must be brought to light one after the other and in due order in the different arts, until these have reached their highest point of development" (v.1456–57).[22] The same law must be valid in regard to the understanding of nature. Knowledge of nature was achieved through a long line of inspired thinkers, the Pre-Socratics and Epicurus, the Epicurean system being, so to say, the entelechy of Pre-Socratic ideas; the victory gained is a victory of human thought, of Greek thought. Yet, if the rational interpretation of nature had begun long before Epicurus, the fight against religion must likewise have started long before his time. The two are identical, as Lucretius himself says, and it was a commonplace that Pre-Socratic philosophy had disregarded the divine agency and that it was atheistic.[23] Lucretius could no more consider Epicurus the first fighter against religion than he could consider him the first interpreter of nature. Even the victory wrought over religion was the accomplishment of generations.

In short, to take the eulogy on a Greek and his achievements

[21] Nec me animi fallit Graiorum obscura reperta/ difficile inlustrare Latinis versibus esse. Cf. K. Büchner, *Beobachtungen über Vers und Gedankengang bei Lukrez*, *Hermes*, Einzelschriften 1 (1936), 113: "Die Klage über die Schwierigkeit passt für den Anfang, wo man noch nicht weiss, wie man ihrer Herr werden wird. Der unbestimmte Plural *Graiorum obscura reperta* 136 und das leicht abwertende *obscura* würde verwundern in einer Zeit, in der der eine Epikur wie ein Heiland von ihm verehrt wird. . . .". I agree with Büchner in so far as he stresses the incompatibility of this statement with the belief in the savior Epicurus. Yet, *obscura* is hardly meant to belittle the content of the findings of the Greeks; the philosophical theories are abstract, hard to understand (cf. also I.933), and light has been brought into the matter only by Epicurus (III.1). Moreover, the words do not necessarily prove an early date but are indicative of Lucretius' considered judgment about the philosophical achievements of Epicurus and his relation to his predecessors; cf. also II.8: doctrina sapientium.

[22] Munro's translation, *loc. cit.*; cf. A. O. Lovejoy, G. Boas, *Primitivism and Related Ideas in Antiquity* (Baltimore, The Johns Hopkins Press, 1935), 237: "If the Ms reading of the end of line 1456, accepted by Giussani, Merrill, and Rouse [and Diels], is adopted, the translation should be: '[men's] intellects saw one thing after another brought to light, etc.'"

[23] Cf. e.g. Plutarch *Nicias*, ch. 23, 1ff., and above all Plato *Laws* XII.967 C.

as a praise of the Pre-Socratics and of philosophy is not only in accordance with the facts, it is also in accordance with Lucretius' views of the development of natural philosophy. Moreover, one can hardly deny that the encomium thus understood is a fitting introduction to a poem dealing with the nature of things.[24]

So far it has been shown that Lucretius must have considered the Pre-Socratics the first to interpret nature and to oppose religion. But is it likely that he wishes to admit this belief openly, that he desires to eulogize others than his master? Lucretius is an Epicurean and the Epicureans, one might say, are wont to exaggerate the praise of their hero beyond all fairness and justice to others. I shall not insist that the followers of Epicurus were hardly ever as intransigent and enthusiastic in their love for the master as ancient and modern criticism intimates.[25] Nor shall I say that Lucretius is least of all likely to be averse to giving to other Greeks the credit which was rightly theirs, because he delights in everything Greek and admires Greek literature and learning as a whole, not only Epicurus or Epicurean books.[26] Certainly for Lucretius too, Epicurus is the greatest philosopher, the "glory of the Greek race" (III.3); "he who surpassed in intellect the race of man and quenched the light of all, as the ethereal sun arisen quenches the stars" (III.1043–44).[27] Yet this belief does not prevent him from attaining an objective evaluation of Epicurus' original contribution to philosophy.

In three places Lucretius expressly states his opinion of Epicurus' historical rôle in the development of philosophical thought. He was the first, the poet says, who was able "amid such thick darkness to raise on high so bright a beacon and shed a light on the true interests

[24] As to the relation of the *laus inventoris* to the preceding and to the following verses, see note 32.

[25] Cf. the ironical report in Cleomedes, *De Motu circulari Corporum caelestium*, ed. H. Ziegler (Leipzig, Teubner, 1891) about Epicurus: ὁ μόνος καὶ πρῶτος ἀνθρώπων τὴν ἀλήθειαν ἐξευρών (162, 17–18); καὶ τὴν πρώτην ἐν αὐτοῖς (*sc.* τοῖς φιλοσόφοις) τάξιν ἔχων (166, 15–16). Obviously it is the founder of the school who alone and first has shown the truth (see note 33). The enthusiasm for the master as expressed by the Epicureans is not an isolated phenomenon, cf. e.g. Epictetus I.4. 29ff.; I.17. 16.

[26] Cf. W. Y. Sellar, *The Roman Poets of the Republic*[3] (Oxford, Clarendon Press, 1889), especially 302ff., with whom I agree against the more recent tendency to stress Lucretius' relation to Epicurus and to think less of Lucretius' familiarity with Greek literature as a whole (most strongly Regenbogen, *op. cit.* [see note 5], 15: "Sein Griechenerlebnis ist ein Epikurerlebnis;" in spite of his belief that Lucretius' enthusiasm for Epicurus is gradually developing, cf. *ibid.* 79).

[27] Munro's translation, *loc. cit.*

of life" (III.1–2); he was the first who "found out that plan of life which is now termed wisdom, and who by trained skill rescued life from such great billows and such thick darkness and moored it in so perfect a calm and in so brilliant a light" (V.9–12); he was the first who "bestowed sweet solaces of existence" (VI.4–6).[28] In all these instances, then, Lucretius puts the emphasis on the practical side of Epicurus' teaching, on what he did to make life bright, sweet, and happy. It is he who "cleansed men's breasts with truth-telling precepts and fixed a limit to lust and fear and explained what was the chief good which we all strive to reach, and pointed out the road along which by a short cross-track we might arrive at it in a straightforward course" (VI.24–28).[29] This happiness was the one thing which men in Epicurus' time still lacked after everything else had been provided for as far as possible (VI.9ff.). In other words, for Lucretius no less than for any other Epicurean the historical merit of Epicurus consists in his showing the way to true happiness.[30] That it is which the master was the first to accomplish; that constitutes his incomparable deed, his own discovery; that, and that alone. Epicurus is the instigator of practical wisdom, not of theoretical speculation. Wherever the Epicurean Lucretius evaluates the historical achievement of the founder of the school in clear and unequivocal words, he proves himself of unbiased objectivity in his judgment; he never claims more for his master than can be claimed in conformity with the facts.

What interest, then, could the poet possibly have in ascribing to Epicurus at one place what was not his achievement but that of others? One might object: this one place is the opening passage of the whole poem; here Epicurus, and nobody else, must receive the tribute of his follower; the poet has to be partial on this particular occasion. Such an objection can be readily disposed of. All agree that the poem is not complete; moreover it has been shown that eulogies on Epicurus himself were not provided for in the original plan and, in the various prooemia, were added only later.[31] I dare not decide whether Lucretius had no desire to give an encomium

[28] Munro's translation, *loc. cit.*

[29] Munro's translation, *loc. cit.*

[30] Cf. Sextus Empiricus *Adv. Mathematicos* XI.169 (Usener Fr. 219): Ἐπίκουρος μὲν ἔλεγε τὴν φιλοσοφίαν ἐνέργειαν εἶναι λόγοις καὶ διαλογισμοῖς τὸν εὐδαίμονα βίον περιποιοῦσαν.

[31] Cf. Regenbogen, *op. cit.* (see note 5), 79: "Der Typus des Epikurelogiums war im Vordringen."

of the master at the beginning of his poem, or whether he intended to write one when putting the finishing touch to his work. However that may be, the argument in question cannot invalidate the objective reasons against the claim that the praise of a man of Greece, as it stands, is meant to refer to Epicurus.[32]

A second objection carries more weight. Lucretius, it seems, feels primarily indebted to Epicurus for liberation from religious fears. How, then, can one believe that he would praise the Pre-Socratics and philosophy in general for the victory over religion? Must not Lucretius be partial in his appreciation of Epicurus' accomplishment in this particular regard because he sees in the destruction of religious fears the greatest gift bestowed upon him by the Epicurean doctrine?[33] In the verses in question, however, Lucretius does not speak of his own philosophical experience; he rather speaks of a certain historical situation, of human life at the time when religion was all-powerful, and of the first attempt to break its might. The victory which he describes, be it a victory of the Pre-Socratics and of Epicurus, or of Epicurus alone, is a victory of the past; through it mankind has been liberated long ago. Yet, Lucretius owes the knowledge of this victory, like that of all truth, to Epicurus; he therefore, like the adherent of any philosophical doctrine, owes his salvation to the master alone. That he rightly praises others for what they have achieved would not detract in any way from his personal gratitude to Epicurus.[34]

[32] Concerning the relation of the *laus inventoris* to the previous and to the following verses only so much can be said here: Lucretius is afraid that his book, being so difficult to understand, will be treated with contempt (I.52–53). The eulogy, stressing the greatness of the consequences of natural philosophy, is apparently meant to refute such an attitude of the reader. In the same way Lucretius also later on answers possible objections of Memmius or of the reader (I.80–82; 102–06). Thus the whole complex of verses (I.50–126) seems to be a unity. In accordance with the analysis given above it must be stressed against Büchner's stylistic considerations intended to prove a later date of the verses (*op. cit.* [see note 21], 103ff.) that the Iphigenia example belongs to the eulogy; for the date of the verses cf. also Regenbogen, *op. cit.* (see note 5), 79.

[33] Cf. Regenbogen, *op. cit.* (see note 5), 57, who summarizes the opinions of scholars on this subject; cf. also *ibid.* 55: "Ihm (*sc.* Lucretius in contrast to Epicurus) ist die religio die unheilvolle Macht schlechthin." Cf. also Bailey, *loc. cit.* (see note 19), 290–91: "The keynote of the whole poem is the passionate desire to convince the reader of the truth of Epicureanism as the salvation from the superstitions of religion."

[34] This distinction between personal indebtedness and objective evaluation explains why Lucretius can speak about Epicurus and his philosophy as he does in such passages as III.14ff. There is no reason for the assumption that verses 62ff. even re-echo Lucretius' own experience (contrary to Regenbogen, *op. cit.* [see note 5], 56: "Das ist das Bild, das des Dichters Phantasie geschaut hat—das ist der Druck, unter dem er selbst geächzt hat"; see also note 41).

Moreover, one should not overemphasize the importance of religion for Lucretius' thinking and consequently not overestimate the importance which the liberation from religious fears through Epicureanism has for the poet's mind. This is especially true with regard to those religious tenets which are dealt with in the encomium, namely the belief that God is the fabricator of the universe, that the heavenly phenomena are regulated by him.[35] To be sure, such a conviction is still a force which influences men, and it will continue to influence them, as the poet admits: "what wounds for us, what tears for our children's children" (v.1196–97).[36] Yet, this religious fear, powerful as it still is, no longer *dominates* the human soul: "For when we turn our gaze on the heavenly quarters of the great upper world and ether fast above the glittering stars, and direct our thoughts to the courses of the sun and moon, then in our heart, where it slept oppressed by the other evils, that fear too awakens again and raises its head, the fear that we may haply find the power of the gods to be unlimited, able to wheel the bright stars in their varied motion" (v.1204–10).[37] No longer, then, is human life oppressed by religion as it was in the beginning when it "to view lay foully prostrate upon earth crushed down under the weight of religion, who shewed her head from the quarters of heaven with hideous aspect lowering upon mortals" (I.62–65).[38] The human heart now is oppressed instead by human passions, and fear of the gods is but a re-awakening of old beliefs which are evoked only by certain events, by the sight of the moving stars, by

[35] According to Lucretius natural philosophy must fight against the belief in the divinity of the heavenly movements and the belief in divine punishment after death, the one represented by wrong concepts concerning the gods and their power, the other represented by false myths told by priests (cf. e.g. I.62ff.; 102ff.; 127ff.). This is the true Epicurean distinction, cf. Epicurus *Sententiae selectae*, 11ff. (Usener, *op. cit.* [see note 16], 73ff.).

[36] Munro's translation, *loc. cit.*

[37] Munro's translation, *loc. cit.*, except for the words: "in our heart—other evils" (lines 1207–08) which Munro translates: "into our breasts, burdened with other ills, that fear as well begins to exalt its re-awakened head." In my interpretation of the lines in question I follow F. Bockemüller, *T. Lucreti Cari, De Rerum Natura Libri Sex* (Stade, gedruckt als Handschrift, 1873), I, *ad locum;* cf. also Diels' translation, *op. cit.* (see note 7), II. The contrast to prooemium I seems to me to decide in favor of Bockemüller's opinion, yet the argument would not be altered even if Munro's interpretation (cf. also Giussani, *op. cit.* [see note 2], IV, *ad* 1205ff.) is accepted. In the same way Lucretius stresses the increase in religious fears on account of circumstances in III.54. In regard to the attitude as such which must be distinguished from the relapse into old beliefs possible even for those who have learned the truth (v.82ff.; VI.56ff.) cf. Horace, *Ode* I.34.

[38] Munro's translation, *loc. cit.*

terrifying thunderstorms, or earthquakes (v.1218ff.; 1236ff.).[39] Men no longer live in the belief in God as the arbitrary ruler of the world; they live in the sins of their hearts, as the poet sees it; what they most need, therefore, now just as in Epicurus' time, is not so much liberation from religious fears as liberation from their desires, knowledge of the right way of living, and this right living itself; what they are striving for is true joy and happiness.[40] The fight against religious fears, important and necessary as it is, does not constitute the whole content of Epicurean teaching. It is only one aspect of the doctrine, and not even the most momentous one, though it is, of course, especially emphasized in a book dealing with the nature of things; after all, for Epicurus natural philosophy had its value mainly as a weapon against false beliefs concerning the might of the gods. Yet, ethics was the primary concern of Epicurus and of the Epicureans. There is no indication that in this respect Lucretius felt any different from the other members of the school or from his own contemporaries.[41]

If, then, for Lucretius the quintessence of Epicureanism lies not in its negative but in its positive teaching, he can hardly have had any hesitation in acknowledging even in his very heart what is true: that Epicurus in his fight against religion and in his interpretation of nature did no more than carry on, and carry to the winning post, the torch which had been handed down to him by his predecessors. I do not think that one can hold to the belief that Lucretius ever intended to ascribe to the master what was not rightly his and what not even Epicurus claimed for himself.

[39] Fear of death, on the other hand, is pictured as an emotion troubling "the life of man from its inmost depths and overspreading all things with the blackness of death, allowing no pleasure to be pure and unalloyed" (III.38–40; Munro's translation, *loc. cit.*). More emphasis, then, is put on this aspect of religious fears (see note 35) than on the other (cf. also I.127–130), again, as it seems, in agreement with Epicurus, cf. *Epistula tertia* 125 (Usener, *op. cit.* [see note 16], 61).

[40] I think that Lucretius' testimony as to the religious attitude of his time (v.1204–10) is more important than any conclusions that can be drawn from other sources; concerning the divergent views of scholars in regard to this problem cf. Regenbogen, *op. cit.* (see note 5), 8–9.

[41] Therefore I cannot agree with such statements as that of Regenbogen, *op. cit.* (see note 5), 58: "Wohl kann man sagen, dass diese Zeit vorüber war, als Lukrez schrieb—aber zum ersten, wie in manchem anderen auch, so besonders in seiner Vorstellung von religio und ihrer Macht ist Lukrez ein Anachronismus in seiner Zeit." For Lucretius and religion in general cf. G. D. Hadzsits, *Lucretius and his Influence* (New York, Longmans, Green & Co., 1935), 103ff. The truly Epicurean attitude of Lucretius is emphasized not only by the prayer to Venus but also by such utterances as II.172: dux vitae dia voluptas; cf. also II.16ff.

the year is 346/5. The spacing of the type is of course not intended to imitate the original at all closely, but the occasional gross irregularities, as in IG II² 2797 and 2798, diverge unnecessarily much from the originals. These instances are exceptional; in the main the setting of the type, the work mostly of one veteran craftsman, is unimpeachable, and the student will not be misled who remembers that in monumental work especially the masons spaced their letters regularly.

That some 101 inscriptions were first studied, and are published for the first time in this fascicule, by the editor himself, will not surprise those who have known him. Johannes Kirchner received his doctorate in 1883, finished the *Prosopographia Attica* in 1903, and has now edited some 5300 epigraphical texts in IG II², not to mention many in Ditt., *Syll.*³; in 1935 appeared his valuable *Imagines Inscriptionum Atticarum*. In August 1935 he arrived in Athens to continue work on the last fascicule of texts in IG II² (the sepulchral monuments), and by June 1936 he had checked over all the *ca.* 12,800 inscriptions in the Epigraphical Museum, had examined practically all the other known grave monuments in Athens, including those in the Agora Excavations, and had taken part in an exploration of Attica which turned up about 100 more unpublished inscriptions (*Hermes*, LXX [1935], pp. 461 ff.; *Ath. Mitt.*, forthcoming). To congratulate such a scholar is superfluous. One thinks rather of what the example offered by his soundness, keenness, and vigor means today for classical studies of every sort, wherever pursued.

STERLING DOW.

HARVARD UNIVERSITY.

PIERRE BOYANCÉ. Études sur le Songe de Scipion (Bibliothèque des Universités du Midi, Fascicule XX). Paris, E. de Boccard, 1936. Pp. 192.

In the first part of his book Boyancé gives the text of the *Somnium Scipionis*—according to Ziegler's edition (p. 12)—and its translation into very clear and adequate French. Then he discusses the most important philosophical ideas of Scipio's speech: his conception of the world (ch. II), of the soul and immortality (ch. III), of glory and the great year (ch. IV). Boyancé prefers this method of writing several essays to that of writing a commentary (p. 9) because of the main purposes which he has in mind: to show that Posidonius is not the philosopher whom Cicero follows and to determine the theories which really moulded his thinking. For Boyancé considers the myth of the *Somnium* to be original (ch. I) only in the sense that he ascribes originality to Cicero as a writer, not as a thinker (p. 9).

The Posidonian influence on the *Somnium* has already been disproved by Reinhardt, Heinemann and Harder, as Boyancé is well aware (p. 38). Since his book appeared, Bignone too has rejected such an assumption (*L'Aristotele perduto* I, 1936, pp. 240 ff.). Yet the older theories have a strong hold on the interpreters; it is, therefore, not improper to deal once more with them. Besides, Boyancé's discussion of the arguments brought forward for and against the thesis often contributes, beyond the immediate problem, to the understanding of the philosophical doctrines involved. What he says about the term αὐγή and its meaning in the various Stoic systems (pp. 65 ff.) is especially interesting and valuable. In this argumentation there are but few mistakes. His claim, for instance, that Cicero did not admire Posidonius as a stylist (p. 45) can hardly be accepted. After all, Cicero sent one of his writings to Posidonius for correction (ut ornatius de iisdem rebus scriberet [*ad Atticum,* II, 1, 2]).

On the other hand, Boyancé is right, I believe, in establishing the importance of Cleanthes for the solar-theology (pp. 78 ff.; 174); therein he agrees with R. M. Jones. But the possibility of the influence of Heraclides Ponticus is very uncertain (pp. 74, 137). The fact that friends of Cicero were interested in problems which are treated by Cicero too (pp. 168 ff.) does not prove anything about the historical dependence of the statements made by Cicero. Nor is it a convincing procedure to reconcile, as does Boyancé, Cumont's theory that the deification of Hellenistic kings is relevant for Cicero's belief in the immortality of statesmen with Harder's contention that these are different things (pp. 141 ff.). Finally, since the sentiments alone of the *Somnium* are considered to be Roman, whereas the ideas as a whole are declared to be Greek, it is difficult to understand how the idea of the immortality of the statesman should be a Roman conception (p. 173).

I hesitate the more to enter into any argument about these points because a decision must necessarily be based on considerations outside of the *Somnium.* The mere interpretation of the text, however, is not yet far enough advanced, and it is astonishing that Boyancé did not go into greater detail with this problem. Where he deals with the composition at all, he accepts in general Harder's analysis of the *Somnium* (R. Harder, "Über Ciceros Somnium Scipionis," *Schriften der Königsberger Gelehrten Gesellschaft,* VI [1929], Heft 3). Although he is so bitterly and ironically opposed to the logic of "Quellenforschung"—and this with good reason—he himself is primarily, even exclusively, interested in discovering the sources. But many questions concerning the understanding of the text are still unsolved, the answers to which must affect the discussion of the more general problems.

To give an example, I take the main theme of the *Somnium*, the rejection of human glory. Boyancé is satisfied with characterizing this attitude as being equally far from the confidence in human glory, expressed in *De officiis*, as from the disillusion regarding human glory, shown in *De finibus* (pp. 158-9). Harder says that the rejection of human glory is the philosophy of a man whose expectation for just recognition of his merits has not been fulfilled in this world; he therefore seeks a compensation in the life to come (p. 149). But Scipio, having urged the statesman to despise glory among men and having described how limited in space and time this glory is bound to be, concludes therefrom: quocirca si reditum in hunc locum desperaveris, in quo omnia sunt magnis et praestantibus viris, quanti tandem est ista hominum gloria . . . (VI, 25). Scipio then declares that the acquisition of human glory cannot counterbalance the loss of immortality. In the *Somnium* immortality is promised only to the just and pious statesman—ea vita via est in caelum (VI, 16). He who abandons these principles can no longer hope (desperaveris) to return to the heavenly abode, although he may thus acquire the recognition of his compatriots. But the tenuousness of what he then would gain cannot be compared with the stability of what he is in danger of losing. In such a case he must make his choice: he should despise human glory; he should look up to the heavens (igitur alte spectare [VI, 25]) and not devote himself to the earth. For the aim of the statesman is not the reward of men but the eternal requital bestowed on him by God (illa divina virtus non statuas plumbo inhaerentes nec triumphos arescentibus laureis, sed stabiliora quaedam et viridiora praemiorum genera *desiderat*, [VI, 8]). If it is demanded of him, he cannot hesitate to give up the one for the other. Cicero himself alluding to the *De republica* writes to Atticus: quod si ista nobis cogitatio de triumpho iniecta non esset, quam tu quoque approbas, ne tu haud multum requireres illum virum qui in VI. libro informatus est. Quid enim tibi faciam qui illos libros devorasti? Quin nunc ipsum non dubitabo rem tantam abiicere, si id erit rectius. Utrumque vero simul agi non potest, et de triumpho ambitiose et de re publica libere (*ad Atticum*, VII, 3, 2). This is no attitude of indifference concerning human glory; it is not the renunciation of what the world does not grant and which is therefore sought after in another world. Rather is it the repudiation of a good that one can get but because of a moral standard does not feel allowed to accept. It is, therefore, impossible to determine the source of Cicero's remark as a Hellenistic declamation against glory, comparable to the reflections of Marcus Aurelius (Harder, pp. 131, n. 4; 133). Nor is it necessary to suppose that the Romans, in general, had not the same esteem for glory as the Greeks (Boyancé, p. 160).

Cicero's demand does not mean that the statesman should never indulge in human glory. If it is acquired in a justifiable way, he may rejoice in it. Scipio himself says: principem civitatis gloria esse alendum (V, 9), and he declares that the state would remain safe as long as homage is paid to the princeps (*ibid.*). Boyancé tries in vain to reconcile those statements, not taken into account by Harder, with his interpretation of the myth; they are irreconcilable. At no period of his life did Cicero renounce glory as such. In *De finibus* (III, 57) it is Cato who is speaking, not Cicero as Boyancé wrongly presumes (p. 156). Scipio knows that the philosopher alone is able earnestly to treat the vanity of all glory (I, 26-29). The man of active life must believe in the value of human endeavor.

Scipio admires the philosopher on account of his superior attitude toward glory; he admires the philosophical discussions as such (I, 29). This is symbolic for the philosophy of the *Somnium*. There is no primacy of the active life over the theoretical one, as is generally assumed (Boyancé, pp. 139 ff.; Harder, p. 119). It is true that the active life is stressed much more than is usually done in the Hellenistic systems; but the philosopher and the statesman both have the same claim to immortality as is expressly stated in the *Somnium* (VI, 18). This admission is not a "Bruch" in the composition (Harder, p. 120), nor a contamination of two sources; for that nothing on earth is nearer to God than statesmanship (I, 12; cf. VI, 13) is said in defiance of those who assert that the life of the philosopher alone leads to the salvation of man. In the introduction to the whole treatise Cicero defends and establishes the right of political activity against the current philosophical doctrines of his time; he must do so, he says, because otherwise the purpose of his book would be meaningless. But nothing indicates that he goes so far as to dethrone the theoretical virtues or to claim that the value of philosophy is less than that of political activity. He coördinates the statesman and the philosopher, and this was bold enough an adventure in those days. It is, however, not the theory of Dicaearchus, which Cicero certainly knew (*ad Atticum*, II, 16, 3; VII, 3, 1). It is the philosophy of the Academy or, at least, the philosophy of Antiochus (ut quisque optime natus institutusque est, esse omnino nolit in vita, si gerendis negotiis orbatus possit paratissimis vesci voluptatibus. Nam aut privatim aliquid gerere malunt aut, qui altiore animo sunt, capessunt rem publicam honoribus imperiisque adipiscendis, aut totos se ad studia doctrinae conferunt [*De finibus*, V, 57]).

Boyancé speaks of a dogmatic Platonic belief in immortality (p. 176) which Cicero embraces in the *Somnium*. But the myth is a dream, which must not be understood only psychologically (pp. 50 f.). Scipio is the friend of Panaetius who does not recognize the truth of dreams; the contents therefore remain mere conjecture (cf. I, 15). Cicero explicitly emphasizes that all these things are only dreamed by Scipio; one is never allowed to forget this fact (contrary to Harder's opinion, p. 148). At the moment in which he relates his dream Scipio seems rather to dream than to narrate what he has dreamt (St! quaeso, inquit, ne me e somno excitetis [VI, 12]). Human glory is rejected not because of a dogmatic belief but, so to speak, on account of a postulate or a probability alone.

Cicero, in writing his books on the state, proves himself first of all to be a sincere follower of the Academy and to be consistent in his views on the principles of political activity. This fact—and many others which I cannot mention here but which should and could be ferreted out by a careful interpretation of the text—have to be taken into consideration before it will be possible to give a convincing analysis of the sources. Until this has been done, I do not think it permissible to pass judgment, as Boyancé does, on the originality of Cicero either as a writer or as a thinker.

LUDWIG EDELSTEIN.

INSTITUTE OF THE HISTORY OF MEDICINE,
THE JOHNS HOPKINS UNIVERSITY.

GERDA BUSCH. Untersuchungen zum Wesen der τύχη in den Tragödien des Euripides. Heidelberg, Winter, 1937. Pp. 75.

Not the oldest, but the most long-lived ancient conception of fate, τύχη is the power that one associates particularly with Greek tragedy, and above all with Euripides. One's off-hand impression would doubtless be that the action of his plays, like the language, is full of τύχη. But that the references to chance on the part of the characters are out of all proportion to the actual *rôle* of chance in the plays is the somewhat surprising conclusion of this dissertation.

Dr. Busch begins by analyzing the meaning of the word τύχη in its various contexts, as it is qualified by some ninety different epithets, favorable or unfavorable (the latter being far the more numerous), or as it stands in relation to other words. Next she deals with the moral implications of the word: the inscrutability, and the moral dangers, of luck; its opposition to virtue; the possibility of man's collaborating with τύχη. There follows a discussion of the relation between τύχη and other powers (χρεών,

CICERO: "DE NATURA DEORUM", II.

Man hat immer wieder gefragt, wem Cicero bei der Darstellung der stoischen Philosophie im zweiten Buch der Schrift über die Natur der Götter folgt. Ist es Poseidonios oder Panaitios oder wer sonst? Setzt Cicero die Rede, die er den Stoiker Balbus halten lässt, aus mehreren Vorlagen zusammen? Die widerspruchsvolle Darstellung, die schlechte Gedankenfügung gab Anlass, wenigstens einzelne Abschnitte als Zusätze herauszulösen, wenn man schon im grossen und ganzen eine Vorlage annahm.

In der Tat ist der Aufbau der Rede des Balbus schlecht und widerspruchsvoll. Aber komponiert Cicero sie so schlecht, weil er die verschiedenen Materialien nicht einheitlich verbinden kann, so dass man auf verschiedene Vorlagen schliessen darf? Folgt er etwa einer einheitlichen, aber schlecht komponierten Vorlage? Oder sind Aufbau und Widersprüche aus dem Zusammenhang des Dialoges zu erklären, so dass sie nicht durch die Eigenart der Vorlagen sondern durch eine bestimmte Absicht Ciceros bedingt sind und darum keine Rückschlüsse auf sein Material erlauben?

Diese Fragen sind noch kaum gestellt worden. Um sie zu beantworten und damit die namentliche Bestimmung der Vorlage zu ermöglichen, analysiere ich den Aufbau der Rede für sich allein, ohne jeden Zusammenhang mit den Hypothesen über Poseidonios oder Panaitios.[1] Erst dann wird man, wieder

---

[1] O. Regenbogen hat in einer Uebung über de natura deorum II (Heidelberg, 1928-29) aus anderen Gründen diese Art des Vorgehens als allein möglich bezeichnet. Von ihm übernehme ich die Methode, die Ergebnisse der Untersuchung sind von den damals gefundenen unabhängig.

in einer Untersuchung für sich, die Inhalte prüfen und nach ihrem Zusammenhang und ihrer Herkunft fragen können.[1]

Balbus gliedert die Rede, in der er die stoische Lehre über die Natur der Götter darlegen will, nach einer allgemeinen stoischen Einteilung in vier Teile : den Nachweis der Existenz Gottes, die Untersuchung über die Natur der Götter, die Erörterung der Weltregierung durch Gott, die Darlegung der göttlichen Fürsorge für die Menschen (§ 3, 260, 22 - 261, 3).[2] Er will aber jetzt nur die beiden ersten Teile behandeln ; den dritten und vierten, deren Thema zu umfangreich ist, will er auf eine andere Zeit verschieben (261, 3-5). Cotta, der Akademiker, der an diesem Gespräch teilnimmt, bittet Balbus, über alle Fragen zu sprechen (261, 6-7).

Balbus beginnt den Beweis der Existenz Gottes mit den Worten : « Eigentlich scheint der erste Teil meines Themas gar keiner Erörterung zu bedürfen » (§ 4, 261, 8).[3] Denn was ist klarer und gewisser, wenn man den Himmel sieht, als die Existenz einer göttlichen Macht (261, 9-17) ? Darum gab es von Anfang an auch nur eine Meinung darüber, die mit der Zeit immer fester und sicherer wurde, im Gegensatz zu den lächerlichen Fabeln, die die Zeit widerlegt (§ 5, 261, 18 - 262, 5). Bei allen Völkern wurde die Verehrung der Götter immer grösser, mit Recht. Theophanien (§ 6, 262, 8), Weissagungen und Vorahnungen (263, 3) — von denen einzelne Beispiele

---

[1] Von Gesamtuntersuchungen über Cicero und die stoische Philosophie nenne ich R. Hirzel, Untersuchungen zu Ciceros philos. Schriften, Leipz. 1877 (zitiert : Hirzel a. O.) ; K. Reinhardt, Poseidonios, Mü. 1921 (zitiert : Rhdt. I) und Kosmos und Sympathie, Mü. 1926 (zitiert : Rhdt. II) ; I. Heinemann, Poseidonios'metaphysische Schriften II, Bresl. 1928 (zitiert : Hnm. II) ; Untersuchungen zu einzelnen Problemen werden an den in Frage kommenden Stellen genannt werden.

[2] Die Zitate beziehen sich auf Cicero, ed. O. Plasberg, fasc. II, Teubn. 1911 ; die Hinzufügung der Paragraphen soll das Auffinden der Stellen auch in anderen Ausgaben ermöglichen. In einem fortlaufenden Zitat aus einem Paragraphen steht dieser selbst nur an der ersten Stelle.

[3] « Ne egere quidem videtur oratione prima pars ».

aus der römischen Geschichte angeführt werden — beweisen die Existenz Gottes (§ 6-12, 262, 6 - 266, 17). «Daher steht unter allen Menschen aller Völker das Ergebnis fest; allen Menschen ist nämlich eingeboren und in ihr Herz gleichsam eingegraben, dass es Götter gibt. Welcher Art sie sind, ist strittig; dass sie sind, leugnet niemand» (§ 13, 266, 18-20).[1]

Dass aber alle Menschen einen Begriff von Gott haben, führt Kleanthes auf vier Gründe zurück (§ 13, 266, 20 - 267, 1): auf die Weissagungen (267, 2-3), auf die nützlichen Wirkungen des Klimas, den Reichtum der Erde und die Menge des Nützlichen überhaupt (267, 3-5), dann auf die Naturerscheinungen und Wunderzeichen, die die Menschen erschrecken (§ 14, 267, 5 - 15), schliesslich auf die wunderbare Bewegung und Schönheit der Sterne (§ 15, 267, 15 - 268, 6). Was durch Kleanthes erklärt werden soll, wurde am Anfang gesagt: die Entstehung des menschlichen Gottesbegriffes. Nach der dritten Begründung wird das auch ausdrücklich als Folgerung noch einmal abgeleitet: durch die Wunderzeichen erschreckt, ahnten die Menschen, dass es eine himmlische, göttliche Macht gibt (267, 14-16). So kamen sie also zum Begriff Gottes. Nach der vierten Begründung aber, am Schluss des Ganzen, wird wiederum das Ergebnis festgestellt, doch anders gefasst: der Augenschein lehrt, dass die Konstanz der himmlischen Bewegungen nicht zufällig sein kann (267, 18-19). Wie man beim Besuch eines Hauses, eines Gymnasiums, des Forums, beim Anblick der Ordnung aller Dinge, der Disziplin nicht meinen wird, das sei ohne Ursache so, sondern einsieht, es müsse jemand da sein, der befiehlt und dem gehorcht wird, so muss man noch viel mehr annehmen, dass die wunderbare Ordnung des Weltalls von einem verständigen Geist geleitet wird (267, 19 - 268, 6). Es werden also bestimmte Erscheinungen nicht als zufällig sondern als Wirkung eines Geistes begriffen, es wird die Wirkung eines Geistes in der Welt behauptet und das Verhältnis dieses Geistes zu den Dingen bestimmt. Es wird also nicht gefolgert,

1 «Itaque inter omnis omnium gentium summa constat; omnibus enim innatum est et in animo quasi insculptum esse deos, quales sint, varium est, esse nemo negat».

wie nach Kleanthes, auf den diese Schlüsse doch zurückgeführt werden, gefolgert werden müsste, dass darum alle Menschen einen Begriff von Gott haben. Aber das lässt sich auch gar nicht schliessen. Denn aus den Wunderzeichen folgt zwar der menschliche Begriff von Gott. Aus der Ordnung der Dinge aber folgt nur die Tatsache einer ordnenden Kraft. Auch von den beiden ersten Argumenten, die aus Kleanthes entlehnt werden und aus denen eine Folgerung nicht ausdrücklich gezogen wird, führt wohl die Weissagung auf den Begriff Gottes, doch die Beobachtung des Nutzens nur darauf, dass die Welt nicht zufällig sondern die Schöpfung einer rationalen Kraft ist.[1] Es zeigt sich also eine merkwürdige Zwiespältigkeit der Argumentation und zugleich eine Veränderung des Themas, zu dessen Erörterung die Schlüsse des Kleanthes am Anfang eingeführt wurden. Ohne darauf hinzuweisen, redet Balbus nicht allein von der Entstehung des Gottesbegriffes, sondern auch von der Wirkung einer rationalen Kraft in der Welt.

Dieses Problem ist auch der Gegenstand der folgenden Ausführungen. Denn Chrysipp sagte, wie Balbus fortfährt: « Wenn es etwas in der Welt gibt, das die Fähigkeit und Kraft des Menschen übersteigt, so muss, was es bewirkt, mehr sein als der Mensch. Die ewige Ordnung des Himmels und Alles, was ewig ist, kann nicht durch einen Menschen bewirkt werden. Es ist also das, wodurch es geschaffen wird, mehr als der Mensch. Und wie sollte man diese höhere Kraft nicht Gott nennen? Denn wenn es nicht Gott ist, was kann in der Natur der Welt mehr sein als der Mensch? Er allein besitzt ja Ver-

---

[1] Diese Erklärung der Bedeutung der einzelnen Argumente wird sich später noch auf einem anderen Wege bestätigen (vgl. S. 152, 1). Fälschlich glaubt Hnm. (II 172, 2; 174) an eine inhaltlich gleiche, fortlaufende Gedankenreihe, weshalb er den Sinn der Sätze und ihr Verhältnis zu anderen Ausführungen unerklärlich findet. Hirzel (a. O. 204,1) unterscheidet einen verschiedenen Sinn in der Art, dass in den einen Ausführungen die Entstehung des Götterglaubens, in den anderen die Rechtfertigung enthalten sei, eine Ungenauigkeit, die er zuerst Cicero, dann der stoischen Lehre zuschreibt. Ueber die Erklärung dieser merkwürdigen Vermischung zu einander nicht passender Gedanken vgl. S. 164.

stand, das Höchste von Allem. Ein Mensch aber, der nichts in der Welt für mehr als sich selbst hält, ist wahnsinnig. Es gibt also etwas Besseres (in der Welt), es gibt also Gott (in ihr). Oder könnte man glauben, dass ein Haus für die Mäuse gebaut sei, weil man den Herren des Hauses nicht sieht? So ist die Welt die Wohnung der Götter, die in ihr wirken und die die Gestirne bewegen » (§ 16, 268, 7 - § 17, 269, 2).[1] Es ist also das, was die menschliche Kraft zu bewirken unfähig ist, Wirkung einer göttlichen Kraft. Vorher war die Ordnung des Himmels, seine Schönheit, als Wirkung eines Geistes in der Natur begriffen worden. Jetzt wird sie als Wirkung des göttlichen Geistes verstanden. Das Dasein Gottes ist dabei vorausgesetzt, nur von seiner Wirkung in der Welt ist die Rede.

Die anschliessenden Sätze zeigen dann die Vollkommenheit der Welt. Alle höheren Regionen sind, wie es heisst, besser als die niederen. Die Erde ist die tiefste Region, und doch zeigt die Geschicklichkeit des Menschen auf der Erde schon Sinn und Verstand. Es muss also einen höheren, göttlichen Sinn und Geist geben, denn woher sollte sonst der menschliche Geist kommen? Die Welt (mundus), aus der Alles kommt, was der Mensch hat, muss auch dieses Beste, Verstand, haben, da sie doch selbst das Beste ist. Es ist also Verstand, göttlicher

[1] Diese Ausführungen richten sich gegen die epikureische Lehre von den jenseits der Welt und ohne Einwirkung auf sie lebenden Göttern. Nach stoischer Ansicht ist eben diese Welt das Haus Gottes, in dem er lebt und wirkt; darum auch vorher der Vergleich mit einem Haus. Dass die Argumentation des Chrysipp nicht etwa das Dasein Gottes sondern seine Wirkung beweist, wird sich wieder später auf anderem Wege bestätigen (vgl. S. 151). Hirzel (a. O. 205) zerlegt diese Sätze in zwei Beweise. Einmal sei gezeigt, dass alle Ordnung nicht ohne vernünftige Ursache sei, dann dass diese Welt unmöglich nur der Menschen wegen da sein könne. Aber diese Beweise müssen zusammenhängen, weil nach der Gleichsetzung der wirkenden Kraft mit Gott (268, 14), die zuerst unbegründet ist, erst die Begründung gegeben werden muss, wie es in den dann folgenden Sätzen geschieht. Es wäre wahnsinnig, nichts für mehr als den Menschen (268, 17) und diese Welt allein für die Wohnung des Menschen zu halten (269, 2). So wird zweimal erwiesen, dass Gott in der Welt ist, also mit der die menschliche Kraft übersteigenden Kraft identifiziert werden kann. Das gilt auch gegen Hnm. (II 174).

Verstand in der Welt; sie hat Alles, was es gibt, es mangelt ihr nichts (§ 17, 269, 2 - § 18, 269, 22).

Vollends zwingt der Zusammenklang der Dinge am Himmel und auf Erden, einzusehen, dass die Welt durch einen göttlichen, alles durchdringenden Geist zusammengehalten wird. Wie könnte sonst eine Bewegung so mit der anderen übereinstimmen, wenn nicht eine göttliche Kraft da wäre, die Alles in seiner Bewegung erhält (§ 19, 269, 22 - 270, 7)? Nicht nur die Schönheit und Ordnung der Welt, nicht nur ihre Vollkommenheit beweist, dass ein göttlicher Geist in ihr wirkt, auch die Sympathie der Dinge, die Erhaltung und Dauer in der Bewegung zwingt, an den göttlichen Geist zu glauben.

Nach der Erklärung des menschlichen Gottesbegriffes wird also die Wirkung einer göttlichen Kraft in der Welt gezeigt, die Natur Gottes wird als wirkende Kraft, also in ihrer Qualität begriffen. Es folgen Schlüsse des Zenon, durch die bewiesen wird, dass der mundus Gott ist (§ 21, 270, 15-20), dass er Verstand, Leben und Empfinden hat, vor allem deshalb, weil er lebende und verständige Geschöpfe aus sich schafft (§ 22, 270, 20 - 271, 10). Es wird also gesagt, *wer* Gott ist, nämlich der mundus, nicht, wie im Vorhergehenden, *dass* Gott in der Welt wirkt und schafft. Damit ist die Natur Gottes in ihrem Sein begriffen.[1]

Sicher wird in den zenonischen Schlüssen nicht die Existenz Gottes erörtert, ebensowenig wie in Allem, was Balbus seit den Argumentationen, die er aus Kleanthes nahm, vorbrachte. Aber Balbus behauptet auf einmal, er habe bisher nur die Frage untersucht, ob es Götter gibt. Denn er beginnt nach den zenonischen Schlüssen eine Abhandlung über die Wirkung des Feuers mit den Worten: « Aber da ich angefangen habe, anders vorzugehen als ich am Anfang sagte — ich leugnete

[1] Ob in den zenonischen Schlüssen mundus Welt oder Himmel bedeutet, lässt sich erst später entscheiden (vgl. S. 154). Auch für den Sinn der Schlüsse und ihren sachlichen Unterschied von den vorhergehenden Ausführungen wird sich später wieder ein anderer Beweis ergeben (vgl. S. 161). Die Natur Gottes kann einmal so begriffen werden, dass man fragt, wer ist Gott (also in ihrem Sein,) dann so, dass man fragt, wie wirkt Gott (also in ihrer Qualität).

nämlich, dass dieser erste Teil meiner Rede einer Erörterung bedürfe, weil es Allen klar sei, dass es Götter gibt — so will ich dennoch gerade das durch eine naturwissenschaftliche Untersuchung bestätigen » (§ 23, 271, 11-14). [1] Balbus behauptet also, er habe, ohne ein Wort davon zu sagen, seine ursprüngliche Absicht geändert, er habe länger von dem gesprochen, wovon zu sprechen eigentlich nicht nötig war, er habe im Vorhergehenden Beweise für die Existenz Gottes gegeben; er ist nach seinen Worten noch im ersten Teil seiner Rede, in dem Beweis der Existenz Gottes. Aber diese Behauptung über den Sinn seiner Ausführungen steht zu ihrem Inhalt in offenbarem Widerspruch. Auch die jetzt folgende Abhandlung über das Feuer soll die Existenz Gottes beweisen. Wie er schon vorher von seiner ursprünglichen Absicht, über das erste Thema kurz zu reden, abgewichen ist, will er auch weiter noch von der Existenz Gottes sprechen. Es fragt sich, ob er das wirklich tut.[2]

In der Abhandlung über das Feuer (§ 23, 271, 14 - § 32, 275, 14) ist zuerst allgemein von der Wärme die Rede. Die Wärme bewirkt Ernährung und Wachstum; so lange sie da ist, ist Leben da, wenn sie vergeht, stirbt der Mensch (§ 23, 271, 14-20). Die grosse Bedeutung des Feuers für den Lebensprozess hat Kleanthes auf viele Arten erwiesen (§ 24, 271, 20 - 272, 5). Wärme ist in der ganzen Welt das Lebensprinzip, was sich leichter einsehen lässt, wenn man sich einmal die Natur des Feuers richtig klar macht (272, 5-8). In allen vier Elementen ist nämlich Wärme enthalten (§§ 25-28, 272, 8 - 273, 13). Die

---

[1] « Sed quoniam coepi secus agere atque initio dixeram (negaram enim hanc primam partem egere oratione quod esset omnibus perspicuum deos esse) tamen id ipsum rationibus physicis id est naturalibus confirmari volo ».

[2] Es heisst als Einführung dieser physikalischen Erörterung, dass durch sie das Beweisthema eben physikalisch erwiesen werden sollte. Das Beweisthema ist die Existenz Gottes oder nach dem scheinbaren und von Balbus gewollten Zusammenhang der Inhalt der zenonischen Schlüsse. Von diesen selbst war behauptet worden, dass sie einer breiteren Darstellung bedürften, um nicht so leicht widerlegt werden zu können (§ 29, 270, 8 ff.) So viel ist sicher. Worauf in den die zenonischer Schlüsse einleitenden Worten haec zu beziehen ist (Rhdt. II 112 ff.), dazu vgl. S. 161.

Erde hat Samen und Leben durch die Wärme (§§ 25-26, 272, 9-18). Das Wasser könnte ohne die Wärme nicht dauern (272, 18 - 273, 6). Ebenso steht es mit der Luft (§ 27, 273, 6-11), auch der Aether, der alles Leben gibt, ist feurig (§ 28, 273, 11-13). Wie alle Teile der Welt muss also die Welt selbst durch eine feurige Natur erhalten werden, zumal die Wärme das Lebensprinzip, das Prinzip der Erhaltung ist (273, 13-19). Wie könnten die Teile haben, was dem Ganzen fehlt? So ist bewiesen, dass es eine Natur gibt, die die Welt erhält und bewahrt. Diese Natur muss aber auch Sinn und Verstand haben (§ 29, 273, 20-21). Damit ist der Gedanke weiter fortgeschritten; denn bis jetzt war nur gesagt, dass eine solche Natur vorhanden sei, dass sie Feuer sei. Dass die Natur, auf die alles Schaffen zurückgeht, mit Sinn und Verstand begabt sein müsse, ist eine neue Behauptung, die im Folgenden bewiesen und erweitert wird (273, 21 - § 32, 275, 14).[1]

Jede Natur, die nicht einfach sondern mit einer anderen verbunden ist wie die Welt, die mit dem Feuer verbunden ist, hat ein Prinzipat. Das, worin das Prinzipat einer Natur liegt, ist der Ursprung jedes Handelns, das Wertvollste (273, 21-274, 5). In den Teilen der Welt ist Sinn und Verstand, also auch im Prinzipat der Welt, und zwar in höherem Masse. Es ist also die Behauptung, dass das Prinzipat, anders ausgedrückt die die Welt zusammenhaltende Natur, Sinn und Verstand hat, erwiesen und zugleich erweitert, indem der Natur als dem Prinzipat ein besonderer höherer Sinn und Verstand zugeschrieben wird, als er den Teilen eignet. Weil aber dem Prinzipat der Welt dieser höhere Sinn und Verstand zukommt, muss die Welt Gott sein, muss Alles in ihr durch eine göttliche Natur von vollkommener Verständigkeit zusammengehalten werden, die Welt muss weise sein (§ 30, 274, 5-12).[2] Dass die

---

[1] In gleichem Sinne versteht Plasberg die Aufeinanderfolge der Sätze, wenn er sagt (zu 273, 20): «ex proxima conclusione id repetitur, quod ad universam argumentationem faciat esse aliquam naturam qua mundus contineatur, additurque eam naturam non carere sensu ac ratione, quod deinceps explanatur».

[2] Prinzipat der Welt und Welt ist ebenso gleich bedeutend wie Prinzipat des Menschen — Seele — und Mensch.

Existenz dieses höheren Sinnes und Verstandes in der Welt ihre Göttlichkeit zeigt, ist wieder eine weitergehende Behauptung, die in der Aussage, dass ihr als Ganzem ein höherer Sinn und Verstand als einem ihrer Teile zukommt, noch nicht liegt.

Den Beweis dafür geben die folgenden Ausführungen (274, 13 - § 32, 275, 14), in denen auseinandergesetzt wird, die Wärme der Welt sei wegen ihrer besonderen Eigenschaften zur Bewegung der Sinne viel geeigneter als die menschliche Wärme, und darum müsse die Welt Empfindung haben. Die besondere göttliche Art des Empfindens folgt dann aus der Selbstbewegung der Welt, die unter Berufung auf Platon behauptet wird (274, 13 - 275, 6). Damit ist der eine Teil der aufgestellten Behauptung, dass die Natur, die die Welt zusammenhält, oder die Welt selbst Empfinden und Leben eines Gottes haben müsse, bewiesen. Dass auch ein höherer, göttlicher Verstand in der Welt ist, der zweite Teil der Behauptung, wird anschliessend durch eine logische Ueberlegung gezeigt (275, 7-14). Das Ganze muss mehr von dem haben, was die Teile haben. Ein Teil der Welt, der Mensch, hat Verstand, also hat die Welt (mundus), das Ganze, mehr Verstand, sie *ist weise*, wie eben nicht der Mensch, der es nur *werden* kann (vgl. § 36). Dieser Schluss vom Teil auf das Ganze ist für die Abhandlung über das Feuer charakteristisch (vgl. § 28, 273, 13 ff.; § 30, 274, 5).

Damit sind alle über die Natur der Welt gemachten Aussagen erwiesen. Es ist gezeigt, dass die Welt — sicher ist mundus in diesem Zusammenhang immer als Welt zu verstehen — göttlicher Natur ist und durch ihre göttliche Natur zusammengehalten wird und dauert (273, 15; 274, 12).[1] Es

---

[1] Die Interpretation der Abhandlung über das Feuer hat meist zur Herauslösung einzelner Teile geführt, während man doch keinen Satz herauslösen kann, wenn das Ziel des Ganzen, der Erweis einer göttlichen, lebendigen, die Welt erhaltenden Kraft erreicht werden soll. Und dieses Ziel der Darstellung ergibt sich wieder aus dem bis dahin einheitlichen Fortschritt der Sätze. Rhdt. (I 225-26) streicht die Sätze §§ 29-30 heraus schon wegen der logischen, nicht wie im Vorhergehenden naturwissenschaftlichen Argumentation. Verei-

müsste aber eigentlich, nach der Einleitung des ganzen Abschnittes, in der Abhandlung über das Feuer die *Existenz* Gottes bewiesen werden, so wie Balbus es darstellt, nicht das, was in der Welt geschieht, auf seine göttliche Ursache zurückgeführt und dadurch die *Wirkung* Gottes in der Welt, also seine qualitative Natur gezeigt werden. Von ihr war auch vorher schon die Rede in den an Kleanthes und Chrysipp anknüpfenden Beweisen, die in der Behauptung einer Sympathie der Teile endeten (§§ 18-19, 269, 18 - 270, 7).

Anschliessend an die Abhandlung über die Eigenschaften des Feuers und das Prinzipat der Welt soll dann in einer weit ausgreifenden Paralleluntersuchung die Natur der Götter bestimmt werden (§§ 33-44, 275, 15 - 279, 25),[1] wie es deutlich als Anfang heisst (ad deorum naturam 275, 16). Das ist das Thema des zweiten Teiles der Rede, von dem also schon vorher geredet worden sein muss und von dem auch geredet wurde. Der erste Teil der Rede muss demnach zu Ende sein. Entsprechend der Ankündigung wird gezeigt, dass der mundus Gott ist (§§ 33-39, 275, 17 - 277, 20) und dass die Gestirne Götter

---

nigung von logischer und naturwissenschaftlicher Erklärung ist aber für diesen Text charakteristisch (vgl. 269, 18 - 270, 7 ; 274, 22 ; 275, 7). Fragt man nicht nach der Vorlage sondern nur nach dem Zusammenhang der Gedanken, so ist nichts auszusetzen. Das gilt auch gegen Hnm. (II 277), der andere Sätze streicht, wenn auch weniger als Rhdt., und den Rest mit inhaltlicher, hier also nicht zu diskutierender Begründung für einheitlich hält. Rhdt. (I 227) hat auch die Sätze § 32, 275, 7-14 als leichte Ueberarbeitung der früher berichteten zenonischen Schlüsse (§§ 21-22) von den vorhergehenden naturwissenschaftlichen Sätzen als Zusammenhang für sich getrennt. Dass schon die Verwendung des Begriffes mundus, die hier und in den zenonischen Schlüssen verschieden ist, ihre Zusammenstellung verbietet, dagegen den Anschluss dort, wo die Sätze stehen, fordert, ist sicher (vgl. S. 138-39 ; 154). Auch die Sinnbestimmung der Darlegung über das Feuer wird sich in einer späteren Ueberlegung rechtfertigen (vgl. S. 155).

[1] *Und auch* dann, wenn man von den ersten einfachen Naturen zu den letzten vollkommensten vorwärts schreitet, muss man zur Natur der Götter kommen (« *atque etiam* si a primis incohatisque naturis ad ultimas perfectasque volumus procedere, ad deorum naturam perveniamus necesse est »).

sind (§§ 39-44, 277, 21 - 279, 25),[1] also wieder wird das Sein der göttlichen Natur erwiesen.

Zuerst wird die Intelligenz und Weisheit des mundus (§ 33, 276, 15), die ihm von Anfang an eignen muss (§ 34, 276, 24), und daran anschliessend auch seine Göttlichkeit aufgezeigt (§§ 36-39, 276, 24 - 277, 20). Pflanzen, Tiere und Menschen haben bestimmte, von einander der Art und dem Wesen nach verschiedene Reaktionen. Ueber dem Menschen steht aber noch ein viertes, vollkommeneres Wesen, das von Natur gut ist und weise (275, 17-26). Dieses vollkommene Wesen muss es geben, da die Natur von sich aus zum Vollkommenen strebt und an seiner Erreichung nur durch einen hemmenden Widerstand gehindert werden könnte. Die Welt als Ganzes kann durch nichts gehindert werden, weil sie Alles in sich enthält; so muss es in der Welt die Vollkommenheit geben, der nichts hinzugesetzt werden kann. Und sie ist mit der Natur der Welt gleichzusetzen (276, 1-11), die so beschaffen ist, dass sie Alles leitet und durch nichts gehindert werden kann. Es muss also der mundus intelligent und sogar weise sein. Was aber wäre törichter, als dem mundus, der doch das Beste ist, nicht zuerst Leben, dann Verstand, schliesslich Weisheit zuzuschreiben (wie manche es tun)? Der mundus wäre ja weniger als eine Pflanze, weniger als ein Tier und weniger als ein Mensch, wenn er nicht sogar von Anfang an weiser wäre (276, 14-24)[2]. Anders ausgedrückt: der mundus muss Gott sein; denn ausser ihm gibt es nichts, was vollkommen ist. Mit Recht hat Chrysipp gesagt, Alles ausser dem mundus sei um etwas anderen willen da, selbst der Mensch, der dazu geboren sei, den mundus zu

---

[1] Rhdt. (I 228) versucht eine Herauslösung des § 39, 277, 22 beginnenden Zusammenhangs. Er muss allerdings den diesen Zusammenhang einleitenden Satz (277, 21-22) streichen, in dem die Göttlichkeit der Sterne als zweites Beweisziel nach der Göttlichkeit der Welt bezeichnet wird.

[2] An dieser Stelle wird, wie auch sonst, an das, was sich als Folgerung aus dem Vorhergehenden ergibt, zugleich eine neue Behauptung angeschlossen, die dann in den weiteren Ausführungen erwiesen wird (vgl. etwa 273, 20; 278, 15-16 und die Interpretation dieser Stellen S. 138 und S. 143).

betrachten und nachzuahmen. Chrysipp hat auch mit Recht gezeigt, dass im Vollkommenen Alles besser ist als im Unvollkommenen, also muss der mundus auch Tugend besitzen und zwar als ihm eigentümlich von Anfang an. Der mundus ist selbst weise und deshalb Gott (276, 25 - 277, 20).[1]

Und nachdem die Göttlichkeit des Himmels erwiesen ist, soll jetzt die Göttlichkeit der Gestirne gezeigt werden (§ 39, 277, 21-22).[2] Wieder soll also von der Natur der Götter die Rede sein, davon *wer* Gott ist, nicht davon, *dass* Gott ist (§§ 39-44, 277, 22 - 279, 25). Die Gestirne sind aus den beweglichsten und feinsten Teilen des Aethers geboren, von ganz reiner unvermischter Natur, warm und leuchtend, so dass man ihnen mit Recht Leben, Empfinden und Intelligenz zuschreiben kann (277, 22-25). Dass sie aus Feuer sind, hat Kleanthes erwiesen. Denn er zeigte, dass die Sonne Feuer ist, und zwar Feuer, das dem im Menschen entspricht. Darum muss die Sonne lebendig sein, und auch die übrigen Sterne müssen Leben haben (§§ 40-41, 277, 25 - 278, 15) — offenbar weil für sie dasselbe gelten muss wie für die Sonne, wenn sich die Feurigkeit auch

---

[1] In diesem Zusammenhang ist offenbar unter mundus der Himmel zu verstehen; schon die Ableitung, die zuerst gegeben wird, legt das nahe. Denn es wird, ausgehend von den ersten unvollkommenen Naturen, wie es heisst, über Pflanzen, Tieren und Menschen, einzelnen Naturen also, ein viertes vollkommenes Wesen postuliert, das geschaffen ist durch die ganze Welt, deren Streben nach Vollkommenheit durch nichts gehindert werden kann. Dieses vollkommene Wesen, allen einzelnen Wesen überlegen, muss doch auch selbst ein Einzelwesen, also nicht die Welt sondern der Himmel sein. Später wird noch einmal ein Vergleich des mundus mit Pflanzen oder Tieren oder Menschen, also Einzelwesen, durchgeführt (276, 17 ff.), denen allen der mundus überlegen sein soll. Dabei ist mit keinem Wort etwa wie vorher auf die Ueberlegenheit des Ganzen über die Teile angespielt, es scheint also wieder der Himmel gemeint zu sein. Evident ist das im letzten Teil (§§ 37-39). Von welchem Wesen ausser vom Himmel kann man sagen, dass es für nichts anderes da sei, da doch alle übrigen Teile der Welt, sogar der Mensch, nicht um ihrer selbst willen sondern zu etwas anderem da sind, da doch allein der Himmel Alles in sich umfängt und es nichts gibt, was nicht in ihm wäre.

[2] « Atque hac mundi divinitate perspecta tribuenda est sideribus eadem divinitas ».

allein oder doch am deutlichsten an der Sonne zeigen lässt und jedenfalls nur an ihr gezeigt wird.

Alle Sterne müssen lebendig sein, weil sie im Aether *entstehen* (278, 16). Das ist, wieder in Form eines Anhanges zu dem, was sich aus dem Vorhergehenden ergibt, eine neue Behauptung, die durch die folgenden Sätze bewiesen wird (§ 42, 278, 16-279, 4). Da nämlich auf der Erde, im Wasser und in der Luft Lebewesen entstehen, schien es dem Aristoteles absurd, dass in dem Teil der Welt, der zur Erschaffung von Lebewesen prädestiniert ist (im Aether), kein Lebewesen entstehen sollte. Die Sterne nehmen den Aetherraum ein (andere Lebewesen — und Lebewesen sind die Sterne ja nach den vorhergehenden Aeusserungen — sind dort nicht zu finden oder nicht bekannt), die Sterne sind also die im Aether *entstehenden* Lebewesen (278, 16-20). Nach der Beschaffenheit des Aethers aber müssen die in ihm entstehenden Lebewesen von schärfster Empfindung und grösster Schnelligkeit sein. Es muss also in den Sternen, die im Aether geboren werden, Empfinden und Intellekt sein (278, 20-279, 4). War vorher nur von der Lebendigkeit der Sterne die Rede, von ihrer Feurigkeit, die dem Feuer im Menschen entspricht, so ist jetzt aus ihrer Entstehung die besondere, bevorzugte Art ihres Seins erschlossen.

Und um ihrer besonderen Eigenschaften willen sind sie nicht etwa Menschen sondern Götter. « Es muss in den Sternen Empfinden und Intellekt sein, wodurch bewirkt wird, dass sie in die Zahl der Götter aufzunehmen sind » (279, 2-4).[1] Wieder hat sich die Folgerung aus dem Vorhergehenden erweitert. Mit dieser Erweiterung ist aber erst die zu beweisende Behauptung der Göttlichkeit der Sterne aufgestellt. Der Erweis der Lebendigkeit, und zwar eines bevorzugten Lebens, ist dafür nur die Voraussetzung. Die überlegene göttliche Intelligenz der Sterne folgt nun daraus, dass sie im höchsten Teile der Welt leben und dass ihre Ernährung eine besonders feine ist (§§ 42-43, 279, 4-10). Vor allem aber wird die Art ihrer Empfindung und Intelligenz aus der ewigen Konstanz ihrer Bewegung deutlich,

---

[1] « Consentaneum est in his (sc. astris) sensum inesse et intelligentiam, ex qua efficitur in deorum numero astra esse ducenda ».

die nicht zufällig oder zusammenhanglos ist und also nicht etwa durch Natur oder Zufall gegeben sein kann sondern durch freiwillige göttliche Eigenbewegung (279, 10-17). Aristoteles hat ja gezeigt, dass jede Bewegung allein von Natur oder durch eine gewaltsame Einwirkung oder durch Freiwilligkeit zu erklären ist. Eine Kreisbewegung kann nur freiwillig sein, da von Natur der Körper nur nach oben steigen oder nach unten fallen kann. Dass etwa die Sterne gegen ihre Natur von einer Macht, die mehr ist als sie, bewegt würden, ist unmöglich (§ 44, 279, 17-25). Die Freiwilligkeit der Gestirnsbewegung und damit ihre Göttlichkeit folgt also aus ihrer regelmässigen Bewegung, die eine Kreisbewegung sein muss ; das wird einfach behauptet, ohne jeden Beweis. Für Balbus ist damit die Auseinandersetzung über die Göttlichkeit der Gestirne zu Ende.[1]

Die Untersuchung über die Göttlichkeit des Himmels und der Sterne war als eine Paralleluntersuchung eingeführt, die auch zur Natur der Götter führen sollte (§ 33, 275, 15-17 ; vgl. S. 140) ; es muss also schon vorher davon die Rede gewesen sein, *wer* Gott ist, obwohl Balbus ausdrücklich behauptet hat, vorher immer die *Existenz* Gottes behandelt zu haben. Die Ausführungen über den Himmel und die Sterne wären als Parallele zu den zenonischen Schlüssen aufzufassen, wenn in ihnen unter mundus der Himmel zu verstehen ist und wenn bei den Geschöpfen, die der mundus schafft, an die Sterne zu denken ist (vgl. S. 136). Es sollten ja die zenonischen Schlüsse noch ausführlicher behandelt werden, weil sie wegen ihrer Kürze zu leicht widerlegt werden könnten (§ 20, 270, 8 ff.). Diese ausführlichere Darlegung würde aber dann nicht unmittelbar anschliessend folgen, zwischen Ankündigung und Durchführung hätte sich ein Zusammenhang ganz anderen Inhaltes geschoben, die Abhandlung über das Feuer. Ist es so, dann

---

[1] Rhdt. (I 228) hat den Aristoteles-Schluss als einen Zusatz bezeichnet, mit Unrecht. Die Ausdehnung des Aristoteleszitates wäre in einem anderen Zusammenhang zu erörtern. Mir scheint überzeugend, dass vom Aristoteleszitat bis zum Schluss des Sternabschnittes ein untrennbarer Zusammenhang geht, wie W. Jaeger sagt (Aristoteles, Berl., 1923, S. 145 ff.); Rhdt. (II 61 ; 81 ff.) bestreitet das. Fa, die ganze Erörterung ist einheitlich.

disponiert Balbus schlecht, er trennt Zusammengehöriges und verbindet, was nicht zusammen passt. Können aber nicht die zenonischen Schlüsse gemeint sein, so fände sich in Allem, was Balbus gesagt hat, nirgends eine Untersuchung, zu der die Ausführungen über den Himmel und die Sterne eine Parallele wären.

Balbus deutet diese sachlichen Schwierigkeiten mit keinem Wort an. Er spricht ruhig weiter, als sei Alles, was er sagt, an seiner rechten Stelle. Ja, nachdem er jetzt so lange über die Natur der Götter geredet hat, für die er einen zweiten Beweis zu geben behauptete, sagt er auf einmal: « Wer das sieht und leugnet, dass es Götter gibt, der ist nicht nur unwissend sondern auch unfromm. Und es macht nicht viel Unterschied, ob er das leugnet oder ob er jede göttliche Fürsorge und Handlung bestreitet. Wer nicht handelt, der lebt nicht, wie mir scheint. Die Existenz der Götter ist also so klar, dass ich nicht glauben kann, es sei bei Verstand, wer sie leugnet. Es bleibt nur übrig, zu überlegen, welches die Natur der Götter ist » (§§ 44-45, 280, 1 - 281, 6).[1] Balbus behauptet also, bis jetzt überhaupt nur von der *Existenz* der Götter geredet zu haben. Er behauptet, erst jetzt das zweite Thema, die *Natur* der Götter, behandeln zu wollen, von dem er doch schon vorher nach seinen eigenen Worten geredet hat.[2] Die Widersprüche und Unklarheiten häufen sich immer mehr.

Aber Balbus beginnt den zweiten Teil wirklich wie etwas Neues mit einer Erinnerung daran, wie schwer es sei, sich

---

[1] « Quae qui videat non indocte solum verum etiam impie faciat, si deos esse neget. Nec sane multum interesset, utrum id neget an eos omni procuratione atque actione privet; mihi enim qui nihil agit esse omnino non videtur. Esse igitur deos ita perspicuum est ut id qui neget vix eum sanae mentis existimem. Restat ut qualis eorum natura sit consideremus ».

[2] Auffallend ist auch der Anschluss der den ganzen ersten Teil abgrenzenden Worte an die Betrachtung über die Kreisbewegung der Sterne. Wer das (die Regelmässigkeit der Kreisbewegung) nicht sieht — ist sie eigentlich so auffällig sichtbar? — ist unfromm, nicht nur unwissend, wenn er die Existenz der Götter leugnet. Vgl. dazu S. 159.

Gott in einer anderen als der menschlichen Gestalt vorzustellen. Es ist unnötig, diese Schwierigkeit ausführlich zu behandeln, nachdem Cotta schon in seiner Erwiderung auf die Rede des Epikureers Velleius darüber geredet hat (§ 45, 280, 6-11). Zu dem präformierten Begriff von Gott, nach dem er Leben haben und das Vollkommenste sein muss, stimmt zuerst (ut primum 280, 12), wie Balbus meint, dass der mundus selbst Gott ist und darum Leben hat (280, 11-16). Damit ist also das Sein der göttlichen Natur bestimmt. Der Einwand der Epikureer, die glauben, dass der mundus nicht Gott sein könne, weil ein runder, sich bewegender Gott lächerlich wäre, ist hinfällig. Es muss Götter geben, die das Mächtigste sind, und sicher ist nichts mächtiger als der mundus, der also Gott sein muss (§ 46, 280, 16-26), wie sich auch aus seinen Wirkungen später leicht zeigen wird (280, 26). Für jetzt genügt gegen diesen Einwand ein Hinweis auf die Schönheit der Kugelgestalt, ihre Herrlichkeit an sich und ihre einzigartige Fähigkeit, Gleichmässigkeit der Bewegung und Konstanz der Ordnung zu ermöglichen. Wegen all dieser Eigenschaften ist nichts törichter, als anzunehmen, dass der mundus nicht rund sei oder eine andere Gestalt habe, oder dass es gar viele mögliche Gestalten des mundus gäbe. Wenn Epikur nur gelernt hätte, wieviel zwei Mal zwei ist, hätte er das nicht behaupten können : sed dum palato quid sit optimum iudicat, « caeli palatum » ut ait Ennius non suspexit. Fixsterne und Planeten lassen durch ihre Bewegung die Bewegung des mundus, des Himmels, die nur in einer Kugelform denkbar ist, und die Rundung der Sternbahnen erkennen (§§ 47-49, 281, 1 - 282, 14).

Es folgt eine Schilderung der Bewegungen der verschiedenen Sterne (§§ 49-55, 282, 15 - 285, 9). Und zwar werden zuerst die Sonnenbahn und die Mondbahn beschrieben (282, 15 - 283, 13), dann die Bahnen der 5 Planeten (283, 13 - 284, 23) und die der Fixsterne (284, 24 - 285, 9) ; denn auch die Fixsterne bewegen sich. Anfangs liest sich diese Beschreibung wie eine Ausführung derBehauptung über die zwei Arten von Sternbewegungen, durch die eben die Bewegung des Himmels und die Kreisform der Sternbahnen erschlossen war (282, 9-14). Doch im Verlauf der Darstellung wird die Beschreibung der Sternbahnen überhaupt zu einem reinen Lob der Regelmässigkeit und Konstanz der Bewegung. Und überraschender Weise schliesst die Schilderung der Planetenbahnen (§ 54, 284, 20-23) und der Fixsternbahnen (§ 55, 285, 5-9) mit der Konsequenz: wegen der wunderbaren Regelmässigkeit ihrer Bewegung müssen die Sterne Götter sein. Davon aber war bis jetzt keine Rede. Die Beschreibung der Sternbahnen dient zur Begründung einer neuen, hier unvermittelt auftretenden These, die aber mit Aussagen des ersten Teiles übereinstimmt, wo auch am Schluss die Göttlichkeit der Gestirne erörtert worden war. Der entscheidende Grund dafür war die wunderbare Regelmässigkeit ihrer Bewegung, die nur behauptet, nicht bewiesen wurde. Und doch ist die Regelmässigkeit der Sternbahnen nicht ohne weiteres einzusehen, wie ja schon die falsche Bezeichnung der Planeten als irrender Sterne (§ 51, 283, 13 ff.) zeigt. Je weniger selbstverständlich aber die Regelmässigkeit der Sternbahnen ist, umso nötiger wäre ein Beweis für sie. Sonst ist die Behauptung, dass die Sterne Götter sind, nicht sicher. Was am Ende des ersten Teiles fehlt, steht nun im zweiten Teil ohne Anschluss an die unmittelbar vorhergehenden Ausführungen, in plötzlicher Veränderung der Themastellung.[1] Wieder zeigt sich ein Bruch in der Darstellung des Balbus.

Da alles himmlische Geschehen voller Ordnung und Regelmässigkeit ist, muss es durch einen Geist bestimmt sein, wird jetzt gefolgert (§ 56, 285, 10-16). Darum kann es kein Irrtum sein, wenn man qualitativ die Natur des mundus, des Gottes, mit Zenon als die eines Künstlers bestimmt, der nach seinem eigenen Gesetz Alles schafft, was ist. Der mundus bewegt sich wie ein Mensch, sein Verstand, den man mit Recht *πρόνοια* nennen kann, sorgt dafür, dass der mundus möglichst geeignet sei zum Bestehen, dass er nichts entbehre und dass vor allem in ihm wunderbare Schönheit und aller erdenkliche Schmuck sei (§§ 57-58, 285, 17 - 286, 10). Nachdem also zuerst von der

---

[1] Schon Plasberg sagt (zu 280, 14), dass die Beschreibung der Sternbahnen inhaltlich von dem Nachweis der Bewegung des Himmels durch die Nennung der Planeten- und Fixsternbahnen zu trennen sei, er setzt also auch einen Bruch der Darstellung zwischen 282, 14 und 15 an. Vgl. Rhdt. I 217.

Gestalt des Himmels, dann von der Regelmässigkeit der Sternbahnen und der aus ihr folgenden Göttlichkeit der Sterne geredet war, wird jetzt das Wesen der unwandelbaren Ordnung des Himmels erklärt. Der mundus, der Alles in seiner Umarmung umfasst, also der Himmel, ist wie ein schaffender Mensch. Man erwartet, dass sein Schaffen näher geschildert würde, die aufgestellte Behauptung liest sich wie der Anfang und die Disposition eines neuen Themas.[1] Aber Balbus begnügt sich mit dieser allgemeinen Behauptung über die Natur und das Handeln des mundus und zieht sogleich einen Schlussstrich: es war vom mundus im Ganzen die Rede, von den Sternen, und damit ist schon eine Reihe von Göttern erschlossen, die wirken und deren Handeln sich ohne Anstrengung und Mühe vollzieht (§§ 59-60, 286, 11-21). Dieser Schluss kommt wiederum vollkommen unerwartet.

Balbus spricht jetzt noch von den Naturen anderer Götter (§§ 60-72, 286, 22 - 287, 17). Er behandelt zuerst die Vergöttlichung alles dessen, was die Natur den Menschen an Nützlichem geschenkt habe (§§ 60-62, 286, 22 - 287, 17), dann die Vergöttlichung von Menschen (287, 18 - 288, 8), die aus dem Naturgeschehen erkennbaren Götter (§§ 63-69, 288, 9 - 293, 4), schliesslich die erdichteten Götter (§§ 70-72, 293, 5 - 295, 5). Damit ist er schon am Ende seiner Ausführungen über das zweite Thema, das so schwierig sein sollte: « ich glaube, deutlich genug gezeigt zu haben, dass es Götter gibt und wie sie sind » (295, 4-5).[2]

Vergleicht man also in den beiden ersten Teilen der Rede des Balbus die Absicht der Darstellung mit der Ausführung und prüft die Aufeinanderfolge der Argumente, so ergeben sich grosse Schwierigkeiten. Balbus spricht lang und ausführlich über die Probleme, die nach seiner immer wiederholten Behauptung gar keiner Ausführung bedürfen (§ 4, 261, 7; § 12,

[1] Rhdt. (I 218) hat zuerst das Fehlen der Ausführungen an dieser Stelle und den Dispositionscharakter der fraglichen Sätze erkannt. Ueber die Bedeutung des Wortes principium (§ 57, 285, 18) vgl. S. 164.

[2] « Ac mihi videor satis esse deos et quales essent ostendisse ».

266, 18; § 23, 271, 11), er braucht für die Behandlung dessen, was selbstverständlich und klar ist, viel mehr Zeit als für die Behandlung des Themas, über das Alle verschiedener Meinung sind.[1] Diesen Anstoss fühlt er selbst, er sucht ihn damit zu entschuldigen, dass er sagt, er mache es eben anders, als er es sich am Anfang vorgenommen habe (§ 23, 271, 11). Noch schwerer wiegt ein anderer Einwand, dessen sich Balbus nicht bewusst ist, über den er wenigstens nicht spricht: Dreiviertel der Ausführungen über die *Existenz* der Götter gehören nicht zum Thema. Denn er redet ja nur am Anfang des ersten Teiles wirklich von der Existenz Gottes (§§ 4-12, 261, 8 - 266, 20). In Allem, was dann folgt (§§ 13-44, 266, 20 - 279, 25), erörtert er dagegen nicht die *Existenz* Gottes sondern er zeigt nach kurzen Ausführungen über die Entstehung der menschlichen Gottesvorstellung, *wer* Gott ist und welches die *Wirkung* Gottes ist (vgl. S. 135).[2] Alle diese Ausführungen gehören aber eigentlich nicht in den ersten Teil sondern in den zweiten, in die Erörterung über die *Natur* der Götter, die dieses schwierige, wirklich strittige Problem im Verhältnis zum ersten Teil viel zu kurz behandelt. Dazu kommt, dass wieder im zweiten Teil Ausführungen, die angekündigt werden, fehlen. In beiden Teilen werden Zusammenhänge nicht zu Ende geführt oder unerwartet neue Ausführungen schlecht eingefügt, wie die Gedankenfolge überhaupt oft schlecht ist. Verschiedene Ausführungen weisen über die zunächststehenden Darlegungen hinweg auf frühere zurück (die Abhandlung über das Feuer auf die Erörterung der Sympathie; die Erörterungen über die vollkommene Natur des Himmels auf die zenonischen Schlüsse; die Beschreibung der Sternbahnen auf den Beweis der Göttlichkeit der Sterne aus der Konstanz ihrer Bewegung). Die gleichen Probleme werden in beiden Teilen behandelt (die Göttlichkeit des Himmels und die Göttlichkeit der Sterne). Von all diesen Schwierigkeiten sagt Balbus nichts.

Aber das Merkwürdige ist, dass Cicero sich ihrer bewusst ist,

---

[1] Der erste Teil umfasst 403 Zeilen, der zweite 287.

[2] Von den 403 Zeilen des ersten Teiles behandeln also ungefähr 300 Zeilen nicht die Existenz Gottes, das aufgestellte Thema.

dass er all diese Anstösse genau sieht und sie durch Cotta in seiner Kritik an der Rede des Balbus im 3. Buche tadeln lässt. Denn an den Anfang seiner Widerlegung stellt Cotta die Frage, warum Balbus so viel von den Dingen geredet habe, die angeblich klar sind, von der Existenz der Götter, die gar keiner Erörterung bedarf (§ 8, 348, 5-7).[1] Balbus sucht sich jetzt damit herauszureden, dass auch Cotta vor Gericht so viel Argumente wie möglich vorbringen werde, selbst wenn die Sache klar sei. Man kann nicht fragen, warum wir mit zwei Augen betrachten, was wir mit einem sehen können (348, 8-13). Aber Cotta erwidert: « Was klar ist, verliert nur durch Argumentation.... Weil du selbst kein Zutrauen hast, dass die Sache so selbstverständlich ist, wie du wohl möchtest, hast du mit vielen Argumenten die Existenz der Götter zu erweisen versucht » (§ 9, 348, 16; 349, 2-3).[2]

Aber Cotta behauptet auch, dass von den Ausführungen des ersten Teiles der Rede des Balbus das meiste gar nicht zu dem Thema gehört, das Balbus zu behandeln vorgibt, und zwar all das, was nach den Beispielen aus der römischen Geschichte vorgebrachte wird, also die Ausführungen von den Kleantheszitaten an bis zum Ende des ersten Teiles (§ 13-44). Denn nachdem er die von Balbus in dem Abschnitt über den sichtbaren himmlischen Gott, die Weissagungen, Theophanien und Orakel vorgebrachten Argumente für die Existenz Gottes (§ 4-12) widerlegt und als falsch erwiesen hat, wenn er sie auch wenigstens als Argumente zum Thema gelten lässt,[3] sagt er: « Bis hierher kann ich nicht einsehen, dass es Götter gibt, wenigstens soweit ich mich dir anvertraue, Balbus. Ich glaube

---

[1] « (Requiro) primum illud cur quom (perspicuum in) istam partem ne egere quidem oratione dixisses quod esset perspicuum et inter omnis constaret deos esse, de eo ipso tam multa dixeris ».

[2] « (Perspicuitas enim argumentatione elevatur).... sed quia non confidebas tam esse id perspicuum quam tu velis, propterea multis argumentis deos esse docere voluisti ».

[3] Dass Cotta (§§ 10-15, 349, 10 - 351, 20) die Argumente nach einander bespricht, die Balbus (§§ 4-12, 261, 9 - 266, 20) vorgebracht hatte, zeigt die Gegenüberstellung des Textes in den Verweisungen des Plasberg'schen Apparates.

zwar an ihre Existenz, aber die Stoiker können sie nicht beweisen. Denn Kleanthes hat, wie du sagst, geglaubt, auf vier Arten sei der Begriff Gottes im Menschen entstanden. Ueber die Weissagungen haben wir geredet. Was Wundererscheinungen angeht, am Himmel, im Wasser oder auf der Erde, so lässt sich nicht sagen dass es nicht Menschen gibt, die glauben, dass Gott sie schicke. Aber das steht nicht zur Diskussion, ob es Menschen gibt, die an die Existenz der Götter glauben; ob es Götter gibt oder nicht, das ist die Frage. Denn die anderen Argumente, die Kleanthes vorbringt, das eine von dem Nutzen, der uns zuteil wird, das andere von der Zeitordnung und der Konstanz der himmlischen Bewegungen, die werden von uns behandelt werden, wenn wir über die *Fürsorge* der Götter reden, über die du, Balbus, am ausführlichsten gesprochen hast. *Eben dahin* verschiebe ich die Erörterung dessen, was Chrysipp sagt..., den Vergleich der Schönheit eines Hauses mit der des Kosmos und die Erörterung der Uebereinstimmung und des Zusammenhanges der ganzen Welt. Die kurzen Schlüsse des Zenon verschiebe ich auf den *selben Teil* meiner Rede, den ich eben erwähnte. Zu *gleicher Zeit* sollen alle Ausführungen, die du naturwissenschaftlich argumentierend machtest, über die Kraft des Feuers und über die Wärme, aus der Alles entsteht, erörtert werden, und zwar dann an ihrer *richtigen Stelle*. Alles, was du sonst gesagt hast, als du zeigen wolltest, dass es Götter gäbe, weshalb der mundus im ganzen und Sonne und Mond und Sterne Sinn und Verstand hätten, verschiebe ich auf die *gleiche Zeit*. Von dir will ich nur das immer und immer wieder wissen, welche Gründe dich denn überzeugt haben, dass es Götter gibt» (§§ 16-19, 351, 20-353, 3).[1] Cotta behauptet also, von den Argumenten des

[1] « Non igitur adhuc, quantum quidem in te est Balbe, intellego deos esse; quos equidem credo esse, sed nil docent Stoici. Nam Cleanthes ut dicebas quattuor modis informatas in animis hominum putat deorum esse notiones. Unus is modus est de quo satis dixi, qui est susceptus ex praesensione rerum futurarum; alter ex perturbationibus tempestatum et reliquis motibus; tertius ex commoditate rerum quas percipimus et copia; quartus ex astrorum ordine caelique constantia. De praesensione diximus. De perturbationibus

Kleanthes gehörten zwei zur Erklärung des Gottesbegriffes und seiner Entstehung, aber schon das sei eine Verschiebung des Themas, dem zu Folge die Existenz der Götter erörtert werden solle, nicht die Frage, ob es Menschen gibt, die an Götter glauben, oder wie sie zu diesem Glauben kommen. Die anderen beiden Argumente des Kleanthes aber gehörten ebenso wie alle übrigen Ausführungen des ersten Teiles zu einem ganz anderen, neuen Thema, nämlich zur Erörterung der göttlichen Providenz.[1] Denn ihre Erörterung wird ja von Cotta in die Besprechung dieses neuen Themas verwiesen, wo sie dann an der richtigen, ihnen zukommenden Stelle behandelt werden sollen; sie hätten also eigentlich auch von Balbus in diesem Teil seiner Ausführungen vorgebracht werden

---

caelestibus et maritimis et terrenis non possumus dicere, cum ea fiant non esse multos qui illa metuant et a dis inmortalibus fieri existument; sed non id quaeritur, sintne aliqui qui deos esse putent: di utrum sint necne sint quaeritur. Nam reliquae causae quas Cleanthes adfert, quarum una est de commodorum quae capimus copia, altera de temporum ordine caelique constantia, tum tractabuntur a nobis cum disputabimus de *providentia* deorum, de qua plurima a te Balbe dicta sunt; *eodemque* illa etiam differemus, quod Chrysippum dicere aiebas,... quaeque in domo pulchra cum pulchritudine mundi comparabas, et cum totius mundi convenientiam consensumque adferebas; Zenonisque brevis et acutulas conclusiones in *eam partem* sermonis *quam modo dixi* differemus; *eodemque tempore* illa omnia quae a te physice dicta sunt de vi ignea deque eo calore ex quo omnia generari dicebas *loco suo* quaerentur; omniaque quae a te nudius tertius dicta sunt, cum docere velles deos esse, quare et mundus universus et sol et luna et stellae sensum ac mentem haberent, in *idem tempus* reservabo. A te autem idem illud etiam atque etiam quaeram, quibus rationibus tibi persuadeas deos esse».

[1] Die Reihenfolge der Kleanthesargumente hier ist von der im 2. Buch § 13 gegebenen verschieden. Es folgen 1 3 2 4 statt 1 2 3 4. Sachlich entspricht das ganz den Ergebnissen der Analyse über Inhalt und Beweisziel der Arguments, vgl. S. 134. Wie man die verschiedene Reihenfolge an beiden Stellen erklären muss, wird sich zeigen (vgl. S. 164). Cotta betont zwar die Fremdheit der beiden ersten Argumente im Sinnzusammenhang des ersten Teiles, schliesst sie aber doch trotz seines Einwandes aufs engste an den ersten Teil an und verweist sie nicht, wie die anderen Argumente in einen anderen Teil. Vgl. dazu S. 159.

müssen. Gemeint ist damit die Untersuchung über die Natur der Götter, also der zweite Teil der Rede des Balbus. Denn in seiner Widerlegung dieses zweiten Teiles bespricht Cotta die Argumente, die er aus dem ersten Teil herauslöst und in die Erörterung der göttlichen Providenz verweist (§ 20, 353, 12 ff.). Cicero ist sich also klar darüber, dass alle diese Ausführungen nicht in den ersten Teil sondern in den zweiten Teil gehören.[1]

Cotta übernimmt aber die Argumente des ersten Teiles in den zweiten nicht etwa in dem Zusammenhang, in dem Balbus sie vorträgt, sondern er zerlegt sie vollkommen und verbindet sie mit den einzelnen Argumenten des zweiten Teiles der Rede des Balbus zu einer neuen Ordnung. Sie passen also so, wie Balbus sie anordnet, nach seiner Meinung nicht zu einander. Cotta spricht zuerst wie Balbus (§ 45, 280, 6 ff.) von der Schwierigkeit, sich Gott in einer anderen als der menschlichen Gestalt vorzustellen (§ 20, 353, 15 ff.), dann wendet er sich gegen den Schluss, dass nach der präformierten Idee Gottes zuerst der mundus Gott sein müsse; dieser Schluss

---

[1] Sicher müssen die aus dem ersten Teil herausgelösten Abschnitte in den zweiten Teil, in die Erörterung über die Natur der Götter eingeordnet werden. Es ist nicht etwa mit dem Verweis der dritte Teil gemeint, in dem gezeigt wird, dass die Welt durch göttliche Vorsehung geleitet wird, wie Plasberg (zu 352, 12) meint. Er verwies bei den beiden Kleanthesargumenten auf den dritten Teil der Rede des Cotta. Nun fehlt allerdings gerade die Besprechung der beiden Kleanthesargumente in der Widerlegung des zweiten Teiles, und so hat es eine scheinbare Berechtigung, an den dritten Teil zu denken, in dem die beiden Argumente zwar auch nicht behandelt werden, der ja aber überhaupt lückenhaft erhalten ist. Doch da die Behandlung all der anderen von Cotta genannten Beweise für die selbe Stelle wie die der Kleanthesargumente zurückgestellt wird (352, 14; 19; 20; 353, 1) und alle anderen im zweiten Teil der Widerlegung des Cotta vorkommen, muss auch ihre Erörterung für diesen zweiten Teil angesetzt werden. Wenn sie nicht ausdrücklich genannt werden, so wird sich zeigen, dass überhaupt nicht alle dort behandelten Abschnitte ausdrücklich genannt werden. Dass die Providenz der Götter in die Erörterung ihrer Natur gehört, geht auch daraus hervor, dass Balbus selbst im 2. Teil von ihr sprach (286, 6).

ist falsch (§ 21, 353, 19 ff.). Die Behauptung, der mundus sei Gott, ist auch nicht durch die kurzen Schlüsse des Zenon erwiesen (§ 22, 354, 4 ff.) ; hier ordnet er also die Beweise ein, die Balbus im ersten Teil zwischen der Lehre von der Sympathie und der Abhandlung über das Feuer (§ 20, 270, 8 ff.) in schlechtem Zusammenhang gebracht hatte.[1] Nachdem Cotta so die Göttlichkeit des Himmels widerlegt hat, lehnt er auch die Behauptung ab, dass die Sterne, deren wunderbare Ordnung den Balbus so sehr entzückte, Götter seien (§ 23, 353, 4). Er widerlegt damit, was über die Göttlichkeit der Sterne am Ende des ersten Teiles (§§ 40-44, 277, 21 - 279, 25) und zugleich das, was im zweiten Teil darüber gesagt wurde; die letzten von ihm aus dem ersten in den zweiten Teil verwiesenen Argumente sind jetzt erörtert.[2] Nach der Widerlegung der Göttlichkeit des Himmels und der Sterne wendet sich Cotta gegen die von Chrysipp und Xenophon vorgebrachten Gründe und gegen die Lehre von der Sympathie (§§ 25-28, 355, 20 - 357, 3). Damit trifft er die Ausführungen, die in der Rede des Balbus im ersten Teil zwischen der Erklärung der menschlichen Gottesvorstellung und den zenonischen Schlüssen standen, also am Anfang des ganzen von Cotta aus dem ersten Teil herausgelösten Zusammenhanges (§ 13, 268, 7). An die Erwähnung der Sympathie schliesst Cotta eine dem Karneades entlehnte Polemik gegen den Gedanken der ewigen Erhaltung (§§ 29-34, 357, 4 - 360, 8), die in den Ausführungen des Balbus natürlich keine Entsprechung haben kann,[3] als Anfang einer

---

[1] Durch die Einordnung der zenonischen Schlüsse an dieser Stelle zeigt sich, dass in ihnen mundus als Himmel verstanden werden muss, wie es im ganzen Zusammenhang und vor allem in den abschliessenden Worten klar ist: nihil.... eo pulchrius.... nihil ornatius aspectu motuque costantius (355, 3-4). Die Ausführungen über die Vollkommenheit des Himmels schliessen also wirklich an die zenonischen Schlüsse an.

[2] Dass Cotta wirklich die von Balbus am Ende des ersten Teiles gebrachten Beweise für die Göttlichkeit der Gestirne treffen will, ist, wie mir scheint, dadurch deutlich, dass er besonders gegen den Gedanken der Ordnung polemisiert, auf den sich Balbus vor Allem stützte (vgl. S. 143).

[3] Sie ist als Polemik rein akademisch.

Widerlegung der Lehre vom Feuer (§§ 35-37, 360, 9-362, 4). In der Rede des Balbus folgte die Abhandlung über das Feuer auf die Schlüsse des Zenon (§ 23, 271, 11), der Uebergang war schlecht. Cotta schliesst mit einer Polemik gegen den Gott, der keine moralischen Eigenschaften haben soll (§ 38, 362, 5-18) — eine Polemik, die wieder bei Balbus keine Entsprechung finden kann, weil sie ja gerade eine Konsequenz aus den Thesen des Balbus bekämpft — und mit der Besprechung der anderen göttlichen Naturen ausser den Himmelsgöttern (§§ 39-64, 362, 19-378, 12).[1] Diese Anordnung der Argumente ist einleuchtend. Zuerst wird die Göttlichkeit des Himmels und der Gestirne behandelt, dann die Lenkung der Welt durch den Verstand Gottes, schliesslich die Frage, ob die Welt Gott ist. Im letzten Abschnitt wird die Existenz der anderen Götter erörtert, die es ausser Himmel und Gestirnen und der durch Gott geleiteten Welt noch geben soll. Cotta nimmt jedes Argument in dem Sinn in Anspruch, den es wirklich hat, er darf die Fehler des Balbus mit Recht tadeln. Wenn man so wie er die Argumente des zweiten Teiles mit denen verbindet, die im ersten Teil falsch eingeordnet sind, dann entsteht ein in sich geordnetes, verständliches Ganzes.

Cicero sieht also, dass in der Rede des Balbus die lange Behandlung des an sich keines Beweises bedürftigen Themas zu tadeln ist, dass die meisten der von Balbus im ersten Teil vorgebrachten Argumente gar nicht das zu beweisende Thema angehen, dass sie schlecht zu einander stimmen. Er findet die beiden ersten Teile der Rede des Balbus schlecht aufgebaut. Aber warum schreibt er sie dann so schlecht? Fand er die Fehler, die er kennt und aussetzt, in der Vorlage, der er folgt? Folgt er ihr, obwohl er sie so schlecht disponiert fand, und macht er sich in der Rede des Cotta nur das Vergnügen, zu zeigen, wieviel klüger er ist als das Buch, das er ausschreibt? Dann ist aus seinem Tadel eben nicht mehr zu schliessen, als

---

[1] Die beiden Kleanthesargumente, die in diesen Teil verwiesen wurden, werden also von Cotta nicht genannt. Wo sie einzuordnen sind, wird sich später zeigen, wenn überhaupt die Einordnung der nicht ausdrücklich genannten Stellen behandelt wird (vgl. S. 164).

dass er die Fehler seiner Vorlage erkennt, und dass es ihn freute, den Stoiker auf einem Irrtum zu ertappen und ihn durch einen Akademiker widerlegen zu lassen, um die Ueberlegenheit der akademischen Dialektik zu zeigen.[1]

Standen aber wirklich die Fehler, die Cotta tadelt, in der Vorlage Ciceros, oder machte Cicero sie selbst, um sie dann durch Cotta tadeln zu lassen? Es wäre ein seltsames Lehrbuch der stoischen Theologie, in dem zwei Drittel der Ausführungen zu einem Thema gar nicht zu diesem Thema passen, in dem entgegen der immer wieder geäusserten Ansicht, die Frage der Existenz Gottes bedürfe gar keiner Erörterung, in so handgreiflichem Widerspruch fortwährend von ihr geredet würde, jedoch mit Argumenten, die wiederum ganz andere Behauptungen beweisen. Ein seltsames Buch, in dem das Material so schlecht geordnet ist, dass der Gegner es sofort bemerkt. Oder komponiert etwa Cicero mühselig nach vielen verschiedenen Vorlagen eine schlechte Rede, macht dann alle Fehler selbst wieder rückgängig und lässt den Cotta nach einer von ihm erfundenen Disposition die richtige Rede halten? Wahrscheinlicher ist doch, dass er nur den an sich guten Aufbau eines ihm vorliegenden Buches entsprechend seiner dialogischen Absicht veränderte, um dann die gute Disposition gegen die schlechte, die er selbst verschuldet hatte, durch Cotta ausspielen zu lassen! Ironisch sagte Cotta, nachdem Balbus geendet hatte, zu Velleius: «Du hast doch gemerkt, glaube ich, wie viele Argumente Balbus für seine Sache vorgebracht hat, wie sie zu einander passen und mit einander zusammenhängen, wenn sie schon nicht wahr sind» (§ 4, 345, 20 - 346, 2).[2] Er lässt sich von Balbus bestätigen, dass er sich die Einteilung der ganzen Rede richtig gemerkt hat (§ 6, 347, 15-16),[3] er behauptet: «Ich habe meinem Gedächtnis nicht nur die Zahl sondern auch die Anordnung deiner Argumente einge-

---

[1] Cotta spricht ja zuletzt gegen Balbus; er muss also etwas gegen ihn zu sagen haben, und Cicero ist ja Akademiker (vgl. aber S. 45, 1).

[2] A Balbo autem animadvertisti credo quam multa dicta sint quamque etiam si minus vera tamen apta inter se et cohaerentia.

[3] Haec si recte memini partio fuit.

prägt » (§ 10, 349, 8-10).[1] Dann findet er Alles, was Balbus gesagt hat, schlecht aufgebaut und konstruiert einen neuen Zusammenhang. Aber so wie er die Argumente verwendet, waren sie ursprünglich nicht gemeint. Am Ende der Schlüsse des Zenon, die auch an anderer Stelle überliefert sind, heisst es : « Was den Samen des Geistes aussendet, ist selbst vernünftig. Der Himmel sendet den Samen des Geistes aus, also ist der Himmel, der die himmlische Ordnung leitende Gott, vernünftig, worin zugleich die Existenz dieses Gottes gegeben ist » (Sextus Empiricus, adv. math. IX, 101).[2] Auch die übrigen von Zenon berichteten Schlüsse sind Existenzbeweise, die von der Ordnung der Welt ausgehen (a. O. 75 ; 104) ; Balbus aber verwendet sie, um die Natur Gottes zu bestimmen. Auch der Sinn des Xenophonbeweises ist nach Sextus die Existenz Gottes (a. O. 92-94). Und Kleanthes wollte nach seinen eigenen Worten in den Ausführungen, denen Cicero die Argumentation über die Vollkommenheit und die damit gegebene Göttlichkeit des Himmels nachbildet, einen Beweis für das Dasein Gottes geben (a. O. 91). Ebenso führt die Erörterung des Prinzipatbegriffes bei Sextus zum Nachweis der göttlichen Existenz (a. O. 78 ff.). Für Cotta dagegen sind alle diese Schlüsse keine Existenzbeweise, ja er tadelt gerade an Balbus, dass sie von ihm als Existenzbeweise verwendet werden. Wie kann er das tun ? Erfindet Cicero das ? Oder muss man nicht annehmen, dass er diese charakteristische Veränderung des ursprünglichen Beweiszieles der Schlüsse in einer Vorlage fand, dass er sie sich gemäss seiner Absicht, den Stoiker durch den Akademiker widerlegen zu lassen, für die Rede des Akademikers vorbehielt, den Stoiker aber die umgeänderten Argumente im alten Sinn verwenden liess und so in Widersprüche verwickelte,

---

[1] Mandavi enim memoriae non numerum solum sed etiam ordinem argumentorum tuorum.

[2] *Τὸ προϊέμενον σπέρμα λογικοῦ καὶ αὐτὸ λογικόν ἐστιν. ὁ δὲ κόσμος προΐεται σπέρμα λογικοῦ. λογικὸν ἄρα ἐστὶν ὁ κόσμος. ᾧ συνεισάγεται καὶ ἡ τούτου ὕπαρξις.* Zur doppelten Bedeutung des Begriffes *κόσμος*, durch die der Schluss auf die Existenz möglich wird, vgl. St. V. Fr. II 527. Darum ist auch jede Aenderung von *τούτου* (*τοῦ θεοῦ* Bekker dub.) unnötig.

die der Akademiker dann mit Leichtigkeit löste? Diese Annahme wäre, wie mir scheint, dann richtig, wenn sich nach Cottas Angaben ein Buch rekonstruieren liesse, in dem die jetzt nicht zu einander passenden Teile der Rede des Balbus passend an einander kämen. Die ungeordneten, fast chaotischen Darlegungen des 2. Buches müssten nach der Ordnung des Cotta ein organisches Ganzes werden, die Hinweise und Andeutungen, die jetzt in der Rede des Balbus unverständlich sind, müssten Sinn gewinnen. Wie sollte es dann Zufall sein, dass Alles zu einander stimmt, wie sollte man dann annehmen, dass die einzelnen Bestandteile von Cicero aus den verschiedensten Vorlagen zusammengeschrieben worden wären? Ich versuche also, nach dem Tadel des Cotta die Rede des Balbus zu rekonstruieren, so wie sie lauten müsste, wenn es nicht die Absicht Ciceros wäre, sie durch Cotta widerlegen zu lassen.[1]

---

[1] Hnm. (II 244 ff.) hat, so viel ich weiss, als Erster ausdrücklich darauf hingewiesen, dass die dialogische Absicht Ciceros bestimmend dafür gewesen sei, wie das Material in der Rede des Stoikers verwendet würde. Der Akademiker soll Recht behalten. Hnm. sagt: «Nicht der Stoiker bestimmt Aufbau und Stoffauswahl des Akademikers, wie es selbstverständlich bei Cicero den Anschein haben muss, sondern der Schriftsteller legt jenem die Gedanken, die der Akademiker widerlegen wollte, und zwar in der Reihenfolge, in der dieser sie widerlegen wollte, in den Mund» (II 170). «Nicht Vermutung sondern Tatsache bleibt aber, dass er im Interesse des akademischen Vortrages eine durchaus unstoische Gliederung als stoisch ausgegeben und nach ihr den Vortrag (des Balbus) einzuteilen fingiert hat» (II 169). Aber das kann unmöglich richtig sein und reicht zur Erklärung keinesfalls aus. Denn Cotta widerlegt die Argumente des Balbus ja gerade in anderer Reihenfolge, als Balbus sie vorbrachte. Cicero kann also nur die Argumente an falscher Stelle verwendet haben, damit Cotta die falsche Verwendung tadeln kann. Nach der Einteilung des Cotta kann man positiv über die Existenz der Götter und über ihre Natur reden wie Balbus oder negativ wie Cotta. Diese Einteilung ist stoisch; es kommt nur darauf an, dass sie richtig durchgeführt wird. Reinhardt hat sich diese Frage überhaupt nicht gestellt. Seine Theorie, dass die Rede des Balbus aus drei verschiedenen Vorlagen, aus Poseidonios, einem Eklektiker und einer Syllogismensammlung zusammengeschrieben sei, gründet sich auf die Beobachtung von Anstössen der Darstellung und auf allge-

Vor Allem durften dann die ganzen Ausführungen über die Wirkung Gottes in der Welt, die zenonischen Schlüsse, die Abhandlung über das Feuer, über den Himmel und die Göttlichkeit der Gestirne (also der Inhalt der §§ 13-44) nicht im ersten Teil, der von der Existenz Gottes handelt, sondern erst im zweiten Teil stehen. Der erste Teil kann nicht da schliessen, wo er jetzt schliesst. Cotta sieht schon in den Argumenten des Kleanthes, die Balbus an erster und an dritter Stelle anführte, nur die Erklärung dafür, dass es Menschen gibt, die an Gott glauben, nicht einen Beweis für die Existenz Gottes. Aber er schliesst sie eng an die Argumente für die Existenz Gottes an, denn er übernimmt sie nicht etwa in den zweiten Teil (vgl. S. 152); für Balbus war ja auch die Allgemeinheit der Gottesvorstellung ein Beweis der göttlichen Existenz. Mit diesen beiden Argumenten ist nach Cotta der erste Teil zu Ende, alles Andere gehört, wie er sagt, in den zweiten Teil; darum muss hier also der Abschluss des ganzen ersten Teiles gelesen werden: « Wer das sieht, der ist nicht nur ungelehrt sondern auch pietätlos, wenn er nicht glaubt, dass es Götter gibt » (§ 44, 280, 1-2).[1] Wer was sieht? Wunderzeichen, wie sie jüngst im octavianischen Krieg zu sehen waren; so schliesst ja die Argumentation nach Kleanthes.[2] Ungelehrt und pietätlos ist es, die allgemeine Uebereinstimmung der Menschen nicht zu kennen und sich durch sie und die Beispiele der Geschichte nicht belehren zu lassen. Schon einmal hiess es, es sei töricht und pietätlos, die Existenz der Götter zu leugnen (§ 6, 263, 2), sie nicht durch die Beispiele der eigenen Geschichte belehrt (§ 7, 263, 9 docti) anzuerkennen. Die abschliessenden Worte haben also hier

meine Erwägungen über den Inhalt. Aber die Lösung dieser Frage ist für Rhdt.s These von entscheidender Bedeutung. Wenn Cicero die Fehler selbst machte, kann man unmöglich aus seiner Darstellung ohne weiteres auf die Vorlage schliessen, sondern man kann über sie erst urteilen, wenn die ciceronischen, bewussten Fehler rückgängig gemacht sind.

[1] Quae qui videat non indocte solum verum etiam impie faciat si deos esse neget.

[2] Die römischen Beispiele sind natürlich von Cicero eingesetzt, und durch sie mag auch der Vorwurf der Pietätlosigkeit bedingt sein.

Sinn ; in der Rede des Balbus waren sie unverständlich. Die Erörterung über die Existenz Gottes, die eigentlich nur Hinweise auf die Selbstverständlichkeit der göttlichen Existenz gibt, ist jetzt so kurz, wie sie sein muss, wenn der Redende ehrlich davon überzeugt ist, dass sie keiner langen Erörterung bedarf.[1]

Es folgt der zweite Teil über die *Natur* der Götter. Cotta beginnt die Widerlegung der Argumente des Balbus mit einem Hinweis auf die Schwierigkeit, sich Gott in einer anderen als der menschlichen Gestalt vorzustellen (§ 20, 353, 15) und schliesst daran die Erörterung über die Göttlichkeit des Himmels (353, 16 ff.), wie es auch Balbus tat (§ 45, 280, 6). So war also der Anfang des zweiten Teiles auch ursprünglich aufgebaut. Am Ende des ersten Teiles war die Allgemeinheit der Gottesvorstellung behauptet und ihr Zustandekommen nach Kleanthes erklärt worden, am Anfang des zweiten Teiles wird von der präformierten Idee Gottes auf die Göttlichkeit eines bestimmten Wesen geschlossen. Der im Menschen liegende Begriff muss realisiert werden. Mit dem Schluss von der Idee Gottes auf die Göttlichkeit des Himmels war in der Rede des Balbus die Widerlegung des epikureischen Einwandes gegen diesen Gedanken fest verbunden ; Cotta erwähnt sie nicht. Aber man kann sie wegen des inneren Zusammenhanges von dem Vorhergehenden nicht trennen, sie muss ursprünglich an dieser Stelle gestanden haben.[2] Erst beim Uebergang zur Beschreibung der Gestirnbahnen war in der Darstellung des Bal-

[1] Da die in der Rede des Balbus falsch stehenden Worte noch so deutlich auf die Zusammenhänge Bezug nehmen, in denen sie ursprünglich standen, muss Cicero die Vorlage zuerst ganz übersetzt und dann erst bei der Komposition des 3. Buches geändert haben. Weitere Beweise dafür vgl. S. 162, 164.

[2] Man kann bei der Rekonstruktion der Vorlage natürlich nicht in sich zusammenhängende Ausführungen der Rede des Balbus zerreissen. Cottas Widerlegung geht zu summarisch vor, als dass man auf den Hinweis verzichten könnte, der in einem guten Anschluss von Sätzen der Rede des Balbus liegt. Nur so können auch die von Cotta nicht namentlich bezeichneten Stücke untergebracht werden, an richtiger Stelle, dort nämlich, wo sie dem Sinne nach hingehören.

bus ein Bruch. Cotta lässt diese Beschreibung nicht sogleich folgen, er widerlegt zuerst die zenonischen Schlüsse (§ 22, 354, 4 ff.), die, wie er sagt, die Göttlichkeit des Himmels bestätigen sollen. Diese Schlüsse standen bei Balbus an falscher Stelle und ohne Verbindung (vgl. S. 136). Schliesst man sie wie Cotta an die Widerlegung des epikureischen Einwandes gegen die Göttlichkeit des Himmels an, dann gewinnt man einen passenden Zusammenhang. Denn nun wird zuerst von dem Begriff Gottes auf die Göttlichkeit des Himmels geschlossen, ein Einwand der Epikureer gegen diese Gleichsetzung von Gott und Himmel abgewehrt und dann in Polemik gegen die Akademie der Beweis der bis jetzt ja nur behaupteten Gleichsetzung durch die Einführung der zenonischen Schlüsse gegeben. Dabei wird zugleich das Thema wieder in seinem ganzen Umfang aufgenommen und nicht nur, wie gegen Epikur, eine Einzelheit verteidigt. « Die ganzen Behauptungen, die zur Diskussion stehen, entgehen dann, wenn sie ausladend und breit behandelt werden, wie ich es im Sinne habe, leichter den Schmähungen der Akademiker, wenn sie aber so, wie Zenon es tat, kurz und sehr prägnant bewiesen werden, sind sie leichter zu widerlegen » (§ 20, 270, 8-11),[1] so begann Balbus die zenonischen Schlüsse. Diese Worte blieben in seiner Rede ohne Entsprechung (vgl. S. 144), jetzt aber passen sie sich ein.

Für Cotta sind die zenonischen Schlüsse der letzte Beweis für die Göttlichkeit des Himmels, er wendet sich dann zur Widerlegung der Göttlichkeit der Gestirne (§ 23, 355, 4 ff.). Aber schon die Einleitung der zenonischen Schlüsse, wie sie wenigstens bei Balbus lautete, wies darauf hin, dass es noch andere, dem gleichen Thema geltende Ausführungen geben müsse. Die Schlüsse des Zenon sollten ja ausführlicher bewiesen werden, weil sie in ihrer Kürze zu leicht widerlegbar schienen. Balbus erörterte die Göttlichkeit des Himmels noch einmal ausführlicher, nach allgemeinen Erwägungen über die Notwendigkeit, dass das Vollkommene existiere (§ 33, 275, 15 ff. ;

[1] Atque haec cum uberius disputantur et fusius ut mihi est in animo facere, facilius effugiunt Academicorum calumniam ; cum autem, ut Zeno solebat, brevius angustiusque concluduntur, tum apertiora sunt ad reprendendum.

vgl. S. 140). Ursprünglich aber musste die ausführlichere Darstellung unmittelbar auf die zenonischen Schlüsse folgen. Sie muss also hier eingefügt werden. Der Himmel ist Gott, Zenon beweist das wohl, aber zu kurz; ich mache es anders, ist die Gedankenfolge, und der Uebergang lautet: « Und auch, wenn man von den ersten unvollendeten Naturen zu den letzten vollendeten aufsteigen will, muss man zur Natur der Götter kommen » (§ 33, 275, 15-17).[1]

Der ausführlichere Beweis der Göttlichkeit des Himmels ging unmittelbar anschliessend in den Beweis für die Göttlichkeit der Sterne über. « Und nachdem die Göttlichkeit des Himmels erkannt ist, muss man den Sternen die gleiche Göttlichkeit beilegen » (§ 39, 277, 21-22).[2] So hat auch Cotta nach der Widerlegung der Göttlichkeit des Himmels die Göttlichkeit der Sterne bestritten. Seine Anordnung ergibt sich also von selbst, nachdem die zenonischen Schlüsse und die mit ihnen zusammenhängenden Ausführungen hinter der Widerlegung des epikureischen Einwandes gegen die Gleichsetzung des Himmels mit Gott eingefügt sind. In der Vorlage wurde offenbar wirklich zuerst die Göttlichkeit des Himmels, dann die der Sterne bewiesen. Balbus sagte ja auch ausdrücklich, dass nach der präformierten Idee Gottes *zuerst* der Himmel Gott sein müsste, ohne in der Aufrählung fortzufahren (§ 45, 280, 12; vgl. S. 146). Wenn aber auf den Beweis der Göttlichkeit des Himmels der Beweis der Göttlichkeit der Sterne folgt, dann ist dies « erstens » inhaltlich begründet, wie es formal in dem Uebergang nachklingt: « Nachdem die Göttlichkeit des Himmels erkannt ist, muss die Göttlichkeit der Sterne behauptet werden ».[3]

---

[1] Atque etiam si a primis incohatisque naturis ad ultimas perfectasque volumus procedere, ad deorum naturam perveniamus necesse est. Damit sind wieder Schwierigkeiten in den Ausführungen des Balbus beseitigt (vgl. S. 144).

[2] Atque hac mundi divinitate perspecta tribuenda est sideribus eadem divinitas.

[3] Plasberg zu 280, 13 sagt also mit Unrecht, dass das primum keine Entsprechung habe, wenigstens was die Vorlage angeht. Auch hier hat Cicero zu ändern vergessen, als er die Umstellung vornahm. Vgl. im Vorhergehenden S. 160 und im Folgenden S. 164.

Weitere Ausführungen über die Göttlichkeit der Sterne werden nicht gemacht. Dieser Abschnitt (§§ 39-44, 277, 21 - 279, 25) ist der letzte, der nach der Widerlegung des epikureischen Einwandes einzuordnen ist. Damit ist aber zugleich die Lücke ausgefüllt, die sich in der Rede des Balbus hier fand; er schloss an den Gedanken, dass der Himmel Gott sei, die Beschreibung der Sternbahnen an. Der Nachweis, dass die Sterne Götter sind, trifft jetzt unmittelbar auf jene Beschreibung des regelmässigen Laufes der Gestirne (§ 49, 282, 15 ff.), die nicht zum Vorhergehenden passte und zudem eine Doppelung der im ersten Teil gebrachten Gedanken war. Inhaltlich gab sie den notwendigen und geforderten Beweis der früher, im ersten Teil aufgestellten Behauptung (vgl. S. 177). Jetzt schliesst sie sich auch formal mit ihr zusammen.

Diese Beschreibung der Sternbahnen, zu der man ohne weiteres von der Behauptung der Freiwilligkeit ihrer Bewegung herüberlesen kann,[1] endete eng anschliessend bei Balbus in einer Definition der Natur des Himmels, die wieder nach Zenon gegeben wurde (§ 57, 285, 17 ff.). Hinter dieser Definition aber schien etwas auszufallen. Was über den Verstand und die Tätigkeit des Himmels gesagt wurde, las sich wie die Disposition neuer Ausführungen, die aber fehlten. Cotta schliesst an seine Widerlegung der Göttlichkeit der Sterne die Widerlegung der von Chrysipp und Xenophon vorgebrachten Argumente, sowie die Besprechung der Sympathie und der Lehre vom Feuer (§ 25, 355, 20 ff.). Er nennt die zenonische Definition der Natur des Himmels überhaupt nicht, aber sie gehört untrennbar zum Erweis der Göttlichkeit der Sterne und ist die notwendige Voraussetzung für das Chrysippzitat, die Xenophonstelle, die Lehre von der Sympathie und vom Feuer.[2] Inhaltlich jeden-

[1] Die Behauptung der Göttlichkeit der Sterne schliesst: restat ut motus astrorum sit voluntarius. Die Beschreibung der Sternbahnen beginnt: primusque sol.... Freiwilligkeit und Göttlichkeit, wie es am Ende der Beschreibung heisst, sind identisch (vgl. S. 144).

[2] Cotta erwähnt die Definition Zenons erst, nachdem er die von Chrysipp und Xenophon gegebene Argumentation widerlegt hat (§ 27, 356, 19), nur um seine Definition des Naturbegriffes polemisch abzuheben.

falls wird in diesen Ausführungen gesagt, was nach der zenonischen Definition hier gesagt werden müsste, was aber bei Balbus fehlte. Es wird die wunderbare Schönheit und Vollkommenheit der Welt bewiesen, es wird der Zusammenklang aller Teile und ihre Erhaltung durch die Sympathie als Wirkung des göttlichen Geistes erklärt. Am Schluss der zenonischen Definition wird gezeigt, dass durch die Wirkung des Himmels, des göttlichen Verstandes die Beständigkeit, die Mangellosigkeit, die vollkommene Schönheit der Schöpfung geschaffen werde. Die Disposition ist also jetzt erfüllt; man kann mit Recht jetzt den Schlussstrich unter die Erörterung der himmlischen Götter setzen (§ 59; vgl. S. 148). Hiess es bei Balbus am Anfang des zweiten Teiles, die Göttlichkeit des Himmels sollte aus seiner Wirkung später noch deutlicher werden (§ 46, 280, 25), so ist jetzt wirklich durch das Schaffen des Himmels seine Göttlichkeit bewiesen.

Mit dem Chrysippzitat zusammen aber werden die beiden Kleanthesargumente, die Cotta in den zweiten Teil verweist, dann jedoch nicht mehr bespricht, hierhergezogen; sie standen ja in enger Verbindung vgl. dazu S. 134. Es entsteht also eine korrekte doxographische Reihe: Zenon, Chrysipp, Kleanthes; die Ansichten der stoischen Philosophen werden genannt, um die Darlegung der eigenen Ansicht zu unterbauen.[1] Wenn es am Anfang dieses Abschnittes über das Handeln des Weltgottes hiess: « Ich werde nicht irren, wenn ich vom Ersten, der die Wahrheit suchte, die wir finden wollen, Anfang und Prinzip meiner Untersuchung herleite. Zenon nämlich.... » (§ 57, 285, 17-18),[2] so ist dieses Wortspiel jetzt verständlich. Mit Zenon begann die Kette der Beweise für die Göttlichkeit des Himmels, und Zenon ist als Begründer der Schule, wie es wenigstens den Schülern scheinen muss, der Erste, der die Wahrheit suchte. Ausserdem muss auf die Lehre von der Sympathie die Lehre von der Wärme folgen, die inhaltlich dazu gehört und die Cotta nach der Lehre von der

[1] Cicero vereinigte also die verschiedenen Kleantheszitate, um den Übergang vom 1. zum 2. Teil zu gewinnen und verdeckte ihre Unstimmigkeit, indem er sie kreuzweise anordnete (vgl. S. 152, 1).

[2] Zu huius disputationis principium vgl. Rhdt. I 218.

Sympathie ebenfalls widerlegt (§ 35, 360, 9).[1] Damit ist Alles, was aus dem ersten Teil in den zweiten einzuordnen war, eingeordnet, die Lücken des zweiten Teiles sind ausgefüllt. Der Schluss kommt nicht mehr überraschend, die Wirkung des himmlischen Gottes ist ausführlich besprochen worden. Nun kann die Untersuchung über die anderen Naturen der Götter angeschlossen werden (vgl. S. 148).

Es ergibt sich also eine gute Ordnung und eine innere Beziehung der Gedanken. Der erste Teil (§§ 4-12) erweist die Existenz Gottes allein durch den Hinweis auf die allgemeine Uebereinstimmung in dieser Frage, die Uebereinstimmung aller Zeiten und aller Völker (§ 12). Die Schwierigkeiten liegen nicht in der Frage der Existenz sondern in der Bestimmung der Natur Gottes. Die Einigkeit der Menschen in dieser Ansicht wird durch die Erklärung des Entstehens der Gottesvorstellung noch mehr gesichert. Die Erfahrungen, auf die sich Kleanthes beruft, werden überall gemacht; darum glauben alle Völker und alle Zeiten an die Existenz Gottes.

Da die Existenz Gottes sicher ist und jeder Mensch eine bestimmte Vorstellung von Gott hat, kann seine Existenz und eine bestimmte Vorstellung von ihm in Allem, was folgt, als Faktum vorausgesetzt werden. Man muss nur den Gott, den es sicher gibt, erkennen.[2] Nach der präformierten Idee Gottes muss der Himmel Gott sein. Das scheint im ersten Augenblick befremdlich. Die gefährliche Ironisierung eines runden, sich bewegenden Gottes wird abgewehrt und dann die Gleichsetzung von Gott und Himmel, die am Anfang nur behauptet worden war, bewiesen. In Anlehnung an die alten Schlüsse des Zenon wird der Beweis breit und ausladend, ausgehend von dem Gedanken der Vollkommenheit, gegeben. Und wie der Himmel Gott ist, sind auch die Sterne Götter. Damit ist gesagt, wer der Gott ist, dessen Existenz gewiss war.

---

[1] Der Einwand des Carneades, den er zwischen die beiden Widerlegungen stellt (§ 29, 357, 4 ff.), kann natürlich in der Vorlage keine Entsprechung gehabt haben.

[2] Die andere Einstellung zum Existenzbeweis erklärt also die andere Verwendung des alten, sonst für die Existenz gebrachten Materials (Chrysipp etc., vgl. S. 157 etc.).

Gott ist aber nicht nur, er handelt auch. Die himmlische Ordnung ist seine Wirkung. Dass Alles so eingerichtet ist, dass es bestehen kann, dass nichts fehlt, Vollkommenheit also und ausserdem Schönheit und Herrlichkeit die Welt erfüllen, muss die Wirkung der *πρόνοια* sein. Diese Behauptung wird durch Kleanthes und Chrysipp bewiesen, durch die Lehre von der Sympathie naturwissenschaftlich erklärt.[1] Damit ist die Erörterung über die wahren himmlischen Götter, ihre Natur, ihre äussere Form und ihre Wirkung zu Ende. Es folgt die notwendige Abgrenzung der wahren Götter gegen die geglaubten Götter. Einige von ihnen sind mit den wahren Göttern identisch, die anderen sind Erdichtungen und Fiktionen.

Die Vorlage Ciceros ist wirklich ein einziges, einheitlich komponiertes Buch. Man muss sich seinen Aufbau und die Aufeinanderfolge der einzelnen Argumentationen ursprünglich so denken:

ne egere quidem videtur oratione prima pars (§ 4, 261, 7) — itaque inter omnis omnium gentium summa constat; omnibus enim innatum est et in animo quasi insculptum esse deos. quales sint varium est, esse nemo negat (§ 12, 266, 18-20).

Cleanthes quidem noster (duabus) de causis dixit in animis hominum informatas deorum esse notiones. priorem posuit eam de qua modo dixi, quae orta esset ex praesensione

---

[1] Diese Ausführungen beschreiben also in umgekehrter Reihenfolge das, was die Disposition am Ende des Zenonabschnittes als Wirkung des vom Himmel aus die Welt leitenden Verstandes angibt. Rhdt. I 217-18 fand die fehlende Erörterung im dritten Teil der Rede des Balbus (§ 115). Zwar wird auch dort das aptissimum ad permanendum erörtert (315, 10-12). Aber dass diese Ausführungen nicht gemeint sein können, selbst wenn man Rhdt.s Quellentheorie zugeben wollte, beweist der Schluss des Abschnittes (§ 119, 317, 11) der, wie es dort der Zusammenhang fordert (vgl. S. 178), die Cohärenz und Dauer der Teile für bewundernswert erklärt. Es wird also dadurch nicht etwa das Wirken Gottes bewiesen, wie es doch nötig ist und in den von mir hier eingefügten Zusammenhängen geschieht. Ausserdem fehlte bei Einsetzung der §§ 115 ff. die Mangellosigkeit und Schönheit der Welt. Dass inhaltlich unter aptissimum ad permanendum aber die Sympathie der Teile zu verstehen ist, zeigt sich aus diesen Ausführungen, auf die Rhdt. verweist.

rerum futurarum (§ 13, 266, 20-267, 3), (alteram) quae terreret animos (§ 14, 267, 5) — vim quandam esse caelestem et divinam suspicati sunt (267, 15).[1]

quae qui videat non indocte solum verum etiam impie faciat si deos esse neget (§ 44, 280, 1) — ex utraque re et mundi volubilitas quae nisi in globosa forma esse non posset, et stellarum rotundi ambitus cognoscuntur (§ 49, 282, 14).

atque haec cum uberius disputantur et fusius, ut mihi est in animo facere, facilius effugiunt Academicorum calumniam (§ 20, 270, 1) — cur igitur mundus non animans sapiensque iudicetur cum ex se procreet animantes atque sapientes? (§ 22, 271, 10).

atque etiam si a primis incohatisque naturis ad ultimas perfectasque volumus procedere, ad deorum naturam perveniamus necesse est (§ 33, 275, 15) — restat igitur ut motus astrorum sit voluntarius (§ 44, 279, 25).

primusque sol qui astrorum tenet principatum ita movetur.... (§ 49, 282, 15) — (mens mundi providet, ut) in eo eximia pulchritudo sit atque omnis ornatus (§ 58, 286, 10).

(atque Cleanthes id probat duabus causis. primam posuit eam) quam ceperimus ex magnitudine commodorum quae percipiuntur caeli temperatione, fecunditate terrarum aliarumque commoditatum complurium copia (§ 13, 267, 3-5). (alteram) causam esse, eamque vel maximam, aequabilitatem motus (§ 15, 267, 16)....[2] — haec ita fieri.... non possent nisi ea uno divino et continuo spiritu continerentur (§ 19, 270, 7).

tamen id ipsum rationibus physicis id est naturalibus confirmari volo (§ 23, 271, 13)[3] — nam ni ita esset, hominem.... pluris esse quam mundum omnem oporteret (§ 32, 275, 14).

---

[1] Die in runden Klammern stehenden Worte sind eine Veränderung des Textes, die durch die Umstellungen Ciceros notwendig ist, um die ursprünglichen Sätze zurückzugewinnen.

[2] Dass diese beiden Argumente, etwa in diesem Wortlaut, hier stehen müssen, wurde gezeigt (vgl. S. 164).

[3] So ungefähr muss der Uebergang geheissen haben, da die Worte, die Cicero einfügt, um die falsche Ordnung des Balbus zu motivieren und zu verdecken (vgl. S. 136), natürlich gestrichen werden müssen.

dictum est de universo mundo, dictum etiam est de sideribus (§ 59, 286, 11).... — ac mihi videor satis et esse deos et quales essent ostendisse (§ 72, 295, 5).

Alle Widersprüche, die sich in der Rede des Balbus finden, alle Fehler der Darstellung sind von Cicero bewusst gemacht. Man kann aus ihnen keinen Schluss auf seine Vorlage oder seine Vorlagen ziehen. Um zu entscheiden, welchem Philosophen Cicero bei der Darstellung der stoischen Theologie in den beiden ersten Teilen folgt, muss man die Fehler, die sich finden, rückgängig machen.[1]

Nur die beiden ersten Teile seines Themas wollte Balbus ursprünglich behandeln, von der Lenkung der Welt durch Gott und von der Fürsorge Gottes für die Menschen sollte bei anderer Gelegenheit die Rede sein (§ 3, 261, 5). Cotta verlangte, dass er auch darüber spreche (261, 6-7), Balbus antwortete ihm darauf nicht. Nachdem er die beiden ersten Teile seiner Rede einheitlich abgeschlossen hat, beginnt er den dritten Teil sofort, als wenn es immer seine Absicht gewesen wäre, alle Punkte des Themas zu behandeln, mit den Worten: « Das nächste ist, zu zeigen, dass durch der Götter Vorsehung die Welt geleitet wird » (§ 73, 295, 6).[2] Dann teilt er das ganze Thema in drei Abschnitte und definiert es ausführlicher als zuerst: « Ich behaupte also, dass durch die Vorsehung der Götter die Welt und alle ihre Teile im Anfang zusammengesetzt wurden und für alle Zeit gelenkt werden. Diesen Gegenstand behandelt unsere Schule fast allgemein in drei Teilen. Ein erster ist der, der von der Erwägung ausgeht, durch die gezeigt wurde, dass Gott ist. Wenn das feststeht, muss man

[1] Zur genauen Rekonstruktion der Vorlage Ciceros würde gehören, dass noch jede einzelne Veränderung von Uebergängen oder sonstigen Zusammenhängen, die Cicero vornahm, bestimmt würde, man müsste wenigstens hypothetisch erklären, wie er bei seiner Veränderung vorging. Dazu wäre eine inhaltliche Erörterung nötig, die erst in einem anderen Zusammenhang gegeben werden soll und auf die also auch diese Fragen zu verschieben sind.

[2] Proximum est ut doceam deorum providentia mundum administrari.

zugeben, dass durch der Götter Willen die Welt regiert wird. Der zweite zeigt, dass alle Dinge einer mit Empfindung begabten Natur unterworfen sind und von ihr aufs beste gelenkt werden, woraus folgt, dass diese Natur von lebenden Prinzipien herstammt. Die dritte Erwägung handelt von der Bewunderung der himmlischen und irdischen Dinge» (§ 75, 296, 4-12).[1] Balbus behauptet also nicht mehr allein die Leitung der Welt durch die Vorsehung der Götter sondern auch die Zusammensetzung aller Teile der Welt und die ewige Lenkung der Welt durch Gott.

Dann beginnt er sofort die Behandlung des ersten Abschnittes. Entweder gibt es keine Götter oder es gibt sie. Wenn es sie gibt, dann müssen sie handeln und müssen, weil das die höchste Aufgabe ist, die Welt lenken (§ 76, 296, 13-17). Sonst existierte eine mächtigere Macht, durch die die wunderbaren Erscheinungen der sichtbaren Welt bewirkt würden, Gott wäre also nicht das Mächtigste. Gott ist aber das Mächtigste, also verwaltet er die Welt und regiert die ganze Natur (§ 77, 297, 7). Wenn die Götter Verstand haben, müssen sie die wichtigsten Dinge erkennen und auch die Kraft haben, sie auszuführen. Also wird die Welt durch die göttliche Vorsehung verwaltet (297, 14). Da die Götter sind, müssen sie Leben haben, verständig sein, mit einander in Verbindung stehen und gemeinsam die Welt, ihren Staat, regieren. Den Göttern eignet Klugheit und Gesetz wie den Menschen, nur in höherem Masse ; was die Menschen haben, stammt von Gott. Die Götter müssen ihre Kraft auch in Handlung umsetzen, also wird die Welt durch den Ratschluss Gottes gelenkt (§ 80, 298, 8). Und da die Gestirne, der Himmel, die Welt Götter sind, wird Alles durch

[1] Dico igitur providentia deorum mundum et omnis mundi partes et initio constitutas esse et omni tempore administrari. Eamque dispositionem tris in partes nostri fere dividunt. Quarum prima pars est quae ducitur ab ea ratione quae docet esse deos, quo concesso confitendum est eorum consilio mundum administrari. Secunda est autem quae docet omnis res subiectas esse naturae sentienti ab eaque omnia pulcherrime geri, quo constituto sequitur ab animantibus principiis eam esse generatam. Tertius est locus qui ducitur ex admiratione rerum caelestium atque terrestrium.

Gott gelenkt. Der Beweis der göttlichen Weltregierung unter der Voraussetzung der Existenz Gottes ist damit zu Ende: « Und über den ersten Teil ist damit genug gesagt » (298, 13-14).[1]

Die Durchführung des zweiten Punktes der Disposition schliesst sich unmittelbar an mit den Worten: « Jetzt muss ich zeigen, dass Alles der Natur unterworfen ist und von ihr aufs beste geführt wird » (§ 81, 298, 15-16).[2] Bei der ersten Angabe der Disposition (§ 75, 296, 9) sagte er, er wolle zeigen, dass alle Dinge einer mit Empfindung begabten Natur unterworfen sind und von ihr aufs beste gelenkt werden, woraus folge, dass die Natur von lebenden Prinzipien herstamme. In der Formulierung am Anfang des zweiten Teiles fehlt also, wenn man sie mit der vorhergehenden vergleicht, der Begriff der Empfindung, die die Natur doch haben sollte, und die Behauptung, dass sie von lebenden Prinzipien herstamme.[3]

Statt dessen gibt Balbus eine Definition des Naturbegriffes: « Aber was die Natur selbst sei, muss man vorher kurz auseinandersetzen, damit das, was gezeigt werden soll, leichter einzusehen ist » (298, 16-17).[4] Die Einen meinen, Natur sei eine irrationale Kraft, die in dem Körper die notwendigen Bewegungen hervorrufe (298, 18-19). Die Anderen sehen in der Natur eine rationale ordnende Kraft, die einen bestimmten Weg verfolge, Ursache und Wirkung jedes Dinges setze und jeder Kunst, jeder Handfertigkeit, jedem Künstler überlegen sei. Die Kraft des Samens schaffe in der Materie, in die sie eindringt, Alles, was ist (298, 19-27). Die Dritten bezeichnen Alles mit dem Namen Natur, wie Epikur, der so definiert, es sei aller Dinge, die sind, Natur der Körper, das Leere und seine Akzidentien (§ 82, 299, 1-3). « Wenn ich aber sage, durch die

---

[1] Ac de prima quidem parte satis dictum est.

[2] Sequitur ut doceam omnia subiecta esse naturae eaque ab ea pulcherrime geri.

[3] Auch die erste Definition am Anfang des ganzen dritten Teiles (§ 73, 295, 6) und die zweite (§ 75, 296, 4-5), die der Unterteilung vorangeht, unterscheiden sich von einander.

[4] Sed quid sit ipsa natura explicandum est ante breviter, quo facilius id quod docere volumus intellegi possit.

Natur bestehe die Welt und werde durch sie verwaltet, meine ich es nicht wie bei einem Klumpen Erde oder bei einem Stück Stein oder bei irgend einer anderen Sache dieser Art, deren Natur keinen Zusammenhang hat, sondern ich meine es wie bei einem Baum, bei einem Lebewesen, in dem keine Regellosigkeit sondern Ordnung ist und etwas gewissermassen der Kunst Analoges » (299, 3-7).[1] Balbus stellt also seinen Naturbegriff gegen drei andere Naturbegriffe. Der erste (298, 18-19) ist der akademische. Cotta sagt gegen Balbus gewandt: « Die Einrichtung der Welt ist die Wirkung einer Natur, einer Natur die nicht als Künstler schafft, wie Zenon meint, sondern Alles schafft und lenkt durch die jedem Ding eigentümlichen Bewegungen und Veränderungen » (§ 27, 356, 18-21).[2] Er weist die Behauptung des Balbus, die Sterne seien Götter, da sie in ewigem Gleichmass ihre Bahn ziehen, zurück, weil das nicht die Göttlichkeit sondern nur das Wirken der Natur beweise, durch die sie sich notwendigerweise regelmässig bewegen (§ 23, 355, 9 ff.). Die Stoiker, die das rationale Gesetz der Natur nicht kennen, flüchten sich in eine Erklärung durch göttliche Kräfte (355, 17-19). Diese Auffassung umschreibt die erste von Balbus genannte Definition, nach der die Natur eine irrationale Kraft ist, die in den Körpern mit Notwendigkeit die Bewegungen bedingt. Denn wäre sie eine rationale Kraft, so würde der Schluss auf ihre Beseeltheit wie im Folgenden gegeben sein. Die zweite Definition in der fast Worte der zenonischen Definition aufgenommen werden (§ 57, 285, 18 ff.), ist stoisch, es ist die Definition der Schule. Die dritte Definition schliesslich, für die ausdrücklich Epikur angeführt

---

[1] Sed nos cum dicimus natura constare administrarique mundum, non dicimus ut glaebam aut fragmentum lapidis aut aliquid eiusmodi nulla cohaerendi natura sed ut arborem, ut animal in quibus nulla temeritas sed ordo apparet et artis quaedam similitudo.

[2] Naturae ista sunt Balbe, naturae non artificiose ambulantis, ut ait Zeno, quod quidem quale sit iam videbimus, sed omnia cientis et agitantis motibus et mutationibus suis. Die Urnatur hat ihre eigene Kraft und Bewegung (und damit notwendige weitere Bewegungen), sagt Cotta in einem erhaltenen Stück des dritten Teiles seiner Erwiderung (Lact. II 8, 10).

wird, ist auch sonst als epikureisch bezeugt (fr. 75 Us.). Im Gegensatz zu diesen Allen fasst Balbus die Natur als eine organische Kraft. Natur soll ja allgemein so wie bei einem Baum oder bei einem Tier verstanden werden. Darin liegt mehr als im akademischen Naturbegriff, das Organische begreift über das Notwendige hinaus in sich Ordnung und Zusammenhang. Gegenüber dem stoischen Schulbegriff ist die Definition des Balbus enger, es fehlt die Steigerung zur Rationalität und Wirkung des Künstlers. Wenn auch der Baum, das Tier, der Mensch als Schöpfung nicht zu verstehen sind, ohne dass der ordnenden Natur verbindende Kraft und etwas Aehnliches wie Kunst eignet, so darf man ihr doch eben nicht Kunst zuschreiben, und man darf sie nicht mit einem Künstler identifizieren, wie es die Schule tut. Dem epikureischen Naturbegriff aber ist der Naturbegriff des Balbus dadurch überlegen, dass er gegen das rein Mechanische und Zufällige das Organische und Sinnvolle stellt.[1] Die Natur muss, so wie Balbus es darstellt, wenigstens Empfindung haben. Ihre Teile sollen sich nicht trennen lassen, wie die Teile eines Steines, sie sollen

[1] Die im epikureischen Naturbegriff liegende Zufälligkeit zeigt das von Balbus angeführte Beispiel vom Haus und den Atomen (§ 94, 304, 13). Rhdt. (II 94) bezeichnet den ersten Naturbegriff (298, 17 ff.) als epikureisch, er muss dann den ausdrücklich an dritter Stelle genannten epikureischen Naturbegriff (299, 1) als quantitativ von dem vorher gegebenen unterscheiden, der qualitativ sei. Aber es steht in der dritten Definition ja nicht, alle Dinge, die sind, machen die Natur aus, so wie es in der von Rhdt. verglichenen Definition der Epikurbriefe (I 39) heisst. Es wird aller Dinge, die sind, Natur als der Körper, das Leere und seine Akzidentien, also qualitativ bestimmt. Nach Rhdt. würde auch zweimal der epikureische Naturbegriff vorgetragen, dagegen würde der akademische Naturbegriff überhaupt fehlen. Balbus hat aber doch gerade die akademischen Einwendungen als besonders gefährlich für diesen Teil seiner Untersuchungen hingestellt (295,7). Die Epikureer lesen die Werke der Anderen gar nicht und sind in diesen Problemen, wie er sagt, nicht so sehr zu fürchten. Wie soll man also das Fehlen der akademischen Meinung verstehen? Balbus hat ja auch durchaus damit Recht, dass die rein mechanische Erklärung, die die Ordnung nicht verständlich macht, leichter zu widerlegen ist als die von den Akademikern behauptete rationale Notwendigkeit, die eine göttliche Erklärung, wie die Stoiker sie geben, überflüssig machen würde.

zusammenhängen wie die Teile des pflanzlichen und tierischen Organismus. Ihr Zusammenhang ist also ohne Empfindung nicht denkbar.[1]

Nach der eingehenden Definition der Natur wird jetzt die Behauptung, dass Alles der Natur unterworfen sei, in mehreren auf einander aufbauenden Schlüssen bewiesen. Was in der Erde als Baum wächst, lebt durch die Kunst der Natur. Dann aber muss auch die Erde selbst sicher durch die gleiche Kraft leben. Sie hat ja alle Samen in sich, schafft Alles, umfängt Alles, sie wird durch Luft und Aether um sie herum ernährt und nährt diese wieder durch ihre Ausdünstungen (§ 83, 299, 8-13). Da für das Ganze gelten muss, was für die Teile gilt, muss für die Erde der gleiche organische Zusammenhang wie für einen Baum bestehen, und sie steht ja auch mit den Dingen um sie herum in einem organischen Zusammenhang. Denn sie empfängt von ihnen Kraft, wie sie sie ihnen gibt; sie ist also ein Organismus. Dementsprechend war das Besondere des Naturbegriffes, der für die Durchführung des Themas gelten sollte, zuerst durch einen Hinweis auf den Organismus eines Baumes verdeutlicht worden (299, 5).[2]

---

[1] Keinesfalls könnte der Begriff sentiens aber hier stehen. Denn was unter Natur zu verstehen ist, erklärt ja die Aufzählung der verschiedenen Naturbegriffe und die sich daran anschliessende Ableitung des eigenen Naturbegriffes. Wer auseinandersetzen will, was Natur ist, damit man ihn besser versteht, wie Balbus es tut, kann nicht den definierenden Zusatz vor der Definition bringen. Die Definition wäre dann unnötig. Rhdt. (I 234 ff.; II 92 ff.) bezweifelt also zu Unrecht die Einheitlichkeit der Ausführungen, weil der Begriff sentiens fehle. Sachlich ist ja sicherlich in der Definition des Balbus doch die natura sentiens gemeint. Vgl. dazu im Folgenden S. 174. Empfindung ist als primitivste Voraussetzung des Lebens im Organismus gesetzt.

[2] Rhdt. (a. O.) meint, es müsse einfach Natur heissen, nicht arte naturae (299, 8), weil eben definiert wurde, was Natur sei. Der Begriff ars könnte fehlen, es wird sich aber nicht beweisen lassen, dass er an dieser Stelle nicht gesetzt werden dürfte. Der Natur war von Balbus etwas wie Kunst zugeschrieben worden, er kann also von der Kunst der Natur reden. So sagt er auch im Folgenden nicht immer einfach Natur, sondern akzentuiert manchmal den in seinem Zusammenhang wichtigen Teil des Begriffes durch einen Zusatz.

Wenn die Erde durch ihre Natur erhalten wird und lebt, so steht es ebenso mit der übrigen Welt. Wie die Bäume in der Erde verwurzelt sind, werden die Lebewesen durch die Luft gehalten (299, 15-18). Alles aber, was in die Mitte der Welt, nach unten gezogen wird, ebenso wie das, was von unten nach oben steigt und was sich im Kreis um die Mitte bewegt, schafft eine zusammenhängende und einheitliche Natur der Welt (wie vorher die Erde in Austausch mit den sie umgebenden Dingen stand). Aus den vier Arten der Körper und ihrem Wechsel setzt sich die zusammenhängende Natur der Welt zusammen (§ 84, 299, 18 - 300, 4).[1] Dieser in sich unaufhörlich wechselnde Zusammenhang ist entweder ewig oder doch unermesslich lange dauernd (300, 4-10). Jedenfalls wird die Welt durch ihre Natur geleitet (§ 85, 300, 10-11). Denn die Fahrt eines Schiffes, die Aufstellung eines Heeres oder, um Beispiele aus der Natur, nicht aus dem menschlichen Handeln zu bringen, das Wachstum einer Rebe, eines Baumes, die Gestalt eines Lebewesens, der Körperbau, Alles zeigt keine so grosse Sorgfalt der Natur wie die Welt selbst. Entweder ist also nichts durch eine mit Empfindung begabte Natur gelenkt (natura sentiens 300, 15-16), oder die Welt selbst muss durch sie gelenkt werden.[2] Denn wie kann das, was alle anderen Naturen in sich enthält, nicht selbst durch die Natur gelenkt werden ?[3]

[1] Continuata natura ist schon ein überflüssiger Zusatz, da ja unter Natur organischer Zusammenhang verstanden werden sollte.

[2] An dieser Stelle zeigt sich also, dass der von Balbus vertretene Naturbegriff wirklich nichts anderes als natura sentiens ist. Er charakterisiert wieder seinen Naturbegriff durch einen Zusatz, und zwar durch den gleichen, den er ihm am Anfang des ganzen dritten Teiles gab (§ 75, 296, 9).

[3] Rhdt. (II 93) tadelt, dass auf das Handeln der Natur geschlossen wird, obwohl vorher auch vom Handeln der Menschen geredet wurde, und er sieht darum in diesen Ausführungen wieder die Zusammenarbeitung verschiedener Vorlagen (300, 11-15). Aber unmittelbar vor dem Schluss werden Handlungen der Natur genannt, und die Grösse des sinnvollen Geschehens in der Welt soll gerade dadurch gekennzeichnet werden, dass es jedem sinnvollen Handeln, dem menschlichen wie dem natürlichen, gegenübergestellt wird. Man braucht kein Wort vom anderen zu trennen.

Wenn die Zähne des Menschen, sein Körper, seine Reife Ergebnis eines natürlichen Prozesses sind, dann muss der Mensch selbst durch seine Natur entstehen. Das Ganze, das die einzelnen Teile aus sich entlässt, muss ihre Eigenschaften sogar in noch höherem Grade besitzen. Die Welt, die Schöpferin aller Dinge, die Erhalterin aller Wesen, die ja Organismen sind, muss selbst ein Organismus sein (§ 86, 300, 16-25). Alles ist also der Natur unterworfen, die einzelnen Teile der Welt und die Welt selbst. Und der Zusammenhang aller Teile der Welt ist so, dass er nicht besser sein könnte. Niemand hat je sagen können, was in der Welt hätte besser sein sollen, wenn er nicht Unmögliches verlangte (§§ 86-87, 300, 25 - 301, 4). Alles ist also der Natur unterworfen und wird von ihr aufs Beste gelenkt.

Kann aber dieser wunderbare Zusammenhang der Dinge, kann ihre Schönheit zufällig sein, oder ist Alles nur denkbar unter der Voraussetzung eines göttlichen Wesens, das die Welt durch seine vorausschauende Vernunft lenkt? Die Leistung der Natur übertrifft die Leistung der Kunst, die ohne Verstand nicht denkbar ist. Darum kann die Natur nicht ohne Verstand sein (301, 5-11). Da sie aber an sich nur organische Kraft ist, wie sie in einer Pflanze und in einem Tier lebt, also nicht verständige Kraft, muss dieser Verstand durch etwas Anderes als die Natur gegeben sein. Wer ein Gemälde sieht oder irgend ein Kunstwerk, glaubt an einen verständigen Schöpfer. Wieviel mehr gilt das für die Welt! (§§ 87-88, 301, 11-26). Ihr erster Anblick mag darüber täuschen. Schliesslich aber muss man erkennen, dass die Welt und ihre Ordnung nur unter der Voraussetzung möglich sind, dass Gott in der Welt wohnt, sie regiert, lenkt und gleichsam der Architekt der wunderbaren Schöpfung ist (§§ 89-90, 301, 27 - 303, 6). Die Welt, die Natur der Welt ist also das Werk Gottes, sie ist von ihm geschaffen. Wenn Alles einer mit Empfindung begabten Natur unterworfen ist und von ihr aufs Beste gelenkt wird, so muss diese Natur selbst und ihre Ordnung doch von Gott abgeleitet werden, sie ist nicht selbständig. Damit ist das ganze Thema des zweiten Abschnittes behandelt, so wie es in der

Einleitung am Beginn des dritten Teiles formuliert wurde (§ 75, 296, 8-11).[1]

Es muss jetzt das dritte Thema besprochen werden, das als letztes der Erörterung über die Leitung der Welt durch Gott angesetzt war: der Nachweis, dass aus der wunderbaren Ordnung am Himmel und auf der Erde die göttliche Fürsorge für die Welt folge (296, 11-12). Nach der Behauptung, dass Gott der Architekt der Welt sei, heisst es: « Jetzt aber ahnen die Philosophen nicht einmal, scheint es, wie gross das Wunder der himmlischen und irdischen Dinge ist » (§ 91, 303, 7).[2] Balbus beginnt also mit fast den gleichen Worten, mit denen das Thema angekündigt worden war, jetzt seine Durchführung. Formal ist der Uebergang nicht scharf bezeichnet, wie etwa der Uebergang vom ersten zum zweiten Teil (298, 13-16); aber er ist inhaltlich geschickt. Die Bewunderung der in der Welt herrschenden Ordnung hatte den Schluss begründet, dass die Natur der Welt von Gott abhängig sein müsste, noch in den letzten Sätzen war darauf hingewiesen worden (303, 1-4). So ergab sich der Uebergang zu dem Teil, in dem die bewundernswerte Schönheit der himmlischen und irdischen Dinge dargestellt werden musste, ganz von selbst.[3] Noch einmal weist Balbus darauf hin, dass die Teile der Welt, die Erde

---

1 Am Beginn der Durchführung des zweiten Themas (298, 15) fehlten im Vergleich zur Disposition am Anfang des dritten Teiles (296, 8 ff.) verschiedene Begriffe. Aber jeder Versuch, aus diesen Unterschieden eine Ungleichheit der Vorlagen zu konstruieren, scheitert, weil die Durchführung doch das ganze Thema erfüllt. Die Worte fehlen an der zweiten Stelle, weil dort nur aus dem Naturbegriff argumentiert wird und alles andere als seine Konsequenz abgeleitet wird.

2 Nunc autem mihi videntur ne suspicari quidem quanta sit admirabilitas caelestium rerum atque terrestrium.

3 Rhdt. (II 149) sagt: « von dem letzten Unterteil.... wird, kurz bevor er recht beginnt, um der Polemik willen weniges vorweggenommen »; er lässt also 303, 7 nicht den dritten Teil beginnen. Ebenso macht es Hnm. (II 194). Aber das ganze Thema ist ja schon behandelt. Aehnliche unscharfe Übergänge ohne formale Betonung finden sich auch in den ersten beiden Teilen der Rede des Balbus (§ 60, 286, 22) und im Folgenden (vgl. S. 180).

(303, 8), die Luft (303, 10), der Aether (303, 18), die Sterne (303, 21) mit einander in Verbindung stehen. Dieser organische Zusammenhang kann ebenso wenig zufällig sein wie der Zusammenhang im Gedicht des Ennius oder wie der Bau eines Hauses. Die tägliche Gewohnheit hat die Menschen nur für die Schönheit der Welt blind gemacht. Wer sie zum ersten Mal, aus den Tiefen der Erde an das Licht steigend, sehen würde, würde die Göttlichkeit des Schöpfers sofort begreifen. Das Alles kann nur durch die göttliche Providenz geschaffen sein, die Welt muss durch Gottes Fürsorge gelenkt werden. Diese Behauptung folgt aus der wunderbaren Einrichtung der himmlischen und irdischen Wesen (§ 95, 304, 17 - § 97, 306, 8).[1] Die Beschreibung der Schönheit der Dinge will Balbus nicht in subtiler Disputation geben, er will sie gleichsam für die Augen sichtbar machen (§ 98, 306, 9-11). Er zeigt zuerst, was an den himmlischen Dingen (§§ 91-119, 303, 8 - 317, 13), dann was an den irdischen Dingen bewundernswert ist (§§ 120-132, 317, 14 - 326, 5).

Balbus beschreibt die Erde mit ihren verschiedenen Bäumen und Blumen, mit ihren Quellen und Flüssen, ihren Bergen (§ 98, 306, 11-19). Die verschiedensten Tierarten erfüllen die Erde, die Menschen schmücken die Erde mit Häusern und Städten, sie verhindern ihre Verwüstung durch das Ueberwuchern von Pflanzen oder durch die Wildheit der Tiere. Wunderbar ist das Meer mit seinen mannigfaltigen Inseln und Gestaden, mit seinen vielen verschiedenen Tieren (§§ 99-100, 306, 19-307, 12). Die Luft, dem Meere benachbart, ist am Tag und in der Nacht verschieden, sie bildet sich zu Wolken, zu Regen und Winden um, sie ist bald kalt, bald warm (§ 101, 307, 13-18). Ebenso wunderbar ist die Mannigfaltigkeit des die Welt umfangenden Aethers, in dem die von einander

---

[1] Diese Ausführungen sind also nicht Vorwegnahme des Abschnittes über die bewundernswerte Ordnung der Dinge, sondern sie sind die ausführliche Formulierung des Themas dieses dritten Abschnittes. In ihm soll ja nicht eine einfache Beschreibung der Herrlichkeit der Welt gegeben werden, sondern es soll aus ihr die göttliche Fürsorge erschlossen werden.

immer verschiedenen Gestirne ihre verschiedenen Bahnen zurücklegen (§§ 101-104, 307, 19 - 308, 19).[1]

Aber nicht nur die Mannigfaltigkeit und Schönheit der Welt, auch ihr fester Zusammenhang ist bewundernswert. Alles ist gleichsam durch ein Band mit einander verbunden. Die Gottheit hat es so geordnet, dass die Dinge sich mit einander verbinden, ohne sich zu schaden, die Erde mit dem Meer, mit der Luft und dem Aether (§ 115, 315, 10 - 316, 10).[2] Die Sterne verbrauchen fast nichts oder doch sehr wenig von dem Wasser, das sie ernährt. Panaitios bezweifelte, wie man sagt, den Untergang der Welt, die stoische Schule nimmt an, dass sie nicht ewig währt. Wenn aber auch die Welt einmal zerstört wird und die Dauer, die so verherrlicht wurde, aufhört, so entsteht doch immer wieder eine neue Welt, und der Zusammenhang ist wenigstens in diesem Sinne ewig (§ 118, 316, 15 - 317, 5). Balbus schildert noch einmal die Ordnung der Sterne (§ 119, 317, 5-11), und damit hat er gezeigt, dass die himmlischen Dinge von herrlicher Mannigfaltigkeit und Schönheit sind und sich mit einander zur Unversehrtheit und Einheit der Welt in wunderbarem Zusammenklang verbinden.

Er spricht jetzt von dem Wunder der irdischen Dinge, damit klar wird, dass Alles, was ist, nur von einer mit Verstand begabten Natur, also von Gott geschaffen sein kann (§ 120, 317, 13-15): « Ich will nun von den himmlischen Dingen zu den irdischen kommen: was gibt es in ihnen, das nicht das Walten einer verständigen Natur offenbarte? ».[3] Wieder spricht er zuerst von der bewundernswerten Mannigfaltigkeit

---

[1] Cicero legt ein Stück seiner Aratübersetzung ein (§ 104-14), in der noch einmal von der verschiedenen Bewegung der Gestirne die Rede ist. Der Schluss am Ende des Zitates auf eine höchste rationale Ursache entspricht dem Schluss von der Beschreibung der Erde auf die sie schaffende göttliche Vernunft (§ 100).

[2] Es sind die gleichen Teile, von denen bei der Beschreibung der Mannigfaltigkeit der Welt geredet wurde.

[3] Age ut a caelestibus rebus ad terrestres veniamus, quid est in his in quo non naturae ratio intelligentis appareat (unter caelestia ist also hier wie immer in der Rede des Balbus nicht nur das himmlische Geschehen sondern das kosmische zu verstehen. Die Erde ist wie die Luft als Teil der Welt zu den caelestia gehörig).

und Schönheit der Dinge, dann von ihrer bewundernswerten Dauer und Einheitlichkeit.

Ganz verschieden ist das Wachstum der Pflanzen (317, 15-318, 3). Wie gross ist die Verschiedenheit der Lebewesen, wie gross ist die Kraft, die angewandt ist, damit jedes in seiner besonderen Art und Verschiedenheit von den anderen existiert. Ihre Nahrung ist immer verschieden, und dem entsprechend ist es ihr Organismus (§ 121, 318, 9-16). Verschieden ist die Art, in der die Tiere die Nahrung gewinnen und verzehren (§§ 122-127, 318, 16-322, 7). Verschieden ist auch die Art, in der sie sich verteidigen, jedes hat seine eigenen Waffen (322, 8-323, 2).

Und was tut Gott alles, um diese verschiedenen Dinge zu erhalten? (§ 127, 323, 3-4). Für den Samen der Pflanzen ist gesorgt, damit sie immer bestehen (323, 3-10). Der Körperbau der Tiere macht die Fortpflanzung möglich, sie ziehen ihre Jungen mit Liebe und Sorgfalt auf (§ 128, 323, 10-324, 15). Das alles kann doch nicht zufällig sein, sagt Balbus wieder, um an sein Thema zu erinnern (323, 19-324, 1). Auch die Menschen sorgen für die Erhaltung der Tiere (§ 130, 324, 15-19).[1]

Die unendliche Mannigfaltigkeit der Erde, ihre immer neue Schönheit ist für den Menschen eine Freude (324, 20-325, 9). Und Alles, die Winde, die Flüsse, die Berge helfen zur Erhaltung der Menschen wie der Tiere, der Wechsel von Tag und Nacht schützt die Lebewesen. So ist für Heil und Erhaltung

[1] Rhdt. (I 209; II 144) hält die Sätze über die Erhaltung der Dinge für einen Zusatz. Da aber die Unterscheidung von Mannigfaltigkeit und Erhaltung geradezu das Einteilungsprinzip aller Ausführungen ist, kann man diesen Abschnitt nicht herauslösen. Man kann auch nicht wie Rhdt. sagen, dass die Erhaltung der Dinge das einzige, wesentliche Thema dieser Ausführungen sei (I 209, 1), dagegen schon W. Theiler (Die Vorbereitung d. Neuplatonismus, Problemata, 1931, 105). Die Beschreibung der Verschiedenheit und Schönheit der Dinge wird von Rhdt. wie von Hnm. (II 196) nicht berücksichtigt. Inhaltlich braucht man in diesem Abschnitt ja auch nicht mehr die § 58 fehlenden Ausführungen zu sehen. Keinesfalls würde zudem die Disposition des § 58 in der Beschreibung der Dauer, wie sie der dritte Teil gibt, durchgeführt werden.

in dieser Welt durch göttlichen Ratschluss aufs wunderbarste gesorgt (§§ 131-32, 325, 9 - 326, 5).

Balbus hat jetzt bewiesen, dass die Welt durch göttliche Fürsorge geleitet wird. Er hat zuerst gezeigt, wie er es nach seiner Einteilung wollte, dass die Götter, wenn es sie gibt, die Welt regieren müssen. Dann hat er dargestellt, dass Alles einer mit Empfindung begabten Natur unterworfen ist, die es aufs beste lenkt und die selbst von geistigen Prinzipien, von Gott herstammt. Schliesslich hat er die bewunderungswürdige Einrichtung der Welt, die Schönheit, Mannigfaltigkeit und Dauer der himmlischen und der irdischen Dinge beschrieben und auch daraus die göttliche Fürsorge abgeleitet. Die ganze Einteilung ist also von ihm so, wie sie gegeben wurde, durchgeführt worden.

Er beginnt dann den vierten Teil, in dem er zeigen will, dass die Götter für die Menschen sorgen (§ 4, 261, 2), ohne scharfe formale Abgrenzung vom Vorhergehenden: « Wenn nun einer fragt, wofür denn alle diese wunderbaren Dinge geschaffen sind..., wenn man sich Alles überlegt, so kann man nur glauben, dass der Götter und Menschen wegen die Welt und Alles in ihr geschaffen ist » (§ 132, 326, 7-18).[1] Die Götter sorgen für die Menschen (326, 15).[2] Das lässt sich leichter einsehen, wenn vorher die Einrichtung des menschlichen Körpers, die menschliche Gestalt und die menschliche Vollkommenheit erkannt ist (326, 15-17).[3]

---

[1] Sin quaeret quispiam cuiusnam causa tantarum rerum molitio facta sit.... fit credibile deorum et hominum causa factum esse mundum quaeque in eo mundo sint omnia. Auch Werner Jaeger (Nemesios von Emesa, Berl., 1914, 127) lässt an dieser Stelle den vierten Teil beginnen. Hnm. (II 277) meint: « Der vierte Teil, der anscheinend § 154 beginnt, denn schon § 133 hatte Cicero erklärt, dass alle diese Herrlichkeiten nur des Menschen wegen dasein müssen ». Aber die §§ 133-153 gehören schon selbst in den vierten Teil.

[2] Mit dieser Formulierung ist das Gleiche gemeint, was vorher so ausgedrückt wurde: die Welt ist um der Götter und Menschen willen gemacht. Erst die zweite Formulierung aber entspricht genau dem Wortlaut in der Einteilung am Anfang (§ 4, 261, 2).

[3] Faciliusque intellegetur a dis immortalibus hominibus esse provisum, si erit tota hominis fabricatio perspecta omnisque humanae naturae figura atque perfectio.

Balbus schildert ausführlich den menschlichen Körper und die Funktion seiner Teile (§§ 134-39, 326, 17 - 330, 3). Wenn der Körper das Werk der sinnvoll schaffenden Natur ist, so hat Gott die spezifisch menschliche Gestalt, den aufrechten Gang des Menschen geschaffen (§ 140, 330, 4-10). Dadurch bedingt sind die Sinneswerkzeuge des Menschen in seinem Kopf wie in einer Burg angeordnet, nur die Empfindung ist über den ganzen Körper verteilt, so dass das Unangenehme von den Sinnen fern gehalten wird (§ 140, 330, 11 - § 141, 331, 5).[1] Nachdem Balbus so die Einrichtung des menschlichen Körpers und die spezifisch menschliche Gestalt behandelt hat, zeigt er die menschliche Vollkommenheit. Augen, Ohren, die Nase, die Zunge können ihre Aufgaben wirklich erfüllen, die Sinne der Menschen übertreffen die der Tiere (§§ 144-146, 331, 6 - 334, 4). Ausserdem haben die Menschen allein Verstand und Vernunft, die Gott ihnen gibt (§ 147, 334, 5-18), sie können sprechen, eine göttliche Fähigkeit, die die Natur durch wunderbare Bildung der Sprechwerkzeuge unterstützt (334, 18 - § 149, 335, 14). Durch die Vollkommenheit der Hand, die die Natur wunderbar gebaut hat, erobert der Mensch die Welt (§ 150, 335, 15 - § 152, 337, 13), er allein dringt bis zum Himmel, indem er mit seinem göttlichen Verstand die Bewegung der Gestirne und das Wesen der Gottheit erkennt (§ 153, 337, 14-22). Es fehlt an seiner Vollkommenheit nur die Unsterblichkeit, die aber zum glücklichen Leben nicht notwendig ist. Der Mensch ist den Göttern gleich (§ 153, 337, 18-22), das kann nicht zufällig so sein (337, 23-26).

Nachdem Balbus den Körperbau des Menschen, seine Gestalt und seine Vollkommenheit beschrieben hat, die vor der Darstellung der Fürsorge Gottes für den Menschen erörtert werden sollte, zeigt er, wie Gott für den Menschen sorgt.

---

[1] Rhdt. (II 139 ff.) streicht die Aussage über den aufrechten Gang als Zusatz. Aber dann wäre es unmöglich zu sagen, die Sinneswerkzeuge sind im Kopf wie in einer Burg angeordnet, auch wird ausdrücklich gesagt, wie gut es ist, dass Ohren und Nase hoch oben sitzen. Primum 330, 6 wird fortgesetzt in autem 330, 11. Ebenso urteilt, wenn auch aus anderen Gründen, W. Theiler (a. O. 105) und Ph. Finger (Rh. M. 80, 1931, 314).

Alles in der Welt ist um des Menschen willen da (§ 154, 338, 1-3). Die Welt ist die Stadt der Götter und Menschen, für die allein Recht und Gesetz gilt (338, 4-11). Die Bewegungen am Himmel sind ein Schauspiel für die Menschen, die allein sie verstehen (§ 155, 338, 11-18). Die Erde mit ihren Früchten, alle Tiere sind für den Menschen geschaffen (§§ 155-161, 338, 11 - 341, 4). Die Felder, die Berge, was über der Erde ist und was in ihrem Innern verborgen ist, ist für die Menschen da (§ 162, 341, 4-10). Schliesslich sorgen die Götter für die Menschen dadurch, dass sie ihnen die Zukunft enthüllen, ein Wissen, das es sicher gibt (§ 163, 341, 11-342, 6). Die Götter sorgen für Alles, sie sorgen für die Welt, sie lieben die Welt und die einzelnen Menschen. Darum enthüllen sie ihnen die Zukunft (§§ 164-167, 342, 5-343, 17). Jetzt hat Balbus auch das letzte Thema seiner Untersuchung in einheitlich fortschreitender Erörterung behandelt. Die Beschreibung des menschlichen Körpers, der menschlichen Gestalt und der menschlichen Vollkommenheit, die er zuerst gibt, erleichtert ihm den Beweis dafür, dass die Götter in Allem für die Menschen sorgen. Damit ist Balbus am Ende seiner ganzen Rede.

In den beiden letzten Teilen der Rede des Balbus finden sich also keine formalen Anstösse. Er bespricht die Themen, die er angekündigt hat, die Durchführung stimmt mit der Disposition überein, die Gedanken hängen eng zusammen. Kein Satz lässt sich vom anderen trennen und etwa als fremd erweisen; man kann aus formalen Gründen nicht sagen, dass Cicero verschiedene Vorlagen verarbeitet. Die ganzen Ausführungen könnten so, wie sie gegeben werden, aus *einer* Vorlage genommen sein.

Darin liegt ein wesentlicher Unterschied des dritten und vierten Teiles von den beiden ersten, in denen die formalen Schwierigkeiten erst rückgängig gemacht werden müssen, um die Vorlage zu erkennen, ein Unterschied, der, wie mir scheint, inhaltlich bedingt ist. Der Akademiker Cotta kann die stoischen Ansichten über die Lenkung der Welt durch Gott und über die Fürsorge Gottes für die Menschen inhaltlich widerlegen, wie ja auch Balbus selbst diesen Teil seiner Rede besonders durch die Akademiker bedroht findet (§ 73, 295, 7).

Auch gegen die Natur der Götter, wie die Stoiker sie definieren, kann der Akademiker Einwendungen machen. Das Dasein Gottes kann er nicht bestreiten, oder darf er wenigstens nicht bestreiten. Cotta sagt nicht mehr, als dass die Beweise des Balbus nicht ausreichen, oder nicht beweisen, was sie zu beweisen vorgeben. Der Akademiker kann den Stoiker also nur formal widerlegen. Darum musste sich Cicero die Mühe machen, formale Anstösse in den ersten beiden Teilen zu konstruieren, während das in den letzten beiden Teilen nicht nötig war.[1]

Ob der dritte und vierte Teil nun aber wirklich einem Autor gehören und ob es der gleiche ist, auf den die Vorlage der beiden ersten Teile zurückgeht, diese letzte Frage lässt sich erst in einer inhaltlichen Untersuchung der stoischen Theologie lösen.

LUDWIG EDELSTEIN.

---

[1] Da die formalen Schwierigkeiten des ersten Teiles durch Umgruppierung des ersten und zweiten Teiles entstehen, sind beide Teile formal schlecht aufgebaut, obwohl die Schwierigkeit nur durch das erste Thema bedingt ist. Dass der Akademiker Cicero den Akademiker Cotta nicht unbedingt Recht behalten lässt, zeigt sich deutlich am Schluss des Ganzen. Dem Velleius scheint die Rede des Cotta wahrer, dem Cicero die Rede des Balbus der Wahrheit ähnlicher und näher (§ 95, 399, 15-17).

In spite of the judicial detachment with which the authors have properly conducted their researches, they reveal unmistakable admiration and respect, indeed something close to affection, for the god who has commanded their prolonged attention. And they make good the justice of their kindly feelings for the kindly god at almost all points. In one matter, however, in my opinion, they claim too much. "The god was concerned," they say, "not only with the life here but also with the Beyond." In support of this they bring forward two pieces of evidence: the connection between Asclepius and Demeter, and the last words of Socrates as given by Plato at the end of the *Phaedo*. With regard to the former, they draw unjustifiable conclusions from the testimonies (especially 565a), and they allow their imagination to make too much of the justifiable conclusions. As for the latter, we are, to be sure, dealing with a passage which has exercised commentators since ancient times. In the very article of death Socrates says: "Crito, we owe a cock to Asclepius. Pay it and don't forget." Following the lead of the Neoplatonist Olympiodorus, the authors maintain that Socrates is thinking of Asclepius, not as the healer of disease, but as the reviver of the dead, because for Socrates death is life and life is death. Now this may in a sense be true, but it does not argue any eschatological function for Asclepius. The words may be understood more simply. For Socrates, life's fitful fever is over, and he is content. For such a boon he must express his gratitude, and with paradoxical irony, half serious, half whimsical, he bids his friend do what he cannot do himself and make a thank-offering to the god who cures the ills of men. Asclepius is still the great physician, as the authors have fully and sympathetically represented him throughout the book, not a god who promises and assures a blissful life beyond the grave.

IVAN M. LINFORTH

University of California

GALEN ON MEDICAL EXPERIENCE. First Edition of the Arabic Version with English Translation and Notes. By R. WALZER. Published for the Trustees of the Late Sir Henry Wellcome by the Oxford University Press, London, 1944. Pp. xi, 164.

Only two fragments of Galen's book *On Medical Experience* have been preserved in the Occidental tradition. Natorp has recognized their philosophical and historical importance. From Walzer's edition and translation of the entire treatise, which Ritter discovered in 1931 in a twelfth-century Arabic manuscript (p. v), it now appears that the essay as a whole is unusually interesting from a general point of view. How experience is brought about, whether reason or sense perception is the basis of knowledge, this question is discussed with regard to medicine, yet with arguments mostly derived from philosophy. More than one tenth of the content is devoted to a *collegium logicum* dealing with the intricacies of the *sorites* (pp. 114–119; cf. 96 f.).

On the evidence of the fragments known, that give the exposé of a dogmatist and an empiricist respectively, the treatise *On Medical Experience* has been identified with a work of the young Galen in which, as he says in the catalog of his works, he reproduced a discussion between Pelops and Philippus, physicians of his own time (Deichgräber, Fr. 23a [*Die griechische Empirikerschule,* 1930]). Walzer accepts this identification. That one can do so only with certain reservations has recently been shown by Temkin (*Bulletin of the History of Medicine,* XIX, 1946, p. 242). The Arabic version does not mention Pelops and Philippus. Here the participants in the debate are described as a follower of Asclepiades — who lived in the first century B.C. and revived the atomic theory in medicine — and as an empiricist, be he Menodotus, Serapion, or Theodosius (p. 87). And although Philippus was an empiricist and Pelops a dogmatist, there is no indication that they adhered to the specific systems referred to by Galen. Moreover, according to the preface (pp. 86 f.), the work is written for publication, while Galen claims that he put down the words of Pelops and Philippus as an exercise for himself, and that the manuscript was published by others without his knowledge. It would, therefore, seem necessary to assume that Galen reworked the treatise in later years and changed it a good deal. To me, it seems even more likely that the book in question is not identical at all with the youthful writing of Galen quoted by him without title. He himself names the essay *On Medical Experience* among others on the empirical school which he composed when he was an older man (Deichgräber, Fr. 1, l. 8). Like most of these works, the newly found treatise has a decidedly empirical bias: contrary to Natorp's suggestion, it is the empiricist, not the dogmatist who carries the day (p. viii; *S. B. Berl.,* 1932, pp. 449–451). The fact that Galen distinguishes his own views from those which he presents (p. 87) also speaks in favor of a late date of composition.

However that may be, the book is typically Galenic. The peculiar flair of Galen's rhetoric is unmistakable even in the translation from a translation. This is also a compliment to the skill of Walzer. The details of his rendering I am unable to judge. Walzer's previous work warrants the merit of his new enterprise in which he collaborated with H. A. R. Gibb, G. Levi Della Vida, and J. Schacht (p. xi). In view of the difficulties of such an undertaking, one will not be astonished if in some cases the correctness of the translation can be challenged. Two instances in which this has been done are of particular interest for the student of ancient philosophy. According to Walzer, Diogenes of Apollonia is mentioned by Galen among the physicians, and a medical work of his is quoted (p. x; cf. Diels-Kranz, *Die Fragmente der Vorsokratiker,* III⁵,1937, p. 653). It has been suggested (Temkin, *op. cit.*, p. 243) that in the one passage (XXII, 3) Diocles is the easier reading, and that in the other (XIII, 4) Diogenes is a mistake of the scribe which he himself corrected in the immediately following Diocles.[1] In my opinion, the correctness of this suggestion is proved by the content of the statements made. Diogenes can hardly be said to have lived after Hippocrates (XIII, 4); he was at best a contemporary of his, while Diocles indeed belonged to the following generation.[2] Again, it is attested that Diocles wrote a work in which he collected the diseases and their causes and remedies in one treatise, a feat ascribed by Walzer's rendering (XXII, 3) to Diogenes. Galen himself in other writings quoted Diocles' book *Περὶ πάθους αἰτίας θεραπείας* (Wellman, Fr. 37; cf. 43). The list of new matter of philosophical importance to be gained from Galen's treatise (p. x) must, I think, be corrected accordingly.

As regards the content of the book, this is not the place to enter into an analysis of the data which it contributes toward an understanding of the practical aspects of empirical medicine. Although they are not numerous, they are nevertheless important. Nor can I discuss here the other medical information furnished by the new treatise which, together with Galen's famous *Subfiguratio Empirica,* provides the only continuous description of the teaching of empiricism.[3] Yet it seems appropriate to ask which philosophical doctrine was advocated by the empiricists. That they were skeptics is generally agreed upon (e.g., L. Robin, *Pyrrhon et le Scepticisme Grec,* 1944, pp. 181 ff.). The issue

[1] Diogenes and Diocles sometimes seem confused even in the Greek tradition. Cf., for example, Diels-Kranz, II, p. 57, 3, where Diels, following Tertullian and Theodoretus, reads Diocles (Kranz keeps Diogenes in the text). Diels's emendation is accepted by Wellmann (Diokles Fr. 14, [*Die Fragmente der sikelischen Ärzte,* etc., 1901]).

[2] Whatever the exact date of Hippocrates' life, Galen, at any rate, supposed him to be a contemporary of Socrates. For Diogenes, cf. J. Burnet, *Early Greek Philosophy,* 1930, p. 353; *Greek Philosophy,* I, 1928, 123.

[3] Walzer's notes give the most important parallels in medical works (p. x) and are quite helpful. One might only have wished for more comments on the text, which is sometimes difficult to understand. I note a slight mistake which I wish to correct. Petron is not a physician hitherto unknown (XIII, 7; p. 160). He is mentioned in the Meno papyrus (cf. W. H. S. Jones, *The Medical Writings of Anonymus Londinensis,* 1944, p. 78). He lived after Hippocrates and before Herophilus (*ibid.*, p. 16). Galen (XV, p. 436 K) says of a certain Petronas exactly the same which he says of Petron; the two are apparently identical, as has been maintained by some scholars.

is whether they were followers of Pyrrho (Deichgräber, pp. 279–281; cf. Walzer, *S. B. Berl.*, 1932, pp. 465 ff.), or of the Middle Academy (Edelstein, *Quellen u. Studien z. Geschichte d. Naturwissenschaften u. d. Medizin*, III, 1933, pp. 253 ff.). Additional proof for the correctness of the latter contention is, I think, given by the new treatise through which one gains a clearer picture of the technical elaboration of the concept of experience, the basic dogma of the school.

Experience, to the empiricist, is achieved by "seeing-very-many-times." Such an observation of the phenomena is sufficient not only for the discovery of simple isolated things but also for that of the other things (pp. 127 f.). It is not in need of the support of the *logos* (pp. 128–154). It constitutes in fact the method by which everything is found out, while the *logos* is quite incapable of making all discoveries by itself (pp. 98–126). What is here described as the accomplishment of "seeing-very-many-times," Galen in other writings on empirical medicine attributes to the "imitative experience," which, in contrast to simple experience by chance, or experience by intentional trial, gives reliability and constitutes art or science (Fr. 15, Deichgräber, and pp. 291 ff.). Now this confidence in the results of experience is irreconcilable with the teaching of Pyrrho and Timon, who distrusted sense perception no less than the *logos* and exercised suspension of judgment in regard to both. It is, however, in agreement with the attitude of the Academic skeptics in whose doctrine the concept of probability came to play an ever-increasing role. Whatever the attitude of Arcesilaus, whatever the details of the theories of Carneades, the Middle Academy certainly differentiated between sense impressions that are simply probable and those that are probable and tested, or probable, tested, and irreversible (Sextus, *Hypotyposeis,* I, 227 ff.). Just as the Academics applied repeated and circumspect observation to the objects of daily life, so the empiricists proceeded in regard to the objects of medical concern and thereby gained probability, as did the followers of Carneades.

Another more specific influence of Carneades on the empirical doctrine is evidenced by the use which the representative of empiricism makes of the *sorites*. It is, to be sure, not he who introduces the argument. The Asclepiadean speaker has first referred to it in his attack on the concept of "seeing-very-many-times" (pp. 96 f.), and he has applied it in the form of the "dilemma with regard to motion" (XX, p. 123). He wishes to prove that it is not many observations, but really one observation, that constitutes experience. (In a like manner, the *sorites* is used in Sextus, *Adversus mathematicos,* I, 68, against the definition of grammar given by Dionysius Thrax which, if not empirical in origin, is at least identical with the empirical concept of experience [Deichgräber, p. 325]). Yet the dogmatist feels himself that he is on dangerous ground (p. 96). And the defender of empiricism is not slow in pointing out the weakness of his adversary's position: "You are ignorant of the strength and bearing of this argument — were this not so, you would never have dared use it on an occasion so unsuitable" (p. 115). For to him, the *sorites* is the fallacy of adding and subtracting, of increasing and diminishing, and in this specific meaning it serves to refute the basic presupposition of dogmatism. It shows that the *logos* is incapable of understanding reality, as far as reality is made up of divisible objects. For the same purpose, the *sorites* is applied by a follower of Carneades in Cicero's *Academica* (II, 28, 91 ff.). Indeed Carneades and his pupils were renowned for turning this fallacy against the dogmatists (Zeller, *Die Philosophie der Griechen,* III, 1, 503; 511), thus transforming an argument that had been invented by the Megarians to destroy the trust in sense perception into one that undermines the reliability of reason. As for the difficulties into which the empiricist himself is driven by the *sorites,* he does not deny them (cf. also p. 47, 1 ff., Deichgräber); rather does he circumvent them by admitting that he is unable to solve the absurdity (pp. 123 ff., esp. 126). Such a subterfuge is permissible to him as a skeptic, while it is not permissible to the dogmatist. For Carneades has proved that the dogmatic philosopher cannot escape the power of the *sorites* by "coming to rest" at will. His opponent is likely and justified to urge him on, and thus to refute him in the end (*Academica,* II, 29, 93).[4]

It is not only in the concept of experience and in the use of the *sorites* that the empiricists and the Academics concur. There exist other similarities (cf. Edelstein, *loc. cit.*). Chronological considerations are also in favor of a dependence of empiricism on the Academy. The school was founded, it seems, by Serapion (200 B.C.; cf. Deichgräber, p. 254 ff.). At that time Academic skepticism was at least as important as Pyrrhonean skepticism. Moreover, the movement instigated by Pyrrho, which had never been widespread, ceased to exist in the second century B.C. when the empirical theory was brought to completion. If the empiricists occasionally refer to Pyrrho or Timon and show admiration for them, they do what the Academics did likewise. Arcesilaus was conscious of the fact that he continued the Pyrrhonean tradition (Zeller, III, 1, p. 490). Both these doctrines nevertheless remained different from that of the old skepsis. Sextus, who writes in defence of the revived teaching of Pyrrho, justly claims that a true skeptic cannot subscribe to the school of empirical physicians, but must adhere to that

[4] In my discussion of the *sorites,* I have drawn much material from Walzer, *S. B. Berl.,* 1932, pp. 464 f. However, I disagree with his evaluation of the significance of the argument within the empirical teaching.

of the methodists (*Hypotyposeis*, I, 236 ff.). The latter, in the first century A.D., incorporated Pyrrhonism into medicine, while the empiricists were, and remained, followers of Arcesilaus and Carneades.

In my opinion, it is for an appreciation of the history of the Middle Academy that the empirical teaching provides material, and for this task much indeed can be learned from the newly discovered book of Galen.

LUDWIG EDELSTEIN

The Johns Hopkins University

ARISTOTLE, ON COMING-TO-BE AND PASSING-AWAY. Some Comments. By W. J. VERDENIUS and J. H. WASZINK. Leiden, E. J. Brill, 1946.

This excellent little dissertation is not so much a book as a series of notes and remarks which are in the main "a criticism of the commentary by Professor H. H. Joachim." There is no doubt that Verdenius and Waszink have made their mark in the study of Greek philosophy and must from now on be listened to with special respect. Certainly, Verdenius, to judge from his other work and from this is a figure of brilliance.

The authors show great range and skill in their use of the results of linguistic investigation and realize to what an extent interpretation of an ancient text is almost purely a matter of linguistic discipline. Indeed, the unique contribution of the book and of Verdinius' other work lies in the very clever union of philosophical ability and insight with the knowledge of Greek linguistics.

Thus, the discussion on certain problems in the study of growth can be regarded from the double aspect of an exercise in the meaning and use of Greek particles, among other linguistic problems, and of a philosophical study in the meanings of the terms matter and form as an elucidation of a particular discussion of the problem of growth. The two procedures reinforce one another and are indeed not to be separated.

A typical example of the procedure should illustrate very well the character of the book. Part of the Greek text is printed, then the first words of Joachim's translation are quoted. (The selection is from pages 25 and 26.) "Nevertheless, since there is also a matter out of which corporeal substance itself comes-to-be. . . ."

The authors then remark that the use of the word *also* is here rather strange, because in the preceding lines it was this very corporeal matter itself which was under consideration. This, of course, is to make the Aristotelian argument somewhat nonsensical or at the least to alter

artificial and of little practical use. But it is necessary to realize that originally the syllogism was not a method of inquiry, but a method of communication. The premises were a means of compelling a respondent in a dialectical conversation to assent to a preëxisting conclusion. Even in the "scientific" syllogism the mental process is actually from conclusion to premises, not from premises to conclusion. An examination of the historical background of Aristotelian logic, especially the relevant passages in Plato's works, provides a true perspective of the syllogism and dispels the misconception caused by the attempt to interpret the syllogism as a method of inference from known premises to an unknown conclusion (pp. 71-4).

Besides the syllogism Kapp also discusses problems involving other topics of traditional logic, namely, concepts, judgments, and induction. For each topic he finds the specific historical setting of Aristotle's views, the disregard of which has caused a misinterpretation of Aristotle by traditional logic. As in the case of the syllogism, this historical setting is found in the works of Plato. The correct understanding of many parts of Aristotle's logic, Kapp says, "depends on unprejudiced interpretation of Plato's rather than of Aristotle's writings" (p. 60). For example, most of the "difficulties in Aristotle's logic of the judgment disappear completely when we consult Plato's *Sophistes*" (p. 58). The problem of false reasoning, as Aristotle presents it in the "Sophistic Elenchi," "would be incomprehensible or at least unbelievable to us, if we did not have a dialogue of Plato, the *Euthydemus*" (p. 63). The "obvious divergence between Aristotle's notion of induction and the modern concept of intuitive induction" (p. 82) is explained by reference to the *Meno*. Thus Aristotle is expounded primarily on historical and philological, rather than on analytic grounds.

The most serious limitation of this book, in my opinion, is its brevity. In barely 87 pages the author covers many of the central problems of Aristotle's logic, in relation to both subsequent and antecedent philosophical writings. Necessarily, technical details are for the most part omitted; and whole regions of relevant material, such as ancient post-Aristotelian logics, are dismissed with only casual mention. Hence the reader feels that although Kapp's interpretations are often attractive and plausible, a fuller discussion would be required to render them entirely convincing.

PHILLIP DE LACY.

UNIVERSITY OF CHICAGO.

EDITH OWEN WALLACE. The Notes on Philosophy in the Commentary of Servius on the Eclogues, the Georgics, and the Aeneid of Vergil. New York, Columbia Univ. Press, 1938. Pp. 200.

Rarely is the question asked in what sort of intellectual climate the ancient commentators on poetry were at home. Important and interesting as it would be to use their writings as a means of reconstructing the trends of thought prevalent in late antiquity, they are almost exclusively considered in their relevance for the understanding of the works of the great poets. The book under review, therefore, deserves praise on account of the subject chosen: it endeavors to represent the philosophical problems discussed by Servius, to ascertain whether in dealing with them he exhibits a consistent point of view, and, if this proves to be the case, to determine to which of the known systems his philosophy may be related (p. 5), thus throwing light upon the philosophical situation in Servius' time (cf. p. 182). The method applied in this study is meritorious as well; for the answers to the questions raised are not derived from a haphazard investigation of a few selected passages. A collection of all the utterances concerning philosophy that are found in Servius' commentary on Vergil precedes the interpretation (chap. I, pp. 11-69; for the arrangement of the testimonies, cf. pp. 6-9). The examination of the various topics (chaps. II-VI, pp. 70-175) first takes the entire material into consideration, then sifts the decisive ideas for closer inspection as to their essential unity, and ultimately characterizes their distinctive hue. Thus a sure foundation is laid for gaining durable results.[1]

That the remarks of Servius are uniform in their standpoint has, I think, been proved conclusively; this is a result which is well in agreement with the fact that Servius' commentary seems to be the work of one author.[2] Certain ideas are advocated throughout the whole exegesis of Vergil: existence is believed to depend on God as well as on the elements (p. 77); the soul is considered immortal (p. 7). It has also been shown, I believe, that although the specific form of these tenets is reminiscent of fourth-century thought (pp. 180-2), Servius cannot simply be classified as a Neo-Platonist, as had been casually suggested by Siehler, the only one who seems to have given attention to Servius' philosophical affiliation (cf. p. 2, n. 8). Servius, who mentions Plotinus once and Porphyry twice (p. 3, n. 11; pp. 53, 55, 61), in some respects goes further than Plotinus (cf., e. g., pp. 142-4; reincarnation), in others he is less decided than the Neo-Platonists (cf., e. g., p. 135; the nature of the soul).

In Servius' philosophy, the author rightly says (cf. especially the "Conclusion," chap. VIII, pp. 182-90), Platonic and Stoic influences are noticeable along with those of Pythagoreanism and Orphism. Is there also "a strong strain of Epicureanism," as she maintains (e. g., p. 183)? Is the greatest distinction of Servius' notes "the very fact that they make Neo-Platonism, Platonism, Stoicism and Epicureanism lie down together and not war, one with another, but reveal such harmonies as they have" (p. 86)? In my opinion Epicureanism, contrary to the author's assertion (e. g., p. 83, n. 67), remains for Servius the only system that is irreconcilable with the other philosophies. For he does not accept any of the typically Epicurean views, neither their mechanistic explanation of the genesis of the world, nor their belief in free will and in the utter destruction of the human being through death. The author herself has made this evident (cf. pp. 77; 161-2; 127). Moreover, Servius shows a dislike for the Epicureans which he does not evince toward any other

[1] I wish to draw the reader's attention to chap. VII, pp. 176-9, where the bearing of the present investigation on the so-called "Servian question" is outlined.

[2] Cf. M. Schanz, *Geschichte d. Römischen Litteratur*, II, 1 (1911), p. 121.

philosophical sect. Like his contemporaries and earlier opponents of Epicurus, he calls the philosopher's theory of the sun "stupid"; he stigmatizes Epicurean theories as irreligious; he calls the Epicureans superficial; he censures their delight in pleasantries even as regards serious matters.[3] Is this not the usual attack on the Epicureans, made in Servius' day, in which the author maintains that he has not taken part (p. 190)? To be sure, Servius is not a full-fledged anti-Epicurean. That he often expresses ideas in Lucretius' language need not indicate more than his aesthetic appreciation of this poet (cf., e. g., pp. 183; 101). But by adducing Epicurean testimonies where he could equally well have quoted Stoic sources (p. 99), and by noting the agreement between the Epicureans and other philosophers where this is possible (cf. *Aen.*, VI, 596, 741; Wallace, pp. 50; 48), Servius evinces interest in Epicurus' dogma and fairness and justice toward his doctrine. This, but no more, it seems to me, is characteristic of Servius' notes.

Now, while "a strong strain of Epicureanism" in Servius' time would indeed have been as unusual a trait in the philosophy of a non-Epicurean as the author declares it to be (p. 183), willingness to give the philosopher Epicurus credit when he deserves it was not uncommon in that period. Thus Themistius, the rhetor and philosopher of the 4th century, who was not an Epicurean, did not condemn Epicurus' ethical teaching altogether but refers to it in his orations and in his philosophical writings.[4] Consequently it is unnecessary, on account of Servius' stand in regard to Epicurus, to assume that Servius did not belong to any of the philosophical schools, that his is "partisan support only of the truth" (p. 190). It is quite right that such an attitude, in his eyes, was the philosopher's ideal as contrasted with stubborn insistence on the school dogma (p. 168). But subjectively every philosopher is only and solely the defender of truth. Servius' censure of Lucretius as being a partisan of Epicurus rather than a seeker for verity (p. 125) is the usual belittling of the enemy, and the ethos of *Plato amicus magis amica veritas* is one that has been maintained by members of all philosophical creeds. Rather than ally Servius with "humanists" as were Lucretius, Horace, and Cicero in Shorey's opinion (p. 190), it seems more adequate to characterize Servius' philosophy as eclecticism. Just as Themistius is an eclectic Aristotelian who integrates into his philosophy Stoic and Platonic and even Epicurean conceptions, so Servius' thought, although basically Stoic and Platonic, is not alien to admixtures deriving "from the tenets of all the existing sects," as the definition of ancient eclecticism has it (Diogenes Laertius, *Prologue*, I, 21).[5] Probably such a philosophical point of view, among grammarians, rhetors, and the educated of late antiquity

[3] Cf. *Aen.*, IV, 584; *Georg.*, III, 525; *Aen.*, VI, 264; *Ecl.*, 6, 41—Wallace, pp. 34; 64; 54.

[4] Cf. F. Ueberweg-K. Praechter, *Die Philosophie des Altertums* (12th ed., 1926), p. 658.

[5] Concerning Themistius' "weitherzigen Eklektizismus," cf. Ueberweg-Praechter, *loc. cit.* In the beginning of her study Miss Wallace once hesitantly speaks of Servius' notes as representing "the consistent belief of a cultivated gentleman living in a milieu of eclecticism" (p. 86; cf. p. 156, syncretism).

in general, was much more in vogue than has as yet been recognized. The example of Servius, whose commentary enjoyed so great a popularity, seems to warrant this inference.

In conclusion I should like to stress more strongly than has been done in Miss Wallace's book the caution with which the philosopher Servius treats of Vergil's philosophy. It may be that to him, too, the poet is omniscient, that he defends the correctness of his statements even where they are untenable, that he suppresses hostile criticism.[6] But he does not expect the poet to write as an accomplished and consistent philosopher. On the contrary, with Servius it is a fundamental maxim that the poet uses, and should use, the respective philosophical dogmas as is fitting for his purposes. Only he who like Lucretius intends to expound a certain philosophical doctrine must stick to it throughout his work; other poets are allowed to vary in their opinions as the sects themselves differ one from the other.[7] In short, Servius accepts Horace's motto for his poems as the true slogan of poetry: *nullius addictus iurare in verba magistri / quo me cumque rapit tempestas deferor hospes* (*Epist.*, I, 1, 14-15); he sees Vergil as Sellar, among modern interpreters, has seen him: as an eclectic who borrows from many sources according to his needs. It is perhaps for this reason that Servius has such a fine appreciation of Vergil's art. Instead of looking for inconsistencies he distinguishes between those passages in which the poet speaks in his own name and those in which he speaks in that of one of his characters. He permits him to express himself according to the opinion of the many, or in allegorical fashion; he grants him poetical license although he insists that Vergil infuses philosophy into poetry.[8] The *lex operis* to which Metrodorus, another interpreter of Vergil, referred in explanation of the poet's seeming shortcomings in astronomical knowledge (*Georg.*, I, 229; p. 32 Wallace) is the highest principle of Servius' method of interpretation. This is indeed a great achievement for someone who has a philosophical standpoint of his own. Modern criticism, I think, could sometimes learn with profit from Servius' teaching. He seems to have been one of the first who consistently brought to bear on the understanding of poetical works the conviction which Lessing in his evaluation of Pope pleaded in so masterly a fashion: that a poet is not a metaphysician.

LUDWIG EDELSTEIN.

THE JOHNS HOPKINS UNIVERSITY.

---

[6] Cf. Schanz, *loc. cit.*; H. Georgii, *Die antike Aneiskritik* (1891), pp. 35 ff.

[7] Cf. *Aen.*, X, 467; pp. 63-4 Wallace; for the contrary attitude taken by others, cf. *Georg.*, IV, 219; pp. 12-13 Wallace.

[8] Cf. *Aen.*, X, 467; *Ecl.*, 3, 105; *Aen.*, V, 527; *Georg.*, I, 243—Wallace, pp. 64; 36; 19; 21.